Walking With the Earth Mother

Jim Graywolf Petruzzi

Table of Contents

Acknowledgments

This book, like everything I write, is a creation of all the circles of which I am a part. The learning, sharing and experiences I have had with so many people and circles of people are what have given me the material needed in all my writing. That is why, in my first book, it was said: "It is all about Jim, but not about Jim at all". That still holds true. My walk, my successes and failures, my joys and pains and the stories I tell act as surrogates for the stories of all in my circles. I truly hope this makes sense, as it is key to understanding how best to use any knowledge or ideas you may gather here. So I begin by extending my heartfelt gratitude and thanks to all with whom I have walked, am walking and will walk in this life's journey. It doesn't matter if our connection was harmonious or contentious—the lessons were shared, the journey enriched, the growth attained.

And I extend this gratitude to all, not just the two-leggeds with whom I have shared time, space and energy. I thank the four-leggeds, the winged ones, the creepy-crawlies, the Standing People, Rock People, the Ancestors, my spirit guides and animal guides, Father Sky and Mother Earth and all other creatures, entities and sources of energy. How's that for an extended circle? And yet that is the way of it—at least for me. Each part of life and creation has value and each has given me something. Hopefully I have also given back to all—whatever I was able, as best I could.

And, I especially acknowledge the Creator—Great Spirit or whatever name you chose—without whose permission and assistance I could write and share nothing. Without whose gifts I would have no talent for sharing my stories and the stories of others.

As for thanking individuals, where do you start? I thanked many in the previous book and probably could have thanked many more. In this book I again thank my half-side, Sue, for being with me. For all she has done to help me have the space writing takes. For now walking with me on the Red Road, each serving the greater good individually and serving jointly as well. My past wives—Nadine and Bonnie—for the time we journeyed together and the lessons you taught me. My healer Tammy, without whom my body would have finished its collapse and I would no longer be in this realm. And who remains a steadfast friend—a sister—to this day. I thank my brother, Jim Francek and his half-side, Pat, for the support and guidance when I was struggling to escape my dark time of the soul. As I do Donna, my sister, for her untiring willingness to be there for me when the pain was at its peak. My brother, Jack Martin, I thank for his constant help and support and his steadfast friendship. And, as importantly, his example of an unwavering commitment to personal healing even when the results seemed slow in coming and his example of 'giving back' as he walks forward. Dale, a friend who stood with me just after my losses had piled up—thank you brother. My mother, my stepdaughter, my friends and relatives I would also thank for their contributions to this book.

Here, when thanking humans, I send special thanks to my grandchildren—Lyra and Dashiell. All that I do now—alone and through Sanctuaries of the Earth Mother—I do for future generations. My grandchildren act as loving reminders of that commitment. Thank you both. I hope one day when you are ready, you read my works and act on some of what I say. What a beautiful legacy that would be.

On the spirit side—the Blue Road—I first again thank my ex-wife, Bonnie. Our thirty-two years taught me so much I would not begin to enumerate these lessons. And her continued help from the other side is a continued blessing. My father next, for he ignited in me an ever-growing love of and connection to nature and all its creatures. What a gift! Thanks Dad, I still see you holding the ladder for me. And all the others I have known and loved who now live there—on the other side.

To all my Earth walking teachers and guides I say Mitakuye Oyasin—all my relations. And to my spirit teachers—Black Elk and White Buffalo Calf Woman and all the others—I thank you: Pilamaya. Without all of you on both sides of the 'screen' I would still be sleep walking through this life.

Finally, but extremely close and important to me, I honor my animal guides in the Native tradition. Wolf of Many Colors, my long time guide and protector, and all the Wolf people, I thank you for allowing me to be one of your pack. The Eagle people, another of my long-time totems, I thank you for eyes that see far and spirit that soars. And all the other creatures with whom I communicate and to whom I listen, I thank you.

Foreword

Ah, FRIENDS. IT IS GOOD TO SEE YOU SITTING HERE IN CIRCLE WITH ME again. And welcome to all the new faces I see in the group. As I wrote my first book—*White Man, Red Road, Five Colors*—it became clear to me I would write others. And, as some of you walked that first journey with me, you also suggested there was more to be shared. More for all of us to explore and learn together. So it was no surprise when I sat down yesterday to do some Sanctuaries of the Earth Mother paperwork that I pulled up two blank sheets on the computer and let two titles flow from my spirit. Nor was it a surprise that I reopened this one today and began writing—began the next part of our spiritual trek together. I begin capturing this journey with great pleasure and joy and little of the fear and doubt that dogged my earlier writing.

Sue, my half-side, tells me there are many books waiting within our earlier journey through *White Man, Red Road, Five Colors*. She is probably correct—we shall see. I will write as often as Spirit guides me to do so, with no expectations of what that may mean. I see that while any and all of the books we create together will be connected in many ways, I know each may also be read as a stand-alone piece. So, while you new souls to this adventure may wish to read the first book to better understand where my spiritual journey began, you can also enjoy this journey without doing so. I wish to repeat little from the first book here, but I will share a couple quick things for you new folks.

My first book shared my journey with my indigenous teachers, especially my Lakota teachers. I shared how I came to walk the Good Red Road and how I learned different healing methods and spiritual ceremonies from my teachers in the American West, Central America and in other parts of the Earth Mother's realm. I also shared the visions I had some years back, which have begun to now manifest before me and the others with whom I walk in the physical world. These visions center around the Sanctuaries of the Earth Mother—something I think you will hear more about as we walk together here once again. I say—I think—because I did not know where the previous book was taking us as I wrote it, nor do I know where this journey leads. That, my friends, is a manifestation of my belief that, "it is all about the journey, not the destination". As my friends here from the last walk know, I did not read the first book until it was complete. I was aware of some of the things I captured, but very surprised when I read other sections of that book. Stories appeared I did not expect to tell and other stories I was certain I would share were not present. Who knows, maybe some will appear this time around.

This book will center around my more recent life with, probably, some stories and facts from the past. And maybe some visions of the future. If things are repeated—in different ways or through different stories—they often have special meaning and I suggest you explore them carefully with your heart and mind. The journey of *White Man, Red Road, Five Colors* stopped as I was leaving Fort Collins Colorado about 1998, although I shared the conversation I had with Two Bears years later. I believe this book will begin in the fall of 2008, as I attempted to recover from a long journey into the dark time of my soul— a journey I will share in the other book whose title came yesterday. I'm not sure when I will be able to write of this time, but I know it is important that I do share this walk. What I experienced as I lost everything I thought I owned will have special significance in these times we now inhabit. As will this journey of rebirth and growth we have already begun, here in my initial impressions of what is to come. Or we may travel other roads as this evolves.

Those who have read the first book, and those new to our circle—I hope you visit the Sanctuaries of the Earth Mother home page as I am writing this and share your thoughts, suggestions and ideas so that I may add them to what I write for the circle in the future.

As I told the original circle, people will get different things from the books I write. Each of you I hope will follow the ancestor's advice given to me by Two Bears and others: "Take with you whatever you can use and leave the rest behind". Enjoy the stories, enjoy the people with whom I have walked, enjoy the fun and sorrow, and consider musing over the teachings I will offer from time to time. I am certain there will be things for you to take away with you and, hopefully, share back with this circle and others.

Most of the people you will meet here in *Walking With the Earth Mother* are different than those in the first book, but a few will re-surface and rejoin our walk. This is the way of many indigenous people—people come and go as your work together dictates. Some stay a long time, some are with you briefly and are gone. Some re-appear, some do not. It is how you connect with others when they are present that allows you to grow and expand, so I have tried to practice understanding and acceptance when someone leaves suddenly or stays longer than I would like. I capture my interactions with the people I have shared space with as accurately as I can, without judgment. As I do with myself and my own actions. My teachers in this part of my walk will continue to appear, but less often as I step up to my own place of grandfather and teacher. My spirit teachers and guides remain with us but, again, some you have yet to meet them as you join our circle here.

I feel certain the main character of this book is a presence I have been honored to walk with this entire life—the Earth Mother. I believe nature and our role in it and connection to it will play a strong part in this book. We will see if I am correct as we move ahead. It is after all, the Earth Mother—our home—we need to now make peace and come back into harmony with. So why would she not have a strong voice in this book?

As I opened the first book, so too I open this book by thanking you for joining me here in a good way so we may journey and learn together.

JIM GRAYWOLF PETRUZZI
Hota Sugmanitu tanka (Graywolf)

Black Elk and the Earth Mother

PART OF BLACK ELK'S VISION

"The sixth Grandfather was really Mother Earth, the Earth Spirit. The Earth Spirit took Black Elk outside the lodge and told him the Earth Power would be with him. In time, the two-leggeds would desperately need Mother Earth's help.

Black Elk was instructed to set the red stick in the center of the yellow hoop. There, the tree was to grow, and around it people would gather. In time the tree would bloom.

Black Elk saw the Earth becoming sick. The animals, the winged ones, and the four-legged ones grew frightened. All living things became gaunt and poor. The air and the waters dirtied and smelled foul. Below, Black Elk saw a blue man living in and empowering the sickness. The powers of the four directions, represented by four horses, charged the blue man, but were beaten back. The Grandfathers called upon Black Elk. His bow changed into a spear, and he swooped down on the blue man, killing him. When the blue man fell, all life came back upon the Earth; all things became fresh and healthy again."

From "*Black Elk Speaks*" by John G. Neihardt

WORKING WITH THE EARTH MOTHER FOR THE BENEFIT OF THE SEVEN GENERATIONS

"Both the Hopis and Mayans recognize that we are approaching the end of a World Age. . . . In both cases, however, the Hopi and Mayan elders do not prophesy that everything will come to an end. Rather, this is a time of transition from one World Age into another. The message they give concerns our making a choice of how we enter the future ahead. Our moving through with either resistance or acceptance will determine whether the transition will happen with cataclysmic changes or gradual peace and tranquility. The same theme can be found reflected in the prophecies of many other Native American visionaries from Black Elk to Sun Bear."

— Joseph Robert Jochmans

From the website www.adishakti.org

Walking With the Earth Mother

1 | Rising From the Ashes

Hᴀɴɢ ᴡɪᴛʜ ᴍᴇ ɪɴ ᴛʜᴇ ʙᴇɢɪɴɴɪɴɢ ᴏꜰ ᴛʜɪꜱ ʙᴏᴏᴋ. Sᴏᴍᴇᴛɪᴍᴇꜱ ᴡʜᴇɴ we walk together we experience our pains—with little fun or joy attached. This is, in fact, the balance to those times of pure joy we hopefully each have had. While this beginning may be less than easy reading, it is important in order to continue our walk together with an understanding of what teachings may arise later.

In the summer of 2008 I had no spirit. My wife of thirty-two years, Bonnie, had finally succumbed to breast cancer in May, the story I am certain I am to tell in *Light in the Dark Time of the Soul*—the other title that appeared to me a few days ago. Before her death several others very close to me had died and several more were to follow in the six months following her exit from my life. My house was gone, my savings depleted from medical expenses, I had no job and I had a small mountain of medical bills due doctors and hospitals on both coasts. I do not wish to re-tell the story of Bonnie and our last four years walking together here, but I need to share enough so you understand where I stood emotionally, physically, mentally and spiritually at that time. I was certain I would follow Bonnie to the spirit realm shortly after she left. I was tired of the pain I had been experiencing for years and saw no reason for going on alone. I barely had a hold on my spiritual practices and that road I had walked so happily before. I functioned like a zombie, going through the motions with little feeling or comprehension around my actions. Shortly after Bonnie died my sister took me to get a dog—Onyx, the Labordoodle who walks with me today. He was my one pleasure and a focus for keeping my brain functioning. It is from these ashes of my life to this time that I will begin our journey here.

I have shared in other places and with other people that the Phoenix of mythology rises only from the ashes. He/she does not rise to be re-born from a partially burned building or life. If just your foundation still exists, do not expect to see this glorious legendary winged one rising with you to the heavens. Phoenix rising from the ashes means FROM the ashes. Now, in the summer of 2008, I truly understood this teaching. I stood amidst the ashes of what I thought I owned—what I thought I was—trying to decide in my spirit whether to stay on this material world or step into infinity. My brain told me to lie down in the evening and invite in my own death. To ask Great Spirit to take me with the Ancestors, as I had had enough in this life. I no longer saw beauty or color, nor felt pleasure or joy. Even nature, my life-long sanctuary of beauty, held no allure for me. And yet, even as I asked for death in my sleep, each morning I awoke again, with a small puppy waiting to be rubbed and taken out for a romp. And so I arose and began the daily ritual of movements that had become my existence.

Even while walking through this gauntlet of pain and self-pity I had many people reaching out to me for support and guidance. Some were from my work with the group Natural Leadership Way, some from my past spiritual road and others who had found me along the way and sought my aid on their own healing journey. I welcomed the phone calls and emails from these fellow travelers of life, but waited for my infrequent clear-headed moments before I responded to them. And of course, I had my own circle of support to keep me going, especially important because they allowed me to just hear a voice and know I was not totally alone. That feeling of being totally alone is one that can generate extreme fear and thereby block any forward motion you might otherwise make. And it was persistent. I would think I had escaped its clutches for a while only to sit down and feel the cold grip of aloneness and fear grabbing at my heart.

My days were taken up with doctor's appointments, grief abatement groups, walking, alternative healers and occasionally a visit to one of a few close friends or relatives. The house I rented was surrounded by open land and farms, so Onyx and I could walk, sit under trees or sit by a stream. Then I would spend an hour picking ticks off of us.

Okay, I'm getting depressed again just sharing this with you. I think you see where I was at. Mind, body and spirit were at rock bottom as I stood standing surrounded—metaphorically—by the ashes of my past. I was certain, as I had been for some time, that I would never get back to the open, natural places I so loved in the Mountain West. Yet something within caused me to continue rising each day and face life. I was not looking for pity; my mind was doing that well enough itself.

In mid-July I began taking my Chanupa, my sacred pipe, outside and opening it to the seven directions, asking Great Spirit to take this burden off of me. And I asked for guidance—from the Universe and the Ancestors—for what I was to do. I was not allowing my anger, no, my rage, over what had happened to me to surface yet. I invited a few people who asked to come to my place to come and I conducted healing ceremonies with them, but knew the energy and spirit you needed for such work was not with me. Still, if I could guide them in a way to think, I felt I was doing what was needed.

Each night I awoke at 3 AM, as I had for many years—and still do to this day. This is a powerful time for me, with either pleasant or unpleasant energies coming at me. It is a time I may awaken from a dream and understand some meaning of the dream images. Or I may wake in a sweat, feeling panic from something I 'almost' remember. My animal guides or spirit guides may come to me or I get a clear message of what Great Spirit wants me to do next. Like I said, power time for me. Not good or bad, but powerful. Usually by 4 AM I was back asleep—sometimes to remember everything in the morning, sometimes with just a vague idea of what had come to me. Now, in my depression and isolation, I used this time to pray to Spirit and ask for release from the Earth realm if my work was done.

So this night I awoke at 3 AM with a start and my heart racing was not very different than many other nights, except I could still hear the echoes of a powerful voice (although voice does not express it well as it permeated my entire being) asking, "Do you really wish to drop your robes now?" Dropping your robes in this context, as used by many Native nations, meant to die and move into the Spirit world. I lay there sweating and shaking; wondering if I was awake or asleep. And wondering if I was remembering a dream I had awakened from and/or if I actually heard a voice. Onyx was tightly plastered to my left side, in a world of doggie dreams as he twitched and yipped in his sleep. I did not speak or think an answer to my questions, as my mind was truly confused, like it was most times then. I sat with the question in my head, assuming it had come from my own inner being. And, after a few minutes, I remember thinking, "No, I don't wish to die just yet. I don't think I do anyway. Oh, I don't know. Anything is better than this." Then, I must have slept since I awakened at 6 AM, when I took Onyx out to relieve himself. Then I lay back in bed, as I did many days, for hours—unable to think or move, experiencing mental and physical pain and emotional suffering. Finally I got up and called a good friend, Jim Redhawk, and began my day. The night before came back and I mused over it all day. Was I being given the choice by Great Spirit to stay or leave? I had heard of this happening from other spiritual guides and teachers. Or was it my own mind asking itself the question?

After I washed, I took a ride into Maryland and parked near the Conowingo Dam, where bald eagles flew. I had brought a drum and Onyx and I walked a couple of miles down the river trail, and then sat as I played and mused. My brain was controlling my decisions and actions these days and I struggled to return that leadership to my heart. It is in leading with my heart that my best work has always emanated, but my heart was too empty to do this now. And so, fear and doubt crept into everything from the workings of my mind. This day I was surprised however, as I felt the stirrings of the energy I was familiar with coming from my heart. I sat there for quite a while, watching eagles and other waterfowl fly by as I drummed and meditated. I don't know how long I sat, but when I began to rise, my numb legs failed me and I crumbled to the ground. Onyx thought this was great fun, so I rubbed his belly as I waited for my circulation to return. Then we walked back to the car and drove home.

That night I went to bed asking for help with my confusion around living or dying and worked on sending my energy out of my mind and into my heart as my mentors had shown me. It often took a long while for me to fall asleep, with my brain running full tilt with questions and fears. Finally I must have slept, because I again awoke at my 3 AM time. And, again, the same question was ringing in my ears and vibrating down my spine, "Do you wish to die now?" I got up and began pacing, with a small, black lab following me from room to room. After about an hour I lay back with no real answer in my head. I thought, "Well, maybe I won't wake up in the morning and the decision will be made for me. But, for now I don't think I want to die". And, of course, I didn't die but rather I awoke at 7 AM—in a deep, dark depression. "Damn it, damn it. Damn it!" I yelled. "I'm sick of this! Enough pain and sadness. This can't all be happening. I must be in a nightmare." Any of you who have gone through a time like this will probably recognize this type of reaction. You feel so powerless—so defeated. Luckily, Onyx was making it clear he needed to go outside, so I had a reason to push myself up.

After a breakfast of a large bowl of oatmeal and sweet coffee, Onyx and I went for a walk in the fields behind the house. We hiked to a huge grandfather tree I had sat under many times over the past six months. Here I sat and wrote some of my thoughts and impressions as they came to me. I sat there a couple of hours as Onyx chased rabbits and jumped in and out of a nearby stream. Then I went back to the house and dressed for a grief-sharing meeting. That night I skipped dinner, as I had also skipped lunch, and sat listening to flute music as I burned sage and tried to slow my fevered brain down. This often worked for a while and gave some respite from my tortured existence. I went to bed early and lay listening to more flute music. I was still unable to read or write much at all—a persistent problem for a number of years to that point. And the opposite of my ability and joy in reading and writing in the past. Actually, it was not until my first book started to flow from me that this inability began to ebb. I said 'began to ebb', as it still is an issue at times—with physical and mental pain blocking my ability to read or write.

Three in the morning came and so did the question again. But this time somewhat differently. All through my body and awareness I heard and felt, "Do you wish to live or die? There is still much for you to do. Yet it is your choice. This is the third and last time you will be given the choice. After this, you stay here and finish your work." And I quickly responded in my heart with, "I wish to stay and finish". And I felt great fear and surprise—and relief—as I fell back into dreamtime.

In the morning I awoke with a clear head, but physical pain in my legs and knees. I took an Aleve, got up and limped outside with the four-legged who walks with me. And I watched the sun come up and a group of three blue herons fly by. Then I turned towards the house and was surprised to see four turkey vultures spaced along the roofline. I noticed the flowers poking out from around the west corner of the house—flowers I weeded and watered, but had no interest in enjoying. It hit me that this was the first time I was seeing, feeling and enjoying nature in a long time. It didn't last too long, but it was wonderful to see the colors again. I went back inside and made coffee as I marveled that I had decided to stay on this Earthly realm and continue my journey. My brain screamed at me, "Are you nuts!" But my spirit felt it was right, even if I was totally surprised by this answer I had given.

In the past I had been asked things by Great Spirit, spirit guides and flesh-and-bone teachers repeatedly—in this multiple way I was asked about living or dying. And I often used repetition—repeating a question—with others in my work. It is a valued way of teaching and emphasizing points. As well as giving the one you ask the repeated question time to think and contemplate. Many of the things I share as we walk along, friends, I have covered in my first book, especially teachings of my indigenous guides. I won't repeat most of these things, as it will slow our walk forward together. A few I will repeat, as some understanding may be needed by each of us. I may, later, share some of my vision again as well. We shall see. It is unclear to me now, but I am certain we will all know if that is needed as we move ahead. Feel free, at any time, to visit or revisit *White Man, Red Road, Five Colors*, for elaboration on the customs and teachings covered there or Google for information on any customs or ceremonies I may mention that are foreign to you.

Please don't think for a minute that, suddenly, I was healed of my depression, doubt, fear, regret, remorse or physical pains. It rarely works that way. In fact, sitting here writing this for us, I am still working many of these things through. As we all do. Healing and growth are a process, not something you can pop a pill for and be done with. The old ones understood this. It is Western medicine and its practitioners that have led us to believe in the 'silver bullet'—the instant cure. That is because they work on symptoms, not causes. We have spoken of this at length in our earlier walk. That said; there was a shift in my awareness and being. A willingness to at least try some other things now that I had committed to Great Spirit my agreement to complete my work here.

This question of "Why am I here?" has walked with humans as long as we two-leggeds have existed. I have come to believe there are two primary reasons for each of us being here—to work on ourselves and hopefully, grow as beings and to perform some functions or services needed by the universe. We will examine this more as we walk here I believe, but it is important we speak of it now. Some humans seem to have elaborate, continued reasons for being here, others seem to contribute some small piece of knowledge or understanding and then fade away. You cannot judge the importance of anyone's walk—their purpose for being. Those who try to reach for some big purpose, often contribute nothing—being too obsessed with their egos. Those who fear what they have to contribute, or the gifts they have been gifted, often hang back and give less than they could. I have spoken before about this with the lesson Two Bear's gave me often—"Do not try to be more than you are, but do not be less than you are either." Two Bears, as a principal Lakota teacher of mine early on in my walk on the Red Road, was fond of repeating teachings until he thought I had some understanding of his meaning. Those who have walked with me before remember well many of Two Bears stories and lessons. If you do not 'play your role' in the jigsaw puzzle of our life here on Mother Earth, Spirit often gives you another chance. Then another is chosen to play the role if you are un-able. This is not a judgment, but simply the Universe needing to continue with its evolution. When I committed to staying on this planet to fulfill my role, whatever that is, I understood that I would have to continue my healing and growth. I expected no glorious rebirth, but rather a slow, sometimes difficult travel forward. Hopefully I am fulfilling the mission Great Spirit wished from me. I believe I am, because in the times in the past when I was not connected to my inner self, the God 'within', and the 'God without'. I was aware that something was out of harmony—out of balance. That, relatives, is one good way to judge if you are fulfilling your purpose. Ask yourself frequently—"Am I in balance? Am I in harmony with my world and those in it"? If the answer is no, it may be time for some major introspection.

Many days I would get frustrated and angry as I continued to deal with the physical and mental pain I was working through. During prayer or ceremony time I would ask Wankan Tanka (Great Spirit) "Why I did not feel less pain"? I had agreed to stay. "Why the continued suffering"? Then on occasion I would get periods where I was relatively pain free and my brain was clear. I would give thanks and hope that was the end of it, only to have the pain return.

I have worked with many people who speak of similar walks with pain. For some it's physical, others mental, still others report emotional turmoil and depression. I can understand how they feel as I also work through these issues. Actually I now understand one reason I have been given this pain and suffering to deal with. It is so that I can understand many levels of pain that others experience. For people who talk about losing everything I can relate to my own dark time of the soul and all I 'lost' and therefore be able to connect in a very real way. I guess it's a variation on the old saying, "If you want to learn how to paint, go ask an artist". Or you want to know how to swim, or play a sport or any other area of life—ask someone who knows. Two Bears, spoke of this many times. He also had many physical ailments that came and went. And he often offered a prayer of gratitude for all these pains taught him. At the time many years ago, I thought he was truly insane. Why give thanks for such a 'negative' thing? That was until I understood it was not negative—or positive. It simply was. And it was painful and distracting. But negative? Who is to judge positive and negative?

In my work with Natural Leadership Way, I conducted a conference call once a week. Sometimes one or two called in—sometimes the circle was twenty-five. It never mattered. All who needed to be there were there. A truth I now follow in all things. I do not worry about who shows up, or calls in, or reads a book or works with me. Whoever needs to be present—is. This removes a lot of stress and anxiety from anything you might do. And any negative judgments of your own work—even if only a few seem to take advantage of it. A few days after the third time I spoke my desire to live the next conference call was scheduled. I was tired and my head was on fire. It felt as if I could fry an egg on it. And it felt like someone had shoved a twenty-pound bag of mulch in it—in space that would hold three pounds at best.

But, at seven in the evening I dialed in to see who might appear—hoping for a few so it might be over quickly. Four people were already on-line. Okay, this should go quickly I thought. I should be off in thirty minutes. For those who read White Man. . ., you are very familiar with the word 'should'. It is a word, I hold, that needs to be eliminated. There are no shoulds. There are only things you could do or might do; but as soon as you accept you 'should' do something you lose all objectivity and allow yourself to be controlled—either by your own mind or someone else's desires. But I was still 'shoulding' a lot this summer. Some horrible 'shoulds' reared up at me then—I should have been able to do more for my wife; I should have been able to save my aunt; I should have been able to heal myself quickly and so on. These big 'shoulds' can trap you in black space forever. Please. . .please, work on 'should' as we travel together. Remember you 'shouldn't should'—a title I will use for a book down the road.

Friends, I apologize if there seems to be so many 'teachings' appearing so quickly here. It surprises me somewhat—as if anything could any longer. When I write I attempt to empty my mind, go into my heart and let whatever Great Spirit sends to me flow onto the pages. Some would say it is all too easy for me to empty my mind. That's okay—I smile with them. And accept some truth there. But in reality, it is extremely difficult to empty the mind and only be in the heart. Many of you know this from past attempts. If you have never tried it, why not give it a go? It will help you see where I come from in my work. It is a powerful place to work from, as long as you have no expectations about how long it will take to accomplish anything or what the product may look like at the end.

Back to the call. I asked for each of us on the line to check in—share a little about how they felt, what they were doing or whatever else came to them. Or simply pass if they wished to remain quiet. As we began this opening of the circle, 'bings' announced three more callers. As I welcomed them, several more arrived. "Okay everyone, let's wait a few minutes to see if any others are arriving late. No sense in being interrupted each time we begin the check-in," I began. "Is everyone okay with that?" I asked. Several yeses and okays came back to me from the circle, so I took this as consensus agreement. "So, who was in nature today and wants to share something they experienced with any of their senses?" I asked.

"I would like to take that Jim," I heard the voice of Mary Ann say. And she did take it as she spoke about her walk along the Pacific coast where she lived and the seals that came near the shore to bark at her. She spoke about how connected she felt to the natural world as the wind blew her hair, the seals barked and the waves slapped the rocky coast. "Thank you for showing me how to 'feel more' in a walk I often take, Jim. I was so aware of how everything connected today," she finished.

"Welcome, Mary Ann, but you always knew this. You just needed someone to remind your spirit how it worked," I responded.

No one else came on the line as Mary spoke and I answered. "Okay, I think we are all here. It's a quarter past the hour. I think there is about ten of us now, so let's do brief check-ins and then open a new topic. Work for everyone? Who wants to begin?"

"I would love to," Sam said. "I'm having some issues with people at work. I would like to put this into the circle and maybe someone will connect with me on it later. It seems. . ."

Bing, bing, bing, bing. Four more arrived. Usually everyone is on by five after. I often ask for timeliness so we don't repeat ourselves and disturb the flow. Bing, bing. Two more.

"It seems we are all straggling into tonight's circle. Odd, but let's deal with it," I said.

"I guess I'm a little angry about this," Jack put in. "I was on time and I feel a lack of respect by those coming on this call late."

"Maybe a challenge by the way we are coming on the call today. Maybe a test. Did you notice no one came in while we were waiting and Mary Ann shared her story? Then we began checking in again and more people arrived."

"Sorry, circle. I was late. An issue with the kids, but I really wanted to be on tonight," someone spoke as I finished.

"Yeah, okay," said Jack. "I've been late before so I guess I can't be angry. Can we start now?"

"Sure, let's skip check in. There seems to be twenty or more of us on now. Let's simply each speak our name into the circle and say one word that you wish out there. How you feel. What you see. Anything," I answered.

And so we rapidly moved around the circle. Then we did a reading from Jamie Sam's *Medicine Cards* book and started talking about

the teaching she put forth. We often did this, with one person call-
ing out a page number and another opening to it and reading what
Jamie had written. Tonight's page was all about balance and tim-
ing. It sure fit in with the healing road I was currently on. Finally,
after about an hour and a half, we were ready to wrap it up. At least
I was.

"Well, folks, I ask someone to come forward with a closing prayer
or thought and we can wrap for tonight," I spoke to the group.

"Jim," Pam interrupted. "Could we talk for a few minutes after the
call? Or tomorrow morning as I drive to work?"

"I'm tired, so the morning works better for me if there is no
urgency".

"No, great. I'll call when my cell phone works".

Then Paulette asked to do a reading from Thoreau's book *Walden
Pond*. When she finished, I gave thanks for the circle to the seven di-
rections and we all began 'binging' back out.

I have just spent some time sharing this phone circle meeting
with you since I wished to show how circles, although strongest when
they physically meet, can form and share over great distances almost
equally as well. We had people from across Turtle Island (the U.S.)
and four from Europe on this call and we managed to feel complete
when we finished. While we used the phone and shared words and
energy through its medium I believe people will re-learn how to do
this energetically from spirit to spirit without electronics again in
the near future—if we are willing to work at it. I truly believe we
once had this skill, as many of my indigenous teachers told me, but
slowly lost it when we ceased "exercising" that "muscle". Why did so
many indigenous people around the Earth Mother have similar ideas,
words, thoughts, art, teachings, etc., in the distant past? There are many
theories given—and maybe the answer is a combination of them. But
I believe this talent of sharing through heart and spirit is part of the
answer. A large part. Like so many other talents and skills we have lost
or have weakened as we grew to depend on machines and technology
for our lives and connections.

Back to our main road, my friends. As I hung up the phone I felt fairly good and had nice energy. Onyx, who had been peacefully laying beside me listening, got up and began his 'tail pump' announcing his patience was thin and bladder full. We walked outside to find a full moon looking down on us. I sent gratitude to Grandmother Moon as we walked into the fields behind the house. In a few minutes I began to feel the darkness move back into me and the pain return to head and spine. We finished our walk and went back inside, where I made some hot Sleepytime tea so I might get a little rest. Onyx slurped some water and finished his meal from earlier in the evening. It was about ten o'clock now and I turned on both the TV and the stereo, along with every light in the house. Then I sat at my computer to reply to emails.

This is a technique—noise and light—many of us use to drown out the sound of our own spirit talking to us or to make it impossible to listen to our mind, body or spirit. If we can't hear about something from our being that is out-of-balance, we don't need to deal with it. It's another fear-based reaction we humans have perfected. Do you wonder what I mean? Do you wonder if you ever do it? When is the last time you sat quietly out in nature—no talking, no phone, no thinking about other things—for a period of time, even only twenty minutes? When was the last time you turned all the electronic communications devices in your home off at once and just sat? Try it today. Go outdoors, preferably to a natural area like a park or woods trail, and sit for twenty to forty minutes. Clear your brain of its thoughts and see what you think, feel, smell, see, hear or sense. Just reach out through your heart and stay connected as long as you can. Then write about what you experienced. You will be amazed that the more you develop this skill, the more you will learn directly from nature.

Want a bigger challenge? Turn off your TV's, stereos, and any other distracting sights and sounds in your home for an entire day. Do your work in a place without these intruding. And see how much you accomplish. The first time you may get little done since it may make you uncomfortable to do things without your 'white noise'. So try it again and see how you do.

I was using everything to stop me from thinking and thereby, I thought, I would stop hurting even worse than I was. I still sometimes catch myself doing this. Sue and I will sit down to discuss something—with the TV on. Or I will sit at the computer to write—with music playing. Of course, there are many other distractions used to stop from growing energetically—constant action, liquor, drugs, and on and on. But I'm talking about the sensory robbing, seemingly innocuous ones now—the TV's, stereos, computers and the like. I have a good friend who, each time I call him at his home I hear his TV playing loudly in the background and some audio coming over a radio or his computer. He is often also talking to someone else in his household or on another phone as he speaks to me. This is a person who does not like change and fears what is coming. So, presto, if he drowns thought out with noise and distraction, his fears stay below the surface. The only problem with this (as I have learned from personal experience) is that sooner or later these fears—these issues—will come out. And the longer they are repressed, the worse their bite when they do emerge.

The next morning the phone rang and, as I knew it would be Pam, I picked it up.

"Morning, Jim here," I answered quietly.

"Hi Jim. It's Pam. On my way to work—so we can talk as I drive. Great call last night. I slept through the night. How was your night?"

"Okay, I worked on the computer a while, then went to bed," I lied by omission. I had worked for a couple of hours and then I did go to bed—but got almost no sleep.

"Good," Pam responded. "Look, I've told you about stretching my comfort zone and trying to pull together a weekend gathering. I would like to hold one in three weeks. Could you come and lead us in building a lodge? And running some ceremonies? I know you might not be up to it yet, but I had to ask."

"Boy, I don't know Pam. It takes a long while to build a lodge in the right way, with the right prayers and ceremonies as we do so.

I've built a number, but always with my teachers leading. And I don't know if I'm emotionally up to leading ceremonies or sweats. I can't sing for three years after Bonnie passed over, as I was taught. I don't know. Let me think about it and get back to you. How many people? Who?"

"Maybe fifteen. I would put the invite out to the Natural Leadership Way circle first and invite a few friends from here, where I live. Let me know as soon as you can please, so people have some time to plan."

"I will." We chatted for a while, then she reached work and we hung up. I pondered her request all day, then called two of my teachers from the past, and luckily reached Two Bears. I laid out what Pam had asked and then asked his advice.

"Jim, this is your call," Two Bears told me. "Are you ready for this? You did good to tell her this would be something the group creates, but not necessarily a traditional lodge. And I agree—no singing for you for three years. This is the way my grandfather taught me. It is okay to lead prayers and chants, drum or ask others to sing. If you do this thing, ask Spirit for guidance before beginning and for permission to create this 'new way'."

"Thank you, Uncle. I need to sit with this. It feels right, but I wish you were here."

"No, this is about you now. Your way, your time. I will be there in spirit."

We hung up soon after this, with me feeling I had his blessing if I decided to do this thing asked of me. I did fear looking like a weakling or a fool. Pure ego coming forward here. So I worked hard to not let that influence me. I called Pam the next day and told her I would give it a go. We set the date and I released it from my thoughts for a while. In a few days I called my friend, Jim Redhawk in Connecticut to see if I should stop for him on the way to Pam's. Jim was part of our circle, my close friend and also a pipe carrier. I felt better knowing we could do this together.

"Ho, Redhawk. How goes your walk?" I asked.

"Good brother. Just working on a presentation I need to give a potential client company next week."

"Good. I was just planning for the weekend at Pam's. Shall I come up the day before so we can drive up together?"

"Oh, Jim. I can't make it. Too many things going on and I need to generate some income. Maybe you can stop on the way up or back."

Oh hell, I was stopped dead. Not make it? I was counting on him to be a support. I never thought about him not going. Jim loves center stage. He is a performer by heart, so I thought he would relish this opportunity. Now what should I do. Cancel? Go alone? Damn!

"Wow, Papa," I said, using Jim's nickname. "I guess I just assumed you would be along. I don't know if I can do this yet. I'm going through so much doubt and pain."

"I know you can do it, but it's your call. Everyone will understand, however you decide. Look, I need to go; I'm on a conference call in a few minutes. Will you call in the morning?"

"Sure. We can talk more then."

Jim is one of those few people who were helping me through this pain I suffered. He was there whenever I needed advice or just someone to listen to me. There must be a reason I was being sent by the universe to do this alone. So, hell, I'd do it—however it came out. I could stop at Jim and Pat's on the way up and the way back if I chose to do so. We could talk and do ceremony together.

So I committed myself to go and lead this weekend of ceremony. I had committed to the only person that really mattered in this case—myself.

2 | The Story of the Phoenix and the Red Road

I HAVE SPOKEN ABOUT HOW I FELT MY WORLD WAS IN ASHES AROUND ME, which allowed for the Phoenix—me in this case—to rise from these ashes and begin to heal. I know the story had meaning for me prior to the timeframe of this book, during the timeframe of this book and onto the present day. And I also know it is relevant to what some of my friends and those I guide on their healing road are currently undergoing. So my guess is it will have relevance for some of you, my friends of this circle, even if you have heard the story before.

There are many variations of the legend of the Phoenix rising from the ashes. This is one of those stories. This story is told, in very similar fashion, throughout many ancient cultures around the world. I will now share one of the versions I was taught by my Mayan teachers in Central America.

Picture two Mayan elders sitting at a fire with me deep in the jungle in the backcountry of Belize in Central America. We have brewed a pot of very strong black coffee, which we sip as we share stories and teachings. Both of these elders are friends of mine and have been teaching me myths and stories each time we meet. As I then share some stories my Lakota elders had given to me. We always enjoy this story telling before they instruct me in healing with herbs or spirit healing with songs and ceremonies. Both Umberto and San, my teachers tonight, are full-blooded Mayan—something not too common any more. And both come up to my mid-chest when we stand. They kid me about me getting nosebleeds from being up that high and I joke about how many extra steps they need to match my stride. We always laugh a lot when we are together. Being with them is one of the joys of my trips to Central America. I hope you can see us clearly now two short, brown men and one tall olive-skinned man sitting at a fire in the jungle drinking strong, black coffee. Birds calling and an occasional animal grunt from the jungle around us. Strong natural scents are wafting through the air, which tickle my nose and spirit. Smiling and laughing as we share stories and jokes. Good, I see you have the image better now. Sit, pour a cup of coffee and join us now. Not too close there. . . the fire is hot.

"The eagle and the condor are the same energy, one in the North Americas and the other in the Southern Americas," Umberto speaks as we discuss the power of the winged-ones in our parts of the Americas. "There are other birds with the energy of 'all that is above' [Father Sky in Lakota terms] in other areas of our Mother's land." [Earth Mother]

"Yes," I picked up his thought, "What of some of the mythical birds many cultures have shared? The Roc? The Phoenix?"

"Ah," San put in, "Umberto tells the story of the Fire Bird very good. Umberto, will you tell it to us?"

"I will. The Fire Bird—what you call the Phoenix, Jim—is in stories around Na'lu'um, your Earth Mother. What do your Native American friends have as Phoenix stories?"

"I think the Thunderbird is the closest to the Phoenix. A huge spirit bird that rewards those walking in a good way and renders apart those sowing harm or ill will. And I have also heard some Native American elders speak directly of the Phoenix."

"There, you see. Already we have several names for this being. Yet the general way of this great bird seems the same for each. So I will tell you of Phoenix, as I know him from my grandfather and his before that."

"The Phoenix—the Fire Bird—first came into existence to assist the sun with keeping the days light and bright," Umberto continued. "He came with beautiful feathers in the colors of the rainbow. Ahau, the God who made all, sent him to also help those who were just and honorable and strike down those who were evil or caused their people to suffer. Phoenix was to live a 500 year life so his work here would not be disturbed."

"Umberto, speak of how he filled the sky with light when he flew," San put in.

"Okay, San. I will tell what I remember. But you have heard this many times. Let Jim enjoy what I have to say here now."

"I feel like I'm getting ready for a bedtime story," I laughingly chimed in. Sometimes our story telling went this way, with comments and jokes every few minutes. Other times we were quiet and serious. I was never sure what dictated the energy, but it always seemed right.

"My grandchildren listen better than you two," Umberto smiled and said. "But, yes San, it is said the sky all around the Fire Bird burned with a white light when he flew. Honest men smiled, knowing he may decide to help with their load and evil men shook, fearing he might soar down and rip them apart. Phoenix is huge and his feathers are made of fire so he is not to be missed. So was the power and glory of the Fire Bird, the Phoenix."

Umberto paused, refilled his cup with coffee, took a sip and leaned back against a rock behind him. "But even with all this power, the Phoenix could not live forever. It is not the way of the universe or of Ahau. He dies after 500 years of being in the skies. And here is the wonder of the Fire Bird: Everything around him is destroyed by fire burned to ash like this fire before us. The place he lived, his nest, the trees, all around him to ash. Then he sets himself on fire and his own flames eat him to ash as well. Here is where there are many things people believe about the Fire Bird, because now he arises and lives again for another 500 years. And so the circle begins over. Some say his ash creates a golden fire from which a new, young Fire Bird comes. Others say he leaves an egg on the ground before he sets himself on fire and that the fire of his burning hatches this egg so the new Fire Bird comes out. What matters is he comes out of the ashes of all he knew and the ashes of his physical body to soar again and continue his work."

"Is the Phoenix or Fire Bird a bird of prophecy like the condor, Umberto?" I ask.

"No, Jim. The Condor, it is said, will help welcome in a time of peace when he flies north and flies through the skies with the eagle. That is what I have been told. I think this is like the story about the Fifth Earth we approach that your Native teacher gave you. That is different than the Phoenix story that I just told you."

And that was the story of the Phoenix as Umberto told it to me. I heard this story of the Phoenix, with some small variations, from four different people in Central America, as well as others in Europe and elsewhere. The basic story always being the same. And I was always drawn to the fact that the Phoenix in each story, no matter where I heard it, always rose from total ashes. I have shared this teaching with many, especially those who feel they have lost everything. And, for myself, I hung onto this story when everything was in ashes around me. Phoenix does not rise from a partially burned building, but from ashes. And he is consumed in his own flames first. Some say everything burning around the Phoenix is because his own flames lit it. He was responsible for everything burning. Maybe so, but I know, once the ashes surround you, you need to burn whatever you no longer need out of you before you, like the Phoenix, can truly rise again.

Before we get back on the journey where I am beginning to rise from the ashes, I think I need to say a little about the Red Road. "Walking the Good Red Road" is a phrase used by many Native American people of various nations that indicates a person who is walking in balance, living in a good way, serving the greater good and following the wishes of the Creator—Great Spirit / Wankan Tanka. And one does not need to be Native to walk the Red Road.

People of all races, religions or cultures may walk the Red Road. It is a way of living, a way of journeying through life. It is behavior as well as beliefs and attitudes. It is a way of living and 'doing' with reverence—walking so you do not harm other life. All other life. Respecting Mitakuye Oyasin...We Are All One. Walking in balance sounds easy, but to truly walk in balance, honoring all creatures and customs, takes a great deal of patience and practice. It involves engaging all aspects of your psyche—mind, body, emotions and spirit. You learn what it is you are here on this life journey to learn and do if you are able to remain on the Good Red Road. Being human, however, even those of us who pay attention to walking the Good Red Road sometimes see we have wandered off the path. When this happens it is time to stop and consider what it is you need to do in order to step back on the Red Road. The Good Red Road is considered to run from North to South—the place of energy and warmth and action (South) to the place of cold, thinking and slowing down (North).

It is important to remember we do not always walk the Good Red Road alone. We must connect with other creatures along the way to learn our lessons fully and thereby allow our spirit selves to grow and advance. As Back Elk put it in his teachings:

"The Red Road is a circle of people standing hand in hand, people in this world, people between people in the Spirit World, Star people, animal people, stone people, river people, tree people . . . . . The Sacred Hoop."

From *"Black Elk Speaks"* by John G. Neihardt

Black Elk has been, for many years, my primary teacher from the Spirit World—or the Blue Road. After we are done our walk in this life we enter the Blue Road—the road of the Grandfathers and Grandmothers...the Ancestors. The spirit road we walk after our body dies here. In our spirit form, we continue to learn by counseling those who remain on the Good Red Road of life. The Blue Road is seen as running from East to West. If you have walked your life in a good way on the Red Road, your time on the Blue Road will be spent in this positive way.

There is, as my teachers shared with me, another road in this living world one may choose to walk—the Black Road. As Black Elk describes this road:

"The Black Road goes from where the thunder beings live (the West) to where the sun continually shines (the East), a fearful road, a road of trouble and war."

From *"Black Elk Speaks"* by John G. Neihardt

When I first began learning of the Good Red Road and the Blue Road, this Black Road 'in the same directions as the Blue' completely confused me. Two Bears spent a great deal of time on the roads we might walk as both a living and a spirit being. In his way, the Black Road is the 'contrary' road chosen while we still live. It is the road of ego and personal gain. It is the road of disharmony and a place where the connection with the Earth Mother has been lost. Sadly, it is the road much of Western civilization has put us on. A road that will, by the prophecies of many, many cultures around the world, lead to our destruction as a race if we do not awaken in larger numbers to its reality. We, as humans, need to come together and relearn how to live in a sustainable way with the Earth Mother and with each other and all other creatures. If you are interested in how one culture looks at this, research Prophecy Rock of the Hopi Nation and read about the meaning of this rock and its symbols.

I believe I will bring Sanctuaries of the Earth Mother into this journey we take together as I did in *White Man, Red Road, Five Colors*. This non-profit organization sprang from the visions I had years ago that were re-awakened in the first book. We have a Sanctuary website (www.SOTEM.org) I invite you to visit where soon, there will be places we can communicate together. And Facebook groups as well. This because I want these journeys we take together—current and future journeys—to be shared in a new way. To be shared via electronic means like websites and then through our spirits once we have developed those skills. Think about this aspect and see if it moves you. For now I will say only this about the Sanctuary project and process—and in another's words:

"Let us put our minds together and see what life we can make for our children."

Sitting Bull
Hunkpapa Lakota Sioux holy man

I have now dedicated the rest of my life's journey to trying to pass a better legacy on to our children as I practice and teach new ways and the old ways of living in harmony. This walk evolves each day and I continue to remind myself of a truth I have lived by for a long time. This helps keep me from getting frustrated or impatient. And that truth, once again, is. . . . "It is all about the journey and not the destination". In fact there is no destination on either the Red or the Blue Road. You could easily argue there is a destination on the Black Road—the end point of destruction. So let's not walk that road or even invite its energy into our trek.

I believe strongly that if no, make that when, enough people have awakened and realized they must leave the Black Road, we will enter that time of peace and harmony the prophecies have spoken of: The Fifth Earth that my indigenous teachers have told me of. It is this legacy I hope we shall collectively leave for the seven generations to follow—our children's, children's children.

Black Elk spoke of where his people would walk if they stayed on the Good Red Road. I believe this holds for two-leggeds humans in general. So, in Black Elk's words, once again, I capture what will happen when we step onto the Good Red Road together:

"From where the giant lives (the North) to where you always face (the South) the Red Road goes, the road of good, and on it shall your nation walk."

From *"Black Elk Speaks"* by John G. Neihardt

That nation, as I see it, is the nation of all creatures—all humans, four-leggeds, winged ones, finned ones, creepy-crawlies and all other beings upon the Earth Mother. I see the Phoenix—Fire Bird, Thunder Bird or whatever name assigned it as one of Great Spirit's monitors of how we walk this road together. He aids us or rains down destruction on those who cannot walk in this good way. The destruction he rains down is really only a reflection of their own doing. Either way, he aids us.

Have you seen what has happened as we consume resources in an unsustainable way? Look at the gulf. When our consumptive ways alter the environment? Read about the new weather patterns. These are the ways we need to shift, finding new, more sustainable ways to walk.

3 | Gathering My Spirit

THE DAY FINALLY CAME FOR ME TO HEAD NORTH—UP TO NEW Hampshire where Pam lived. It looked like we would have between fifteen and twenty people attending. I loaded up the car with my ceremonial items and some clothes and took Onyx to my sister's place, where he would visit. He would romp happily with her dogs, cats and horses while I was gone. Still a puppy, I was sure he would get into some mischief, but she had animals everywhere so I knew she would deal with him. He shot out of the car and headed for the barn as soon as I opened the door. I called him back, fearing he might reverse direction and head to the road that fronted her property. He was not road or car savvy—in fact, he still is not. He seems to say, "Hey, this is my world. I don't trouble anyone. Let them respect my space." He's right, but we all know how oblivious many drivers are. The fact that we have lived places where there are few roads nearby has also decreased his ability to have a healthy respect for their dangers. We played together for a half-hour, and then I told him what I needed to do and asked that he behave while at Donna's—my sister's—house.

I have always talked to animals—whether talking to those animals who walk as my companions, like Onyx, or animals in the wild. And I assume they understand what I am saying—in the words, spirit and energy I put out. I have found, most times it works. They accept what

I have to say and cooperate with me. People often watch me doing this and either shake their heads up and down or from side-to-side. If up and down, usually with a smile, I know they get it and may speak with creatures this way as well. If side-to-side, usually with a frown, I know they pity the poor addled human before them. Which group do you think I often choose not to connect with? No, no—no answer is needed. It was a rhetorical question.

I see as I look at our circle each of you is smiling or nodding your head up and down. No surprise there—those who would shake their head side-to-side have probably already walked from us. Maybe some of them will return later. I hope so. This walk, this journey, needs many. And there appear to be more of us in this circle all the time. That's a good thing—we will gain more strength as we journey together.

I headed up through Chester County in Eastern Pennsylvania where I lived, and on into Bucks County, where I had lived for four years in the past. My head was in pain and it was difficult to focus. I stopped three times when the pain got too intense or I felt I was a danger to others. This sort of thing had been happening for some years now, as you will learn when I am able to face the pain of writing about my dark time of the soul, as I know I must.

I was a day early, so I could stay at Jim and Pat's for the night and not push my minimal energy reserves too far. Driving in the East is no fun anymore. Too many cars and too many people for my likes. Yet sometimes, I manage to find back roads. Not as easy to do as it is when I am living in the mountains in the West, but possible. I would look for some on this trip, which would make the drive more pleasurable. I got off the expressway in Connecticut about six hours later and tried to follow Jim's elaborate directions from there. I immediately got lost and was on less-travelled roads along a fast rushing river. I stopped and rested on the banks of the river for almost an hour, allowing my screaming nerves and mental fears to wash through me and recede slightly. Then I got back in the car and followed my instincts. Twenty minutes later I came out just up the road from Jim's place. I gave thanks for the back road, the river and the guidance to my destination.

It was near dinnertime and Jim had hoped I would make that. So I went up and knocked loudly as he had instructed me.

"Ho, Red Wolf! How are you, brother!"? Jim greeted me as he came to the door, stepped out and we embraced.

Our circle, being an astute one, learning from each other and paying attention to details you probably just noticed my name change. I was, at that time, called Redwolf. It was this name my Native American friends gifted me as I learned the ways. It is more recent that this shifted to Graywolf. It changed while I was connecting with Great Spirit one day not long ago and I checked in with Two Bears to see what he thought. But that's already covered before, so just be aware, please, that I was Redwolf and am now Graywolf. It is different energy and affects my work now.

"Ho, Redhawk, I'm fine. And you?"

"Wonderful. It's great living here near our daughter and grandchildren."

Jim and Pat lived many years in Colorado—Colorado Springs and Woodland Park—and it is there that I first met them. Jim loves Colorado—his soul lives there. But a couple of years before this, they had left Colorado and moved back to Connecticut to be with their family. And I am certain it is a wonderful thing for him to be near the kids, but I know he longs for the mountains. It was there that Jim had also been introduced to the Red Road and had begun learning Lakota ways. Pat, I believe, is just as comfortable in Connecticut with the little ones.

"Where's Pat, Papa?" I asked Jim.

"She'll be here any time. Had a meeting after work."

And, as he said this, she pulled in the driveway.

"Hi Pat," I greeted her as I approached her. We hugged and we all moved inside.

One of Jim's 'addictions', like mine, was food. It was one of the things he used for comfort and to block truly delving into his spirit. His addiction was more pronounced than mine, with Jim at about 350 pounds and me at 265 at this time, but a problem we shared. And

Pat, even less pronounced, felt the same pull of addiction. So they whipped out some papers and began telling me about Greysheet and the eating style they now used. At the same time they brought out scales and began weighing all their food for dinner. I thought, "Wow, this is nuts. Too extreme." And, as we ate, I told them I was glad this eating style was working for them, but that it was too extreme for me. They continued to tell me of its virtues and I listened, happy it was aiding my close friends.

After dinner, we cleaned up and I washed and lay down a while, as the depression, a daily visitor, was peaking again. After a while I went downstairs to see what my hosts were up to. Jim had taken out his Chanupa and his sage and tobacco.

"How are you feeling, Jim? Are you up to doing a pipe together?" he asked me.

"I feel like crap. But, yes, lets. It often helps for a while. And it's been too long brother."

I went upstairs and retrieved my pipe and tobacco and went back down to the den. Jim and I used to sit outside his home in Woodland Park and do a pipe as we watched the clouds move across Tava—Pike's Peak in Colorado.

"Pat, you doing this with us?" Jim called up to his wife. "We're almost ready. You need to hurry on down if you are joining in."

"Yes, I want to. I'll be down shortly," she answered sweetly.

Jim, by nature, likes control and plans, so I wondered how his 'hurry down' and Pat's 'down shortly' might mesh. Ah, those small points of difference and contention mates have and I no longer had, although I longed for it. Out of these thoughts, my cloud of depression began to rise again and the pain in my head and eyes worsened. I was glad to have this pipe to do so I would be distracted for a while.

This was not the way to do a pipe, to distract yourself from pain. But at this time, I did what I needed to, to survive. Once I began a prayer, talk or ceremony my spirit was totally engaged, which was what probably helped with the pain for a while. But on starting, my reasons were more self-serving—block the pain!

I sat, cross-legged, as was my way, on the floor in the middle of the den. Jim, with his large girth, had to sit on a sofa across from me. I took out my Chanupa and cleansed it in the smoke from the sage Jim had begun burning. Then as we waited for Pat, I got up, went outside and had a cigarette. Another of my addictions, tobacco in the form of cigarettes. Another way to not look inside and to block what I might see. I smiled as I thought, "Well, at least I have plenty to work on— food, tobacco, pain, depression and inertia."

When I went back in Pat was coming down the steps, glasses of water in hand. We sat and Jim, in his deep, glorious voice began opening the ceremony to the seven directions. We took turns as he opened the East and then nodded at me to open the South. From there we went in turn, from West, to North, to Father Sky, to Mother Earth to Great Spirit within us and around us. Each of these directions is spoken to with a prayer, welcoming in any help we need for those for whom we do the pipe and giving gratitude for the help we know we will receive. You never do a pipe for yourself—that is not the way— but you do a pipe for any who ask or for all people in general. In so doing you are also including yourself, but the pipe was not gifted to ask Great Spirit for your own benefit.

I have spoken of the Chanupa, its origin and use in my previous book. If you wish to know more you can go to that book, or research the Internet or a library. I also cover some of the ceremonies in that book in great detail. More about these things may come to us here, as we walk together, but, if not, you now know where to look.

After we finished our pipe ceremony together we sat and talked for a while. And had tea to which I added some crackers. It was comfortable, but I needed to get up early and never knew how much sleep I might actually get, so I got up to turn in.

"Are you ready for this weekend, Jim?" Jim asked me.

"I don't know. I wish you were coming."

"Just didn't work out. Sorry. You'll do fine I'm sure. Anything you are able to do will be welcomed. Who is coming?"

"I'm not sure, Papa. From Natural Leadership way there is Pam, of course, Mary, Quentyn—I think, Sue and maybe a couple of others. The rest are people Pam knows and has worked with in some way."

"Well, try and get some rest. You need more tea or anything else?"

"No thanks. I will take some of the sleep supplement I have and some natural calming herbs for my nerves and see if I can get some sleep."

"I've got my Overeaters meeting at 6:30 AM tomorrow. Every day, in fact. Want to come?"

"I don't think so, Jim. I'll rest, eat something and leave about 8. Will you be back by then?"

"Oh, yeah. Bacon and eggs? And some fruit?"

"Great. What can I do?"

"Nothing. Coffee will be on when you get up."

"Thanks, brother. Good to be here. Thanks for all the support and help."

"Welcomed. As you would do for me. Good night."

"Ho. Sleep well. Enjoy your meeting in the morning."

I lay in bed, twisting and fighting the pain in my head and the memories washing over me until two AM, when I finally dropped off; which only changed the media—as the memories and feelings came in my dreams. At three AM I was wide-awake—as always. I listened to flute music until I fell asleep again. Then I got up about 6:30.

After breakfast I left for Pam's—about a five-hour drive. I got there in the early afternoon, parked, got out of the car and approached her house. Pam came out and gave me a big hug—thanking me for coming. I went in and met her partner, Jeff, and her two boys—Sam and Doug. Pam and Jeff had cleared some land up the hill behind their house where they wanted to build the sweat lodge. We went out to take a look.

"Looks good to me, except it's circled by rocks, Pam. We might have to use them as a part of the sides. Okay?" I asked.

"Sure, whatever you say. There are rocks everywhere, so we might as well invite the Rock People to join us," she answered.

"Feels good. We will see how far we get. You know I told you I have seen it take four or five days to build a lodge. We have one and a half days to build this and still have enough time to go in and do ceremony. But, Spirit will guide us and we will go in, no matter how far we get with building it. Work for you?"

"Yep, it's your call, but I think we can do it," Pam said.

"Well, let me bring my things in and then I will want to spend some time up here doing prayers and clearing with sage and tobacco. After that I want us to prepare the holes for the willow twig supports so I can bless them as well."

"Great," Jeff said. "I have more willow branches than you asked for, but wanted to be certain we had what was needed."

"Good. Please bring them over near the lodge clearing before I start, Jeff. I want to smudge them and take a look at what you have. Then, if you will, dig that fire pit another two feet down. You positioned it where I asked. Thanks."

"Got it," said Jeff, who went off to do as I had asked.

"Jim," Pam said, "You are getting Sam's room. He will be staying at a friend's house. And you don't donate to the pot to help with costs— you came a long way and are our spiritual guide."

"Normally I would argue, Pam. But you know what I am going through emotionally and mentally, so I welcome the space."

I had arrived a day and a half before the gathering attendees so I could prepare myself and work on the lodge. This was the first time I was erecting a lodge without multiple elders involved, so I went up the hill past the lodge and sat with sage and sweetgrass and prayed.

"Wankan Tanka, Great Spirit. I ask your permission to conduct these ceremonies in 'the best way I know how' this coming weekend. And I ask your permission and guidance to erect this lodge so we may have a sacred place to connect with you, the Earth Mother and each other," I began. "Two Bears, Uncle and guide, I invite in your spirit and energy as we begin this retreat. I know you said you would be here and I thank you for that spirit presence. Ancestors of the four colors—white, red, black and yellow—I ask you to be with me during these days. I am ill, lonely and in pain. I need your support and energy to do ceremony in a way that will help all here and those they come for. Animal guides, please be here to protect this circle and this lodge. Wolf people, my pack, please circle this lodge we are about to build in the four directions and keep it safe from any negative energy that may attempt to intrude. Wolf of Many Colors, you who have walked with me so long, please sit next to me all weekend and walk beside me when I move. I will need to lean on you at times, a new thing for me. I ask these things not for myself, but so that I may serve others and help to heal the sacred hoop wherever it is broken. Mitakuye Oyasin."

Then I walked back down to the place where the lodge was to be built to begin the clearing of the land of any negative or dark energy and to welcome in all spirits wishing to help me with this lodge.

"Thanks, Jeff. That's plenty of willow branches," I told Jeff as he carried more branches towards the lodge area. "They look good and strong and are a good length. I'm sure we'll have plenty with what you've brought over. Let's start digging the fire pit deeper now. Okay?"

"Yep. I'll get a shovel now."

"Bring two. I could use a little exercise before doing more work on the spirit side of things," I called after him.

He came back with two long-handled pointed spades—perfect for this rocky soil. We began deepening the fire pit and I also added to its diameter. In about twenty minutes I stopped, panting a little.

"Jeff, is it okay if I start the clearing words? I've had about all the digging I can handle for now."

"Sure, I'll finish this up and then sit with you if I may."

"Absolutely. I think Pam was picking some things up at the market. Maybe she can come out when she returns. I really want her energy here as well."

I really liked Pam. She had strong energy and spirit, even if she still hid some of this from herself. She always contributed a lot to the conference calls and I had even asked her to guide a couple when I was unable. Pam was late thirties I believe—a single mom with three sons, two of whom still lived with her. I think she had lived with Jeff for a couple of years when I first met him. Jeff was more traditional, but a good, clear spirit as I sensed him. And he obviously wanted this weekend to go well and was willing to do whatever he needed to contribute.

I began by smudging the whole area and asking for the Ancestors to work with me to remove any negativity from the area. By smudging the area I mean I lit a handful of sage and one of cedar and burned it in the shell I had for that purpose. I used one of the sacred feathers gifted me in the past to move the aromatic smoke around as I walked the area where we would work. Then I marked with tobacco, the places where I would dig the holes and insert the eight upright willow branches. As I finished this Pam came walking up and Jeff paused in his digging and came over.

"Good timing, you two. This will be a good place for a lodge, but difficult to work with. You chose well, Pam, but we will need to see how we deal with these huge boulders. We won't move them, so we will make them part of the lodge."

"There really isn't any place without rock, like I said, and I thought these huge ones would bring Rock People energy to the lodge," Pam responded.

"Oh, they will, I'm sure," I smiled as I spoke up. "With these Rock People as part of the lodge and the Rock People we will heat and bring in, we will have rock energy to spare!"

"What should we do now?" Jeff asked.

"Let me smudge you two then, Pam, will you please smudge me. After that I'll dig the holes for the uprights, put tobacco and sage in them and say a prayer at each. Then we can sit and talk about tomorrow."

Just digging the small holes for the willow uprights—maybe three inches across—took time and persistence; hitting rocks all along the way. But finally I had them as I wanted and I began, from the East, going to each, putting in the tobacco and sage, and welcoming the earth and the willows to our lodge. Pam and Jeff followed along with me. When we were done, we sat in front of where the lodge door would be facing East to the new day.

"I used the boulders for extra support wherever I could and dug a willow hole there," I explained to Pam and Jeff. "In a while I will put a willow branch in each hole, where they will sit until tomorrow. We need to dig more within the lodge area so we have level ground, then I need a shallow fire pit dug in the middle of the lodge. About eight inches deep, no more. This pit will hold the Grandfathers—the rocks—when we bring them in. Can you do that, Jeff?"

"I'll work on the leveling," Pam spoke up.

"And yes, I'll add the pit," agreed Jeff.

By that evening we had the land for the lodge ready both physically and spiritually, the willows in place, the two fire pits dug and a huge pile of wood ready to be burned when the time came to heat the Grandfathers for the Sweat ceremony in the Inipi—the lodge. And we could not have looked dirtier or more tired than we did.

"Let's sit, drink water, and talk a little more about this weekend," I requested.

We sat around the large fire pit and Jeff made a small fire.

"Pam, I still don't know if we can finish this lodge in a good way tomorrow. But we will be far enough along to do a lodge tomorrow night or the next. What are your thoughts?"

"I'd like to do one each night, if you are able."

"You do like to think big. Maybe we can. Let's do tomorrow night and then see how we all feel. What time will people arrive tomorrow?"

"Two people are coming this evening and several more early tomorrow so we can get working. The rest as they can depending on how far they need to come."

"Good," I said, nodding my head in approval. "I doubt many, if any, have ever been in an Inipi, so I want to honor that newness. Yet I also need to honor the way a lodge is run and do everything as Two Bears taught me. This honors him, me, us and especially the Inipi Great Spirit is allowing us to build here. So, after we finish our work tomorrow we will all sit in circle and I will teach about the Inipi and some protocol things I will need followed. Good with that?"

"Yes," they said in unison.

"Great, now can we go wash and eat something? I'm famished," I said.

"Me, too," agreed Jeff.

We went inside and found Pam had made a fine dinner, which had been simmering on the stove—just waiting for us. Pam's sons joined us and we ate after a short prayer of gratitude to Wankan Tanka from Pam. Then I went and lay down for a while, with the brain pain and body spasms racking me. I was furious with myself, life and the universe as I wondered why I needed to continue this humiliating pain. Wasn't I doing my Spirit work? After an hour or so the pain eased enough so that I ventured back into the living room. Two people, a man and Sue, had arrived separately. I met them and we gathered up some drums and rattles and sat down for a lively drum and chanting session. I drummed, but did not sing following the directions for the mourning period I had agreed to.

After a couple of hours, I excused myself and went to my bed. I lay there for several hours before sleep—tortured, sweaty, stressful sleep—came to me. I managed to sleep for about four or five hours—good for me at this time. I was up at seven AM to pour myself some coffee, eat some scrambled eggs Pam had made and head out to the lodge. I had prepared some long, narrow pieces of cloth in the four colors to help bind the willow branches together. And Jeff had gathered some vines that I had also requested. We all stood around the lodge and I said a prayer to the seven directions. Then I asked Pam to smudge us all, followed by the lodge—inside and out. This complete I asked Sue, the woman who arrived the evening before, to smudge the fire pit and the area around the lodge out to about ten feet from the lodge. I then gave directions on how we would bend the willows and tie them together at the top, after which we would begin weaving other willows parallel to the ground through the uprights. These would also be tied in place. We would create a door in the East as we went, securing branches around its edges.

After several hours of smudging willow branches, bending them, breaking some, earning ourselves scratches and cuts, we had the willow 'ribcage' complete. Then another hour to re-arrange and re-tie some branches to give better shape to the lodge. All of this was more difficult with the boulders we needed to work around but, when we were done, this was one secure lodge!

"Good work all," I congratulated. "Now, how about some lunch?"

"Coming up," said Pam. And she and two others went to put food out. Shortly after we all followed them in. It had begun raining and the wind was picking up, so eating outdoors was not an option. When we got inside Quentyn arrived. Quentyn had been on the calls for months and I truly valued his words and wisdom. I felt he was a brother before we ever met. Quentyn was about my age; late fifties and thin. He also had obvious physical problems, with a painful-looking, leg scraping walk. And on his face—a huge smile. Something I would learn over time Quentyn almost always carried. Right behind Quentyn came Marge, another member of Natural Leadership Way. Marge was about fifty and had been a Catholic nun for twenty-five years, recently out of the order. I hugged them both, as did Pam, with great gusto. It was good to see them. Then three other people arrived. And finally a recent member of the conference calls, Sue, Pam's best friend, arrived. Hugs all around, then lunch for those who wished it. I went out to see to the lodge and pray about next steps.

After lunch Jeff built a larger fire in the fire pit and used sheets of wood to block some of the rain. It was pouring now, nonstop and heavy. Yet Jeff was determined we were going to have hot rocks to do a lodge. I gathered four of the others and we began putting blankets over the ribs of the lodge. It was difficult keeping them as dry as possible as we lashed them on. Then we put plastic sheets over the blankets to keep the downpour from drenching the blankets and 'raining' inside the lodge. Next we created a lodge door with branches and blankets and tied it into place. The lodge, in spite of everything, was built and in the right way with prayers, smudging and blessings.

Now I began speaking to Great Spirit and the Ancestors once again, giving thanks for allowing this to happen so quickly and well and asking for the rocks to be hot if I was to run a lodge that night.

Sometime later I called people into a circle and began instructing in the ways of the lodge. People asked their questions, which I answered as best I could, and then we went off to dress and spiritually prepare for lodge. At a little before seven PM we gathered in Pam's living room before going out to the lodge. We had thirteen who wished to do a lodge that night, so I knew it would be tight. In spite of my instructions about the lodge and what was expected of those who entered, one woman came wearing a swimsuit with metal fastenings. She also wore no skirt, that the women were asked to wear, and she wore a lot of metal, which all were asked not to wear. I called her aside.

"Carol, right?" I asked.

"Yes, it is," she answered.

"Carol, I apologize for not being clear, but women need to wear a long skirt into lodge. A bathing suit underneath is okay if you wish, but you need the skirt. And that bathing suit will not work—you have a lot of large metal clasps as part of it. No metal goes into lodge. It is not natural and so needs to be left outside. And it will burn you badly, another good reason for no metal."

"Well, I was not told any of this before I came and this is the suit I have. I have no skirt with me. I will wrap towels around the metal so I don't get burned," Carol said, huffily.

"I'm sorry, Carol. But you cannot enter the lodge without a skirt or in that bathing suit. I would ask Pam, or the other women, if they have something you can borrow. But you will not come in that way."

"I came a long way and I will do your lodge this way," she said angrily.

"I tell you once more, you will not. If you force the issue, there will be no lodge and you may explain to the others after I tell them why I have cancelled it."

At that she turned and stomped off, fire shooting out of her eyes at me. There are some things that can be allowed in the lodge. Some 'gray areas' that the water-pourer (the one conducting the lodge) can decide. But some things, like proper attire, are not optional in my teaching. I have not often blocked someone from a lodge, but have done it when the energy or respect was not right.

Ten minutes later as I spoke more with the group, Carol returned with a skirt over a loose blouse of some sort. I do not know who helped her, but I would now allow her in, even if I did not like her negative energy.

Marge called me aside as the others started out to the lodge. I asked them to wait outside of the lodge as I spoke with Marge. Marge, you will remember my friends, was the ex-nun of the group.

"Jim, I really want to come in, but I am afraid," Marge shared quietly.

"Marge, you must do what you feel comfortable with. I will run a lodge that is not too hot. And we will sing and chant, but nothing that should discomfort anyone. We all pray to the Creator—whatever name we each assign that entity. Then, when we share around the circle, you are free to enter a prayer in your way if you wish. At the end of each door, as I told you all, anyone may leave if they have had enough."

"Okay, I want to try," Marge said, a bit shakily.

I knew Marge with her strong Catholic foundation, might have difficulty with this ceremony. A ceremony viewed as pagan in the eyes of the church. So I respected her willingness to enter.

We walked up to the lodge where everyone waited, getting wetter by the moment. I asked Pam to smudge each person as they entered and asked the women to begin by going in and moving around the circle of the lodge fire pit in the direction of the sun, east to west.

After a few minutes we were in the lodge and I asked Jeff, who was serving as rock carrier, to bring in seven rocks. He brought in seven bright red rocks. I was amazed that he had been able to heat them this well in the downpour and saw this as affirmation that I was ready to pour the water. After he brought in the rocks, Jeff entered and sat next to the door—on the side opposite me. And so we began.

I had asked others to bring in rattles and flutes as they wished and had allowed Pam to bring in a drum, a second to mine. On the second lodge, the following night, I would ask Sue to bring in hers. So we did a lot of music making and chanting, but I sang no lodge songs as I had committed. I will not relate the entire lodge (I covered entire lodges in the previous book), but I will share some interesting happenings.

A lodge is divided into four 'doors', the time between when you close the door flap and begin praying, singing, speaking, etc. and the time the water pourer asks for it to again be opened. More rocks—seven each door—are then brought in. It is during these open doors I allow people to leave if they need to do so. Once someone leaves, I rarely allow them back in, but I invite them to sit with the fire and continue to be part of the circle. The emotional impact of a first lodge can drive some people into such a level of stress and fear that they feel much hotter than they are. There is no dishonor in this, it happens. It happened to me in my first lodge. If you are able to face this fear and continue—wonderful, you are working on yourself in a good way. If you need to leave that is also fine. Maybe you will try another time—maybe not.

After some opening drumming at the beginning of the second door I sent the 'talking stick' around the circle, so each person had the chance to speak if they wished. Marge did a short prayer in her churches tradition, which was a welcomed addition to the lodge and made her much more comfortable, as she told me later.

In the third door, after I had asked for my Chanupa to be brought in and we had smoked it in the circle, we began drumming and some-one began to sing: A woman with a beautiful, clear voice. As she sang I watched little pinpoints of light begin to form in places around the lodge—most notably in the lower half of the lodge. This lower half was nestled in amongst the boulders as I mentioned. More and more of these beautiful little pinpoints appeared and I poured more water and burned more sage as they did so. I prayed to Wankan Tanka asking for the healing of humans and reconnection with the Earth Mother. And I prayed for all of those close to me who had recently moved to the spirit world. And I prayed for each of those in this lodge. And the pinpoints of light continued to flicker around the lodge. Beautiful. Serene. Stunning. Unexplainable.

As any person conducting ceremony in a good way does, I continually energetically check in with each person in the lodge. With my current physical, mental and emotional state I feared for my ability to do this properly, but I was very pleased to see that my skills in this area were not diminished. I soon sensed strong negativity coming from two in the lodge and identified Carol as one and a man I had hardly spoken to as the other. I prayed for their comfort and asked Spirit not to allow this negative energy to disrupt the lodge. When this happens, as it does on occasion, it is important to 'wall off' this negative energy or, if it is too intense, to ask those bringing it into the lodge to please leave. I did not have to do this, as I was certain no one else in the lodge was being disrupted by his or her fears and doubts.

The third door ran long as I was fascinated by the light show and the energy we were building as a circle. Finally, I asked Jeff to open the door. He threw up the flap and prepared to exit for the last seven rocks.

"A moment, please Jeff," I stopped him. "Sit and let us speak around the circle."

He sat back down and I sat in silence for a minute or two. Just letting the energy flow and build. A skill Quentyn had guided me in exploring.

"Does anyone wish to share anything they have seen or heard before I ask Jeff to bring in the Grandfathers for the fourth door?"

"Well," said Pam haltingly, "It makes no sense, but I saw a lot of small lights moving around the bottom of the lodge."

"I saw them, too," piped up Quentyn. "Beautiful little spots of light that flickered and moved around. Sometimes they were alone, sometimes in clusters."

"I also saw them," said Sue. "I thought it was my eyes."

Several others spoke up indicating they had also seen them. And some began proposing 'logical explanations' for these lights. There was luminescent algae on the rocks; the minerals on the rocks were reflecting light; the heat and herbs were causing flashes in our eyes and so on. Of course this did not explain how or why they moved about—forming clusters and breaking free at times. Nor did it explain the large increase in energy many in the lodge felt when the lights appeared. In fact, I have seen, heard, smelled and felt many amazing, logically impossible things in lodges and in other sacred ceremonies I have been a part of. But I have never seen this dancing lights phenomenon before this lodge and the one the following night or since. It was, at least to date, something unique to this lodge and this time and place. My sense of it was the spirit people were in attendance at that lodge in a big way and the lights were their spirits connecting with us. Whatever the lights were about, they have remained in my conscious memory ever since. Maybe it was to show me I could survive and rise from the ashes and that a partner in my work was there with me, even if I would remain unaware of this for quite some time. Would, in fact, tell all who would listen that I wished my dog and I to be left alone, in the mountains, so I might do my work. I wanted no partner or other strong connections. The lights were that for me I believe, as I know they carried other messages for some in the circle of that lodge. Powerful medicine.

On the fourth door, the lights again appeared but from my perspective at least, they were somewhat less bright. And, on a second lodge we did the following night, they appeared only in the fourth door and for a shorter period of time. Maybe those they appeared for, including myself, were subconsciously 'getting the message' and so their work was done.

Over the three days of the gathering we always had about fifteen people in the circle. I believe we had nine or ten who stayed throughout and others from the local community, who came, participated for a while, and left. Some to return at a later time, some not. As it often is. I remember the second night we had nine in the lodge. And we sweated for a long time. Many spirits and animal guides filled the lodge with us. This lodge was more focused and intense then the first night, partly because those with any negativity had departed.

Sunday afternoon we wrapped up the gathering and those of us staying there prepared to leave. Pam was very happy with the event and her ability to face her fears and create it. I left and headed back to Jim and Pat's for a few days.

4 | Visiting the West: Building Strength

I DROVE THE MILES SOUTH, BACK TO JIM'S HOUSE, SLOWLY AND CAREFULLY as I was exhausted. While my energy stayed strong as I conducted ceremony and participated in drum circles, meals and talks, I was back into extreme pain as soon as I rested or went to bed. The fire in my nervous system burned bright and I got little sleep over the four nights I was at Pam's. I pondered this as I drove towards Jim's. No answers came as they still have not. For even now, although the intensity is somewhat less, I move through these times of powerful mind, body and spirit pains. I no longer fight it and I am certain there remains a reason for it, but I do hate the cycles of imbalance it causes.

I also thought about the things still blocking me from working on my healing by accessing memories and feelings deep inside—food, tobacco, white noise and motion. Jim and Pat were taking positive steps on their food addiction. Why was I laughing at this? Why not try it myself? Or was I not strong enough yet? If so—if not now, when? So I decided to speak to them more about the plan they were on. The tobacco I would again try to stop. I realize now my words were wrong "I would try. . .". I would have been better served to state "I will now stop using tobacco except when I use it in sacred ceremony." Words have power and importance, especially now. Never doubt it. In fact, when about a year ago I rephrased my intent to quit tobacco, I was able to quit. Please, examine the words you are using in any endeavor important to you. And when necessary, make apologies to Great Spirit for poor word choice, and re-state your intention in the clearest and best way. It works. Give it a try.

I spent four nights with Jim and Pat and learned about the Over-eater's Anonymous group and the Greysheet Plan. I went to two morning meetings with them and listened to the words of others with differing addictions. I left their house with a scale tucked under my arm and a new intention for how I would eat. And, while I have had my challenges over the past three and a half years, I have managed to keep my weight in fairly good shape. As I can no longer eat wheat or gluten in any food or sugar, I find eating more 'green food' appeals to me because of the discomfort gluten; sugar and starches can cause me. And it helps deal with my pre-diabetic blood sugar level without drugs. I will speak much, much more about prescription drugs, Western medicine and foods when I write the book about the dark time of my soul. I have much to share that I think others will benefit from hearing. And I am sure, much to hear from this circle and those it evolves into, which will help me continue to heal in a natural way.

I finally left Jim's and started the drive back to my rental home in Chester County, Pennsylvania. I left Jim's Connecticut home early in the morning on a Saturday, hoping to avoid some of the horrible traffic between Connecticut and Pennsylvania. I took Route 5 south from his town—the Merritt Parkway. A beautiful passage through woods and trees, but a driving nightmare. Cars flying along too fast on narrow, two-laned stretches. Deer coming onto the road from unseen positions amongst the trees. And cars entering from side roads via short, hard to see ramps. Accidents every day from what Jim told me. And I had seen a few in the times I had driven it. So I was paying careful attention to detail as I shot down the road at the 65 MPH speed limit. I passed two slower cars, and then pulled over as four cars roared by me—doing at least 80. I fast approached another car, doing maybe sixty, so I pulled into the outside lane getting ready to pass. I began to hit the gas so I might pass him more quickly and then get back over as I clearly—and loudly—heard a voice command me. "Slow down! Now! Quickly! Hit the brake now! Stop!" Loud, commanding and. . . the voice of my recently deceased wife. So clearly her voice, I began looking around; my face, I am certain, going white. As I did this I again heard, "Stop!!!" I hit the brake—hard. And pulled back over to the right behind the car I was to pass. I followed along, at fifty miles per hour or so for maybe fifteen seconds, when a huge stag deer broke from the cover of the trees to the left, crossed the north bound lanes and lunged into my south-bound lanes. A car, two in front of me, swerved and just missed the buck. The car I was passing was not so lucky and slammed into the buck maybe sixty feet in front of me. The car and buck both went flying off the road, with car parts flying by me. It all happened so quickly I had no time to stop. And I was in shock. Had I not hit the brake it would have been my car slamming into the buck.

This was not the first time I had help of this sort. I may share some in later books. But it really shook me to my core, especially given the state I was already functioning in. I felt horrible for the buck; as I knew he could not have survived. And I sent my prayers for the driver of the car. I called the state police from home two days later and was told the buck had died quickly and the man, who was the only oc-cupant in the car, was in the hospital but would recover. I sent a prayer out for the buck. And I sent energy and intentions to the driver. Then I did some ceremony around this event for myself. Hearing about the accident from the Connecticut police not only told me the outcome of the accident, but also verified that it had actually happened. There-fore, as there was no other reason for me hitting the brake that way, I had also heard the voice. I had committed to remain here on the Earth Mother, and finish my work in the Universe's plan; therefore I was warned so as not to exit before the play was over.

I drove the rest of the way home slowly and carefully, as you all might expect—with no incidents. I stopped at my sister's to pick up my partner and buddy, Onyx, and stayed for a good, home-cooked meal. I told my sister, another of the small circle who had helped me survive the dark time of my soul and still helped me survive, of the incident with the deer. Since she had been with me several other times in the immediate past when my wife, Bonnie, had made contact, she was not surprised. She was surprised that I actually heard a voice. The other contacts had been through animals and signs.

Jim Redhawk called me the day after I got home so we could talk through my feelings. I told him of the deer and the voice. He was curious, but not surprised. When you have walked a spiritual road long enough, little surprises you any longer. I told Jim I was planning a trip out West to Colorado. That I needed to get out of Pennsylvania for a while and see if that helped my emotional recovery. And he brought up his friend, Jack, once again. Jack's wife had died of cancer about six months before my wife succumbed.

"Great! I'll call Jack and tell him you will stop for a few days. He has a wonderful house just outside of Santa Fe and up in the mountains. It's right on your way. Then you can drive up through Taos to Colorado."

As I have shared, my friends, Jim was and is like a brother to me. There every time I need him; there to support me when I was ready to check out. Yet, there to also irritate and anger me at times as well. As I know I sometimes do with him. Wherever I am going anywhere, Jim has a short list of people I 'should' visit and 'should' stay with. I never do that—it's not my way. I'm an introvert functioning at times as an extrovert. Jim is pure extrovert. He loves center stage and will do everything he can to grab it; and he shines when there. I avoid it until I am pulled up on 'the stage' to do my work. And I shine when there. Jim is an elaborate planner always filling every hour of the day with a schedule. I let Spirit move me; and plan as little as possible. Interesting we are spirit brothers, eh? Or not? Maybe combined there is balance? I think this is so. But this time, for whatever reason I told him to go ahead and call Jack. I was going to spend some time with a friend in Buena Vista, Colorado, which is pretty much due north of Santa Fe.

"Great! Let me call him now and I'll get back to you in a little while!" And he was gone. All wrapped up in making 'a plan'. And thank Spirit he did. Jack and I needed to meet and needed to walk the road together in many ways. As you shall see when I introduce you to my brother Jack and he joins our circle here.

Jim called back later that afternoon and wanted me to give Jack a call. Jack was ready for my visit and he thought we 'should' talk. Should—groan! But I gave Jack a call and told him my travel plans. A week later I was on a plane to Albuquerque. I picked up a rental car and headed north to Santa Fe. Oddly enough, the rental car was a silver 2007 Toyota Highlander—the same car I own. So I was totally comfortable driving it.

I called Jack on the way north and got directions for reaching his house. About an hour later, I pulled off route 25 at the Glorieta exit—about twenty miles northeast of Santa Fe. From there I drove up the Santa Fe Trail road until I found the dirt road heading up the mountain to his casa. I travelled the two miles up the road as Jack instructed, but missed some landmarks and about a mile later as the road rutted into track, I went back down. Finally I saw a small sign with his number on it and turned in. The driveway wove several tenths of a mile through the trees and up to an adobe-style home, which fit into its environment beautifully. Wow, what a spread. With views down the canyons and only a few homes visible off in the far distance.

As I got out of the car, the door nearest me opened and a man walked out. And so, circle, meet my friend Jack Martin. Not the same brother I now walk with, but the Jack of three plus years ago. A man with a welcoming smile. A man with very, VERY, close-cropped hair; a large gut; and a painful-looking way of walking. A man with as much dark depression surrounding him as I carried—maybe more. We shook hands as he reached me.

"Glad you made it. Good to have you here," Jack began.

"Good to be here, Jack. Damn, what a great place. In nature and part of nature. I see the turbine. Are you off the grid?"

"No. The wind turbine never worked too well. But I do have solar that provides a lot of my electricity and hot water. And the house is straw bale construction. I'll show you later. Tired? Want something to eat?"

"Sure. I stopped and picked up some things, since I eat like Jimbo does now."

"Oh, Jeez. Another one with the scale?"

"In my bag," I smiled as I answered.

"I shouldn't talk. I could stand to lose a lot. How's brother Jim's diet going?"

"Meal plan, not diet. I think he's lost about seventy pounds the last time he checked."

"That's amazing," Jack said, shaking his head. "Never thought he could do it. He was over three hundred and fifty pounds you know?"

"Yep. It's an amazing thing to watch."

"Come on it and I'll show you your room options."

And so started a four-day visit to Jack—the first of many. We talked for long stretches, late into the night. We shared our stories of depression, grief, loss, regret and the like. And how we might better deal with our losses.

That first afternoon we sat and shared some about our past. And the connections were fascinating. First, as a reference point, Jack is ten years older than me. I already shared how we both lost our wives to cancer six months apart. We are both from Philadelphia. A couple of Philly boys—both walking very different roads now. And we lived only a few blocks apart in Southwest Philadelphia. Walking the same streets—with me ten years behind him. Playing in the same ball yards and vacant lots. Jack making mischief down near Hog Island Lumber Company, where my father worked. And, a little later, Jack's family moving to the western suburbs, to Springfield. And my family moving to the western suburbs, to Prospect Park. Again, only a few miles—and ten years—apart. The same pizza parlors; the same hoagie shops; the same hamburger joints; our sports teams playing each other. And now, all these years later, sitting here on a mountaintop in New Mexico. Both Westerners, both with lives which had taken dramatic turns into the painful realm. Both knowing the huge majority of those we grew up with still lived a short distance from the old stomping grounds in the Philadelphia suburbs. And so we wondered why this was and why we were here in this way. It's only recently I've seen the answers begin to appear.

With all these similarities, we were also very different in some ways. Again, that 'balance' thing. Jack and I were both business people. Me with retail and wholesale businesses and Jack with a steel company. Jack is strongly Conservative and I am a strong Liberal. Jack made out well when he sold his company and still has the means to live without too much economic worry. I did well selling my businesses, but lost most of what I had during my wife's illness. Jack, like Jim Redhawk, is also a planner, although less extreme. He likes to know where you are going to be and when you are going to be somewhere and I wait until I am there. And, with all the similarities and all the differences, we hit it off from the beginning.

Each night at Jack's I again tossed and turned in physical and emotional anguish. Jack booked a massage for me with a friend and that helped relieve the pressure enough for me to function. I tried to read, since Jack had a good selection of books available. But as it had been for seven years to that point, I was unable to read more than a page. And unable to write more than a page as well. This angered me as much, or more, than the pain I endured. As an avid reader, being unable to read was a true curse. And as someone my peers for years had praised for my writing abilities, being unable to write withheld one of my major assets from me. I see now that the time was not right and so my body and mind would not allow me to write. I hope to understand more of this as I travel along, but. . . no expectations there. If I understand more I will share it with you. If I don't, so be it. It is, after all, all about the journey, not the destination. Ah, repetition merits study.

When I left Jack's I travelled north and spent a day in Taos, a town I had always liked and felt at home in. Leaving there I headed north into central Colorado, past the Sand Dunes National Monument and towards Buena Vista. As I headed up Route 285, still in New Mexico, I suddenly pulled to the side of the road. I leaned my head back with my brain screaming at me and watched pictures play across the screen of my inner eyelids and listened to the voices in my head. Knowing by now I was not loosing my mind, I just waited it out. I think I see now that my heart is ready for the images, sound and smells that come to me on occasion. My brain however 'freaks out' and cannot take it. I work diligently to mesh the two so my heart can lead and allow these messages to flow. When it was over I continued on my way. Driving through so many places my wife and I had driven through was painful almost beyond endurance. I cursed my luck and anything else that came to mind. At times, I cried out in rage and pain, which was a great relief valve for the grief I was going through.

I spent about five days with my friend in Buena Vista, a small town I had also visited many times in my past. We spent a lot of time walking and talking. She had suffered a major loss a couple of years before she was still trying to recover from. We had connected while I was in Colorado Springs and it was good to re-connect. The pain still dogged me, however, and, on several occasions I was unable to hike some trails I knew. My body began spasming and my spinal cord rang out. As I backed off these trails, the pain receded. Interesting, eh?

On the other hand, I gave gratitude each morning to Great Spirit for allowing me to be here. When my own illness was at its peak and I could barely get out of bed, I was sure I would never see my beloved Rocky Mountains again. And here I was.

Some time after this visit I angered my friend from the high country and she broke off contact with me via an angry email. I miss that connection and that friend, but realize people come and go in our circle as is needed. She may re-appear later on my walk. Or she may not. Either way she remains a good friend and a part of my circle as I move forward.

From Buena Vista I drove to Vail, where I spent a few days with my good friend Kat. Kat was another of the Natural Leadership Way inner circle and a person of great spirit and energy. Kat and I spent a couple of days reconnecting and talking. Then I headed back to Santa Fe, stayed at Jack's for a night and flew home to Pennsylvania.

Another friend you will meet later, maybe in this journey, maybe in a later book and journey, is Tammy, the healer who saved my physical body a few years earlier. Three weeks after Bonnie died, Tammy invited me to a Healing From the Core workshop in West Virginia. I knew I could not, and would not, do this and Tammy knew I could, and would. And so... I did. Now a Healing From the Core New Years workshop was scheduled for January in Sedona, Arizona. Tammy and another good friend from the same group, Dale, thought they would attend. I also booked a spot. Then both Tammy and Dale had to back out. I searched my soul and decided to go. I flew out to Phoenix and rented a car. And, once again, got a 2007 silver Toyota Highlander. Coincidence, friends? Do you still really believe in those? Hmmm.

I drove up to Sedona, about one hundred miles north of Phoenix, and searched for the house Chery, a group member and friend from the West Virginia workshop, had booked for ten of us. After I took a familiarization ride around Sedona, I found the place, surrounded by the red rocks of the area. I was enthralled by the beauty and energy of Sedona. This was going to be a powerful ten days, of that I was sure.

I pulled into the driveway of our rental house and was welcomed by the few friends already there. It was a large, sprawling house and thirty feet away from it, a smaller guesthouse. It had a pool and wonderful views of the red rocks in every direction. My roommate, Joel from Florida, would arrive the next day—so I had a room and bathroom all to myself for the night. The workshop was not going to start for two days yet, but I had wanted to allow time for whatever physical effects from the travel I encountered to work through my system.

The next day others in our group began to arrive. The sisters from Scotland—whose energy I loved—came about the same time that Joel showed up. Fran and Gary, from Jackson Hole, got in that afternoon. They had an interest in Native American spirituality and I had spent a good amount of time with Fran in West Virginia sharing some of the knowledge I had. This group that now arrived I knew I would do circle work with in the future. Some of this has already occurred and more I see is yet to come. And then all the others began arriving. It was good to see them: I felt at home; I felt that I was with family.

This paradoxically, gave me strong, painful reactions all through my nervous system.

That night we gathered at our rental house to meet and talk and hear from Suzanne, the creator of the Healing From the Core process. She had invited a local musician, Jesse Kalu, to come, meet us and play his flutes. This began a relationship for me with Jesse that holds to today. Jesse is from Micronesian, the U.S. Virgin Islands. He has lived in Sedona some twenty years and had been working with Suzanne for a number of years. He leads hikes to sacred places around Sedona for Suzanne's groups and plays music at least one evening during the workshops. And his music is special and powerful. He carries about ten flutes with him, each being a different style and each made by Jesse from bamboo around Sedona. He mimics animals, birds, sea-life and the elements when he plays—transporting you to another place. People come again and again to hear him play at different venues around Sedona. He is the most serene, peaceful, connected person you could image when he is playing his music. When he puts down his flutes and lives daily life he becomes fractured, frantic and disconnected from what others are saying. It's an amazing difference and one visible to all who know him. I think it is all about balance once again. When he plays his music he is truly in a place of high art. He is totally connected with the music, the listeners and the Universe. Therefore, when he is not playing the flutes, he rolls all the way to the other end of the spectrum. The two states, when combined, produce a balance-of-spirit.

Jesse and I immediately hit it off. Maybe because my spirit was also fractured now—with personal examples of energy and behavior at both ends of the scale, as I have been sharing with you. I had brought my Chanupa, as Suzanne had requested, and Jesse had many questions. I felt we would do some one-on-one work while I was there. Two days later, Jesse took the group to the Birthing Cave where we hiked into a powerful canyon. The cave it was named for looked like a woman's birth canal and was used by the Native American women as a place to gather when one of their group was preparing to give birth.

Jesse climbed into the rocks as we ascended from the trail to the cave. Then some of us entered it, one-at-a-time. As others sat around the cave, Jesse showed me a medicine wheel, out-of-the-way, some distance below the cave. It was there I burned sage and sent prayers and requests to Great Spirit. I did not realize this would become a special place for myself, and others, down the road.

The next day, Jesse offered to take me to meet his ex-wife, an energetic healer. Jesse had an ex-wife and many, many ex-girlfriends. His spirit and magnetism while playing attracted them and his everyday energy eventually drove them away. A difficult road for anyone to walk. I told Suzanne I would miss the morning sessions and possibly the entire day. She was aware I needed to work on my healing in ways outside of the sessions and I had no role that day, so I felt comfortable in this decision. We went and met Kim, Jesse's ex-wife in the morning. She had made coffee, so we sat and talked for some time. I liked Kim and felt there were things we could work on together. Then she began talking about the non-profit healing and teaching institution she was working on and I saw the connection. We talked about my non-profit work and she became excited, asking me to assist her. I said we could talk more later.

When we left Kim, we headed back to the hotel the workshop was being held at. Jesse pulled over and asked me, "Jim, I really want you to meet a local artist, Bearcloud. Can we stop by his gallery?"

"Sure, Jesse. I'll get back when I need to. Let's do it."

And so we drove to Bearcloud's Edge of Town Gallery—one of two he had in Sedona at that time. We went in and Jesse asked the woman there if Bearcloud was in.

"No, I think he is home working on his art, Jesse."

"Abbey, this is Jim. I really hoped Bearcloud could meet him. He walks the Red Road and has done a lot of non-profit work; I know they would connect on the Chameleon Project."

"Oh, wow. Let me call Bearcloud and see what his schedule is."

Abbey got on the phone and Bearcloud answered, something, I learned later, he did not often do when at home painting.

"Ok. Yep. Good. Wait, let me ask," Abbey said into the phone.

"Bearcloud says he would really like to meet you. He lives up the canyon and wants to know if you can wait forty-five minutes or so?"

"Sure, if it's okay with Jesse."

"Fine with me. I need to run some errands, so I can come back in a couple of hours," Jesse answered.

"Bearcloud," Abbey said back into the phone, "Jim can wait. He'll be here. I'll give him the tour."

Jesse left and Abbey and I chatted as she showed me around the gallery and introduced me to the Chameleon Project. I was fascinated by everything I saw and heard. The Chameleon Project was a non-profit project based around the visions of Bearcloud and the crop circles of years past and present. Go to www.chameleon-project.org for more on this.

Some customers came in about fifteen minutes later and Abbey went to wait on them, so I began roaming the gallery, slowly taking in Bearcloud's art. Some art appeals to me and some leaves me cold. Bearcloud's spoke to my spirit. Then I rounded a corner and came upon a painting *Guide My Path, Send Me Visions*, which stopped me cold, captivating my full attention. The wolves in the painting virtually spoke to me as I stood there. Tears welled in my eyes and began rolling down my cheeks. It was the strongest reaction I had ever had to a piece of art. If you want to know what the painting looks like, circle, go to my first book since Bearcloud used the painting in creating the cover for me. Or visit his virtual gallery at www.bearcloudgallery.com. I stood there mesmerized for thirty minutes until Bearcloud entered the gallery.

"Aho, Jim?"

"Yes. Good to meet you, Bearcloud."

We spoke about his art and the Chameleon Project for over an hour. I was really tuned into his energy and the work he was doing.

"So," he said. "I am doing a lodge Friday night. Can you come?"

"I am here with a workshop group, but I think I can make that work. It's been way too long for me and I would be honored to go into your lodge."

"I see. Good," he answered. "Do you think you might want to help in some way with the Chameleon Project?"

And I spoke it as it came to me—no one more surprised than me, "Yes, I know I do. I believe I will be moving here very soon. I have met you and a couple of others I know I have work with."

"Cool beans," he answered with a smile.

And so, after a few days in January, I knew I would be moving to Sedona—where I knew only a few people and had no means of generating a living. Thank you Spirit for showing me the way.

It was a powerful lodge that Friday night. I had no idea it would be the first of many or that I would serve as fire-keeper and rock carrier for Bearcloud at times in the future. I just knew I was home when I entered the lodge.

Fellow travelers, if you visit whatever place I am living in these days, you will find my copy of *Guide My Path, Send Me Visions* hanging in a place of prominence.

I felt years younger while I was in Sedona and my fellow workshop attendees told me this as well. Yet, when I left to drive to the airport in Phoenix I had to pull off the road as I was assaulted by pictures and stress-like reactions. I sat there over an hour and almost missed my flight. But I did make it and flew home ready to prepare for my move. I intended to be in Sedona before March 21, the Spring Equinox.

5 | Preparing for the Journey

I ONLY HAD A COUPLE OF MONTHS TO MAKE THIS MOVE BY MARCH 21 if I was serious about it. I had a gathering at Jim Redhawk's in February and a lot of work doing a give-away. In a give-away, you gift possessions you no longer need to others or gift possessions to others who need them more than you do. My intention was to gift virtually all I still owned. I wanted to start clean and unencumbered by my past. At least as much as I was able to do so. My first step would to be to ask my stepdaughter what she wanted of her Mother's things or mine.

I also had six people working with me as their healing guide who I needed to work with, as I got ready for the move. So, in order to get it all done I took my Chanupa and sage and Onyx and I went off for some long walks. I needed to do some journeying and meditating before beginning any of the work of moving.

One trip we took was back to the Conowingo river walk. We left early on a Saturday morning and walked about four miles down the trail, watching the eagles, hawks and other water birds as I always did. Then we played for a while—well, Onyx played and I did as he asked. I threw sticks out into the water and he swam out and got them. Onyx will do this for hours on end if you allow it; he is a true water dog. This day was no exception and I threw sticks for about forty-five minutes, when I saw him starting to tire and I knew we still had to walk back. We walked about half of the way back as I looked for a place to stop. Finally I saw a nice grassy field behind some trees, but within sight of the river. Perfect. I had only seen two people during the several hours we had been walking and playing, so I didn't expect to be disturbed.

I burned some sage and prepared my pipe for opening to the seven directions. As I got out my tobacco a family of four: mom, dad, one boy and one girl appeared heading down the trail in my direction. I continued preparing my pipe and hoping they would respect my space.

As they got nearer the little girl being about ten, ran over and asked, "What are you doing?"

The father came and took her hand, guiding her back to the trail and said to me, "I'm sorry. We'll move out of your way in a minute. Sorry again."

"No problem," I answered. Although in that time and place it was.

"Are you an Indian?" the little boy asked. He seemed about the same age as the girl—maybe ten or eleven.

"No. I have learned some things from Indian friends," I answered, as Onyx jumped up and ran over to play with the kids. Oh, well, I guess I was sunk. "You are all welcomed to come over and I will tell you what I am doing," I said with an insincere smile.

It was not that I didn't want to teach or lead circles as I had been trained to do, but it was my state-of-mind and trying to see my way to making the move West that had my preferences at 'I hope no one comes along'. But, as the kids quickly took me up on this—petting and hugging Onyx as they did, I felt suddenly good about having a circle as I did today's ceremony.

"Are you sure?" the mother asked.

"Yes, if you wish it."

"I'm sure the kids will pester you with a hundred questions. Is that okay?" she continued.

"Yes, I'll tell them when it is time to do some prayers and you all can stay or go as you wish. But you guys will respect that and be still, right?" I asked the kids.

"Oh yeah," they yelled as they hugged Onyx some more and looked at my pipe and my ribbon shirt.

And so the family began asking questions that I answered as I continued to get ready and then I began to tell them about praying to the seven directions. The kids wanted to stay and the parents, after again asking if it was okay, agreed.

As we were getting our little circle ready for me to smudge everyone, two teenage girls came up the trail. They looked over our way as they approached and one, a cute blond girl with close-cropped hair wearing a Colorado sweatshirt smiled broadly and came over towards us. She stopped about ten feet from us, smiled even broader and nodded pleasantly. I smiled back and waved them over.

"Hi, I'm Sandy and this is my friend, Sarah," she said as she came up to the circle. "We are taking classes at Lehigh University and heard about the eagles here so we came to see them. I'm from Colorado and haven't seen anyone doing a pipe ceremony in two years. I miss it. May we join?"

"Certainly," I answered. "I am Jim and this family of four are new friends who came up a little while ago just as you did. I'll let them introduce themselves—but, first, this is Onyx, spirit dog and master companion. He'll be doing ceremony with us."

Everyone then shared introductions and brief bio facts around the circle. I added more sage to the bowl and asked our new friend from Colorado if she would like to smudge us so we could begin.

"I'd love to! Thank you so much, Jim. This is the best thing that has happened to me in months!" And she took a feather from my medicine box and began smudging the group—starting with Onyx. Now I really liked her energy.

I explained a little more about what we would be doing, the drumming and prayers. Then I explained my slow drumming would match the heartbeat of the Earth Mother while I would speak quietly allowing them to journey in spirit wherever they chose. Or to sit quietly and enjoy the smells and sounds around our circle here by the river.

We drummed (with the one drum I had with me), chanted, and they all had the opportunity to journey as I spoke through the one-two rhythm of the heart drumbeat. We were there a little over two hours much to everyone's surprise, when I brought them back to the here and now.

"That was amazing," the mom said as she rubbed her eyes and breathed in deeply.

"So cool," said our youngest, Tad, the little boy.

"Can't we do more?" asked Alice, the little girl.

"Not now, Alice," I told her. "Everyone is tired. I know I am."

"Ah. Okay."

"Tell you what. Anyone in this group who wants to learn more is welcomed to come to my house next Sunday. I'll give you all my number. If you come, bring some food and we will share afterwards."

"Wow, can we mom?" Tad asked.

"We'll see, Tad."

"I'm coming," said Sandy, the girl from Colorado. "May I bring another friend?"

"No problem," I answered, wondering why I was offering this, given the way I felt.

"Can I pay you something for today's wonderful gift or next week's if we can make it?" the dad, Frank, asked.

"No, Frank. When I lead something like this it is my responsibility to do so when asked. I never take pay for it. You can bring some food, tobacco and sage if you like, but that's all you will need."

"I guess we're coming," mom, Janice, said with a smile.

"It came to me as we began our ceremony that there were seven of us in the circle today—one for each of the directions I opened with prayer. That's a powerful way to go. See you next week. I may invite a few more people. Be welcomed to do the same." And I got up, called Onyx who was exploring a log by the water, and started towards my car realizing as I walked how much I had enjoyed this circle. Then, as I began thinking about those no longer around my circle I began to quietly weep. The ride home was dark and somber for me, but I was glad for the day. I knew I was to head west to Sedona and would soon begin preparing for that.

Sue, from the gathering at Pam's, called that evening and I told her about my circle forming around the pipe. She was now one of those I was assisting on her healing journey and some huge changes she wished to make in her life's journey. We talked for a while as she drove home from work and then I had to get off and feed Onyx, who waited quietly but with big eyes.

After feeding Onyx, I sat at my computer and answered a batch of emails; then I returned a call to another Susan with whom I had worked as a healing guide and still aided on occasion. I had not heard from her for several months and wanted to see how she was doing. Susan had gone through some very dark times—still was and would be for a long time, maybe forever. But at least now she was working at healing rather than wishing for death. Similar to me in that respect. Susan had lost all three of her children in a horrible car accident about a year before someone sent her to me. Even then, with all the pain I was going through, I saw the irony of my working with a Susan while my own wife was taking her last walk on this life's road. And yet, much like the ad hoc pipe circle, it helped me get through each day as I was helping Susan. Life can be interesting and twisted— as can the spiritual road. But at least not boring. Susan asked if I used the healing blanket she had sent me about a year before. And of course I did. When someone works with you on your healing or conducts ceremony for you and your circle over time, it is customary to gift them a Pendleton Native American blanket. She had given me a beautiful one with a dragonfly woven into the middle. The dragonfly is a bringer of rebirth in the Lakota way. I still have it on my healing table to this day and am certain I always will. We spoke for about thirty minutes then agreed to speak longer the following week, as we were both tiring.

While this computer work and phone call was going on I had the stereo playing, the TV on and the lights blazing from every lamp. The blocking of painful memories I mentioned earlier. I turned off the TV and lowered the stereo and decided to sit and attempt to write about my day. I got one sentence down and my head screamed, my nerves jangled and I could feel my blood pressure rising. I stopped in disgust and threw down the pen. Maybe I would try again tomorrow.

On occasion, over the past five years, I had been able to write short pieces and share what I thought even if I was only sharing with myself at the time. And I remembered a piece I had written a couple of months ago before deciding to go west. I searched for fifteen minutes before I found it. It seems I need to share this with you now, my fellow travelers. And so, here it is.

Doors to the Spirit World

Four doors to the den—boltholes to run to when in danger in the field to the north and above my house. The holes set in the four directions. I found the hole to the West the first day I crossed the field—four days a go. The field was hay cut a few days before that. Until then there was no good way to cross and I would never have seen the entranceways. All in its time. I looked at the West hole that day and felt the soil around it. Fox or groundhog? Or something else? It was the right size for a fox and, since I often watch them frolic in the field East of me, I thought this might be home to Brother Fox and clan.

Onyx and I continued our walk that day and went about our business back at the house. But I didn't feel complete. So I went back the next day and found the East hole. Same size. The 'back door' I thought. Again Onyx explored the holes and ran off across the field. I looked at them and then followed him to the stream and woods beyond. That night I led some drumming at a new drum circle I attended. I was asked for some teachings and taught about the Rock People, as that energy has been strong in me of late. There was a lot of fear and angst around the current changes in the World and the Rock People teach us strength, grounding and patience when faced with these emotions. I then did a circle clearing and healing with sage and my Chanupa—un-smoked, but present. One of the other healers there, Tim, offered a healing through sound. I welcomed this. It also brought to mind the sound healers who have come into my space of late: Pam, Hank and Ash. His words to me were, "You walked in an open field or meadow recently and visited a large tree beyond it in woods. But I sense you missed the message—or the full message." That was right on and I knew another walk would come the next morning.

The next morning Onyx and I headed over to the fields. I stood to the side of the West hole and looked over the field. I wondered about the holes I had found and what message I continued to miss. I slowly walked the field—ignoring Onyx and letting him chase butterflies. In a couple of minutes I found the boltholes between the West and East holes. I looked at them and the broader landscape. It was then I realized the four holes were laid out in the four directions. I sat a while and made some notes in my journal. Four holes— four directions. A string fence to the South of the holes and where I stood. Another wire fence to the North, just before the vineyards on the adjacent property. All of the holes on a slope—good site lines in three directions, but a little blocked to the North. I wondered if their maker had considered the placement for protection and safety.

I called Onyx and as he bounded my way, I headed towards the stream and the woods beyond. As I started up the hill next to the trees, I came across the tree Tim mentioned in my healing. A Grand-father tree. Tall, full and knurly. With exposed giant roots, which made a natural 'seat'. I sat with 'Grandfather' a while after asking his permission to seat myself on his roots. But worry about Onyx going off started me back on our walk. I had moved from two holes to four honoring the directions. And added Grandfather tree's calming presence. Grandfather tree whom I had seen many times as I passed him, but neglected to register. But the message? Still unclear.

I ate and knew it was time to drum and journey; and I feared it once again, as I have too often of late. Unconsciously distracting myself so as not to connect too deeply. I set up my altar and brought out four candles to represent the four directions—and the four matched holes from the field. I asked my animal guides to take me to see whatever more I needed to see. And help me construct the full message nature was giving me in the field and woods.

After some time, Wolf came to me and took me to the bolt holes. He stopped by the West hole and patiently sat and waited. His body language instructed me to do the same. Soon a lemur came from the North. I have never had a lemur as a guide and needed to tap my memory to name his species. He took me down the West hole as Wolf watched us go. Images from my past began coming to me in a controlled rush. He took me deep along the passage and I knew pleasure and pain; joy and sorrow; comfort and regret. As the passage neared the den, he stopped. I sensed from him the teaching, "Remember these things—take joy in them. Know they are where your knowledge of the Ways came from. But you can't live in this passage. The West is closed to you for now. Go back tomorrow to the den holes and ponder them. Study the area and see what you are still missing. Talk to Grandfather tree. Talk to the two-leggeds who need to hear."

He led me back the way we had come. At the entrance he turned me back over to Wolf. They both looked at me. I am not yet ready to go down the other holes, but Lemur will be there to guide me when I return. It will be soon.

Wolf ran and leaped as we journeyed back to the physical realm. He shifted from Wolf to Onyx repeatedly. As I have sensed, Wolf is in Onyx and Onyx is in Wolf. The gift of Onyx was so that Wolf could walk with me in both the spirit and the physical worlds as I go through this change and growth.

I went to bed and laid listening to the wolf CD Pam had gifted me. It always soothes and focuses me. And Onyx likes the howls. I slept a few hours. I wanted to go to the fields when I awoke, but Onyx pulled me the other way. Up the gravel lane leading to my house. I gave in. We walked for an hour through the site near the country road that serves my gravel lane, through where 10 homes will soon appear. Onyx leaped at butterflies, chased a rabbit and generally frolicked. I walked, sweated, felt stress and then relaxation. I had some errands to run. Did I—or was I distracting myself again? When I returned to the house I did some cleaning around the yard, picked up my journal and headed to the field. Onyx ran ahead. He would be outdoors 24/7 if I was willing. A message there, too. One that needs more observation and thought.

I sat at the holes and observed everything with all my senses and, most importantly, with my spirit. Four holes—in the four compass directions. North and South close to each other; maybe three feet apart. East and West about ten feet on either side of the North—South holes. Since I could not walked through this field before it was cropped for Fall, I would not have seen these holes before that. It was not time. Now, apparently, it was.

West is 'older' looking than the others. A larger mound of dirt before its opening from the occupant's excavation. And not much growth around its orb except some old, twisted vine arms reaching around it. The hole goes down and turns sharply left. It was this hole Lemur took me down. Onyx nosed the hole and slowly walked around it. He looked up at me. This passage has been well used and the scent is strong. But it now seems dormant. As Lemur showed me—I am not to live here—in the past—at this time.

I walked the ten feet to the North—South holes. I went to the North as Onyx was already sniffing and eyeing it. It looked much like the

West, but with some greener growth around it and less dirt at the entrance. A sense of current use. The North—the direction of the Medicine Wheel I now see myself standing beside.

Before going to the South hole I was drawn to the East. The East had some entrance dirt and flowers on its border. Late summer flowers that came up fast as the field was cut a week ago. Something came to me from the hole energetically, but I could not put a name to it. Onyx spent some time here, then jumped and raced to North and South. He was having a ball. He went quickly to the South hole, and was raptly engaged in studying it. There is no dirt leading to this hole. Cleaner, more smoothly cut. And a passageway that seems to go straight down and back. Onyx was sniffing some droppings just in front of the hole; fresh scat. Fox scat. So my guess about the occupants was confirmed: It is a fox den—and an active one. This hole had not been used for some time but, with the scat, it was now to be the 'front door', the South. Moving to a time of energy and action. The summer of the wheel. Field birds began singing as we stood at this hole; they had been silent before. And I became more aware of the loud background sound of the crickets scattered throughout the field.

I am excited to reconnect with Lemur. I have seen more and hope I am ready for more teachings and guidance.

As I turned to begin the walk across the field, over the stream and up the path to Grandfather tree, my phone rang. I forgot it was on. It was Sarah, a friend from a drum circle. Perfect timing. We talked as I walked and Onyx leaped, ran, paused, looked back and ran some more. We had not spoken much of late, but I sense her energy often when I journey. We talked about the shift and she shared her uneasiness and edginess, as matches my own. How she felt we needed to 'do'—but do what? I sat on Grandfather tree as we continued to speak. She called me so she could talk to someone who understood and would not think her crazy. I could answer her back with the same understanding. As I can with enough people now that it gives me confirmation that the time for change is now. As the Elders spoke to us through their tears at the Massachusetts gathering, "we have waited so long to share these teachings and work together with the people of all four colors." It is not the color, but the teachings and the level of 'awakeness' that makes the bonds of those of us who will guide through the shift. And show the new/old ways.

Since soon after I got back to the house, I received a lot of 'jolts' through my body, pain in the head and a feeling of walking the physical and spirit world at the same time. As has happened over the past six months. I fear it and welcome it. It seems like a block to more journeying. Blocking what I might learn about what is next on my road? I don't know, but I will face it and journey again tonight, I hope. And put the intention not only about my path, but the path a group is now to walk on the road together. The time is now. The Shift is happening. But the action is what? Patience will bring it. But as the Elders said—we've waited so long.

I hope to add more to this tomorrow. I hope to again face my fears and let my joy and interest guide me tonight. For Spirit to decide.

I did not realize how well this fit into what I have been sharing with you all. And how it explains a little more about my journey, while making other things cloudier. This is often how I have found the Red Road to be. Nothing is totally clear, nothing is set in stone. And yet there are messages and signs if you just pay attention.

The next day I remember walking to Grandfather Tree again and sitting, waiting for a clear time in my head so I might catch my feelings about this elder tree. Onyx decided to chase some deer in the field below us—something he did whenever he saw them. And they did the same with him. So I watched him chase the deer east to west and then two deer chase him west to east. It seemed a game they loved to play. As I did this I captured my thoughts, directed to Grandfather Tree, in the following words.

Grandfather

Grandfather tree. Speak to me.
Roots connected to our Mother.
Canopy intertwined with Creator.
Words, pictures, signs or senses.
I am here to listen.

Grandfather tree. Nourish me.
My spirit is in pain. Matching Mother's.1
An imperfect two-legged trying to understand.
Nourish me through the wisdom of your long tenure.
Send me peace and surety as I sit your roots.

Grandfather tree. Teach me.
My two-legged teachers have given.
I have learned.
My four-legged, winged and finned have taught.
I understood.
The Rock People and Plant People have serenaded me.
I listened.
My spirit guides have led.
I have followed.
Share with me now what more I need from nature.
Polish the edges of my skills and gifts.
Add to me what I need to best walk the Red Road.

Grandfather tree. Ground me.
I am floating and free as I await the next steps.
Ground me so I may see how I am now most needed.
Root me in Mother's soul.
Let my spirit fly as my roots support me.

Grandfather tree. Embrace us.
Channel the light and wisdom of Creator to those who will serve.
Fold the powers of Father Sky and Mother Earth and imbue us
* with their energy.*
Do all this so that the communities that must form do so with love
* and understanding.*
And purpose.

Mitakuye Oyasin
We are all one.

Jim Gray Wolf

I have rarely written poems—prose being my preferred way. Yet my entreaty to the Standing Person, Grandfather Tree, needed to come out this way. I had almost thrown this away, I remember, since I felt in writing it I had said what I needed to. Yet something had stopped me, telling me I would need them for someone or something later. So I had put both pieces in the back of a notebook I kept copies of important emails in. And forgotten about them until this evening that I am telling you about now. I am glad it was for you that I was saving these writings for. I hope they just added something to our walk here.

As we now walk this road I just realized an amazing thing about this poem. I wrote this in 2008 and signed it Jim Gray Wolf. Yet I had not remembered my vision of many years ago that I shared with you in *White Man, Red Road, Five Colors* until 2009. It was when I remembered this vision and a lodge with Two Bears that I was told to change my name from Redwolf to Graywolf. Almost two years after I signed this poem. I will need to put some questions about this to my spirit guides in dreamtime tonight and see what I might learn. It is these types of occurrences, my friends, that we need to pay special attention to. I did not pull these writings out until an hour ago and now see my current name before I was given it. As my friend Bearcloud would say, "Cool beans. . . and that's all I've got to say." For now, that's all I've got to say about the signature on my poem.

I put most of my furniture, carpets and other possessions in storage at my sister, Donna's house. I had intended to give everything away, but my stepdaughter, Dana, son-in-law, Stephen, and two grandkids, Lyra and Dashiell, were now going to move from Los Angeles to Maine, where they hoped to buy a house. A house that would have no furniture. So what better place for my furnishings than Dana's upcoming Maine farmhouse. Other things they would not need—TV's, computer, computer table, extra desks and the like. I donated these to families in Chester County who Donna knew. But before I could physically move the things to Donna's, I had one more East Coast trip to make.

I headed up to Connecticut to Jim and Pat's for a four-day retreat they had put together. Quentyn was on his way from Mt. Shasta, California, and was going to come back to Pennsylvania with me, where we would spend several weeks and then drive together, with Onyx directing from the back seat, to Sedona. I looked forward to seeing my new brother again and spending time working together. Seth, a leadership facilitator like Jim Redhawk and friend through Natural Leadership Way was coming, as were Sue and Marge. Pam had intended to come, but dropped out at the last minute. Another person from the weekly circle calls, Monique, was coming with Sue. Monique had been a problem for some time; monopolizing the group's time constantly by looking for everyone's support and sympathy. Bursts of anger did not help her or the rest of us either. But Jim and I had talked and agreed we would attempt to assist her this weekend and call her aside and lay down the rules if needed. My good friend, Moria was flying up from Texas and another friend, John, was coming with her. In addition, another six or seven friends of Jim's were coming. It would be a full house. We would work on leadership skills and do some self-improvement workshops.

The retreat went really well with everyone, as we were told, getting some powerful lessons to take home and work with further. Monique did become a problem and had to be talked to several times. A couple of months later she would be released from the group since she refused to honor individual or group boundaries. I felt bad about this, but the lesson, once again that 'one' cannot be allowed to damage the entire circle was a good one to have repeated. Sue, Quentyn and I spent a great deal of time together talking and laughing. I took several long walks with Sue in order to work with her directly on the issues I had been guiding her on.

Quentyn and I left a little early the final day since a snowstorm was coming up from the south; the way we needed to travel. Half way into the journey, snow began to pile up and we were reduced to a snail's pace. Suddenly we looked to the side of the car and saw, on a small, once-grassy area now covered by eight inches of snow, a rabbit looking back at us.

"What is he doing out here?" Quentyn wondered. "What meaning does a rabbit appearing have in your teachings?"

"We can look it up later. But being gentle and soft are two aspects. Also being trapped without moving is something you want to consider. And I know it is a sign that something more will appear to you within 28 days. That's all I can remember. But him being out here, in winter, in deep snow, in the middle of the highway is very strange. So let's give it some thought."

About an hour later the snow tapered off and stopped shortly after that. We drove out of the storm into just cloudy skies and cold wind.

Several people had asked to drive to Sedona with me, which I welcomed. I really doubted my ability to drive that far alone given the physical and mental pain too much driving brought on in me. Jim Redhawk had thought to go with me, but had to drop out due to a project. Larry, another friend from Pennsylvania was ready to go, planning out our route, when he suffered a minor heart attack and had to back out. So when Quentyn suggested his plan to drive with me, I was happy to say yes.

Quentyn and I spent the two and a half weeks at my place talking and going out in nature. Then we had some local farm workers come with trucks and move my things to Donnas. After that Quentyn and I slept on the floor, Onyx nestled next to me. About five days before we were to leave, Quentyn's VA doctors in California told him he needed to get back there for tests and treatment at once. I drove him to the airport two days later, went back to my place and packed the car and went to Donna's to spend the night before I headed out. Now just Onyx and I were going—and Onyx is not a good driver. I was afraid, but also excited.

Onyx and I ended up spending two nights in Donna's guest room— the same room I spent two weeks in after Bonnie died. It seemed this journey, the worse of my life by far, had come full circle. We left early on a Saturday morning to miss traffic while we drove through the East.

6 | Heading South to Go West

ONYX AND I HEADED WEST ON ROUTE 30 THROUGH LANCASTER County; home of many Pennsylvania Dutch communities, and a county I had long loved to visit. My emotions were mixed; excitement that I had been able to get this far tempered by a feeling of being completely alone; wonder that I would actually live in the West again and fear of doing this alone. An interesting mix but at the beginning of the journey excitement and wonder were winning the emotional race.

I had no plans about how far I would travel each day or even what route I would take. Why? What was the point? All about the journey, friends. And it was March seventh, so I had fourteen days to make the Equinox should I want or need them all. I had only packed what I needed for the trip in the car—much of the remainder of what I was keeping I had shipped to Kim in Sedona. She was storing my things and giving me a place to sleep until I found something to rent. This at least gave me some feeling of connection on the far side of this journey.

I stopped every hour or two so Onyx and I could stretch and he could romp. We managed to find some good parks to stop in as we slowly meandered through Lancaster. In the western end of the county, I stopped at a small café and had a great breakfast with farm fresh eggs, bacon and fresh fruit. I had been managing to stay on my meal plan and didn't want to drop off now, so I had packed plenty of vegetables for the trip.

I drove as far as Virginia and then decided I would go further south and through Chattanooga, where I had lived for a year and a half. So I got off the road in Virginia to find a place to stay for the night. Now, when I travel with my four-legged buddy, I have no problem getting a motel that is dog friendly. Maybe it's a function of the awful economy— I don't know. But then, early 2009, it was more difficult. I stopped at three motels in the small town I had chosen and was told "no, sorry, no dogs". I was tired and hungry by now and my nerves and head pain were kicking in, so I wanted to lie down and try to sleep. I stopped at a convenience store to get a bottle of spring water, some sugar free drinks and a pack of sugarless gum. I couldn't find the sugar-free drinks, so I asked a man who was sweeping the back of the store.

"Oh, sure man. We have sugar-free pop and flavored water. Look over here," the man answered my question and led me to a shelf way in the back.

"Thanks," I said, "I wish I could find a room as easily. I have my dog partner with me and the three motels I tried coming in to town wouldn't take dogs. I'm tired and don't want to drive the sixty miles to the next town. Do you know where there might be a dog friendly place?"

He looked at me thoughtfully for a minute, but didn't answer at once. He seemed to be mulling the question over. Then he shook his head as if he had found the answer.

"Where you going, mister?"

"Santa Fe, then Sedona in Arizona."

"That's a long trip. My wife, she is from Mexico. A small town just over the border from New Mexico. We haven't been there for about three years now. Gets harder as we get older. But, sorry, no I don't know a motel for dogs. There's only two more hotels on the north side of town and I don't think they would want dogs either."

"I was afraid of that. I'm afraid it will be the same way if I drive the hour to the next town, but I guess I have to."

"What do you do? Why are you going to Santa Fe?"

"Good question, my friend. I was living in Pennsylvania for a while, but my wife died this past spring and I had to move on. Couldn't take it. And I love the West. She and I lived in Colorado a long time and other Western states for shorter times, so I'm going back. What will I do? Well, I will do some non-profit work and work on my own healing. And I hope to meet some Native American people again and continue my spiritual walk. Sorry, that's a lot. I didn't mean to say so much."

"No, no. It's good. You needed to say it. I know where you can stay."

"Great. Not too far a ride I hope. I know it's still early, but I'm spent."

"No. Couple of miles. You will stay with me, Julio, and my wife, Conseto. We have a room and bathroom separate in the back of the house. And we both love dogs. And I think Conseto will want to meet you. She may keep you awake talking, but you will like her. And we have a fence in back so your dog can run a little. What do you think?"

"That's really kind. Don't you want to check with your wife first?"

"No. She will be so happy to have someone to talk to other than me," he laughed as he answered.

"Sure. That is a beautiful offer."

"Good. I get off here in about forty minutes. You can wait and follow me or I will call Conseto and send you over. Which do you like?"

"I think I'll go get something to eat and be back here in forty minutes if that is okay with you."

"No. Not okay. Why do you want to get me in trouble with Conseto? A visitor staying and we don't have dinner together? That is not our way. Please wait and we will have dinner together. I will call Conseto now and we will stop if we need anything extra."

"I'm embarrassed. It feels like I'm imposing too much. . ."

"You worked with Native people you said—right?"

"Yes."

"What is their way? What is yours? Would you feed your guest or send him to the café?"

"Thanks, Julio. You are right. It would be wonderful to have dinner with you and Conseto. But if she needs anything, let me run to the market down the street so we don't waste time when you are done here. Okay?"

"Of course."

He took out his phone and called home. I moved down the isle to give him some privacy. In a minute he hung up and walked towards me with a big smile. He seemed to smile a lot. Through most of our earlier conversation he had a smile on his face, as he still did. I looked forward to the day when I could smile again—a real smile with pleasure behind it. It would come. I just needed a great deal of patience; something I had always been short of.

"Thank you for the gift, my friend. Conseto is so very happy to have a visitor and a dog visitor as well. Our dog died about nine months ago and we have not yet gotten a new friend with fur. He was a beautiful black lab who was with us fifteen years. A very long time for a dog. And, you know what? Conseto asked me your name and I could not tell her. I don't know it yet. Or your dog!" and he laughed out loud at that.

"I am so sorry, Julio. How stupid of me. I am Jim. Jim Petruzzi. Jim Red Wolf if you want the name my Native friends gave me. And my dog is Onyx. He is just over two years old and he is a black Labordoodle—a Lab and Poodle mix. He got mostly all Lab, however, except for his coat, which is curly."

"Just like Amigo, our dog who died. Very strange when these things happen. Do you believe in coincidence, Jim?"

"No, I don't. I believe in a reason for everything that happens—even if we don't see it at the time."

"We will have good talks tonight I think," he smiled these words happily at me.

Julio looked Hispanic. He was short, maybe five foot nine, and slender. His skin was the color of polished wood and his hair was straight black mixed with gray. I thought he was about my age—near sixty, but he could have been younger or older, it was difficult to tell. And I was never any good at ages anyway.

I went out and got Onyx out of the car and watched him take off like a rocket behind the convenience store. Then I saw the rabbit he was after. As the rabbit disappeared he stopped, peed against a tree and lopped back to me looking very happy to be out of the car. Julio came to the door and waved me over.

"Jim, could you go and get a head of lettuce, two tomatoes, and a cucumber? Conseto wants to make a salad, but she is short of those things."

"I'm on my way. Be back in a few minutes."

Onyx ran around from the far side of the car where he had been resting, out of sight.

"This is Onyx? He 'is' Amigo. Even his energy reminds me of Amigo when he was young. Oh, Jim, we may be in second place to-night. Conseto will love this dog. I know it."

"I'm used to being invisible to people when Onyx is around. Especially women. They love him. It is his energy. He loves everyone. I'm glad she will like him."

I picked up what Conseto has asked for plus some mixed fresh fruit and was back at the convenience store in twenty minutes. When Julio came out I followed his van to his place. It was only a matter of ten minutes, but we left town behind and pulled into a treed, private piece of ground.

"This is it, Jim," Julio said as he stepped out of his car. "Let Onyx run. There is nowhere he can get in trouble and no cars come this way. Then we will go in and get ready to eat."

I threw Onyx some sticks for a few minutes as Julio watched, laughing, then called him over and we all went inside.

Conseto was a short, round-faced lady with a big welcoming smile. She appeared to have Native or Hispanic blood. She had on a beautiful, many-colored dress covered by an apron. I put the bags on a table and turned to meet her.

"Hello, Jim. I am Conseto. It is so very good you are visiting for the night. And this must be Onyx. He looks just like our Amigo. How are you Onyx? Come here; let me scratch your head. You are certainly a handsome boy!"

As I had predicted, Onyx was a big hit. It was good he brought me along as well.

We had a fabulous dinner of veggies, salad and polenta with a tomato and basil sauce. Then the fruit I had brought along. We just chatted, laughed and petted Onyx throughout. I felt the pain that had been building in me recede into the 'bearable' range.

When we were done, Julio made a big pot of coffee and we all retired to the living room. The room decorations were interesting to me. There were Native American pieces, Spanish art and art inspired by the Jewish faith. Quite a mixed bag, yet it all seemed to go together and it all had a spiritual energy to it.

"Jim," Conseto began the conversation. "Where did you learn of Native American ways that Julio tells me you mentioned?"

"I began visiting Colorado in the late 1980's and moved there about 1991. That's where I met a lot of Native American people. I was at Colorado State University, running an environmental center for them and teaching in the College of Natural Resources and I started working with Native people from there."

"Are you Native blood?"

"Native olive-skinned tribe, yes. Native American, no."

"Oh, what a good answer. We are all Native, just not all the same kind of Native, eh?" Julio put in.

"Just so," Conseto said as she sagely shook her head. "Tell me more of what you have learned and how you see yourself."

"Wow. That's a big order. How I see myself first: I see myself as a human being who has been blessed to have had teachers of all colors and many cultures. I consider myself part of all five colors of life."

"What five colors?" she asked.

"The traditional four colors—red, black, yellow and white. And the fifth color—green. The green of the Earth Mother. Those five."

"That's interesting. I had not heard it that way before," Conseto said.

"That came to me a long time ago, Conseto, since I am so connected to nature I guess. Some day I might even be able to explain it, or at least share it," I smiled at her.

"Now, what have I learned? I have learned I have an enormous amount left to learn. I've learned we own nothing. We control nothing. We are but one small link in the Sacred Hoop of existence. And I've learned songs and ceremonies and healing practices along the way. And I've learned that I can withstand more suffering than I ever thought possible. How's that for a start?" I asked.

"A lot," said Julio. "I felt your pain in the store. It was why I waited a minute before inviting you. But I saw it was pain you carry, not pain you cause. I ask you to share it only if you wish. Then it is your turn to ask of us."

"Hmmm. Yes, I will share, if I am able. In the summer of 2004 my health went bizarrely bad—at all levels. All the doctors and all the tests only produced drugs, which promptly made me sicker, to the point I almost died. Then my wife's cancer returned after twenty years in remission at stage four—a stage that is not treatable, at least by Western medicine beliefs. And so began our last journey together. A beautiful one—but a journey of extreme pain for me, being the super sensitive that I am. A person who feels everything deeply in mind, body and spirit. The expenses took our home and all our savings. I lost two jobs; one I had to leave so she could get the medical treatments she wished and the other I was fired from when they learned how ill she was. Once the savings were gone I began piling up debts to pay for what her insurance would not cover. Finally, she passed away peacefully at the home we rented in Pennsylvania in May, last year. I thought to follow her quickly, but Great Spirit had other plans for me." I stopped as I was choking back tears and fighting intense sinus pain as I spoke. When I did stop, big tears started running down my cheeks. I tried to hide them, but was unable.

"I'm sorry, Jim. I didn't know. I should not have asked."

"No, Julio. It was good I could speak it. I could have chosen not to answer. So, what about you two? Who are you and what are you? Are you Hispanic or Native or just dark-skinned Swedes?"

Conseto began laughing at that. "It's good you can still joke, Jim. You will survive this. I see it clearly. Your spirit is strong and your healing energy very, very intense. Okay, me next. I am part Mexican, part Tarahumara Indian and part Mayan—a mixed blood. I grew up in a small village in Northern Mexico, not far south of the New Mexico border. My family are all healers on the female side and I leaned from my great grandmother and grandmother. My mother died when I was very young. When I was in my late twenties, Julio and I met. We lived in Mexico for seven years before coming here, where Julio is from. It was after my grandmother died we knew we were to come here and do our work. We went back and forth for a long time, but now it is harder as we get older, but I hope we can go back for a while next summer. I also carry cancer, but it has remained dormant for twelve years now. Julio, tell your story."

"Well, first, I am part Mexican and part Jewish. A hard mix to grow up with. Neither side of my bloodline really accepted me so I was in turmoil as a youth. Got in a lot of trouble. Then when I met Conseto, my life changed. She guided me to accepting myself and then it no longer mattered if anyone else accepted me. I have worked at many trades and we have had times we were well off and times we had nothing. Now, I work a little in the store to have something to do in the daytime when Conseto sees patients for her natural healing work. And maybe I work there so I will meet more people like you," he smiled broadly as he ended his tale with this tongue in cheek remark.

Then we spent a couple of hours talking about our teachers and the lessons they had taught as well as gatherings we had attended and circles we were part of.

"You know, before it gets too late I would love to drum a while," Conseto finally said, bringing to an end our story sharing time. "And

Julio, if you would play your flute I know Jim would enjoy it as much as I do. Jim, I'm sure you have your pipe with you. Would you open the directions for us? Do you have a drum or would you like to borrow one of ours?"

"I have my two eagle drums with me, Conseto and, yes, I have my Chanupa. Let me go get my things from the car and then I would be honored to open the next part of our circle. Onyx probably needs to go out, so I can do that at the same time. I'll be back in a few minutes."

Onyx, who had been laying on the floor, belly up, legs pulled in with a seeming smile on his face, heard his name and rolled over, shook himself and got ready to follow me.

"Get your things, Jim. Let me take Onyx out back where he can run without any worry. It's fenced," said Conseto.

"Sure, if he wants to," I agreed.

Onyx looked at me, then Conseto, then back at me. I said, "Go ahead, boy. Go with Conseto so you can run." At this he turned and shot for the back door.

"Smart dog," Conseto said as she followed him.

I went out and got my Chanupa, my medicine box, feathers, tobacco and one of the eagle drums. Julio and Conseto had plenty of sage around and I saw some sweetgrass and bear root on a coffee table, so I didn't bring those in. Julio had cleared a small table and laid a red cloth over it so we had an altar for our sacred things. We set up while Conseto and Onyx were out back.

When Onyx was done playing, he and Conseto came back in and walked over to Julio and I. Onyx, as usual, jumped all over me like we had been separated for months. Then he sat and watched what we were doing. Conseto got the sage and bear root, put some in a shell and began smudging all of us and the room, chanting a medicine song as she did so. Then she put the smoking bowl in the middle of the altar and sat with us. Onyx moved and lay down between Conseto and me. Whenever ceremony or healing is to begin Onyx finds his place, calms down and brings his four-legged energy to the work. He's done this from the time he adopted me. As I write I am reminded, once again, of the people who truly believe every creature, other than humans, are just 'dumb animals'. They miss so much. They understand so little. My heart goes out to them. If they only truly saw whom the 'dumb animals' really were.

"Jim, would you please open the directions?" Julio asked.

"I am honored by both of you, by this night we have and by your request of my Chanupa," I answered. "I will open the directions, then I would ask Julio to welcome in the Ancestors and ask for their assistance with our walks. And Conseto to please call in the creatures: the four-leggeds, winged, finned and creepy crawlies to help protect us and continue to guide us in our spirit work."

"I shall," said Conseto.

"And I," followed Julio.

"And finally I ask Onyx, our four-legged circle member, to welcome in the pack he and I walk with; the Wolf People. And that he run with them around this property to bring good energy and power," I finished, honoring the non-human creatures of the Earth Mother.

Brothers and sisters, friends of this journey we are on—this walking with the Earth Mother. I will share some of the ceremony we four did that night and let it be a ceremony of connection for us as well as we re-visit these things I have seen and I have done. So I welcome you all to sit around this sage fire with Conseto, Julio, Onyx and I as we pray, drum and chant. I invite you to be part of this circle. Beat your drums or play your flutes as you like. Or chant along with us. Or simply sit quietly and connect with Mother Earth, Father Sky and Great Spirit around us. Do not worry about what you do, as it will be correct. There can be no wrong way in ceremony if you enter with your heart pure and intentions good. Be comfortable, pull a blanket around you if you get cold, and be of the circle.

"Wankan Tanka, Great Spirit, Great Mystery, it is I, Ceta Sugman-itu Tanka, Red Wolf, with my friends Conseto, Julio and Onyx asking you to hear our words—to hear our words of gratitude for all you have given us and all you will be giving us in the future. We ask you to hear our questions or concerns and give us light if it is your wish. We ask you to see the smoke from this sacred Chanupa, which I know will come straight up, white and strong, delivering our prayers to you. We ask these things not for ourselves, but for all the people—two-legged, four-legged, winged, creepy-crawlies, Rock Nation, Standing People (Tree People) and all the others of the universe so that together we may heal the sacred hoop wherever it is broken. Aho, Mitakuye Oyasin—all my relations."

With this I put a pinch of my tobacco in the pipe. This is tobacco I have carried from my first ceremony and, with each new ceremony I add a pinch from whomever else puts tobacco in. Julio began playing his flute softly and I just sat quietly as he did so. He had a beautiful, lilting way of playing this instrument. After a few minutes he ended and I resumed.

"Ancestors of the East—the spring of the medicine wheel—please come, be in this Chanupa circle with us now. East, time of birth and innocence and the home of the gentle creatures; the rabbit and deer. This is the time to trust and learn as you move around the wheel of life. Help us with our prayers here tonight so we may help to heal the sacred hoop wherever it is broken. Ho, Mitakuye Oyasin.

"Ancestors of the South—the summer time—be with us in a good way here tonight. The time of action, energy and procreation—bring this to the circle here. Bring us the heat of the summer and the warmth of the sun. And help take our prayers up to Wankan Tanka so he might see we walk the Red Road in a good way for all the people. We ask this so we may help to heal the sacred hoop wherever it is broken. Ho, Mitakuye Oyasin.

"Ancestors of the West—the fall, the white of the medicine wheel—we ask you to be with us tonight. Wolf people of the West please come and protect this circle and those connected to it from afar as you have protected me this entire walk. The West—the time of using the mind more and body less, we ask for the energy of the mind to enter this circle. The time to prepare for old age while we teach those behind us in our tracks. Help guide us and help us send our prayers to

Wankan Tanka here in this place. We ask this so we may help to heal the sacred hoop wherever it is broken. Ho, Mitakuye Oyasin.

"Ancestors of the North—the black on the medicine wheel. The winter, the time of cold—the time of fear as we approach the end of our journey here, on the Earth Mother. But also the time of joy as we prepare for the East to again rise and the journey to continue. We ask you to be with us and help us guide and teach the younger ones, all the way to the seven generations. Black Elk, who sits in the North. I thank you for your teachings and guidance and ask for your help tonight. White Buffalo Calf Woman, who brought the sacred Chanupa to the people, I thank you for allowing me to learn the ways and ask you to help the four colors of people to now come together and share the ways. Power animals of the North—White Buffalo, Bear, Eagle—I ask you all to lend your strength here tonight. We ask this so we may help to heal the sacred hoop wherever it is broken. Ho, Mitakuye Oyasin."

With each direction I added more tobacco to the pipe, cleansing it in the smoke from the sage.

"Conseto, can we have some low drumming please. And, Julio, some flute, on the last three directions. I see Ancestors and spirits and animal guides all around us and want to honor all with sacred music. And I see others, a growing number, who I don't yet know, but want to welcome to the circle."

Julio and Conseto began to play and Conseto began to sing softly. She had a wonderful voice—like a breeze on a warm summer day washing over your body, bringing comfort and ease.

"Father Sky, we thank you for all the beings in your realm and for being here tonight to work with the Earth Mother. I ask you to join with the Earth Mother now, as I join the male stem of the Chanupa to the female bowl. I ask you to work with her so that we poor humans may again know how to connect with you both as the time of change approaches. We ask these things not for ourselves, but so we may help to heal the sacred hoop wherever it is broken. Ho, Mitakuye Oyasin.

"Mother Earth. You to whom I am most closely connected. You that I have walked with this whole life journey. You that I have tried to learn how to better partner with in a good way as the changes come. I ask you to hear our prayers. I ask you to take our gratitude and requests to Wankan Tanka so he may know they are real and we are real. I ask for more time for two-leggeds to awaken and connect with you in a sustainable, harmonious way. All these things I ask, not for myself, but so I may help to heal the sacred hoop wherever it is broken. Ho, Mitakuye Oyasin.

"Great Spirit within me. Great Spirit around us. Great Spirit throughout the Universe, we thank you for listening to our thanks and our prayers. We ask for the help we need so we may do our work— so we may serve and so we may walk the Good Red Road in the best possible way. Ho, Mitakuye Oyasin."

I put another pinch of tobacco into the pipe and then passed the pouch to Julio as he laid down his flute and I picked up my eagle drum.

"Creator, I thank you for hearing me here tonight in this way," Julio began. "Ancestors—those I know and those I do not—I ask you to be in this circle tonight. Those Jim sees I ask you to be in this circle tonight. We need the help of you in the spirit world as the time of endings and new beginnings draws near. Be with us. Send our prayers to the Universe. All my relations."

And Julio took a pinch of tobacco and added it to the pipe. He then passed it to Conseto.

"Creator. Spirit. God. Universe," Conseto started. "Thank you. This is a special night and special words we are putting out. Thank you. Animal people. Creatures of all types—we ask you in tonight. Into the circle. Into our lives. We ask the wolves to run with Onyx here and so give us honor. We ask you to protect us and this entire circle so we can do what we are meant to do. Heya. All my relations. Heya."

And Conseto finished filling the pipe. I then touched the pipe to Onyx as a means to send his words to the wolves.

With that I took the pipe and held it to the sky as I said a few words to Great Spirit and then touched the end of the stem to the earth as I said a few words to the Earth Mother, ran it through the sage smoke once more, and lit it with a sage twig. I took seven puffs, blowing out one puff of white smoke to each of the directions.

Then I passed it to Julio who sat to my east. He held it aloft and made his prayer then also did the seven directions breaths. After Julio it went to Conseto who also did the seven. We had decided this pipe was to ask for the healing of all creatures on the planet and better connections to the Earth Mother. And we asked for any directions or signs Great Spirit might wish to send us. So after smoking the pipe we played drums and flutes and Conseto again sang in her lilting voice. After about twenty minutes we stopped, put our instruments aside, laid back and cleared our minds for any messages we might receive. After a time we slowly sat back up and reconnected to the present place and time.

"Very good pipe, Jim," Conseto said.

"I agree," I responded. "The smoke was very white and went straight up—always a good sign. Did anyone see, hear or feel anything?"

"Yes, I saw people in turmoil and Conseto and I sitting quietly off to the side," Julio said. "I think we are to stay out of the frantic things about to come and do what we will need to after the changes. That's what I sensed anyway."

"I saw some of my Ancestors and they just looked and smiled. No words," Conseto said. "It was comforting, but I don't know there was any message or meaning in it. At least that I understand now."

"Um. And I saw myself in the mountains some time down the road. Not the red rock desert I now go to, but the mountains. I assume the Rockies, which I love, but it was not made clear to me. I was with others, but could not see their faces. I saw Onyx running with wolves in fine and happy spirit. I also don't know the meaning yet," I added, sharing what I had seen.

"I believe we three will see each other again," Conseto began. "It may be a long while, but we will be in circle together down the road. I am glad of this because I think our spirits have matched in a good way here tonight. There will be no need to push it or stay in touch. We will simply reunite later when it is needed."

"Makes a great deal of sense to me," I responded. "And I am also glad we will have more to do together. Tonight must be a circle to open the walk we take together later."

Then we began talking and eating some popcorn Julio had made—just having fun. Onyx rolled on the floor, going from one to the other of us, having doggie fun. We finally decided to call it a night about 2:30 AM and decided to get up for breakfast and some more talk before I left at 8 AM. Not a lot of sleep—but about average for me.

The next morning we enjoyed the eggs, ham and beans Conseto made, with the coffee and corn tortillas Julio fixed. We talked until about noon, as Julio and Conseto both had a day clear of appointments, and then I began packing the car back up. Soon I was ready to leave and we took turns embracing and wishing each other well on the road. Onyx got several rounds of hugs from both of my new friends, which made him very happy. As we headed to the car, Onyx hung his head—not ready to leave this joyous place. We hugged once more at the car, and then I got in, waved, smiled and turned the wheel Southwest once again. I could have easily stayed there for some time, but I knew it was not where Spirit was sending me and, as we had talked about the previous evening, our time in the same circle was down the road. Still, I admit I felt a great deal of sorrow as I got back on the highway heading towards Chattanooga.

I decided to make contact with a friend in Chattanooga. I had met him while living in the Chattanooga area for a year and a half, running a wildlife and environment organization and a youth corps. I hadn't been in touch with him, John, for a lot of years, too many years, so it seemed a good time to try and reconnect. Worse case, I would stay the night in a Chattanooga motel.

7 | With a Southern Friend

I TRIED AN OLD NUMBER I HAD FOR JOHN AND TO MY SURPRISE HE answered the phone after three rings.

"John? John Davis?" I asked.

"Yep. Who's callin'?"

"Jim Petruzzi, John. From the wildlife center. You may not remember......."

"Come on. Sheeeet. I may be getting older, but I ain't senile. How you doin', Jim? Where are you?"

"I'm about ninety minutes north of Chattanooga, on my way to Sedona, Arizona. You came to mind as I was driving and I tried your old number and... well, here you are."

"Course. You know I ain't one for goin' far from home here. And my health's been on the outs. But, hell, you gonna stop? You remember where I live?"

"I do remember where you live and sure I'd love to stop and visit a while. My dog buddy, Onyx, is with me. That okay?"

"Hell yeah. Come on in, man!"

"What can I bring, John? Some pop or snacks?"

"You're gonna eat with me, ain't ya?"

"Love to."

"Then I got a nice roast pork in the oven and some good, ole brown taters. And, of course, okra. Anything else you want, you bring."

"Done. I'll get a real green vegetable if that's okay with you, instead of that okra stuff."

"Still not your thing, huh? Yep, fine. And bring some pop—that's a good idea. You and Onyx alone this trip?"

"Yeah, John, it's only Onyx and I now. We're moving to Sedona."

"Damn, let's talk all this through later. Seems we got a lot to share and I don't cotton to doin' it over the phone. Okay, Jim boy?"

"Couldn't agree more. I'll see you in a couple of hours. It's good to hear your voice, John."

"You too, Jim. You too. You don't get a lotta friends in life and it's always good to hear from one again."

I hung up and put my head back into my driving—scratching Onyx behind his ears. To his great pleasure and to my feeling less alone. I still felt fairly energized and happy about the whole move effort. Some bouts of nerve and head pain shook me, but not as frequently as they were back in Chester County.

"Onyx, my relative. Does that feel good? Yeah, I see it does. We will stop and see my old friend John in Chattanooga. You'll like him. He's an animal person. That's how I met him while I ran the wildlife center. He brought in an injured badger for care. Showed up every day for two weeks until we were certain that badger would live. Old John can sound gruff—but that's only surface. He'll love you for sure. And he owns a big piece of land. You can romp. It will be like back in Pennsylvania. Maybe he'll ask us to stay the night. Okay, okay, I'll scratch a little more," I said as Onyx twisted to stare up at me when I stopped scratching, looking for a minute's rest.

After a stop at the market, we drove on to John's retreat, as he called it. He was about twenty minutes west of Chattanooga, out in the woods, up on a mountain. John had about thirty acres and he tended it alone. He was about sixty-five, but looked and acted younger. His wife had passed away a number of years ago and he had opted to go it alone. Well, except for two dogs, three cats, some fish, and a pet skunk when I knew him some years before. Who knew what he had now.

I put my brain on idle and just followed my instincts to John's. His land was several turns up back roads, so I didn't know how well I would do. But, without thinking (sometimes the preferred way to go) I turned to the left and then right and on up his long driveway.

I pulled in next to his small barn, got out and opened the door for Onyx. He shot out and bounded across the field to our left. I saw John coming out of the side door, waving. I waved as I headed up towards him. He had aged some and lost some weight—even though he was not a big man when I knew him.

"Ho boy Jim! How are you? You look good. Damn, good to see you," came flowing out of John.

"Doing good, John. It's good to see you, too."

"That streak of black moving across the field back there must be your Onyx."

"Yes. He's thrilled to be out of the car and running. Okay if he runs a while?"

"Sure. He can't hurt nothin'. Let's sit here on this bench until he tires himself out."

"Great, but only until we call him in. He wouldn't tire himself out until late tomorrow—maybe."

"So, if you have a mind to, tell me why you're comin' through this way and why alone. And why are you going to Sedona?"

I filled him in on what I've already shared with you all. He listened quietly, but intensely, as I remembered from the past. When I stopped speaking, he leaned back and blew out air, making a 'wooooooo' noise.

"That's a heavy piece of pain to be carrying Jim. I'm truly sorry about Bonnie. What an intense time those last years must have been. When my wife passed over I sat, numb and uncaring, for three years or more. I still feel the pain at times, so I do have some sense of what you're dealing with. Don't think I could have done what you're doin'. Fact, I know I couldn't."

"I had to do something, John. Sitting back where she passed away was too much. And having all the 'things' of my past around me was a constant reminder of what was no longer there. So, I did what I felt I had to. What about you? What's your story now?"

"Well, not much. In fact, I was feeling sorry for myself before I heard you talk. It's easy to get stuck in that self-pity place, ain't it?"

"Oh, yeah. Way too easy. And it's a place easy to get to, but really hard to leave. But, come on, tell me something."

"I been doing some work with animal rehab down the road in Lafayette and some work with dogs up in Georgia. Finding foster care people for them until we can get them adopted out. Been a good thing for me. I was seeing a woman for over two years. Sandra, a good woman. I had feelings for her. But she wanted to make things permanent and I'm not walking that road. Maybe I'm afraid of pain again or just a coward or a plain, ornery, old cuss, but I don't want to be with anyone all the time. I got my dogs and other critters and that's fine with me. And, I'm dealing with some health issues that are creeping up on me with age. Thanks for not saying I look the same when you got here, by the way, cause I don't. I had cancer and I finished chemo about a year ago. But I'm recovering slow like. And my heart problems seem to have gotten worse. Probably ain't gonna kill me soon, but we all go sometime."

"Sorry, John."

"No need. It's always been one day at a time and will be till we give it up and pass over. And that's how I take it."

Onyx came bounding by and I took the opportunity to call him over. He came, tail wagging, and began to check John out. John passed and, in a minute, Onyx was all over him. We decided—all three of us—that we were hungry, so we headed inside, me with the bags of supplies I had picked up.

We had a good dinner—even with the okra. At least John had fried it, out of respect for me I'm sure. I hate okra that's cooked in oil or boiled; it's slimy to me. Sorry all you Southern friends of the circle here, but that's just the truth for me. But I love grits! Does that help with my slighting okra? I hope so. And, hey, I'm sure I could cook up some things you would hate, too.

Back to my time with John. After dinner we went into the living room and John took down his fiddle.

"You still like the fiddle, Jim?"

"Oh yeah. Especially the way you play it."

"Well, what say I play and we sing and stomp a while. That chat outside has us both sad lookin' and I aim to change that now. You game?"

"Perfect. Can I get my drum?"

"Hell yeah! Wow, we will make some good noise here now."

I went out to the car and brought in my eagle drum and a couple of rattles.

"Nice drum. You gotta tell me more about this part of your life later. You want to carry your bag upstairs before we start? We may go late you know."

"I was going to look for a motel down the road later, John. I don't want to put you out. You didn't even know I was coming through."

"Oh. Come on, boy. Ain't we friends? I wish you was stayin' longer, but I know you got to do what you got to do now. But we sure can have some fun tonight. If it will make you feel better, I'll ask the animals if you're puttin' us out. Ain't no one else to ask 'cept them," he smiled.

"Okay. I'll go get my bag. Actually, I already pulled it to the front of the car. Just in case you asked," I said and laughed as I did so.

"Damn, you are a good bullshit artist, my friend."

And so John began fiddling and I just listened for a while. His fiddle almost jumped in his hands, because his heart was so into it. Onyx paced the room at first, not knowing what to make of this new sound. And, with his sensitive dog-ears, probably feeling the sound vibrations more than I. Then he stopped and lay down with his head on his paws. I scratched his head and then picked up the drum and joined in. Fiddle and drum—an odd mix. But it was a sweet sound we made, at least to us. Onyx was having fun with it also—jumping from fiddle to drum and back. Onyx is not a barker or a whiner, he is so expressive in face and body he doesn't need that. Sometimes, if startled or afraid he barks once, or twice, then explores what caused him to do so. But this night, as our instruments got louder and we played them more frantically, Onyx sat, looked at us, raised his head and began to howl. He howled right along with the music. Then again, and again after that. For the next hour we played non-stop, getting up and dancing around or adding some song or yell and Onyx would throw in a howl or two when he was moved to do so. It was nuts, but great therapy for all three of us. 'Singing' actually more like noise—that I could do since I was not in lodge or ceremony. When we stopped it was only for a bathroom break, a walk outside for the four-legged and some glasses of pop, then we took up our instruments again. This time two of John's dogs came in with us. So now we were three dogs and two crazed two-leggeds. And the music and goofiness began again, except now we had three dogs sharing the howling chores.

We went on for another two hours or so and then stopped, plopping in chairs. We were sweat-covered, hair sticking out, thirsty, tired, and generally spent. But we were also laughing as well as we were able with our dry throats. The dogs were all over us, apparently having loved the nuttiness of the night.

"I ain't had this much fun since I can't remember when. Maybe never," John said through his laughter.

"Me, too. I didn't think I could have this much fun again, even if for only a while."

"Don't go to those dark places again and I won't either. Deal?"

"Deal, John. And a good one," I agreed.

Then John brought out some cornbread he had made and a pot of coffee. My eyes lit up, as I do love cornbread. And this he had just heated, so it was steaming hot. He also brought some whipped butter and I knew we were about to have a cornbread feast. Finally, after gorging on cornbread, we sat and began talking some more. We talked about the past and how we came to become friends—thanks to that injured badger and John's insistence on being informed about its recovery. And about our lives now and into the future. And we played with dogs and listened to some music John put on the stereo. And he asked about the drum again and how it came to be. So I told him about my spiritual road and my teachings by so many different people. This fascinated John, since he was very spiritual, but not religious. A difficult thing to be here in the South, where church and religion are such a big deal to so many. I never heard John say anything negative about churches, but I did hear him say how that 'processed' faith wasn't for him. He'd pray direct—thank you all. In this way, he was much like me. And so he listened intently as I told him about some of my journeys and spiritual teachers.

"Jim, I never knew any of this when you lived here. How's that?"

"I didn't say anything. I had run away from it. I didn't want to be different any more. So I let it be."

"Whew. That's a shame. I'm glad you're pickin' it up again. You need to. We need you to. You got power, boy. I told you that before and I tell you again. There's some kinda energy in you and it's good."

"What do you mean, John? My energy has never felt so low."

"Not your physical energy, but the energy from your heart maybe? Don't know, but always knew you had a lot to do. Enough of this, let's take the dogs out so we can turn in soon. It's almost 3 AM," John suggested.

"I had no idea it was that late. Sure, come on guys, let's go check out the moon and you can all take a pee," I said, rousing the dogs.

We let the dogs run for about twenty minutes as we quietly stood and watched the moon overhead. It was cold, but not unbearable. Finally, as the dogs came up to us, we turned and went in.

"Been a great night, Jim. Sure glad you came this way. Seems like you were just here running the center, but it's almost ten years. Time's funny, ain't it? Goes fast when you want it to go slow and slow when you want it to go fast. Well, if you come this way again, I'm here. Maybe you could stay longer."

"You never know, John. I have no idea what I'm headed for now. But if I wander this way, this is the only place I'd stop. And if you come West, just pick up the phone and come stay with me, wherever that is."

"Good. Don't reckon I'll do that. Never was one for travelling you know. And now, at my age and with the ticker cranky, I'll probably sit right here and wait for people to come my way."

"Well, I hope it works for me coming this way down the road. I'd really like to spend some time out in those woods with you."

And with that we headed to our bedrooms. Onyx jumped up on the bed, rolled over and invited a belly rub. He got a short one and then I lay quietly hoping I could sleep. And, to my surprise, I woke up about nine AM.

I smelled the coffee and cornbread cooking from the bedroom, so I jumped in the shower, shaved and pulled on some clothes. Then I quickly headed downstairs. Onyx was down there already, happily watching John fix breakfast.

"Morning, Jim," John called to me as he reached for a mug so I could pour myself some coffee. "Sleep okay?"

"Better than I have in a long while, John. Thanks. Onyx been out?"

"Yep. He went running with the boys for over an hour. They probably thought they saw rabbits or some such. Pull up a chair and we'll get some grub. Guess you need to be on the road, but you can go with a full stomach."

"Sounds good. Yeah, I have places to go yet, I think. And I want to be in Sedona by the 15th if I can. I promised a new friend to be there before the Spring Equinox on the 21st and I would love to find a place to rent before then."

"I heard that. Nothing like some place to land that you feel is your nest. Well, I made some more cornbread after the way you gobbled it down last night. And eggs, ham, grits and greens."

"Wow. That's a feast. I was already leaving with a full spirit and heart after our music making last night and now, you're right, I'll leave with a full stomach too."

We ate our breakfast and then sat over coffee for a while, until I knew it was time to head out. But that didn't come to me.

"John, I'm thinking we may have to make a little more noise. Is it okay if Onyx and I stay another night? Maybe we can all go tracking through the woods like we used to when I lived here."

"Now that's one great idea. I wanted to hear some more about your travels in Central America. Always been fascinated with that area and the people down there. At least from what I've read. Never been there. And I can show you some beautiful falls and caves I just found about a year ago."

And so I felt like I had remembered and followed the teaching of many of my mentors and the one I often taught as well—it's all about the journey, there is no destination. Why rush through here when John and I were connecting in such a fun way? If I made Equinox— great. If not—what would it really matter?

John and I filled our backpacks with water, leftover cornbread and cheese about an hour later and headed off for the trek John had in mind. We piled in John's truck and drove about twenty minutes and after he pulled up a dirt lane and parked, we started out on foot.

It was a beautiful day now. The sun had warmed things up nicely and there was no wind. Onyx was in doggy heaven as was Max, one of John's dogs who opted to come along.

We hiked through some beautifully wooded areas for about two hours. There were several trails, but they seemed little used. At times the woods were so dense I could hardly see the sunlight breaking through, at other times they were so sparse they allowed the sunlight to paint shapes on the ground. I was remembering how glorious nature was, as I did each time I went out and entered the Earth Mother's natural domains. I knew I would feel better if I did this every day, but my guilt and grief would not allow that yet. In fact, even now, as I write this for you, my explorer friends, there are days I don't do my nature-based healing on myself. Ah, we are each a work in progress. We would all do well to remember that.

Finally I could hear the sound of water splashing and running. We walked a little further and came upon a beautiful waterfall—not large, but big enough to create a steady grumble of water striking rock. So beautiful and so serene that tears came to my eyes. Why couldn't all those I had so recently lost be here with me? Why was I still standing? I don't deserve to enjoy this beauty and peace, while those who looked to me for healing or support are no longer here. And with this, the pain in my body began coursing through me—just as the water dropped over the edge of the waterfall, but in a painful, rather than a peaceful, way. I cried, but only for a few minutes, as was my usual process. I truly wished I could break out into heart-wrenching sobs, but that didn't come. John walked around the falls with the dogs, giving me a little privacy I'm sure. Then I heard a loud splash and looked to see Onyx joyfully swimming after a stick John had thrown. Max followed a moment later and I concentrated on their fun rather than my pain. And, for the time being at least, it worked. The tears stopped and the pain lessened.

Not far from the waterfall was an access hole to some caves John had also found. There are caves and caverns all over this part of Tennessee, some of which I had explored while living here. There was a large chamber fairly easy to reach and we hiked and climbed through its interior for a while. We were not prepared to do any real caving. With the beautiful falls and an open field below it, not going into caves was fine with me. We sat and ate next to the falls, watching the dogs chase each other and then dive into the pond below the falls. After a couple of hours, we began the hike back. We saw a number of hawks on the way out. Hawks are another plentiful element in the Earth Mother's array in this part of the world. As are deer, which we saw large numbers of as well.

We got back to John's house in the early evening and I went to get a shower, being sweaty and, I'm certain, stinky from the hike. The hot water felt great hitting my head and I let it run for some time before I grabbed the soap. Something again triggered a remembrance and tears began to come as depression swept over me. It was over in ten minutes, but left me exhausted. I sat on my bed for a while, until I felt I could put on a 'social' face and help John with dinner.

"You look like hell, Jim. Too much hiking or are your emotions giving you fits?" John asked as I came down. So much for my phony face.

"That easy to see?" I asked.

"The pain is in your eyes. A lot of it and it goes deep. I'm been through this, remember, so I can see that only those who have walked this way could."

"Sorry, John. It's wonderful being here, but the pain and depression come on their own schedule. I seem to have no control."

"Course you don't. How could you? You getting the guilt too?"

"Oh, yeah. That comes a lot. Guilt at being here and guilt at failing those I loved."

"That's a full truck load. And it doesn't pass quickly. Fact, after all these years, I still get it around my wife, my mother and my best friend from the past. It just gets to the point you can take it."

"We're getting sad again, partner," I said. "Let's switch tracks here and just enjoy the moment we have. We got music to make! And food to eat!"

"Boy, I heard that. How did you like those falls today? Not too big, but a lot of water and I am always surprised by its energy."

"Oh, yeah. That was one powerful place. Thanks, John. I even actually enjoyed the beauty of the place and watching the dogs play."

"There's another pair of falls about a three hour hike in from the same general starting place. A large pool below them, with a stream running out the bottom. Ferns all around, some green even at this time of year. I'm blessed with nature's beauty in this area. Couldn't have picked a better place to live."

"I'd love to see those falls too. A third night here?" I was completely surprised to hear myself say.

"Hell yeah! We'll leave early tomorrow. Now let's eat and then play some music."

We went on playing and talking until about one and decided to wrap it up, as tomorrow's hike would be longer and harder.

The next day we had another big breakfast, packed our backpacks with lunch and water and headed out by 8:30 AM. We parked about a mile from the starting point of our previous hike and started out, but in a different direction then the day before. Onyx and Max again came with us and were racing ahead trailblazing for us. It was another beautiful day, almost spring-like in this late wintertime. What a gift! We again hiked through heavily treed woods and open fields and meadows. And we saw a great deal of wildlife on the way; on the ground and in the air. The dogs were in 'bliss state' once again, chasing each other and any critter appearing before them. My legs were weary from yesterday, but my energy was good and my emotional state in positive places. So I enjoyed every minute, while trying not to worry about what emotional or physical curveball would come at me next.

Those from our earlier walk have heard me speak of how I often find myself in the past, present and future at the same time. This is why I can create in words here, for you all, an experience I had years before in great detail. Because I 'am there again'. And why, once I remembered my visions, I could also relate those future events in great detail, because I was living them, at that moment, as well. This skill—talent—gift—whatever you choose to call it, scared the willies out of me for a long time. I was certain I was losing whatever mind I had left. That is no longer so; it simply is something I have come to accept. It can, however, also give me problems at times. Like when I try to 'live in the moment' as so many of my teachers and peers have advised me often. For me the question becomes, "How do I live in the moment when the moment, for me, is made up of the past, present and future?" I've found this to be a paradox that I've never fully unraveled. The best I can do is to try to divorce the past and present elements and focus on the physically 'present' elements. Sometimes, it even works. At least this day, on this hike with John and the four-leggeds I was able to 'be present' and enjoy my greatest teachers work—the creations of the Earth Mother.

The falls John guided us to this day were much higher than the falls of the previous day. The double stream of water created even more musical sounds as they hit the water and rocks at the bottom of their tumble. And, as John had promised, the falls fed a beautiful pond and a stream flowing out the bottom of it. It was an idyllic place to stop, play and rest. It was almost as if I was being rewarded for slowing down and focusing on the journey, not the destination I had in mind. Actually, it was not 'almost like' this at all—I am certain that this was the case.

Onyx and Max again leaped into the water and began chasing sticks as we threw them and then chasing each other, when we were not throwing sticks quickly enough. I started to laugh—a real laugh, something I had had little of for a long time. And it felt good. John and I began hiking around the surrounding area, poking into fields, ground holes, tree stumps and anything else we found. Just taking a day course in the Earth Mother's University. As we moved into a wooded area my eyes were pulled upward. I was sensing an energy that was attracting my spirit, not uncommon for me. I often 'saw' birds and animals before they physically appeared and long before others with me saw them. I was very used to this and grateful for it. Yet when I looked up I saw nothing. I began moving forward, but my eyes were again pulled upward. I stopped and began slowly walking around the Standing People—trees—near me as I carefully gazed up. Carefully gazed up so I did not end up on my butt on the ground. In a few minutes I saw the nest. Although it was large, it was nestled between limbs, along the trunk, in such a way as to make it invisible. An owl's nest. I recognized it from my days at the Environmental Learning Center of Colorado State University. And as I looked, I saw two small, feathered heads poking over the top. Two owlets, probably recently born given it was not yet spring, waiting for food.

John had walked further ahead but now circled back to see where I was. I pointed up to the nest and owlets. He looked up and moved around as he did so.

"What are we looking at, Jim?"

"Follow up the trunk of this tree," I said with my hand on the Standing Person. "When you reach the third large limb branching off to my left, look carefully. Where the smaller branches block some of this limb, nestled close to the tree trunk is a nest. A nest with two owlets."

"Damn, I still don't see it," John said moving to position himself where he could more clearly see where I had directed. "Never did understand how you saw so many birds and animals when we hiked. It's like they hold up signs for you."

"In a way, I guess they do. I think it's their energy that draws me. Anyway," I said digging my binoculars out of my pack, "see if these help."

John took them and began looking for the limb as he adjusted the focus for his eyes. "Yep. There they are. Cute little guys. Kinda early in the year for them."

"It is. But unless you get a really late, heavy cold snap, they'll be fine."

We watched the owlets moving around for ten minutes or so and then headed back to the falls where the dogs still romped in the pond. We ate lunch and, with backpack under my neck and hat over my eyes, I took a short nap. A short nap that stretched into almost an hour. With my inability to get much quality sleep, I sometimes had fatigue knock me out like this. John hadn't minded as he took a short nap and then played with the dogs. Finally, after some good, cold water and some discussion about the merits of today and yesterday's waterfalls, we got up and prepared for the hike back. We went slower, watching for critters along the way. And, of course, only saw a few. We will need to speak more of this later, friends.

After a full afternoon of hiking and talking we arrived back at John's—hungry and tired. The dogs got to eat first, as they made their hunger most evident. No human conventions get in the way when communicating with animals. There is no, "Oh, I can wait. I'm not that hungry." Or, "We can eat whenever you get to it." There is body language, looks and sometimes sounds from animals to let you know, "I'm hungry. My body requires nourishment. Please provide it now." And, when given what they need—a tail wag or eyes thanking you. Which behavior is more efficient and effective? Still so many people say we have nothing to learn from animals. It saddens me, again, how much they miss and will never know. Maybe they will see on a future walk—a future life. Maybe the connection and understanding will come then. I hope so.

We made a good, healthy dinner of salad and several veggies, with some pork in the greens for protein after all our exercise. After dinner, and an understanding Onyx and I would actually leave the next morning, we went to John's living room to again connect. It was colder, so John lit a fire in his over-sized fireplace. It was cozy in twenty minutes or less.

"Jim, tell me more of your spiritual road and what you have learned," John requested. So I began to tell him of my journeys, teachings and ways I attempted to serve.

When I finished, John asked, "Would you do one of your prayer ceremonies here? This old boy thinks he needs one."

"Sure, John. I would be honored." I went and got my sage, bear root, Chanupa and tobacco and we settled in for a ceremony in front of the fireplace. I opened the directions and then asked John for his intention in this pipe he had requested.

"Shoot. I ain't sure. Maybe just to get some understanding of what I could be doin'. And some help for my friends who have health problems worse than mine."

"Good, we will put that into the pipe," I responded and spoke John's intention to Great Spirit for both of us.

When we finished we spent about an hour listening to some flute music on CD's I had brought as we both allowed our spirits to drift where they would; we journeyed, as I had taught John this practice was called.

Then, from John, "Jim, can I call you for guidance as I go forward? Like some of these here other ones do with you? I could send you a little cash when I have it to cover whatever you charge."

"John, I will happily guide you in any way I can. I can't work with many in that way now with my energy still so low and scattered, but I'm sure I will get energy from you as I share whatever I can with you. But, no, I want no pay. Not for this, not now. Another way for me to bring in resources will show when I need it. I'm certain of that."

"Thanks, Jim. Okay, but if y'all need something—tell me and I'll see what I can do. Deal?"

"Deal," I agreed.

Then we made our music again. I don't know how good we were at combining our various instruments, but I do know we were loud and we were having fun. That's more than enough. Finally, we went up to bed, once again, late into the night.

In the morning I packed the car as John made us breakfast and the dogs ran and played. It was sunny, but colder than it had been the past few days—perfect driving weather. John and I sat and gobbled our breakfast as we re-visited the things we had done during my time there. Then we took our coffee into the living room where John had another fire going. We sat and talked. We talked about our joy and pain. We talked about aging and how we needed to adapt—or if we did. And we talked of what we thought we each might do next. Then John asked if we could strike up a little more music before Onyx and I left. Just to see us off with some good energy behind us.

And so began one more mixed-venue music creation. We went on for at least an hour, neither of us wanting to end it too soon. Then, as we got thirsty, we got one more cup of coffee and sat, thanking each other for the past days. This caused us both to begin laughing as we re-alized just how much each of us had gotten from our time together.

Then Onyx and I walked to the car, followed by John and Max and Henry, his other dog 'in residence'. Henry was old and not able to do the hikes any more, but had stayed with the circle whenever we were back at John's house. The elder—giving the best he could.

"I'll be callin' you soon, Jim. You take care on this here trip, you hear?"

"I will that. No rush. No time I need to make my destination. I released that here. And you take care of yourself. Call whenever you wish. When you feel you need guidance or just to chat."

We embraced, two brothers connected by spirit and energy. Two getting ready to take the next part of our journey. I had had a bliss-ful time here, even if the pains came on occasion. I would not forget lessons learned and re-learned as John and I re-connected in such a good way.

8 | A Pause to Contemplate Spirit Lessons

Brothers and sisters, it seems to me our walk following my journey from East to West—from pain and depression to regeneration is moving slowly. We've been trekking some time, it seems, and I see we are in the South of this 'migration' of mine. Yet I know what we have seen and heard what we have needed to see and hear.

For those with me in past journeys you may remember how I write—I revisit the past as it is shown to me and capture the words and thoughts as Wankan Tanka, Great Spirit, directs me. I have not read my own writing as it manifests in the past and will not as we travel through this book either. Some of what I write, when I read the words after I know the book is complete, surprises me. Sometimes they surprise me simply because I have shared something, other times because I had forgotten an incident, or even a person, I write about. And yet still other times I am surprised that some stories or people are not in the pages. Happily, I like being surprised! One other note I feel I need to share again—the people I write of I never judge in either a positive or negative way, especially myself. I just relate what comes and things and events as they happened from my perspective. Often, if I have no permission to use their names, I change the names of people who have crossed my path, but do not change the tales to be told. And other teachers and beings I have interacted with you will probably understand are from the spirit world, they have already crossed over. Black Elk is a fine example. He has been a spirit teacher of mine for many, many years and has appeared to me on the physical plane in different ways. If he appears in this book I will clearly identify him—or others of the Blue Road / Spirit Road, so there is no confusion. For some this working with teachers, guides and friends on the red and blue, the physical and spirit, roads is disconcerting. I hope not so for you. But if it is I ask that you do your best to accept that this is part of my walk and the teachings I share. Since some have asked in the past—no I don't drink nor do any type of drugs. Partly because I am a pipe carrier and partly because I have no need of them now. So whatever you read and hear as we travel together is as it was, or as it is now. Okay, enough said here.

So I will share a group of teachings and thoughts that have appeared, or reappeared, to me in the last couple of days as I wrote. First, as to where I am writing this book so you can look into the heavens and 'see me' if you so wish. Just as I see us settling around the fire for this talk. My first book was written in Sedona, Arizona in a beautiful natural setting, which I know allowed that book to flow as Spirit meant it to. Much has happened since that time. Some of this I will share on this journey, some possibly in a later book. Yes, relatives, there will be more books. I hope that brings a smile and not a frown. For this book and another as I see it evolving in my spirit, I am sitting atop a mountain about twenty miles northeast of Santa Fe, New Mexico. I am house-sitting Jack's house—yes, the Jack you met earlier—for the winter, while he 'soaks sun' in Florida. I am, therefore, in another amazingly beautiful natural setting. As I know I will need to be each time I write. I am curious to see where I land next whenever another book is to appear.

As I write this I am able to look out the windows on a pine and high desert view. Beautiful. I can go out back and look miles down the canyons behind the house and see only a handful of houses way off in the distance. I do not remember how much of this I shared earlier and will not re-read to discover that, as I just told you. So if I repeat myself remember to me that means a piece of information or a story is important. My half-side, Sue, and I take Onyx for walks each day or I should say he takes us. Jack's dog, Noche, who Onyx liked so well and who he followed through the hills, passed over about a year ago. Now when Onyx does go out without us he is on his own. He loves it. Sometimes he runs with the coyotes and, so far, there has been no fallout from this. Ah, I see you want to hear more about Sue, my half-side now, eh? Well, patience, this too will come.

Let me start this section with an observation I made anew while hiking with John.

I realized a long time ago: If you want to find something, don't look too hard. Whenever I look diligently for something I want, like seeing wildlife on part of our hike, I almost never find it. When I want something and put it quietly away in the back of my mind so I am not actively seeking it, I find it. Or, more correctly, it finds me. I have shared this with many people and have heard many say, "That's happened to me many times, but I never thought about it that way." So, my friends of the journey, think about it that way, try it and see if it works for you. I have no doubts that it will if you can control your conscious mind to the point that you really don't actively seek your desire. Yet, it needs to be deeply imbedded in your subconscious. Sound easy? It takes practice, believe me. You will see this occurrence manifest many more times as we travel along the road here.

This not looking too hard for what you need is related to the next thing I will bring up manifesting what you need. In my opinion there has been a lot of nonsense, sometimes-harmful nonsense, out there about manifesting. Books and videos written teaching you how to just keep repeating what you want and if you can hold strong energy around this, God or the Universe will provide it. Money, property, fame, cars or whatever. This goes against almost every indigenous teaching I have ever been given and certainly against what I have experienced. So, pour yourselves some coffee from the virtual pot, grab a handful of peanuts from my spirit jar over that way and let's talk about this for a while.

First, you may have noticed in the paragraph above I spoke about manifesting what you need, while many of the 'quick fix gurus' speak of manifesting what you want. Huge difference there. And you can't just sit down, with no preparation or intention and begin manifesting good things. At least that I have ever observed. Certainly not as the norm. On the other hand, for people awake and ready to help with the changes now happening with our planet, the things you need are manifesting faster and faster. Sometimes even the things you want, if they are in alignment with the energy of the universe, they cause no one harm and you use them in a good way. Being aware that what you asked for has already appeared is sometimes as important as asking. Sounds crazy I know, but so many people ask but don't truly expect to receive, so they miss what is given when it is right in front of them.

Let me share a story from yesterday morning. It's small things I asked for, but it is the process I want to walk through, with your permission. Okay, here is. I was writing this journey for us and some entries in the Sanctuaries of the Earth Mother website and Facebook page. The words were coming to me and flowing on the page, so I did not stop for some time. I never like to put a dam in the middle of a good, swift river flow of words when I don't have to. I never know when the raging river torrent of words and ideas will turn into a trickle from a leaky faucet. Got the picture? Good. So I kept going, getting hungry and thirsty as I did. And feeling my body cramp up and my back get stiff. One thing my brother Jack does not have here in this mountaintop writer's retreat are comfortable chairs to write in. Finally I had to stop a minute to use the bathroom.

As I washed my hands and face before returning to my writing haven I thought, "Boy, I hope we have enough propane to get through the coming storm." The snow had already started and was predicted to last five days with some significant accumulation possible. We already have five or six inches on the ground from the night before. "I had better go check the propane tank gauge. Unless the propane company is on it. I'll look as soon as I go downstairs."

Then, as I straightened up and felt my back complaining I thought, "Wow. I wish I had a nice sunny, spring day so Onyx and I could take a long walk. It would be good for both of us. Oh, well, he loves the snow so we can go play 'catch the snowball' later."

I dried my face and hands and headed back to my word cave—the nice den-like room to the front of the house. As I walked into the room I looked out the window and saw a man pulling a line across the driveway. Yes, of course, the propane man refilling the tank. I smiled and chuckled and, very important to include, said, "Thank you, Great Spirit. The gas will keep us warm and allow us to continue to serve and do our work as you wish. Ho. Mitakuye Oyasin." I thanked the Creator, who had heard my request and allowed it to be so.

Then, as I went to sit down, my back spasmed. Charlie horses all up my left side. I yelled and began stretching them out. As soon as they eased up I looked at Onyx and said, "Okay, buddy. Let's go do our winter wonderland walk now." He, of course, jumped up, tail waving like a flag and body tensed to fly out of the door. I headed towards my coats, gloves and heavy shoes. As I walked to the door I looked out and stopped dead in my tracks. So, you are thinking ahead of me, huh? Well, you're correct. It was sunny. The clouds way off in the distance and the wind had ceased. No snow falling in sight. I put on a sweatshirt and winter coat and headed out, walking stick in hand. I couldn't believe what I was seeing, but I accepted and walked forward into the daylight. Within five minutes of walking down the canyon behind the house I had stripped off the coat and then the sweatshirt and stuffed them in the hiking bag I carried, I had on a tee shirt and jeans and was comfortably warm. The temperature had gone up at least twenty degrees in the thirty minutes I had spent in the bathroom and with the back pain. A lot of the snow on the ground had either blown off the rocks or melted off, so that there were only a couple of inches for Onyx and I to hike through. Then, as we got further down the canyon where a large number of pine and cedar trees grow, the birds began singing. There were twenty or thirty by the songs they made. Spring songs in the middle of a winter snow storm warning. So again, friends,

"Great Spirit. I thank you for this glorious Spring-like time out here in nature. I thank you for myself, but mostly for those I am serving in the best way I am able."

Onyx and I walked for about an hour, enjoying the warm sun, listening to the birds and working the stiffness from our bones. We went up a steep hill and I got some good pictures of an old, gnarled tree, which I posted later in the day on the Internet with the lesson I thought the tree was sharing. Then we headed out to the dirt road that leads to Jack's long driveway and continued our walk back towards the house. When we got in we both drank heavily. I had brought no water because it was snowing heavily and frigid cold—right? I had not planned for the sun and heat, so we took care of our thirst as soon as we were inside. Then I found Sue in the back office and told her about the propane and the walk in the Spring I had hoped for. I had not really even put these things in the form of a request, but rather a 'wouldn't it be nice' form.

"And the darnest thing was not only did the sun come out, but the temperature went way up and the birds were singing. Singing in December," I marveled. "Maybe I'll go out some more, as long as I am taking a writing break."

"I think the Spring walk was just for you," Sue smiled and said. "Look out the windows."

I ducked down to see out the low window in that room and saw the same gray/white, heavy, snow-filled clouds that had been present for twelve hours. And, as I looked, the snow began coming down in large, dry flakes again. We went out back and discovered the wind had returned and it had gotten very cold again. There has been little break in the snow and in the cold, since that time. The spring-like weather lasted for the walk we took and maybe twenty minutes longer.

Please don't think I am saying everything we ask for we get. Even if it is needed at the moment. I am saying if we ask Spirit for something we truly need to walk our path, and the timing is right, we will receive what we need. It may not be what we thought we were asking for, but it will fill the need.

I could write about many more instances of rapid manifestation, but the one above serves the purpose. I have seen similar occurrences with others near me. For myself, while I have manifested many things over time, it is only the past handful of years that I have been keenly aware of it and so have not missed gifts that have come my way. What I do see is that the number of things manifesting and the speed with which they are appearing is getting ever faster. One of my Mayan teachers talked about this fifteen years ago. He told me as the beginning of the Fifth World drew near at the end of 2012 by the Mayan calendar that whatever "we who were working in the white light" would manifest (bring forth in his words) was what we asked the Creator for. And it would appear ever more quickly. And he repeatedly told me to be very careful and specific about what it was I asked for as this time drew closer. Another version of 'be careful what you ask for'. But I have asked for things to better do my work and walk the Red Road lately and found what appeared did not quite do what I needed or was an odd version of what I asked. Each time this occurred I examined the words or thoughts that caused the manifestation and found the words were not clear enough. What another Australian teacher, an aborigine, shared with me on this was, "As we become more able to have appear what we seek, it becomes a matter of we are given what we ask for. Our words create the thing or power that Spirit decides to grant us. So we must become masters of the words we use."

It seems some of you are very interested in these things I share now, others have that look of "this will not serve me". Well, while these things seem simple and maybe unreal to others, they are very elaborate teachings. Simple, but powerful. And not to be used only by those who have studied or prayed or done any other specific list of things. They are for those who are awake or awakening now and wish to serve the greater good. Will first time users of these tools be as adept as long time wielders? Probably not. Were you a great driver the first time behind the wheel? But they will come in handy, even necessary, as we move toward attempting to leave a better, healthier legacy behind us. Or as we work as healing guides or mentors in the natural world, or any of those things which will allow us to live more sustainably and peacefully in harmony with the Earth Mother and each other.

As I mentioned when we were spending time with John and his dogs, I truly remembered and followed my own teaching that it is about the journey, not the destination. This simple line is huge in its import. Do you all see that? Shall I say more? Okay, if you are constantly focused only on some goal or some place you wish to be—the destination—you miss the entire trip getting there. If you ever get there. And, if you do arrive at your supposed destination, then what? Do you continue to grow and learn as a living being? Why would you? You have arrived. And what if this destination is not what you expected? Can you move on or are you stuck, thinking it is truly the end-point for you? Do you see the many threads in this robe, my friends? How intertwined they are?

If you focus on the journey, not the destination, you learn and grow every step of the way. You do not miss things because you do not wear blinders that only allow you to see the end zone. It is where we must live, the journey, to truly evolve as human beings. In Western society this is particularly difficult to do. Why? Partly because we are judged by what we own, not what we are. So our destination becomes a place where we own more than the other players in life. Partly because we have been trained to constantly strive to reach our goals. The goals, whatever they are, become the destination and, again a place of stagnation even if we should reach them.

I remember when Two Bears first started trying to get this lesson across to me. He would have me go for a long hike and not think about where I would end up or what I needed to do or how I would get back. Just enjoy each moment of the journey and stay open to what I learned through each of my senses. It drove me crazy for a long time. Really had me nervous and uncomfortable. Or he would have me sit and write, with no thought as to what I might write or how it might turn out when done. Fear of embarrassment reared up on that challenge I remember. But these sorts of exercises, and I could share many more, do work and eventually break us free of the Destination Addiction. It is then you can truly begin to live, learn, explore and grow. Try these exercises and I'll share more in other places later if they are needed.

And so how do we effectively function if we don't know our final destination? Good question. As we journey here with these stories, events and understandings I am sharing; what will be the destination of this book? Do you know? Because I do not, any more than I did for my first book. Yet many of you are back for another journey together, which gives me great joy, and a lot of you have brought friends along. So we must have journeyed well before and the destination for that book/walk must have been the beginning of the continued journey here. See, you are already learning to better live the journey. Keep it up. It gets even better.

I feel I need to say more about my southern friend, John, who we met in much more detail than I would ever have imagined. This journey sometimes surprises, amazes, elates, annoys and angers me, just like all of you here in the circle. So, I have been trying to 'figure out' if I should (oh, dear, the 'S' word!) say more about the walk John and I shared. I couldn't decide as I batted it around in my head while writing some of this section and walking with Onyx. So I gave it up. Quit thinking about it. And, bingo, I just wrote, "I feel I need to say more about my southern friend, John. . . . .". It was decided for me. There was no need to fret over it, just clear my head and write what comes. A method I am still trying to get better at. Not to 'conquer' or 'master'. Those denote destination points, but rather to get better at. Grow in my skills.

John and I spoke many times in the few months after I visited him. He asked many things and we talked some issues through that we both carried. John had decided after his wife died, years before I knew him that he would not walk with another partner again. That was almost twenty years before my visit with him that we all shared earlier. He had suffered mightily when she passed and her passing was very painful and did not go quickly. We spoke of these things because we both understood. I was lucky, as was my wife, that she did not suffer much pain at all, but I fully understood the slow journey to the end of someone's walk and just how painful to one's mind, body and spirit that is. Especially if you are a sensitive of any level of feeling and ability. So, John had kept that pledge to himself and although he had had a few girlfriends, each time they wished to get more serious, he opted out of the relationship. This I also totally understood, as my desire was to take my four-legged brother, Onyx, and go off into the mountains together, playing and learning from nature with as little human contact as possible. I also wanted no partner, ever. I was done with that and the pain that can / may occur. And I told anyone who would listen or anyone who questioned me that this was my wish and it would be so. I was planning, folks—another thing you really don't want to do too much of right now. But that discussion is for another time.

John, like most of us, had a number of painful issues to work through. He was working some of them, but had become an expert of pushing others down. My job as his healing guide was to assist him in bringing them to the surface and examining them so he could then deal with them in a good way. This is what he asked of me and what I attempted to provide. Most of these issues I won't write about, they were between John and I. But some of the things we worked on he gave me permission to share, as he thought it would help others. One was the battle with his dark side—the part of himself he did not like and wanted to eliminate. We worked a great deal on the fact that each of us has a light and a dark side. What many call good and bad. This I do not agree with. There is no good and bad in our natures or even the things we do, but there are outcomes from the things we say or do that we consider positive or negative. As I was taught, the challenge is to find harmony and balance between the light and dark sides of our nature. And to be aware and accepting of both sides and remaining in the light side as often as we are able. This, again, sounds like simple advice but, even with awareness, staying in the light is not easy. And accepting we will function in the dark at times since we know that part of our nature also exists. John was in a long circular trap of guilt and remorse for "some really bad things I did in the past", as he put it. Knowing he could not change these things, he was having major problems moving forward. This I also understood, as I had similar feelings I was working through. There is a key difference, which is being trapped by guilt and remorse or feeling guilt and remorse and working through them.

John was working diligently on his issues and, at the same time, trying to accept that he had created many positive ripples in the universe and the lives of those he touched by all the strong work he had done in his light side. We humans seem to find it so much easier to blame ourselves for all the 'bad' we have done than to accept credit for all the 'good' we have done. Or, as it really is, celebrating all the time we spend in our light side and simply accepting the time we spend in our dark side.

There is a Native American story about this dual nature of humans that I have liked from the first time I heard it. It is a story I often share to help people understand how they can walk this life in the best way possible, even with the two sides of our nature we all have. I have heard that this is a Cherokee story—but I have also heard people of other Native American nations claim it. Since I have heard it from people of many tribes, I suspect it's been shared so often no one is sure where it first came from. This is as it should be—do we share stories and teachings for our ego or so that someone else may benefit from hearing them? Hopefully so others benefit—in which case who cares where the story originated.

Here is the story in its most common form:

> An old Grandfather said to his grandson, who came to him with anger at a friend who had done him an injustice, "Let me tell you a story. I too, at times, have felt a great hate for those that have taken so much, with no sorrow for what they do. But hate wears you down, and does not hurt your enemy. It is like taking poison and wishing your enemy would die.

"I have struggled with these feelings many times," he continued. "It is as if there are two wolves inside me. One is good and does no harm. He lives in harmony with all around him, and does not take offense when no offense was intended. He will only fight when it is right to do so, and in the right way.

"But the other wolf, ah! He is full of anger. The littlest thing will set him into a fit of temper. He fights everyone, all the time, for no reason. He cannot think because his anger and hate are so great. It is helpless anger, for his anger will change nothing.

"Sometimes, it is hard to live with these two wolves inside me, for both of them try to dominate my spirit."

The boy looked intently into his Grandfather's eyes and asked, "Which one wins, Grandfather?"

The Grandfather smiled and quietly said, "The one I feed."

John had worked on feeding his light wolf, the good side if you wish, for a long time and I, as a friend, saw that his positive contributions heavily outweighed his negative. But John struggled with this a great deal. His religious upbringing, which taught you always did good and always served others first, got in his way a lot. As it does with so many of us. Over time, however, John made great strides in this area.

When you feel you have done too many 'bad' things or acted in a way you do not like too often you can now sit and look at yourself and be certain you are feeding the wolf you wish to be dominant—the dark wolf.

John called—sometimes often, sometimes with months in between—when he felt he needed additional material to think about or he just wanted to talk. Likewise, I would call him if I felt it was a good time to do so. This is how I work with most people I guide and even friends and family I connect with. Not forcing it, but taking the connections, when they come—from whomever they come—and seeing what evolves out of this. I had people calling me daily and others every month. Currently I have only a few who check in or ask my aide. I believe this is because I have so much work to do with my writing and with the Earth Mother that Spirit is giving me the room to do it. When I am to assist more people directly again, the time and space will free up for this. This is how it has always worked and now it's even more important that I listen to the Creator and stay firmly on the Good Red Road. Many of you may be having this same occurrence in your walk now; from working directly with many people on healing and growing to working with fewer as other work appears before you. I suggest not questioning this shift, but being thankful and going with the flow.

After a couple of years John was still determined to go it alone and comfortable in that decision. Much more comfortable than he had been when I visited him. This was a good energy shift for him and I congratulated him on it. The area he had asked me for the most assistance, however, was in manifesting his own healing. Healing of his mind, body and spirit. Since we both were walking this road we were able to 'compare notes' and see where we stood compared to one another. John was upset that he did not seem to heal as he would like. And his spiritual healing from many traumatic, negative early life experiences was stuck, as he saw it. Actually he was moving ahead as he left some of his 'baggage' behind. Then one day he called, all excited. The more excited John became the more Southern his speech became—an interesting phenomenon I had always seen with him and something I often kidded him about. As he had once kidded me about being a fast lane Yankee: Always on the run. That, I was happy to know, had changed.

"Jim, I been a thinkin' about that last call we had, that long one, last month. Sheet, that was a good 'un. Dang, I been thinking on it and praying on it and doin' the journeying you taught me, and. . ."

"Whoa, John. Slow down a little and stop talking so Southern," I laughingly said.

"Sorry, but it came to me last night. I heard voices and could make out what they were saying this time. And I saw old people around a fire. The Ancestors—like you taught me. They were telling me a lot of the things you've been a sayin' to me all this time. And now it began to make sense. I'll tell you what, I didn't wanna wake up. And I didn't for a long time. When I did, I burned some of that sage you sent me and drummed. And just tried to clear this here ole boy head of everything. And more came to me. Some of them ones I was guilty over doin' em wrong came into my head. No, my chest, my heart, I guess. Anyway, they asked why I still suffered over this. And asked if I thought they had never done things they wanted to take back. And told me to let it go. Told me I was wasting time on this that I could be doing more good. More working in a positive way."

"John. Take a breath. Relax. This is awesome. You don't often have huge breakthroughs like this, but you've been working on it for a long, long time."

"Okay, okay. I just gotta get it all out. Maybe you're right. Maybe I was working on this a long time and just couldn't see it. I guess I kinda see that now. But it was when you began setting with me and talkin' with me I started to see different. And feel different. Thanks, Jim. Seems a pitiful thing to give ya'. Thanks."

"Welcome, John. And that's the best thing to give—when it comes from the heart. And thank you for helping me. For letting me see I could step into my strengths even when in pain."

"Since you talked about this thanks thing before, I won't argue with you. I'll just say you're welcome."

"Okay. So what do we move into now? Do you have more questions around this 'open door' for healing you are experiencing?"

"Naw. Mostly I wanted to share it with you and say thanks. You know, I'm seventy-four now. Hard to believe, even for me. And I've been in such a dark place for so long. I see that now. I understand them stories you told too. And I've been feeding the white wolf, the good wolf, in me for months now. And what happensbut these last few days of change. I feel so much lighter now. I could go on to that Blue Road you taught me about and become one of those Ancestors now and feel okay with that," he said as he laughed.

"Hey, the Red Road here is still needing some feet on it. But I hear what you are saying."

"Gotta go. Need to go work with some animals this afternoon. Can we talk longer tomorrow?"

"Sure. Just call. I'll have my cell phone if I'm out."

We talked for almost two hours the next day. John had made some amazing breakthroughs. And I was thrilled to hear the change in him and acknowledge it. I remembered some of these breakthroughs I'd had while listening to Two Bears or Umberto, or any of my other teachers. It's as if a curtain is drawn back from your mind and everything is clear. You can't imagine why you couldn't see or understand something before that is now a shining light. And you wonder how you could have doubted things you did see. Most people are not often gifted with these breakthrough times; so they are to be cherished. And many people are so closed and focused they never have one of these moments. They walk in pain, fear and doubt to the end. I truly feel sorrow for these people, even when they create dark things for others.

We talked about six times over the next month, as John was putting together so many pieces of the spiritual path, and loving it. Anything spiritual scared John at one time, now it was like 'bring it on!' He still had many physical problems, especially with irregular heartbeat, but nothing that was considered too dangerous if he watched his diet and exercised. Then he told me he was going in for some tests and after that, he was taking a trip to spend three weeks with his son in Florida. Wow! This was the first time I even knew he had a son.

John told me the story, which I will not share here. But what I will tell you is that John had not seen his son in seventeen years. He promised to keep connected with me through email and he did, for a time. He sent a long email about how he and his son had re-connected and healed their wounds. And how he felt even lighter again. He joked in the email about how this Red Road stuff and spirit teaching course really worked. He felt so good he didn't know what else to work on.

Then I didn't hear from John for months. Emails went out from me, three, but no responses came back. And I left three messages—also unreturned. One of my rules in life is three times and out. Once I reach out three times in any fashion, I stop. If the person gets back to me at some future time, I move ahead as if nothing had happened. As if there was no time between contacts, unless they bring it up. If they don't get back, then I assume what we were doing together is complete. This has saved me a great deal of angst and anger. Especially since I often have people like John thanking me for all I did for them. When, actually, all I did was show them what they were doing or pass on observations that I thought might help. Just having a safe place and person to talk to is sometimes all I do. Others, however, sometimes get furious with me, ranting and raving, calling me names and often hanging up when they are through with their diatribe. This most often happens when someone sees the truth in something we are talking about or has an awakening or breakthrough they are not yet ready for. Then fear or panic become anger and rage. And the most likely target is the one guiding them. In this case—me. I never take this personally, as I know it is about them, not me. And I have done this myself, as you may remember in my first book. Sometimes they return, sometimes not.

So, while I didn't expect a fear reaction from John given all he had already walked through, I was okay if that was what had occurred. If something else, I would hear about it if and when I needed to.

About two months later, I heard. Another friend from my Chattanooga days posted a note on my message board on the Internet. She was so very sad. Remember John? So kind, so nice, such a supporter and mentor to her. She had just heard he passed away a little while ago: In the past few months for no apparent reason. He didn't wake up one morning. She thought I would want to know.

And I did want to know. I felt the shock that always comes with unexpected death. And sadness, as my reconnection with John was a joy to me as well as to him. Then I smiled and thought about what he had accomplished in the year before he died. He was ready. I knew that. And I was right. Sometime over the following months John began showing up around the fire with the other Ancestors when I did my prayers or journeying. And I could see who he was, as I can with some Ancestors.

Thank you, John, for being you. For being a friend. For all you taught me. For the wonderful model of healing you became. For being there on the Blue Road to help all of us still here in this difficult time before us. You didn't die, you moved over.

9 | Turning West to the Desert

BACK NOW TO THE DAY I LEFT JOHN'S AND TURNED THE CAR WEST, finally. Driving southwest and through part of my past was the way I was meant to go, given the meeting with Julio and Conseto and my reconnection with John. But I was ready to head into the home of the setting sun and into new places, people and things, even if I was dealing with a lot of fear around that. As much as I was excited by this new adventure, I also felt as completely alone in the universe as one could feel, heading to live in a place I didn't know, where there were only a few people I had met briefly. Talk about split down the middle. So it was no surprise when later in the day, I had a major attack of fear, coupled by eye migraines, horrific head and sinus pain and a feeling of being elsewhere. I pulled over, put back the seat, closed my eyes and waited out the worst of it. This usually took about twenty minutes, as it did that day. Then I drove a few miles to a rest stop and got Onyx out so he could take care of business.

For the next three days as I drove across country, I experienced these pains and that feeling of being elsewhere. I kept stopping and waiting them out, but my pace was slow. Luckily, at John's, I had already accepted that it was about the journey, so I put the destination demon out of my head. I skipped visiting a friend of Jim Redhawk. I took motel rooms and tried to sleep at night. After a number of days of this, I arrived back at Jack's mountaintop casa. I stayed the night and Jack and I sat up late talking and sharing stories of our common Philadelphia birthplace. This was good for me as it allowed me to block the pain for a while. The next day I knew I needed to keep moving, even though I would have liked to stay a week and re-gather some strength. I headed down past Santa Fe and on into Albuquerque, where I stopped at Cracker Barrel and had breakfast and several cups of coffee. Then Onyx and I got on Route 40 for the final leg of this particular journey. The weather was getting bad with some late season snow, a lot of wind and frigid cold for March. We took it slowly and, after several stops and about four and a half hours, we pulled into another Cracker Barrel in Gallup, New Mexico. Most of the diners were Native American as were the staff and I felt at home as I sat there. I felt I was truly back in the West I loved.

After a big lunch salad, I decided I was too tired to go on, so I found a motel, checked in and then Onyx and I began a walk around town, down Route 66. It was snowing lightly, but the wind had abated so it did not feel as cold as it had earlier. We walked for a couple of hours, meeting several interesting people along the way. Then we went back to the room and I took a very long, very hot shower. I don't remember much of that night, except I awoke around ten in the morning, which was very unusual for me. The snow had worsened and there was talk that if it or the wind got much worse, they would close Route 40. So we got on the road and headed towards Flagstaff—a town at the top of a canyon, thirty-five miles from Sedona.

I fought weather and my own health that day, stopping often and walking with Onyx in the biting cold. And I stopped for long meals to relax and wake up as best I could. Finally, about 6:30 PM I was approaching Flagstaff. I called my friend Kim, who I was going to stay with. She told me the weather in the canyon was really bad and thought I should go down the Route 17, the main highway instead. I told her I would call if things changed, if not I'd see her in a little over an hour. I turned on the radio and heard Route 17 was closed in both directions. So I scratched that off my list of options. It got snowier and icier as I approached Flagstaff and I decided to go to a motel and finish the ride the next day. The weather was the primary determinant of that, but my emotions were also telling me to stop for the day. Telling me I had some emotional baggage to work on that night. I found a motel and Onyx and I settled in. It was then I picked up a paper and saw it was March seventeenth; I was ahead of the Equinox of the twenty-first. Not 'worrying about my schedule' or 'when I would reach this temporary destination on my life's journey' had actually gotten me there in plenty of time.

The next morning I awoke to much improved conditions. Some light snow fell, but it was coming from a mostly sunny sky. And the winds had dropped off, even if it was still very cold. Onyx and I took a long walk around the area we were in (just below the downtown) and, as usual, several people came up to interact with Onyx. Then I packed and went to breakfast, while Onyx waited patiently in the car. Finally we were ready to begin the thirty-five mile trip down route 89A, the canyon road, to Sedona. The thirty-five mile trip, which was also a thousand mile long trek for me this day. This was a 'Golden Door' day for me. Stepping out of my current present life and into a new life, which was more focused on the future. Any of us changing and growing know the Golden Door well, even if we call it something else. It is a one-way door to a totally new group of life experiences. A scary door to approach and one some people never go through. Once through, you cannot go back. There is no doorknob on the other side. I have worked with many people who stood in front of a Golden Door, some standing there for many years, unable to take that step through. No judgments here, my friends. This is one of the hardest things to do in this physical life. Timing, as always, is critical. If the time is not right, Great Spirit will often not let you step through the door even if you see it. Other times, when you try to force major changes before doing your mental and spiritual 'homework', the door will not show even if your foot is raised.

Well, I stood in front of the Golden Door and struggled to raise my foot and step over the threshold. The foot weighed a ton and the leg muscles seemed to have died. Then, as I surrendered the whole process to the Creator, I felt my spirit move ahead as I started down 89A. It was a beautiful ride—especially after I navigated the upper end of the canyon and reached the area where I would start heading down. Flagstaff is at about 7,300 feet elevation and Sedona 5,000 feet, so there is a huge difference in ecosystems, temperature, weather and, for that matter, people. I pulled into a rest area just before starting the ride down and found twenty tables with Native American artisans selling their wares. This is a permanent fixture of this rest stop, but I was unaware of that at this time. I walked and looked and wanted, but my rapidly dwindling cash supplies allowed me just the purchase of one inlaid medallion. I hung this around my neck, visited the restroom and headed down. What a metaphor for my life at this point—headed down into new experiences. . .whatever they might be. When the red rocks came into view I remembered again why I was so captivated by this area when I had come for the Healing From the Core workshop.

I will talk much more about this Sedona area, I am certain. It is a special and unique place, as it has been for many people of many cultures throughout history. We will discuss its environment, energy, people and purpose is my guess. You may have heard of Sedona from others and my guess is each had something different to say. I will share what I saw and experienced and what the Spirit People have shown me. And I will also probably share what my animal guides let me see about the deeper, inner workings and meanings of the area. Some will like what I have seen and know it to be so; some may be upset with my interpretation. This is as it always is and now, especially now, it is so important to speak your truth and not worry about what others may think. We all need to share our gifts, teachings and understandings in these times, between the four colors of people, amongst all cultures. This is what the prophecies all say, what my teachers have said and what I have heard in my own sacred times. But, let's wait and enjoy that discussion later, when we need another rest from this road we walk together.

About halfway down this descending part of the canyon I saw a parking area with a grassy field beyond it, so I pulled in for Onyx's sake and my own. We parked, as I had picked up a temporary pass at the park headquarters when I stopped earlier. Onyx bounded out of the car and began running around the field joyously. He would run, jump and then wiggle through the grass like a large, happy worm. I couldn't help it, I had to laugh. A real, heartfelt, joyful laugh. Something I had, and sometimes still have, in very short supply. Then he ran at me like a freight train, circling around me and heading across the field again. Then more worm wiggles, followed by some nicely executed rolls. I followed him, laughing as I went, picking up some 'fetch 'em' sticks so we could play. When he saw the sticks in my hand, he began jumping in place, then running around me. I threw one, which he pounced on and then brought it back in my general direction. After about ten minutes of this Onyx stopped suddenly, turned and stuck his nose in the air. He had the scent of something. He turned and looked at me as if to say—actually, 'saying' in dog language—"Can we explore this. I need to go! Please!" So an "Okay, buddy, go get it" sent him racing on his way. I followed as quickly as I could and soon understood what he smelled—Oak Creek, which ran a few hundred meters to our left.

Onyx reached the creek as I crested a small rise and saw the creek come into view. He looked back at me, then turned and launched himself off a boulder, through the air and into the water: The cold, fast-moving water—not that he noticed or cared. When I arrived I began throwing the sticks, one at a time, so he could fetch them and bring them to the 'nest' of sticks he was creating. He was in pure joy. You could see it in every motion and every dog expression. Living in the moment, no cares about later. Ah, we can relearn so much from the other animals, if only we will listen. After about forty minutes—and a slowing down, wet, shivering dog on the banks—later I headed us back to the car. When I got there I pulled out a suitcase and took out a large towel, which I dried Onyx with. His expression and motions of 'thanks' caused more laughs from me. This area is one I would continue to visit on a regular basis the entire time I lived in Sedona and still visit each time we return there.

We drove into Sedona a short time later and I now saw it with different eyes, since I would be living here for however long Spirit decreed. I stopped in Uptown, about four blocks long, and walked around a little. I did so not as a tourist, but as a resident. Interesting how the energy was much different with that mindset. Then I got back in the car and drove to Kim's place. She was there, drinking coffee when I arrived. We hugged, Onyx made his thanks known and I carried in what Onyx and I would need while we stayed there. I would be sleeping on a couch in the living room, as Kim's place was small. But this was fine with me; all I needed was some 'crash' room until I found a place.

"It is so good to have you here," Kim welcomed me. "Your boxes are stacked in that back closet space over there. We will start to find you a place tomorrow. Okay?"

"Great. Finding my own space will make me seem more at home." Kim moved to Sedona from Germany some years before, but still had an accent and was certainly Germanic in her approach to things: Very structured, very organized, very plan oriented. And with Kim, a strong belief her plan was best. Just what I needed while I was still reeling from being in this new world.

We drank coffee and talked a long while, and then her kids came home from school—two boys and one little girl. They are really great kids, as I had met them when I was at the workshop. And my staying there did not seem to throw them. The fact that Onyx was along certainly didn't hurt that cause, either.

We went out later that day and got the rental sheets of houses from the two local rental agents, took them to Kim's and began looking them over. I wanted to be in Sedona or West Sedona for now, near everyone I knew (all four people) and places I would need to go. So we narrowed the list down to six places for the next day. Finding a house to rent was an interesting process. I was trying to keep the expense as low as possible to stretch my meager resources remaining, yet

I felt Great Spirit wanted me to have space to bring in current friends and new friends who would need to stay with me for a while. So I did some journeying over this issue and saw clearly I was to provide space for others for now.

The next day we headed out and started doing drive-bys of the six houses. I made mental notes of what I saw and felt, which I might want to go into. As we approached the fourth house, six hundred dollars a month over my budget, I told Kim, "This is it". It was a long, low, large adobe house with a fenced in back yard. Behind it was only open space—all the way to Standing Eagle Mountain. Three bedrooms, two baths and a large common room along with a nice kitchen and dining room as I could see from the pictures and through the windows. And lots of glass with windows and sliding doors everywhere. Perfect. But I couldn't go six hundred over budget, could I?

We went down to the realtor and I met with the listing agent, telling her how much I liked the house, but that I couldn't afford it. She took my application and credit references and promised to approach the owner. I had offered six hundred less than the listed rental price. On my side was the miserable state of the economy and the fact that there were many unrented homes on the market. Kim and I left the realtor and drove to some of the land she hoped to acquire for the non-profit she was getting started, where I now sat on the board. A place to create a school for teaching and sharing alternative healing methods. Kim was a medical doctor in Germany, before coming here and shifting to energetic healing practices. She wanted to better meld the two approaches in a more holistic way. We walked the property and talked about the issues she was having getting her non-profit status. And we drove by a trail up some of the red rock hills she wanted to take me on at Spring Equinox. This trail led to a place that overlooked all the land she wanted to acquire. Then we went back to her place for some late lunch.

While we were eating the agent called me back, very happy with the credit information and references she had received. She told me she had just spoken to the owner of the house I wanted and he would lower the rent two hundred a month. I declined, telling her that was still beyond my ability to pay. Six hundred less and I could do it. Even at that, the rent would be over what I had hoped to pay, but I felt I needed to give some in trust and surrender that it would all work out. She promised to get back to me as soon as possible. About an hour later, she called back and said he would go down four hundred, but could go no further. It was my choice. I quickly said okay, draw up the papers. I'll come by with a deposit in a short while. These words just came from me—much as the words I write here for us—so I knew Spirit guided my actions. I dropped off a deposit and agreed to sign everything and pay the beginning rent the next day. I was given ten free days to get things ready and move in. I had the place I needed—at least for the time being.

The next day I stopped by the rental office and completed the deal and headed up to the house with a lease and keys in hand. The rental agent told me I was lucky I had bonded the deal the day before because just before I arrived there today a couple came in wanting to rent the house and they were willing to pay the asking price. Lucky? What do you think friends? No, not lucky—guided. When I got to the house I saw that a man was working on the grounds. I had gotten landscaping as part of the deal. I went in and mapped some sketches of the rooms. Kim was coming shortly and we were going to move my boxes over and then think about furnishings. I had none. All my things still sat at my sister's waiting for my daughter to pick them up down the road—right where I wanted them.

Kim came and we talked a little more about the rooms and then went and got my twelve boxes. Now I had an empty house save for twelve boxes. And what did they hold: These things I had decided to ship? Okay, what had I kept? Let's see; clothes, some framed artwork, books, Pendleton blankets, ceremonial articles and music, my CD's. That's it folks. All I decided to keep. Once the boxes were stored in a closet, I broke out sage and cedar and proceeded to smudge the entire house both inside and out. That done, we headed to a bedding store. They were having a huge sale, so I bought two beds and the mattresses and springs for each, getting a great deal in the process. Kim had to then go get her daughter, so I headed out to get sheets and such for the beds and see how much a TV would set me back. Once again, due to the economy, I hit great deals. When I got back to the house the truck with the beds was in the driveway, a day early. So, I had them set up the beds and I put on the sheets and dug out some blankets. Soon I could move in, after I had cooking utensils.

On the Equinox, in the evening, I set out with Kim and a friend of hers to climb the rocky hill and do ceremony as the sun went down. When we got there, we decided to leave all lights behind and navigate the climb back down in the dark, with only our cell phones for light. Easier for them as they had climbed it many times, but a real challenge for me. As I climbed, and stumbled, down the hill, I felt so connected with the Earth Mother I began to cry. I was glad it was dark to hide this from Kim. I had not yet learned how to accept what a powerful tool tears were. That night I slept better than I had in a long time.

Each day I acquired more of what I needed and, on the weekend after I rented the house, I found virtually all the furniture I needed at yard sales. With Kim's help we got it to the house. I even got a couple of really unique pieces at a designer friend of Kim's who was moving away. These and the beds now sit in storage in Sedona until Spirit shows me 'where to next'. In about one week I had all I needed, including a guest bedroom set up for very little money. No coincidence, friends: Spirit provided what I needed to do whatever I was to do next.

I could relate many more stories from this time, but I think it is time we walk forward and explore other events. Ah, the people who would come. Shortly after I got moved in I began to hear from many who would like to come and visit. Some wished to share some time and some good hikes, others wanted some of my time as a healing guide. These people were from numerous circles I was a part of and I welcomed each. Several came quickly and each, no matter why they thought they had come, spent time on their healing up in the red rocks. I had learned many powerful places in the rocks to take people—some from Jesse, some from others I met and several from following my inner voice and so coming upon them. The Sedona area is a haven for such places, especially once you get beyond the places tourists are normally taken.

Then Pam called and wanted to come. Twice we set dates and each time she cancelled. She moved her ticket dates each time, but was unable to come. I knew she was having real problems with a Golden Door, but it was not for me to tell her this. Then she began asking about a third time frame and I told her to go ahead and book it. The next day, she said she was unsure about this third time and would get back to me. Work was an issue, her sons an issue and on. As I hung up, Sue called, needing some guidance. She had been standing in front of a Golden Door for some time and had been unable to walk through. Through to a completely different life—one she said she truly wanted. She asked if she could visit and see how she felt about the Sedona area, having known for some time she wanted to move to the West. She was preparing to leave her husband and needed time and space to see what she might hear from Spirit.

I told her Pam might come—maybe they would come together. Then I got an email from Pam, again saying work made it too hard to come. Followed by her anger when she heard Sue was coming. Not logical, but understandable. I stepped back and let it play out, allowing for whoever came or not as being fine with me. Meanwhile Jim Francek, Redhawk, was coming in a week. Then two other friends behind him. And so it was beginning already, the flow of people into my world in Sedona.

A couple of days after I had arrived in town I dropped in to the gallery and re-connected with Bearcloud. It was good to see him and learn more about the Chameleon Project—the nonprofit he was working on. I quickly joined the Chameleon 'team', ready to do my part to promote this work. Bearcloud invited me to a sweat lodge the coming Friday night and I was thrilled to say yes. I had made one when I was here in January and really wanted to make them a regular event. Feeling that I was moving back into the indigenous practices and ceremonies lifted my spirits and enhanced the feeling of stepping into a new part of my life.

The lodge I had attended in January had started in a stressful way for me. I missed Bearcloud's road and went six miles out of my way before calling him. Then, by the time I found my way, I was late. And there was everyone waiting for me. I vowed no reoccurrence of that for this lodge. We were to go into the lodge at six PM—Bearcloud's usual time. I gathered my things, stopped and bought some food for after the lodge and then stopped to buy some sage and tobacco to gift Bearcloud. All this was customary when attending a lodge. With everything I needed in hand I was on the road to his house by five ten. I got there at five-thirty. This was timing that would become customary for me.

I will take you all into lodge with us, but at a later lodge. For me, this lodge was an affirmation that I was in the right place and needed to move forward, even if the road to my own healing was still stretching out before me. In the lodge I clearly was made to understand I needed to heed my own advice to others and get out in nature, connect with the Earth Mother and all her creatures. It's there that real healing occurs.

I listened to this and started going out to the rocks or the water places for some time every day. Let's visit some of these places.

10 | Visiting Earth Mother in the Red Rocks

THE NUMBER AND DIVERSITY OF OPPORTUNITIES TO GO OUT INTO THE natural world around Sedona are countless. And the weather cooperates, except maybe in the heat of the summer, when you need to more carefully pick your time of day. Jesse took me to a number of places and asked me along to others when he had a group to lead. We soon combined gifts—he playing his flutes from the hills above and me telling stories or doing ceremony down below. It was powerful and it seemed the people who needed this found him. And, while helping Jesse out and getting comfortable with my spiritual ways again, I was learning many powerful places and beautiful hikes. When Jesse was busy elsewhere Onyx and I went out and found new places to explore.

Sedona is a special place; unique in the many things it has to offer. It is the home of a large number of vortices—places of concentrated spiritual energy. And a grid of power lines, many connecting one vortex to another, also exists. The red rocks are also special. They offer numerous places to be alone and many to conduct sacred rites. There are places hard to reach with climbs requiring great skill, and other places just requiring a walk. No matter where you are, any direction you look in offers vistas of unbelievable beauty. Many say there is a lot of masculine energy in Sedona with red, hot rocks being associated with the male force. There is truth in this, but there are also places of great feminine energy there. As well as places of balanced masculine and feminine energy. Whatever energy you feel, if you are sensitive and awake at all, you feel it strongly. The energy can, in fact, be so intense some people need to leave.

In the past, Native American people were very aware of the Sedona area and its energy. In fact, they didn't live in what is now Sedona, but rather came, did ceremony or special events and left. They knew this land was not there for people to live upon, but rather to use for a short time and then vacate and go to their homes. I've had people argue about this with me, but I know it to be true. I have seen the evidence in their footprints on the land. I've been told these things by Native elders of several tribes who were told by their elders and by those in the spirit realm when I journey. This makes total sense once you spend some time in Sedona. It was the non-Native peoples who, not too many years ago, recognized the extraordinary beauty and power of Sedona and began building on its 'natural robes'.

So, many people who live in Sedona tell you of this energy and how it can be difficult to handle it. They tell you of all the people who have come and then left because of this energy. They are partly correct, but only partly. They are totally correct about the energy, which is created by the line grid, vortices and crystals underground. And they are correct that people come and go. But from Native elders and my own connecting with the Earth Mother, I see the reasons for this human migration through Sedona are different than most locals want to accept.

The Sedona area is a place of healing. The energies there, masculine and feminine, are there to assist creatures, human and otherwise, with their healing. It is why Native people came, asked for guidance and healing and left. To be able to ask for this healing and accept the strength of the 'medicine' you then receive you must be prepared for it. People connected with the Earth Mother in a sustainable way and with Great Spirit in a spiritual way are ready to ask for this healing and accept any symptoms of their healing that may manifest. People coming with no Earth Mother connection and little spiritual base come to Sedona to "experience the energy of the place". It's no surprise they often leave quickly.

I know someone who was moving to Sedona with a friend. They had a place rented and were excited to be moving to Red Rock country. He lasted eight hours in town and had to move on. These are the folks who come unprepared and get a blast from the energy there. And, not knowing what it is and feeling the discomfort—physical, emotional and mental—it can cause, they leave in fear. Some at once; some over a few months time period. As always I am not judging here, only sharing what I have come to know. Locals are correct when they talk of this group as coming quickly and leaving even more quickly. Where the story leaves the trail of truth is for people who have been in Sedona for a while. The locals often say, "Well, they took it as long as they could and now had to leave. They just couldn't take the energy and the emotions it stirs."

The story is somewhat different. Remember the Native people who came for ceremony or healing and then left, my friends? Well, it is the same model playing out today for those prepared to do ceremony or ask for healing. I thought this was the case from what elders had told me and by what I was observing, but became certain of it as I walked this road.

Those who come to Sedona and stay a year, two years or a while longer are working through their healing with the gift of the diverse Sedona energies. When they are done with whatever piece of healing they were working on they most often leave. In the old way: In the way it was for the first people there. In my own case I lived right in the heart of West Sedona for two years, right under Standing Eagle Mountain. In the hot, red rock energy and in the heart of several energetic power lines. It was intense. Some of this tale you will hear in more detail as we walk. Then, having dealt with that portion of my healing, thanks to the fire element and the masculine rock energy, I found a place about ten miles south of Sedona, in Page Springs. And lived there for about fifteen months. Amidst creeks, streams, ponds and trees and grass. In a feminine energy pool—nestled in the arms of the Earth Mother. And in a place some Native people did live for longer periods, being far enough removed from Sedona and tempered by the water energy that it was land people could live upon.

That portion of healing for me was complete. I needed to continue on my journey again, as so many Native people had done before me. Yet I return to Sedona on a regular basis—to connect, to hike, to teach, to do ceremony and to just 'be'. Again, like so many Native people have done before me. And so many other people do now.

So, what about people who have lived in Sedona and the lands around it for extended periods of time? Here again—the story some locals would like to be true and the story that is so are similar, but different. The story I have heard so often from locals is that they are all able to withstand the Sedona energies because they are advanced enough on their knowledge, understanding and healing journey that they can handle it. Many say they are there to help others heal. And there are a small number of whom this is true. I know some of them and it is clear that this is the case for them. They have completed the portion of healing they came to Sedona to address and now stay to guide others. As others are guided elsewhere by Spirit to do their work. This makes sense and is what I have been shown. But the majority simply have not been able to complete the healing they are there to do. They are stuck, for whatever reason, on their healing road at Outpost Sedona. Then there are those who are so unaware and disconnected from the Earth Mother that they simply don't feel the discomfort—it does not break into their conscious awareness.

There has always also been a large number of insincere people in Sedona, practicing one mode of healing or spiritual guiding or another without any real understanding of what they are doing. I am being kind—I speak of the phonies and the charlatans. Those there to milk the gullible of whatever they can, however they can. With the global changes we are in the midst of, I've seen the energy of Sedona working on this group more severely than in the past and I have watched many leave town. Many of the true healers and spiritual guides, there in integrity serving as they were meant to by Spirit, are welcoming this exodus. These phonies are often not just immoral and corrupt, but dangerous to those they dupe.

Well, enough of this for now, but I thought it good information to share, since similar processes are occurring in other special energetic locations around the globe. The energies are aligning between these locations and the people there in integrity as the planet changes. I do not know what the final reason for this will be, but I am certain we shall all see the reason quite soon. I have seen this process happening in Mt. Shasta when I was there this past summer and in Santa Fe now, where I sit and write awaiting word from Great Spirit where I need to be next. And I have heard of it and sensed it in many other places. So, story shared, teaching complete. May we now go enjoy the Earth Mother's bounty around Sedona? Good, then let's continue on our way.

One of the first power places I had hiked to in Sedona was the Birthing Cave I mentioned earlier when I was there in January. I began hiking there often since I had found a medicine wheel down below the cave, where I could also open my pipe, do ceremony and journey without people around. Soon after my arrival in Sedona in March, I made another sojourn that way. This time I hiked up past the Birthing Cave and the medicine wheel. I hiked another half mile and came to a rock face, but I could see some faint indication of how others scaled it. I attached my walking stick to my backpack and started climbing up, as I felt strongly I was to continue. Onyx, of course, simply watched me wondering what the holdup was. As I scrambled up over the rocks, he bounded from edge to lip on the rocks and looked down from thirty feet above me. So much for my concern about him scaling this obstacle. Five minutes and one scrapped knee later I stood beside him, sucking in air and looking back down the way we had come. I drank some water and gave Onyx some in my hands and then started up the trail that aimed at another rocky climb leading even higher up the mountainside. We walked that way, taking little excursions to high points I could look out over and I saw that I could see the general area the Wisdom Lodge was located—directly in line from the northwest from where I stood. I will share about the Wisdom Lodge in a short while—file it for now friends.

I decided not to climb higher this day, as it was getting late and chilly and my legs were tired, so I turned and started back down. Onyx looked at me, disappointed, and followed. As we headed to the area I would need to climb back down—more like scramble and slide back down—Onyx took off in the opposite direction. I called and in a couple of minutes—on his own time, he came bounding back to me. He stopped, looked at me, cocked his head, got a mischievous look in his eyes and took off in the opposite direction again. When Onyx does this, I know he usually has something he wants me to see, so I laid my pack down and followed obediently. Not twenty paces from the faint trail I had followed up and back just now was a large ceremonial circle. A circle I had not seen at all, even though it was clearly visible from my trail to anyone who just looked this way. It was about thirty feet across with rock slabs slanted upright every couple of feet. These were for people to sit and lean against when this place was used. And there was a small, flat rock laid on other rocks, in the middle—an altar. The energy here was strong, as was a wind that began blowing suddenly out of the east. I was pondering the fact that I walked by this place twice and did not see it when Onyx looked at me again. I turned to him and he walked to the north of where we stood. I again followed his lead and had a 360-degree view—an astounding sight of red rock formations and desert vistas in every direction. So beautiful it brought tears to my eyes. And some peace and happiness to my heart—both still in short supply in these days.

As I looked around the vista I again saw what a direct line there was to the Wisdom Lodge area. I could even see it clearer from this spot. How powerful—two primary energy ceremony places joined in a visual line and an energetic grid line I felt certain. As I turned to take it all in I also realized, in the direction opposite the Wisdom Lodge, I could see the land of Shaman's Cave and Rock. Now I had a three-point straight line in my awareness: The Wisdom Lodge at one end, this Birthing Cave circle (and me) in the middle, and Shaman's Cave on the other end. These were already three places of great power and significance to me then, as they still are today. Seeing this I went back to the circle and got out my Chanupa, sage and drum and prepared for some private ceremony. Onyx came and lay down within the circle, on the east side. The direction of spring, rebirth and new beginnings in the medicine wheel. We spent the next hour in communion with the Earth Mother around and below me, Father Sky above me and Great Spirit within me and throughout the universe. It was a beautiful hike already and this raised it to a whole new level.

As I hiked out after this I realized how much better my mind, body and spirit were feeling. I was aware of some powerful releases of energy and thoughts that no longer served me as I did my ceremony today, in the circle of the Old Ones. I became acutely aware, once again, of what an amazing healer the Earth Mother is. That being in nature and connected with all things out there is the best, most effective and most lasting healing anyone can ever receive. I have spoken of this at length before, but it bears repeating often. Any of you who do not regularly go off into the natural world, I suggest you begin doing so whenever you can. And sit, doing nothing, and see what your senses bring to you. Connect in with your Creator or the Universe if you prefer and ask for healing. Or ask for help releasing whatever it is you no longer wish to carry. See what happens; see if I speak correctly here. You will experience something and with practice, this will become a powerful tool for you on your walk. If you need guidance, seek someone who has experience in this connecting and ask his or her help. I have guided many in these ways and always welcome the opportunity with those who are truly ready and are asking from the heart. Those you seek will feel the same way.

Being ready is a critical piece of anything and everything we do on our life's walk. I already mentioned it in relation to places with strong energetic fields, like Sedona. How, if you are not ready for change will you be able to stay? It also pertains to spiritual work or teachings. I have seen some people, well intentioned with background in spiritual teachings, unable to enter a ceremony or a sweat lodge or a church. They are not ready for what they will receive. It's a 'safety-valve' of the Universe I believe, making sure someone not ready is not harmed. People sometimes ask about my first book, want it and then tell me they can't seem to read it yet. I know that person is not ready yet for my words and teachings, just like it took me years to read Black Elk Speaks, although it sat comfortably on my shelf. I was not ready. This is in no way a judgment of anyone, nor an affirmation someone is 'less' than anyone else or 'more' than anyone else. It simply is. If you see or sense you are not ready for something you had thought to experience, don't push it, friends. There is no rush in the Universe: When you are ready you will step ahead with it.

This circle of the Old Ones I found near the Birthing Cave in Sedona is a great example of being ready as well. Once, while I sat there drumming and preparing to open my pipe, a group of three people came up the trail. Remember the trail runs just twenty feet from the circle, in full view of it. I stopped drumming as they approached, assuming I would have to now share space—and I was okay with that. They walked towards the circle and me, looking about as they came. As they got to the bend just before the circle, they made the turn and headed uphill, where I had gone the first day I came there. They looked at the circle, they looked at me and they looked at Onyx and did not see us. I wondered at that—they must have heard the drum and seen us. An hour later, I heard noise and voices and realized the three were coming back down. Again, they walked right by never really seeing the area nor Onyx or I. In the months ahead I told two people of this place—two people I knew to be strong of spirit. Each reported back to me that they looked for a long time and found no circle. They had seen everything else up on that ledge, but could not find the circle. A third person I told was thrilled with the time she spent meditating in the heart of the circle. Those not ready, my friends, cannot access what they think they need or want.

A couple of days later I was to take Abbey, a new friend, to the Wisdom Lodge. Abbey carried extra weight, so I knew we would need to go slowly. Not a problem—it's a beautiful hike, but it is uphill with some climbing over boulders along the way. I took my pipe, tobacco, sage, and a drum along with some cheese and fruit and lots of water. The Wisdom Lodge is another power place that Jesse had shown me. We started up the wash, which was the way to the Lodge. Happily the wash is not marked and there is no designated parking along the dirt road it is off of, so few people are aware of its location. As we started out, I thought back on the first time Jesse had guided me here.

"Jim, this is a great hike and a powerful place to sit—the Lodge. But like many places, not everyone is able to get to it. You will know more than me," Jesse shared as we climbed up the trail. "Look at the plants and animals as we go. They change a lot and there are places where the plants all grow together—plants that are usually found in different areas."

"I already noticed some of that, Jesse. But I will pay attention to everything around me now. Thanks."

"These trees guard the entrance to the Lodge is what I the Old Ones told me," Jesse picked up the story again. "If your spirit is not clean they will not let you through. If you are not ready for lessons, they will not let you through. Look at those two downed trees over there," he pointed off to the side.

I looked and saw how their long trunks were twisted like a piece of taffy being pulled. "Wow, that's amazing," I truthfully told Jesse.

"That is the energy of the place as Elders also told me. Imagine what that could do to someone's insides if they were not coming here in the right way," Jesse told me. "I have had to leave many times with people I was taking here, who were turned back. Either they felt ill, or their bodies hurt, or they couldn't breath right or some other symptoms they complained of, which stopped them from going forward. Funny though—we would go back, drive to another trailhead for a different hike and they would be fine."

And so we continued up the wash with Jesse telling me more about the rocks and plants as we went. And I, with my natural resource degrees and connection to nature, told him other facts and stories he did not know. He was very pleased, as Jesse always liked to add to his knowledge base on the areas he walked. About half way up the trail I stopped, feeling a wave of energy flood over me, and a feeling coldness settle down upon me. We sat a few minutes and then went on. Everything seemed changed, but I kept silent until I could connect with this shift. When we reached the area below the Wisdom Lodge we stopped before climbing up.

"Good, no one is here," Jesse began. "Let's go up into the Lodge and I will play my flute if you will lead with your pipe."

"Sounds good to me," I agreed.

The Wisdom Lodge is up against a red rock wall on a small ledge under a rock overhang. All around are red rock walls extending up a couple hundred feet. I slowly made my way up the sixty or seventy feet of scrabble-covered rock to the Lodge. Jesse, being half mountain goat shot right by me and up. The Lodge was made in the past by some indigenous people who used the site. Flat rocks were piled in a circle to a height of about five and a half feet. There was a low doorway left in front for entering and a fire pit inside. I was a little tired by the hike up, but felt very strong in general.

"Jess, the changes in energy on the way up the trail are really noticeable to me. Do you feel them?"

"Sometimes I do. Sometimes hot energy, sometimes cold. Sometimes I feel Ancestors looking at me," Jesse answered me.

"When we got to that ninety-degree turn about halfway up I really felt changes. I'm curious to see if I feel them going back out," I added for him.

"What did you feel?"

"I felt an enormous energy surge and a cool wind, even though no air was moving. As I turned the corner, I felt as if we had stepped back two hundred years. I've never experienced anything like that. Everything got quieter and slower then. And the vegetation changed."

"Wow. That's neat. And no drugs, eh?" he laughed.

"Just a natural high," I laughed back. "Even up here, it's so quiet. You hear no sounds of civilization."

"I have always noticed that part. And the change in plants. I guess you needed to be here," Jesse said.

Suddenly, I felt something shifting in my gut—like a ball of energy moving around. I went off the trail and started heaving, even though there was nothing in my stomach to come up. It only lasted a minute and was gone. Then I rejoined Jesse and we went into the Lodge. After he played his flute and I opened a prayer pipe for us, Jesse climbed up another hundred and fifty feet and balanced himself on a tiny ledge where he began to play again. Jesse did this often, having no fear of heights or falling. Below him I took my drum out and joined him in making music. It was a joyful, musical time and we didn't rush it. Going back down the trail I stopped and had Jesse take my picture in that 'time warp' spot I again felt. It was fairly dark there now and he shot me against a rock wall, but I thought something might come out. I felt the reverse change in place, time and energy I had felt going in and, after making the turn I felt I was back in current time. Jesse also was paying attention and noted how, after that spot, it got warmer and we could hear a Jeep going up the dirt road in the distance. From here on, each time I went to the Wisdom Lodge I felt this shift, as did some others I took there, although they only talked about the energy burst or just 'a feeling'. It was also a spot on the trail that some people were not able to go beyond.

When I looked at the picture Jesse took later, I was amazed by what I saw. There I was, pack on back and walking stick in hand, washed in a shaft of white light coming from above and bathing me from the head down. The light showed only as it came down and struck me, nowhere else. Remembering there was no light when the picture was taken and we were in the natural canyon the wash made only increased the oddity of the picture—and the power implied by it. I kept this picture and have used in on occasion digitally, when I feel it appropriate.

As I continued to re-visit that trip with Jesse, Abbey brought me back to our hike.

"Jim, I'm feeling a little peaked. Can we stop a while?"

"Sure. Drink some water and see if that helps," I said, sitting on a fallen tree.

"Funny, it's not hot and this isn't too steep a trail, but I feel wasted," Abbey continued as we sat.

"It's okay. If you feel too badly, we can head back and go somewhere else for lunch."

"No, no, I want to go on, after I rest. Okay?"

"Sure, Abbey. No rush," I answered her question.

Then I again began feeling my stomach churn and my spine ache—as it had that day with Jesse. I went off the trail a little ways and started drinking some water. As I did, I felt my stomach lurch hard and I was vomiting into the brush. Again it did not last long, but I did bring up everything in my stomach. I felt like I had released a bag of cement after this purging. I think the energy of this area had helped me release some piece of dis-ease and the physical symptom of that was what I was vomiting. This was the second and last time this happened to me on this trail, so I guess whatever I needed to release there was gone. Then I walked back to where Abbey sat, as she drank water and rubbed her legs.

"Let's go on, I had some rest and water and I'm fine," Abbey told me with a wan smile that belied her words. But I shook my head 'okay' and we headed up the trail.

We reached some deadfall we needed to climb over soon after. Not much deadfall and easy to scale, but Abbey again hung back.

"Boy, I don't know, that looks hard to get over."

"No, it's not high. Come right through here and I'll take your hand as you do," I said to reassure her.

"Okay," she said weakly and she began going over the fallen tree.

We continued on and she became more and more nervous and edgy, looking around and jumping at any noise.

"Abbey, you look beat. What say we head back? We are almost half way and can go further another day. We can go down by the creek and have our lunch," I offered, giving her an easy way out.

"Okay. I am really tired suddenly. Let's go," she said and headed back down the trail twice as fast as we had come up. She really wanted out of there. She was not about to be allowed in by whatever spirits looked over the place.

This happened two other times I was bringing people there, so I knew it was no coincidence—as if there ever are any! Abbey never asked to go back to the Wisdom Lodge and I never offered.

Friends had started coming, spending a day or a week going on the land and into the red rocks with me to ask questions, do ceremony or just commune. The larger place I had rented was getting its use. One who came, as I previously shared, not long after I arrived was my brother and healing guide through my dis-ease, Jim Redhawk Francek. He was able to stay five days and I was excited by his arrival and curious where he might ask to go. Jim had continued to work his meal plan and had dropped over a hundred pounds by the time he came to Sedona; an amazing accomplishment. And he looked it—a shadow of his former self. As he was releasing this weight his own 'demons' were surfacing for his consideration and action. As it works, my friends. As we release one of our addictions that we were dulling our senses with, the issues we masked with it will surface. This is a good thing, because they will appear sooner or later to all but the totally disconnected. I remembered from retreats in the past when Jim had to stop and sit and wait for hours for the rest of us because he could not climb a hill or cross a long expanse. Now he had his mobility. Would he use it?

The second day he was with me I asked if he would like to take a hike to one of the sacred places I had told him about. Jesse was free and wanted to come and would play his magical flutes.

"Sure. Great, but I didn't bring any kind of hiking shoes," Jim replied to my question.

"No problem, Jimbo. I have an extra pair of hiking boots that should fit you," I told him, digging a pair out of a shelf in the garage where we were standing.

"Okay, let's do it! Where shall we go?"

"Wherever you want: Wisdom Lodge, Birthing Cave, Shaman's Cave, Oak Creek—you pick one."

"How about Shaman's Cave? You've called me from there when I was home and I would like to see it and open our pipes there. Is it too long a hike for me?"

"It's not too hot today and we'll take our time. Let me get Jesse and we can head out."

I found Jesse waiting out back, playing with Onyx. He grabbed his flutes and I called Onyx and away we went. It's about a forty-five minute drive to Shaman's Cave from Sedona—the last three miles up a deeply rutted dirt lane. It's way out on the land and a beautiful drive through desert and rocks. I could tell Jim was nervous, still adjusting to his new body and not experienced in hiking at all. After a jolting, bouncing ride up the three-mile dirt track I pulled to the side and parked. We all piled out and Onyx went racing down the hill in the direction of Shaman's. In a minute he came racing back up, obviously wondered where in the heck we were. We gathered our things, I handed Jim one of my walking sticks and we headed off down the trail.

Shaman's Cave and Dome is a magnificent place to visit if you are spiritual in any way. Also known as Robber's Roost—thanks to white, western people who must rename everything to cute, catchy names—this domed hill houses a sacred circular place under its north ledge much like the one at Wisdom Lodge. And, on top of the dome where I do my ceremonies, is an interesting array of rock features and areas that hold water after a rain. Native American people have been coming to Shaman's for generations to do ceremonies and to join in gatherings. They have also used it as a place to do vision quests. In fact, Native people from around the region still come on occasion and gather and engage in sacred practices. Some tourists manage to find this place, but if they are meant to be there they will make it and if they are not they will get lost along the way. At least it's far enough off the beaten path that the tour operators don't bring groups there.

For me this is the most sacred, most energetically alive spot in the area. The first time I came here and opened my pipe and meditated for hours, I knew it was my primary place for connecting with Great

Spirit, Mother Earth and my own inner self. When I took people to the three spots to cleanse, heal and grow I always took them to Wisdom Lodge first, Birthing Cave second and, if they made it that far in a good, balanced way I took them to Shaman's Cave. A day for each place, but the most time usually spent at Shaman's. After that three-day healing and spirit immersion they were either fully awake and in joy, or glassy-eyed. Sometimes a little of each.

Jim made it to the top of the dome without incident; but slowly and carefully, watching each footfall. When we arrived, Jesse brought out his flutes and began making his magic.

"That was quite a hike," Jim began. "I don't know that I've ever hiked that far. In fact, I know I haven't. What a glorious thing that I can do that now! I just need to remain careful since I'm not used to my new body yet." As he spoke the tears filling his eyes underscored the power of this day for him.

"It was a joy to see you get here, Jim. And now we can open our pipes and then do some journeying and see what comes to us. Okay?" I spoke these words with some tears in my eyes, matching his.

And so we spent two hours up on the rock talking, walking around the dome's top, doing ceremony and playing with Onyx. Finally we began hiking back to the car. No one was at the rock, on the trail or in the parking lot the entire time we were there. As we began bouncing out the dirt access road a Jeep was coming in. It has been like this every time I have been to Shaman's—whether just Onyx and I, or with a small group. And at Wisdom Lodge as well. I think the spirits of the area provide the peace and privacy to those who need it and can use it in a good way.

Fifteen minutes from the parking area a racket broke out in the sky above us. We all looked up to see an enormous flock of black birds wheeling, diving and circling directly above the car. I pulled over so we could watch this aerial circus. There were hundreds of these winged fliers at the least and the number grew as we watched, with others joining the flock. We sat and just watched, wondering what would come next. In a minute another equally as large flock came in from the west doing the same acrobatic dances. The two groups began merging and splitting apart, this display a part of what they were gifting us with. After about twenty minutes they began flying off and we headed back to the car. This was a display I had not seen before, nor have I seen since. Yet, when I shared this with my brother Jack in Santa Fe, he told me of how he and his wife, Fran, had seen a similar display of avian energy—also just one time. How about you, brothers and sisters—have any of you experienced this? I would welcome hearing about it if you have.

After the flocks disappeared, I looked up I saw two huge winged-ones flying south to north just off to our right side and asked, "Jesse, eagles over there?"

"I don't know. They look too big. They are coming towards us; do we have the binocs?"

"No, I left them on the table at the house. But, yeah, they are huge. I thought herons or such when I first looked up, but they fly like eagles."

"Oh, man. They are condors!" Jesse exclaimed. "They are only at the Grand Canyon. What are they doing here?!"

"Condors? They are huge," Redhawk said, as he had also been raptly looking up.

We all watched them fly over and continue north, the direction of the Grand Canyon, then we finally resumed our journey home. These two sightings were a sure sign of powerful medicine to come our respective ways.

I asked people around Sedona if they had ever seen the condors this far south. All of them said we must have seen eagles. Only one old timer remembered a documented case of a condor just north of Sedona some years back. This had not been eagles we saw that day, of that I am certain.

When we got back to the house, I walked into the back yard to get Onyx's dish and enjoyed the sight of Standing Eagle rock behind us—as I always do every time I see this impressive edifice. I shook my head in sorrow for those who had re-named this imposing rock the Native Americans connected with for generations to Coffee Pot Rock. Oh, well, we each have our walk to take, I guess—some more aware and sensitive than others. Some so focused on making a buck, they miss life.

After Jim Redhawk's visit, there was a short lull in people coming to sit with me in circle. To fill that lull, Jesse told me he needed to move from his place in less than a week. He had been living in a wonderfully secluded little cabin for twenty years. A cabin that a local artist rented to him. His landlord had passed away a year before and his son no longer wanted to rent the cabin out, so he had to move. The problem was Jesse was frozen—he did not want to move and had done nothing about it for the three months he had known he needed to move on. He was in denial. So I offered one of the bedrooms at my place for a while until he could find something. With just a couple of days left before the landlord was threatening him with legal action, we began shifting Jesse's possessions to my place. And the remainder we moved to a storage facility he already rented. A couple of weeks after he moved in, I agreed to let Jesse stay a while, which would also help me with the rent. I wasn't sure about this, but he was a friend and he needed time to transition. The energy at the house had shifted once again.

11 | Shifting Sands

ALL OF THESE THINGS I AM SHARING WITH YOU, OUR CIRCLE, HAPPENED quickly once I walked through that Golden Door and into Sedona—over the course of about six weeks. As I go back to that time to relive these things so I can speak with you about them, I am amazed by what a short time frame this was. I was just allowing my spirit to flow back and connect with Jesse and myself, as we moved his possessions out of his cabin—re-experiencing the angst he was suffering. It took longer than usual for me to 'be' there as well as here 'now' than it usually does. And so I examine that with you for a minute before we move on again.

The primary reason I can write about events or conversations that took place years before, is my ability to move back in time and be in that event or discussion again. Not remember it, but be there again. Likewise, I sometimes move forward in time and share in events and conversations that have yet to occur. For a long time—as I recounted in the first book and will in the book about the dark time of my soul when I am able to write it—I was certain this was a sign of impending insanity. It scared the hell out of me and I did all in my power to block it and even deny it was happening. Then I slowly began to accept it for what it was—a gift I needed to welcome and not fear. This allowed me to realize it was not the beginnings of insanity—especially since when it occurs, it allows me to see, hear and experience what I need to, and then dissipates.

Over the past couple of years, I have been exploring ways to manifest this 'time jumping' when I wish to re-experience something. The most success I have had with that is my writing. When I begin writing I move through time, existing in places as needed. It is difficult to explain unless you have experienced this phenomenon. I am in these places—all senses and awareness functioning. Yet often, I am in the present—all senses functioning—at the same time. A few times I have actually been in three places at once. You may begin to see why this is so disconcerting. As I do pay more attention to this moving about, I now realize it is easier for me to 'be' somewhere else the further back or the further forward then the current time. The closer that time is to the present, the more difficult for me to be present there as well and the less clear the pictures are. As if someone is playing with the control knobs on the TV. I have absolutely no idea why this is or what it means, but felt I needed to tell you. If you see less clarity—if the pictures I paint are not as sharp— I am closer to the present time in the incidents I am recounting.

Back on our main trail here, circle. Although I saw a few of you with wide eyes as I spoke of this 'time jumping'—a term that just came to me as I was writing the paragraph above. Maybe some of you have experienced this? If so, know you are not crazy. And know you can accept this as a wonderful gift when you are ready to do so. Know others are experiencing this as well. That often lessens the fear or anxiety around any novel, or unexpected, things that happen to a person.

After the day with the double swarm of black birds followed by the pair of condors winging north, I had Jesse move in with me. I also had been invited to volunteer for the Return of the Ancestors gathering at the end of April. This was a huge gathering of indigenous elders and teachers from around the globe happening in the Sedona area. Adam Yellowbird, who I would connect with in many ways down the road, spearheaded it. As I learned of this gathering, I heard back from Pam that she had again put her airline tickets on hold and could not visit at this time. This was followed by a call from Sue saying she was ready to come and visit for two weeks and asking permission to do so. I welcomed her and any who asked—having received the message clearly from Wankan Tanka that I was to welcome and work with any who came with a clear heart. As we talked and coordinated on dates and times, I realized she was to visit at the same time that the Return of the Ancestors was occurring. I told her of this and she asked if she might also volunteer. And so it was to be.

As I was sitting at my desk thinking about the revolving door my house below Standing Eagle had become, my friend Seth, from back East, called and said he was coming—asking if I had room for him. Of course I welcomed him as well, then realized he would be here five days and would leave the same day Sue was arriving. So much for down time for me! I would drive Seth to the airport that day and pick Sue up at the same time. I was beginning to feel like I needed a schedule book to keep things straight. So smiling, I simply released this whole train of thought, called Onyx in from the back yard and readied for a hike.

Onyx shot through his doggie door in my bedroom like a cannon-ball, jumping in place, knowing a trek was coming.

"Where do you want to go, relative?" I asked him as I rubbed behind his ears. He twisted his head from side-to-side, as he did when I spoke to him—which gave him an air of listening and considering his answer.

"The Birthing Cave? Or maybe the rock fields up off Schnebly Road? I know—want to go to the creek?"

The word 'creek' always elicited a huge response. He began running in circles, jumping and staring up at me, as if to say, "How can you even ask? You bet! Let's go!" I gathered our things and we headed up the canyon to the West Fork hiking trail, which went up that fork of Oak Creek. It was late morning and we hiked, waded and played all afternoon. Even Onyx, when we reached the car hours later, was spent. So we headed home where I could feed us both. The next evening was a lodge at Bearcloud's, so this time I had spent in nature to clear the head and heart was time well spent.

Sue called again the next day to confirm that she had booked her tickets.

"Great. Turns out Seth will be here just before you. In fact, he will be leaving the day you arrive, so I'll do double duty at the airport."

"So I won't need the shuttle to Sedona?"

"No, with Seth going and you coming it makes sense for me to drive to Phoenix. And I did talk to the people with the Ancestor's gathering, so I have us both signed up to volunteer. We can decide how many days we want to spend at that later," I informed her.

"That should really be interesting," Sue enthused. "Pam will be even more upset with me when she hears this. She wanted to come and spend time with you up in the rocks, and she thinks I botched that up for her. I hate this—she is my best friend."

"She was on the yes-no-yes roller coaster for a long time, Sue. In fact, she told me she couldn't make it before you asked, and then she said maybe she would try, and then she heard you had asked. So I'm certain she blames me as well. It's okay; she needs to work this through for herself. Pam needs to remember when you point the finger out at someone, you are really pointing at yourself. She can come when you are here, or after that or not at all. That is her choice."

"I know, but it still bothers me."

"Then that is for you to work out. If you planned your trip knowing she wanted to be here on her own—that's one thing. If you planned not knowing that—that's another slant. Sit with it, go inside and see what you see. Either way, it will all work out."

"No, I didn't know her plans. And it was a time when I could arrange it around my job."

"Then I suggest you might want to let it go. It can do no one any good. What else do you want to do or see while you are here? Ten days or so, right?"

"Ten days, yes. And, I don't know. I want to get a better sense of the West and see if I still want to move that way. I still have so much to resolve with my marriage and family here. Well, whatever you think I might want to see."

Sue had been working on her spiritual road for many years and, I knew from my healing work with her, standing in front of a Golden Door for some time as well. She had learned Native American ways from tribal people in the East and had a highly elevated connection to animals of all walks. In fact, she worked with a pack of wolves and gave educational programs with them around the Northeast. She was married and living in New Hampshire. Not a bad or painful relationship and place of being, but one that was stifling her spirit. She had nothing in common with her husband any longer and felt a strong need to live in the West and expand the work she was doing in the spiritual realm. This need to go it alone or connect with other circles was something I was seeing a lot of then and even more now. As she told me several times, she felt her window of opportunity to go through that Golden Door was finite and short. So making a decision to come to the West and see what her spirit told her was a huge step for her. It helped, I am certain, that she knew me and would have someone she knew aiding her walk while she was in Sedona.

Seth flew in and took a shuttle from Phoenix to Sedona, where I met him for the short ride up to my house. Seth had been to Sedona a number of times so I didn't have to do the tourist shuffle—the quick ride around town and the surrounding area. Seth had been on the spiritual path for some time, but I was never really certain who he had worked with and what his primary road was. Seth was the person working in leadership training whose work inspired what the group I was part of created with Natural Leadership Way. Yet he was not a part of this work, having I believe, some ego and attachment issues he needed to work through. But that was okay as we all coordinated our work and supported each other. No judgments or finger pointing, thank you friends, just acceptance and connection where it made sense.

Seth is an interesting guy—I like him a great deal and his work helped support me while I trudged through my dark time of the soul. But he is also a very private person needing a fair amount of personal time. So when he disappeared for hours the following day, I should not have been surprised. Jesse, however, was. He thought we were all going to hike and had left time for that. When I saw Seth was not going to appear, I suggested to Jess that we just go. And so we did, enjoying a beautiful day amongst the rocks.

Seth, Jesse and I went to a late dinner that night, after Jesse had played his flute at a local resort. Seth had invited a young woman along who he had met that day while hiking up Cathedral Rock. We all introduced ourselves and proceeded to have a fun dinner. Then we went back to my place, did some drumming and called it an early night.

The next day Seth was meeting an old friend and then he was coming with me to Bearcloud's lodge. So, at five in the evening, we met at New Frontiers Market and picked up some food for after the lodge. After stopping for sage, we headed up the canyon to Bearcloud's. The fire was crackling when we got there and I could smell the sweet scent of the burning pine. I introduced Seth to Bearcloud and Diana, his half-side, and we got ready for lodge. Seth had spoken of his Native American teacher many times and the ceremonies he had attended, including sweat lodges. So when we went out to the lodge and he became visibly nervous and edgy, I was truly surprised.

"Sorry, Jim. I don't think I can go in," he said sheepishly. "I'll just sit outside with the fire. Okay?"

"You feeling okay?" I asked.

"Yeah, just don't feel like I can go in," he responded very quietly.

"Okay. Speak to Bearcloud. It's his lodge and he will need to decide if you may sit with the fire."

So he hesitantly went up to Bearcloud and they began talking. Bearcloud questioned him several times about going in and explained he could leave at any time, but Seth was not budging. Nor was he going in. So he went and sat by the fire across from the lodge. I found this all very strange and wondered how much of what Seth had shared about his teachers and the ceremonies he had attended was based in reality. This fear reaction to the lodge was stronger than almost anyone's I'd seen in the past—including my own at my first lodge. Again, people, as I see a couple of you shaking your heads, I'm not judging Seth—please don't do so, either. I was evaluating how I might connect with him on the spiritual road in the future—or if I would at all. Then I released that question, as Great Spirit would make that call for me—I was certain.

A couple of days later I was doing the Phoenix ramble—driving Seth down to catch his flight and then waiting for Sue to arrive on her's. Seth and I talked about the beauty of the Sedona area on the ride down as I was also watching the landscape going by.

As we got closer to the city the highway began going through one suburban town after another—the sprawl spawned by the Phoenix metropolitan mother ship. This sprawl, which gobbles up open space and natural areas as it feeds on itself; always moving ever further out from the core. As it has from virtually every city across Turtle Island—across the globe, in fact. I can remember when this was not the case. I remember Phoenix and the communities close to it being a city surrounded by natural desert and mountains. A clean city, with fresh air and easy access to places to immerse yourself in nature. And this was not that long ago—maybe twenty years. Now concrete, buildings, highways, traffic and pollution. Lots of pollution—the yellow miasma hanging in the still desert air. Is this the legacy we want to leave for the future generations? For our children? Brothers and sisters, we have our work cut out if we are to improve this legacy. If we are going to leave something for our children, and theirs, that they can live with and not die from.

But I'm transgressing into preaching. Sorry, but it's hard not to care every minute once you are truly 'awake' and so hard not to speak what you see. But I'll save it for another time and another venue.

For now, it was enough that I saw some of this Phoenix sprawl—this stain across the land—eating itself from the inside. Much like humans in anger and fear are now eating themselves from the inside. And why not? Don't those same people who seek to control also build these unsustainable man-made environments? So why wouldn't the creations suffer the same fate as the creators? Town after town going by as we neared Phoenix—and each more empty than the one before it. Houses vacant, shopping centers empty—so empty they no longer listed the stores present on their signs. Whole neighborhoods with cars at only one or two homes. Construction job after construction stopped dead by the falling economy. Was this also part of nature taking charge and restoring balance? Would our economic collapse be part of the huge changes coming? This past summer as I travelled around the country I saw similar things. But I also saw pockets of harmony. I have thought about this a great deal and I am certain it will be another journey we all take together. It is important now to recognize and accept that the prophesized time of change is upon us and that we form healing circles in response to this.

Please don't think I want to see everything collapse. Certainly not just for the sake of collapsing. That is not what the prophesizes are about. Nor what we need to be about as human beings. But what is unsustainable needs to cease and be re-tooled. What is out-of-balance must be put back into balance. Those who lead all aspects of human life need to come into harmony with our environment and the rest of us, we human beings. If this can happen softly and easily, I fully support that. It would put me into a state of joy. If not, however it needs to happen—must happen. That is what the prophesizes speak to. Not the end of the world—but the end of the destructive, dead-end practices we have created or allowed to be created.

When we got to the airport we parked and headed to Seth's check-in area. It was early and I had a couple of hours to wait for Sue. We decided to get coffee and talk a little more. Seth checked his bag and we walked to the Starbuck's.

"When does Sue land?" Seth asked me.

"In a little over two hours if her flights not delayed. I think she was going through two other airports to get a cheap flight."

"Good. You'll get back up to Sedona before dark with any luck."

"I'd like to. So when are you getting back this way?"

"Don't know, Jim. Maybe in a few months. I do love Sedona and, with you here it's even better."

"You know there's room—even if it's a couch, given the way it's been going."

"Boy, people sure are coming your way. That's good; you have a lot to teach them. How long is Sue here?"

"Ten days. We are both volunteering for the Return of the Ancestors."

"I'm really sorry I'm missing that. Let me know how it turns out. So you and Sue have any relationship going?"

"No, just friends through the circle and working with her on her healing journey. You know I don't want to walk with anyone. Just Onyx and I. No more—enough. Not now, not down the road!" I said a little heatedly.

"Whoa. Okay, I hear you. I'm just getting something else. But, anyway. It's been really great. Thanks. Say goodbye to Bearcloud and Diana for me and thank them again. Okay?"

"No problem. There's another lodge this Friday. I'm curious to see if Sue is interested."

"Yeah, well. When you coming East again? Remember my place in Connecticut."

"Thanks, I know. But I don't want to come East until I have to for some reason. I've got heaps of healing to do yet, Seth. And that's what I need to work on."

"Perfect. You can't help anyone else heal while you've still got open wounds. Believe me, I know."

"Our own healing is always a work in progress, but you're right, you can't be in too much 'dis-ease' when you try to assist others. That's why I pick and choose my times now."

"Well, I guess I should start through security. You never know what it'll take any more," Seth said as we finished our second coffee. He picked up his carry-on and we headed towards the security line.

"Been great, brother," I said as we embraced.

"Absolutely. Again, soon," Seth responded as he retuned the embrace. Then he turned to the check-in point and started down the tunnel.

Sue's flight was about an hour late so I drank some more coffee while I waited and thought some more about where it would be best to take her—for her highest good. I began musing the ley lines around Sedona and how that might affect where we would go first. I wanted to provide her with a series of spiritual opportunities, starting with some less energetic than others might be. No need to 'fry her circuits' with too much, too quickly. Especially with the big issues that she was wrestling with—too quick an immersion into the energy pool of some Sedona sites might shut her down and so waste her time here.

Ley lines. What are they? Do they exist? What do they mean around Sedona? To start, here is a definition and some description from http://www.ancient-wisdom.co. uk/leylines:

"Most cultures have traditions and words to describe the straight, often geometric alignments that ran across ancient landscapes, connecting both natural and sacred prehistoric structures together. Usually the names given to represent these invisible lines are translated to an equivalent of *'spirit'*, *'dream'*, or *'energy'* paths. However, apart from the physical presence of the sites themselves, proving the presence of a 'connection' between them is something that researchers have found notoriously elusive.

Amongst the widely differing (and often simplistic) theories that attempt to explain *why* ley-lines and landscape alignments first appeared, the following theories probably say as much about us *now* as at any time in the past, yet we are bound to acknowledge and respect the following writers opinions and conclusions as 'they', the following few, are the giants upon whose shoulders this field of study currently sits:

* The current definition of a Ley-line according to http//:Wikipedia. en.org/ is as follows:

'Ley lines are hypothetical alignments of a number of places of geographical interest, such as ancient monuments and megaliths. Their existence was suggested in 1921 by the amateur archaeologist Alfred

Watkins, whose book 'The Old Straight Track' brought the align-ments to the attention of the wider public'.

This explanation by no means completes the modern definition of a ley-line, as we cannot say for example that all alignments of stones are ley-lines, however old they are. Nor does it follow that all an-cient sites were aligned deliberately, even those that appear to have been."

I mentioned these lines of connecting power earlier, when I was at the ancient circle past the Birthing Cave. The Birthing Cave, Sha-man's Dome, the Wisdom Lodge and many other ancient sites around Sedona are vortexes. The plural of vortex is normally vortices—but not in quirky Sedona. There it is "vortexes", so I will go with the local usage. Vortexes are proposed to be points of power or energy on the Earth. The ley lines are the power lines, which follow the relation-ships and connections between these points. If you plot the ley lines between vortexes in Sedona on a map you create many geometric images—the most well- known is a huge star which covers Sedona and the surrounding land. Coincidence? How about the other inter-locking stars and squares created by the ley lines running between the power spots—some I've mentioned to you—in the area. The deniers will, of course, point to coincidence or wishful thinking and want to see your "hard, visible proof." I'm so glad I was shown there are no coincidences early on my spiritual walk so I don't have this mental block to fall back on.

Scientists have studied the vortex phenomenon in Sedona and other places around the world. As usual, some have proposed theories for their existence and assert they are real and function in ways sci-ence cannot fully explain. Others claim they are a hoax and deserve to be ignored. Having experienced and felt the energies at many of these vortexes, I can assure you they exist and are powerful. It may be more a function of a person's ability to feel and use these places based on their readiness and willingness to do so. Readiness, once again friends. It seems as if it's becoming a theme for this walk. Let's pay attention as we journey on and see if it takes us up any further side roads. Ah, all about the journey, eh?

The vortexes around Sedona are energetically masculine and feminine, as I shared before. I have seen and felt this and know it to be so. And the Earth Mother, in my journeying, has shown me this as well. The masculine vortexes, or upflows, are said to help you fly with the eagles to higher spiritual realms, understandings or perspectives. They are wonderful places to journey or meditate. The female vortexes, or inflows, are said to allow for greater introspection and understanding within. There is much more to be learned about vortexes if you search, but this is enough for us for now.

Remember as we continue on, brothers and sisters, there are still a lot of flaky people in Sedona. Every spiritual story in the world is espoused here, UFO's make regular pit stops, faeries dance each night under the moon and animals and goblins literally talk to those who can hear. Tricky spot here. I don't discount anything, especially given some of the things I have seen and experienced. But I do recognize those who go a little far off the path, either because they like their dreams or to create more myths to make money off tourists. Unfortunately this detracts from the real power and energy of the area. Or maybe not. Maybe it protects it from those who destroy everything they don't understand by hiding it under the silliness of some of the claims. I had not thought of this before, so maybe we need to think about it. Where is it often the best place to hide something? In plain sight—where no one would look because it's too obvious.

Okay, sorry, but that was an interesting thought. As for the vortexes and ley lines in Sedona, there is another important element to consider when you explore their 'being'. That is the beliefs of those who have worked with them for generations—the Native American tribes of the area. Look at all the brochures for visiting Sedona. Check out all the websites for visitors. Ask guides about the original people of this place. You will hear about the communities they built in the Verde Valley, which Sedona sits to the north of. You will hear about relics.

You may, on rare occasion, hear how they did not live in Sedona, but did ceremony there, as I have told you. But I venture that nowhere—nowhere—will you hear or read about the Native presence when the Europeans settled. You will hear some tribal people still live in the area, many on reservations, but you will not hear what follows below, at least without doing some research.

> "The Yavapai and Apache tribes were forcibly removed from the Verde Valley in 1876, to the San Carlos Indian Reservation, 180 miles southeast. Fifteen hundred people were marched, in midwinter, to San Carlos. Several hundred lost their lives. The survivors were interned for 25 years. About 200 Yavapai and Apache people returned to the Verde Valley in 1900 and have since intermingled as a single political entity although culturally distinct."
>
> From http://en.wikipedia.org/wiki/Sedona,_Arizona

Add to the large number of diverse vortex types in and around Sedona, the red rocks which appear to be on fire at dawn and dusk, the number of ley lines created which connect these power spots, and the forced removal of the Native population—and you have the massive energy zone that Sedona is. An area for extensive inner healing for those ready. An area where proper respect for the land and all who have walked it before you will allow you to tap into these energies.

I allowed all these thoughts about the energy of Sedona, the vortexes and the ley lines to run through my being as I considered the places Sue might wish to go. I knew I would offer the three I visited most often—Wisdom Lodge, Birthing Cave and Shaman's Dome. The three connected by ley lines and sight lines. What I was unaware of until seeing the work of some visiting scientists a year later, was just how connected to so many power locations—vortexes—the Wisdom Lodge was. It sits at the central point for a multitude of intersecting ley lines. This, the Wisdom Lodge, probably the least well known of any vortexes in the region—not even appearing on most lists. This also is one of the least visited and most unmarked of the sites. Finally, this vortex was the one where I always experience a shift in time and energy when I visit.

With all my thinking and ruminating, I lost track of time—something I can be particularly good at—and suddenly realized Sue's plane was probably on the ground. I got up and headed towards the incoming flight entrance and saw her coming down the exit ramp as I approached.

"Good to see you. Welcome to the West," I greeted her as I approached, cowboy hat in hand.

"Thanks. I actually made it," she smiled broadly as she answered.

We hugged hello and moved on to the luggage carousel to get her bag.

"So, you didn't get too late after all."

"No, about an hour like they said."

"Well, we have about a two hour ride back to Sedona. Are you hungry or do you want to wait until we get there?"

"Let's wait and get something in Sedona. Okay?" she answered.

"Sure, fine with me."

We started back up the highway with Sue looking all around at the desert scenery.

"This is great. I've wanted to be out here for a long time. I thought the mountains would call me first, but this is a great place to start," she said as she checked out the local cacti.

We drove past the dead and dying communities I had observed on the way down and Sue also saw the look of desertion and desolation all around them.

"Boy, these towns look dead," she commented as we drove by the fifth or sixth of them.

"Causalities of the economy and human ego and greed," I agreed. "Wonder if they will recover if the economy turns around or if this is part of the change?"

About half way between Phoenix and Sedona, you begin the climb from low-lying, hot, dusty Phoenix to Sedona's more temperate

5,000-foot altitude. The first climb up is a five-mile mountain where, about half way up, stands the last of the desert guards, a huge branching cactus. I pointed this sentry out to Sue since it marks the boundary between desert and high desert environments.

"Wow, he looks stately," she remarked, using the same word I had the first time I saw this cactus person.

We had some early dinner in Sedona and then went to hear Jesse play at another local hotel. Jesse plays four or five nights a week at various venues around town. Many people who visit Sedona make sure they stop and listen to his magic flutes—some many times. Sue was also impressed by the spirit and energy of Jesse's work. Afterwards we headed back to the homestead.

Let me step back into current time for a few minutes and talk about a couple of interesting energetic connections I am seeing as we walk together and I write this down. I believe we talked about how I sit atop the mountain near Santa Fe as I write this book—versus the desert place near Sedona where I wrote the first. Both are sanctuaries— both are powerful spiritual energy wells. But today, as I write about a huge shift in my life, energy and work it is December 10, 2011. Just a month since I went to Sedona to go into my birthday lodge on 11/11/11. And the day of the full moon and full lunar eclipse. I got up at a little after five AM this morning and saw Grandmother Moon just beginning to don her eclipse gown. A little while later I saw her colors and watched her finish pulling her robes about her. By eight AM I was sitting here writing the next part of our journey and the next shift in my walk, while I was remembering the winged ones from Shaman's Dome we saw earlier. Interesting? I thought so and therefore I document it for us.

The day after Sue arrived we were going to attend a volunteer 'training' for the Ancestor's event, but had all day before this 5 PM appointment. We talked about it and decided to go to the Wisdom Lodge for a hike. Jesse decided to go along and so we set out after breakfast. First we went to New Frontiers, Sedona's independent, organic market and got some cheese and fruit and some bottled water;

then we drove through town a little so Sue could get a better feel for the area. After that we headed off for the Lodge. We bounced our way up the dirt access road and pulled off to the side of the road as usual, just beyond the wash to the Lodge.

Sue and I spent a couple of hours in the Wisdom Lodge enclosure burning sage and tobacco and connecting to Great Spirit as Jesse sat up high playing his flutes. We did ceremony and then settled back and journeyed wherever our spirit guides wished to take us. I was journeying back to the dark time of my soul and then forward to a place of green meadows and running water. Then again to a place high up with snow on the surrounding mountains. No words or images, just pictures of the natural areas flowing through my head and heart. Finally I got up to throw Onyx some sticks as he felt he was being ignored. A little while later we began the trek back to the car.

At five we were at the Sedona High School for the volunteer meeting. A woman, about forty with long, dark black hair addressed those present and introduced herself as an organizer for the event. She had been hired by the event sponsor, the Institute for Cultural Awareness (ICA). She then went on talking for an hour telling us all about herself and her great accomplishments and all the horror stories from past events that involved volunteer staff. I was truly amazed—by the enormous ego coupled with the complete lack of self-image the woman had and by what she was saying. There never was any training and everyone walked away in disbelief and annoyance. I wondered how many would return for the event as volunteers the next day. And, as I expected, less than half did.

The first day of the gathering was on the high school grounds that ICA had rented. With too few volunteers, a small staff and an attendee turnout higher than expected, it was a crazy time for all. I was asked to work the entrance table as I had a lot of experience with events. Sue worked the grounds as a welcomer. It was a long, interesting day, but well worth the time we spent at it. The next day was to be at a state park and we were scheduled to work a while and then we would be given free time to participate in the various ceremonies. We enjoyed that day as well, but decided that was enough until later in the week. With that decision made, we opted to leave for the Grand Canyon the following day. The ICA gathering was to have a sunrise ceremony at the Canyon's rim two days out and we thought we might decide to attend that as well.

After we left the gathering we went and picked up Onyx. He and Sue had hit it off like I knew they would. And, since he was going to stay with Jesse while we went to the Grand Canyon we wanted to give him some time on Oak Creek. So we went to one of the parking areas along the creek and started walking in along the trail. Sue and I talked spirit healing and energy work as Onyx ran up and down the trail and through the fields on either side—one happy four-legged. Then it was stick-chasing time in the creek—his favorite thing in life. We took turns tossing sticks and watching him dive and swim for them. On the way back to the house, Sue wanted to walk around Uptown a while so we parked and headed out on foot. I advised her to wait until we went up the canyon and into Hopi land before deciding what, if anything, to buy. There are much better deals on the rez then in the tourist traps of Sedona.

I hated leaving Onyx home, but there were few places that would allow dogs in the Grand Canyon National Park. Happily Jesse also liked Onyx and Onyx knew it. Jess would take him for at least a couple good walks each day. So, after taking Onyx for a romp on the trails behind the house, we got our things in the car, ready for the 'Big Hole'. We took sage, flutes, drums and Chanupa—not knowing what we might want or need. Then we headed out, not sure where we were going nor what we were going to do. Ah, the perfect plan, friends—no plan. No matter what happened next it was on this 'plan' and therefore nothing could not go wrong.

We headed up the canyon towards Flagstaff—the same canyon I had first driven down when I arrived in Sedona. This time it felt like home, at least for now. When we got to the top we stopped at the rest area, because I knew Sue would want to see what the Native artists had for sale. She found several things she liked and purchased a few for herself and her grandkids. A fetish necklace, however, she left, thinking it too pricey and saying did not yet know how to bargain with the Native merchants. So, while she walked along the tables, I went back to the woman showing the necklace and negotiated a deal. Then I bought it for her—why, I didn't know. It was more than I spend on most people, yet also something I am prone to do at times. I assumed Spirit wanted her to have the energy of this piece and so had guided me. Whatever, she was thrilled—and surprised—by her gift.

We got to the Grand Canyon by late morning and drove to the old inn, the Grand Hotel, in the middle of the park. This was the original resort hotel of the park. An inn that was always booked months—or years—in advance. I checked with the front desk and found they had rooms in a couple of the out buildings, but nothing in the hotel itself. I left my name and we went and ate in the restaurant, looking out over the canyon. We watched the ravens flying along the rim, at times swooping down on the snow looking for scraps. Raven, in the Native American tradition, is about magic and shapeshifting. He is also a trickster in some tribe's lore, much like coyote. In fact, Raven is in the lore of many people—not just Native American. So their appearance was a sign of power to us, although this did not occur to me at the time.

In retrospect, this was an interesting trip for both of us. For me, Sue was a friend and member of our Natural Leadership Way group as well as the role of healing guide I filled for her. Yet, with my wife and others now gone, I felt uncomfortable with her being 'in my space' here in the West. A discomfort I had felt with some of the others who had come to stay with me, although not as strongly as I now felt it with Sue. For her, her internal work over stepping through the Golden Door before her and walking forward alone into a new area, made this time very poignant. I think she was thrilled and excited by Sedona and the West, but still fearful of the big step, without a safety net, she was contemplating.

We went outside and began to walk the rim. It was cold—very cold—with snow and ice blanketing much of the ground. This white against the crystal-like, hard blue of the sky, white and red of the canyon sides, green-hued trees and shrubs and black ravens combined to paint a beautiful natural canvas of many colors. We walked up a mile or so, enjoying scenic lookouts as we went. Then, with cold feet and shivering bodies, we turned for the walk back.

"This place is amazing," Sue said, wonder in her voice. "Pictures don't capture it at all."

"No. No pictures can convey the size and wonder of the place. And certainly not the energy of it. Do you feel it?" I asked.

"I do. It would be great to see a sunup here," she agreed.

"Well, we can get space in one of the out buildings. Won't be as special or contain the energy of the main lodge, but we can be out here walking at dawn. And can catch up with the Ancestors group if we like."

"Let's," Sue agreed.

When I went back to the main desk I found a note—we had space in the Main Lodge. So we now were ready for sun-up—a frigid sun-up, but that would be even better—and meeting with the Ancestor's group if we opted for that. We went and took a ride around the park and enjoyed overlooks and some walks along the rim at various points. It's nice in the winter because all roads are open to cars and there are limited visitors. We watched the winter birds flying and diving—probably in part to stay warm. The temperature was dropping rapidly and this had an impact on all the creatures of the Grand Canyon. The report was for near zero temperatures that night with the possibility of more snow. The Standing People—the trees—were also dealing with the snow and cold in their own way. Some held a white blanket up to Father Sky, some had shaken their blankets off, with the discarded white blankets laying at their feet, and some were just peeking through a heavy white mantle. It was a beautiful, serene day at the Canyon. We snapped a host of pictures—mostly close-ups as the Canyon does not photograph well, but a few to show the white and red down the Canyon's faces. Finally, when we were starting to get icy cold, we turned back to the Lodge.

We parked and walked to the gift shop and museum near the Lodge. Actually, while Sue went to the gift shop I walked up to the museum in the next building. There I began talking to a ranger, John, who had been stationed in the park for fifteen years.

"This is a great place to be stationed," John affirmed. "Busy as heck in the summer, but beautiful and relatively empty most of the winter. Except for around the Lodge here. I get up early each day and take a long hike along the rim or down the trail. Hate to start my day without it."

"And you have the winter clothes for it. My friend, Sue, and I did not come prepared for this much cold," I told John.

"Most people don't. It's late for this much cold, but it's great by me. I come from back East, where cold and ice are painful. Not here. Not as much humidity and less biting wind."

"Where back East, John?" I asked.

"Oh, been twenty years, but from Lancaster County in Pennsylvania. Where the Pennsylvania Dutch have a large population."

"Know it well. I'm from Chester County. Just below Lancaster."

"Really? How about that. Been in Arizona long?" John queried.

"Nope, just a matter of months. But I'll be staying a while. I lived in Colorado for about ten years, so the West is home to me."

"Yeah, I love Colorado too. My brother is with the Park Service and he's with Rocky Mountain National Park."

"I was in Fort Collins with Colorado State, so I was in that Park all the time. I worked with the park service people there a great deal, since I was in the College of Natural Resources."

"Small world for sure," John said smiling. "How long you here?"

"Just until morning. We want to be outside for sunup and then we are off. Back to warmer, sunnier Sedona."

"You want to go out about thirty minutes before sun-up. That's when the powerful time is—birds waking up, sky just beginning to lighten and no people."

"Thanks, John. Will do."

With that some tourists approached John with map in hand and questions on their lips, so we said goodbye and I went back to the gift shop. Sue and I talked a few minutes and agreed to dinner at eight, which was when they knew they would have a table.

I spent one cold night wrapped in blankets and sheets, wracked with guilt and pain over my being here amidst this natural beauty, while my wife was not. I slept little, but was used to that. I was angry by this continued suffering, but shook it off by the early morning and went downstairs. Sue was there and we went out to greet the sun. It was closer to actual sun-up than I had hoped, but the air was almost brittle—and clean, clear and sharp. Some birds were stirring, especially the ravens once again, and we walked the rim, watching the sun pull himself above the rim of the horizon. We gathered more pictures with the camera and then turned to go back for breakfast in the Lodge. We decided not to join the Ancestors group, but rather to see the dawn ourselves, eat and then head out to the desert. Back in the Lodge restaurant we had pinon nut pancakes with prickly pear syrup and pistachio butter—delicious!

We then took a walk along the rim and enjoyed the views once more—watching the ravens swoop, land, squawk and peck. Then we loaded the car and headed east—out to the land of the Hopi. Sue had decided she wanted to see some of the Hopi lands, so we were going to spend the day driving around the mesas with no intention beyond that. There are three primary mesas in Hopi land, named easily enough, First Mesa, Second Mesa and Third Mesa. On top of each is one of the oldest Hopi communities. First Mesa is the oldest of all, the town having been there for thousands of years. We did not think we would drive through the Hopi communities, having not been invited by any residents, but would rather drive through the desert seeing what the Painted Desert and Petrified Forest had to offer to our senses. We had purchased a few CD's of Native American drum and flute music while at the Grand Canyon and Sue began unwrapping one to put into the car's CD player. I had a fairly large collection of this music, as did Sue, but these were some we did not own. We headed out into the high, barren desert of this area with drums playing and flutes singing from the car's speakers—each of us wrapped in our own thoughts.

We drove out of the snow quickly and into a bright, sunny, but cold expanse of land. Many people I hear talk about the desert, speak about its naked barrenness. I don't see this. I see a stark, but beautiful landscape, teeming with life and vitality if you know where to look. And how to look—looking 'small'—seeing the small things you might normally miss since we humans are accustomed to the big, broad 'brushstrokes' of human creations. While I was taking some pleasure in the views all around me, I was glad we had the music playing so I did not have to speak. I felt very sad and depressed—mostly guilt welling up again I suspect. This brought on a great deal of physical pain especially in my muscles, which were spasming faster than the music was playing. Being used to it I did not try to 'fight' it or stop it, but allowed it to play through my being.

I will spend a great deal of time in the book I write about the dark time of my soul speaking about pain, dis-ease and disease, and how you can not 'fight' it or 'conquer' it, but must come to understand it at the core of your being. To do otherwise allows you to ease some of the symptoms of your pain, but not to heal the causes. This I was just beginning to see a glimmer of meaning in as we drove across the desert. And just minutely seeing the difference between dis-ease and disease. Disease, something physically or mentally out-of-balance in the physical being; can cause dis-ease, a feeling of in-balance in your being. To address the cause of your malady you must also address why it makes you feel so out-of-balance—so in dis-ease. Some have taken to spelling disease as dis-ease to explain, with a smile, why you feel poorly. I see it differently, as I just explained to the best of my ability. They are related, but not the same thing, as I understand it. But both do need to be worked on as one before you can truly address the causes and not just the symptoms of your problems.

All the emotional dis-ease I was feeling and the physical symptoms it caused now resulted in a fierce headache and nausea. Being human, and still too much a product of my Western upbringing, I was embarrassed by this and did all I could to hide any outward show of the pain I was in. And I was fearful—maybe terrified—that I would be humiliated by breaking into tears. Boy, was I still a 'package'. Not that I understand it all yet, but I see when I write of these things, that I have learned some things and come a ways further than I was. Okay, maybe a great deal further. Thank you all for reminding me that I need to accept credit for what I accomplish, as well as blame for what I might have done better. And I remind each of you—pointing back your way—to do the same. So, I was fighting back tears and sorrow, forcing a smile to my lips and pretending to be more engrossed by the music than I was. So much for honesty. I had no idea—being so wrapped in my own issues and pain—that Sue was feeling other, similar things. She was dealing with her issues around change and fear.

About an hour out, shortly after we passed the road leading to the First Mesa community, I saw a place we could pull off and walk. I pulled in without asking and without thinking. This happens to me often and I have now learned to follow these instincts and not question them. We got out of the car without saying a word and began walking towards a drop-off to see what view it offered. There were crevasses and expanses of rock and areas of sagebrush and cacti all around and below us. Sue began walking across one of the rock faces as I stood looking up into Father Sky, watching a vulture soar high above. As she continued to meander slowly away from me, I realized it felt right for us to have some time and space alone with Mother Earth, Father Sky and Great Spirit around us. I slowly turned and headed down a ravine, across some white and yellow rocks, in the direction opposite the one Sue had taken. The further I walked—the further from the car and road and 'others' I moved—the more I let down the wall I had built around my emotions while driving. Suddenly, I began to just sob—sobs that came from the core of my being. As I sobbed my sinuses filled and the back of my head screamed in pain, but I did not stop for some ten minutes or so. This, for me, is good—ten minutes. I still, even with the teachings and understandings I have been gifted, have a great deal of difficulty in just 'letting go' and letting my emotions drain. I can remember twice in my life when I cried and sobbed and yelled for hours—letting a reservoir of emotion and pain leave me. That's it—only twice. Even as I sit here with you sharing all this, I know I need a third time to release in this atavistic, primordial way to truly clear my system and yet I have been unable to do so. Probably timing, my friends—I am not yet ready.

I walked further down the ravine I was in and sat on a nicely rounded, butt-accommodating boulder and bent over, putting my head in my hands. I let images and emotions just flood through my brain as I sat there feeling the Earth Mother beneath me. I felt a lump in my pocket as I sat, so I reached in and pulled out a sage ball. I didn't remember putting it there, but it was perfect timing finding it there now. I put it on a rock, lit it and began fanning myself with the beautifully pungent smoke arising from it. I breathed in deeply, cleansing my inside as the smoke swirled around my outside. I said a short prayer to Wankan Tanka, Great Spirit, and slowly got up. I felt a little better and my head was not swimming through the dark swamp water it had been a few minutes before. So I headed back to the car.

Sue was not to be seen, so I sat on a rock near the car, trying to relax my body and mind a little more. Slowly my muscles unclenched as I breathed in deeply of the desert air. I then saw Sue off in the distance, slowly wending her way back. She also looked contemplative and a bit sullen, so I realized, finally, that she was also working some issues. I had done no healing work with her—other than to ask some questions for her to contemplate—since she arrived. This was primarily because we were doing something most of the time, but also because I was dealing with issues that I did not feel left me open enough to work on someone else.

"Hi. Nice walk?" I asked as she got to where I sat.

"Yes. Very beautiful. And quiet and empty. I just had a lot I was working through and I needed to go off and cry," she answered honestly.

Damn, did I need to be as sharing? I could hear Two Bears, my first teacher saying, "Be careful what you teach. You may have to follow yourself."

"So did I," I fessed up. "Lots of emotion. Cried for ten minutes—more like sobbed—over in the rocks. It was good we stopped here."

"Oh yes. But we can go now."

So we headed out and spent the day listening to music, especially the Native group Ah-Nee-Mah, and watching the glory of the Earth Mother and the Rock People opening out before us. We drove east and north from where we had stopped and then drove down through the Painted Desert. The pastel colors that adorn these rocks and cliff faces have captivated me since the first time I had driven through the region, thirty-five years or more earlier. They are particularly glorious after a rain, which brings out all of their colors and hues. But even now, in the stone cold dry time, the colors were amazing. When we felt we had absorbed enough of the Painted Desert energy, I turned in the direction of the Petrified Forest. Seeing a Native restaurant, I pulled in and we feasted on large, very large, Indian tacos. For those unfamiliar with the West, an Indian taco is ground meat in a sauce (like Sloppy Joe) with cheese, lettuce, tomato and onion all piled in and on a large, hot frybread. Oh, how I want one right now. And I see you in the circle do as well. Sorry, friends. But let's take a break. I need to eat a salad and you may want to get some food. We will come back to our circle in a while. No rush—Indian time. When you all get back here we shall proceed.

Okay, it seems we are all here back in circle ready to move ahead. I brought back tea and some salad, so I may eat and drink as we journey. Do the same if you wish to.

Sue and I spent the remainder of the day driving through the Petrified Forest, where we stopped several times to walk among the ossified tree stumps. This is very interesting energy for those who connect with the energy of natural things. These are Standing People— trees—who dropped their robes and passed on eons before. Yet, as rock particulates—silica and other minerals, I believe—came in and impregnated these former trees they became Rock People as well. So they are now to me neither Standing People nor Rock People, but a mix of both over a long period of time. These Standing Rocks, as I will name them here and now, have managed to exist in harmony with the energy of both of their components. How much we two-leggeds could learn here! The four colors of people—red, white, black and yellow—are required to come together now and share in order to co-create, with the Creator and the Earth Mother, a new way—a new human being.

If rocks and trees—two extremely different entities—can become one why do we humans whose only difference is in the 'paint' used on the outside, have such a difficult time reaching this unity?

What? Say again sister. Ah yes, ego. And fear. And hatred. What was that brother? "We are not trees or rocks". Yes, quite right. But, in the Native way, all things have merit in the universe. No being more important or powerful than any other being. What? "We are sentient". Yes, so should we not be better able to come together? Ah, good, I'm glad you see. Yes, I know I used the "S" word—should. I did so intentionally. Maybe however, with more hard work together we could better fulfill the directions of the prophecies and create together. Let's hold that in our hearts as we walk further and see what else may come of it.

We were about two and a half hours from Sedona when we finished with the Petrified Forest and it was getting late so we turned in the direction of Flagstaff and the canyon below, back to the red rocks of home. Everything is quite a ride out here in the west. You get used to it, but you also learn to watch your time if you don't want to be driving late into the night. We got back to the house just after dusk and Onyx was standing up at the front window as we approached the front door. He was all over me when I went in and I dropped my bag so I could accept his heartfelt welcome. Jesse came out and welcomed us back and told me Onyx had been for a walk a couple of hours earlier. I thanked him and went for Onyx's leash. This is a sign for him to go nutty—jumping and running in circles. Sue said she wanted to come along, so we took him out the front door and through the neighborhood where I lived. I always leashed him at night. If animals were around he would bound after them, wanting to play. And if it was a herd of javelinas, this was bad. Javelinas, or wild pigs as they are called, are actually giant rodents that can do a number on dogs. And this night, it was a good thing I had leashed him because a herd of six or seven javelinas appeared a few minutes later.

The next day we were scheduled to volunteer in the morning for the Return of the Ancestors and then go to a lodge at Bearcloud's in the evening. Sue was excited by the opportunity to go into Bearcloud's lodge, but also nervous, hoping she could last the four doors if it was a hot one.

"Don't worry about it," I advised. "Remember what I told you before. The heat is more a function of your inner doubt and fear than it is of the physical rocks. And, if you have to leave, Bearcloud will open the door. You can sit at the fire and still be involved in the ceremony."

"I know, but I want to make it through."

"Then you will. You did fine in the lodge I poured at Pam's. Hung in for both lodges."

"Yes, but I know you. And you said you didn't pour too hot a lodge—then you did!"

"Was it? I can't tell, because I don't feel the heat. I haven't for some time. I know it's hot when I drip sweat, but it only feels warm to me."

"I wish it was that way for me," she told me.

"If you do enough of them, it will move that way," I assured her.

And so, after a morning of volunteering, we headed to the rocks for a short hike with Onyx. The following day we were going to the Birthing Cave and I wanted to go out into nature for a while to clear my spirit for the lodge that night and the Cave the following day. Before long it was time to get ready for lodge. We stopped at the market and bought food and then the Outpost for sage and tobacco and got to Bearcloud's about five thirty.

12 | Into the Lodge of Bearcloud

WE WENT INTO BEARCLOUD'S AND DIANA'S HOUSE, KICKING OFF our shoes at the door and dropping our bags with a change of clothes for later next to them.

"Ho, Diana, Bearcloud. Lodge people here," I called out to announce our arrival.

"Heah, it's great to see you," Diana smilingly said as she came up and gave me a big hug. "This must be your friend from back east. Sue?"

"It is. Sue, Diana, Bearcloud's wife and my spirit sister. Diana's the one with the same 11/11 birthday as mine. Diana, my friend, Sue, from New Hampshire and from a circle I am part of."

"Hi, Sue," Diana said as she turned and gave Sue a hug too. "Glad you could come."

"Thanks, Diana. It's really great to have been invited. We brought some food. Where would you like it?"

"Oh, in the kitchen that way," Diana said, pointing.

We carried the food in and put it down on the counter. We had brought fruit and cheese and crackers and we smelled chicken cooking and saw salad on the table as well. And others were yet to come.

"So what are you doing here?" Diana asked Sue when we went back to the living room.

"I've wanted to move West for a long, long time. And with Jim here, it was a perfect time to visit and see what I really thought."

"Oh. Wow. So what do you think?"

"I think I'm moving here. As soon as I can get things together and get my divorce in the works. When I get home I'll be telling my husband that's what I am doing. He won't be surprised."

"Boy, there's some change," Diana exclaimed. "A lot of people are going their own road now. As the changes are coming at us, those who are awake to what's happening and have a job to do are just pulling up and going. It's fascinating."

And Diana was correct. Some, like me, were going it alone on a new road because their spouse or partner passed on. Others were leaving their partners and moving in the direction—geographically and spiritually—they needed to go. I was seeing it with a large number of people, and even more as time went on. And others I watched partnering with someone else and moving into their work on the Good Red Road. Interesting times indeed. And they still are, my friends. Let nothing surprise you or throw you off balance. Expect anything and nothing will send you on a detour.

"Ho. Werstay. How are you?" Bearcloud said as he came from a back room.

"Ho, good, relative," I answered as he came up and we embraced lightly in the Native way. Then we shook hands, also lightly, and I said, "Bearcloud, this is Sue. The one I asked to bring to lodge tonight. A friend and one I work with as a healing guide."

"Ah. Aho. It is good to meet you, Sue," Bearcloud said, shaking her hand. Then he gave her an easy hug.

"And one who is about to leave home and husband back East and move this way, Bearcloud," Diana chimed in.

"Oh, I see. Hmmm," Bearcloud said, taking this in. "Well, cool beans. And that's all I got to say," he said with a broad smile. These were words I was to learn Bearcloud liked to use when expressing interest. I asked one time and he told me people down Oklahoma way said, "cool beans" and that's where he grew up and got the expression. It's a good one—light and fun, but attention getting.

"Have you done a lodge before?" Bearcloud asked Sue.

"I have, back East. But I'm not sure if this is the same."

"It will be good. After we go into lodge I will talk a little about what it is and why we are here. And I won't make it too hot. Do you have lodge clothes? Women wear a long dress and no metal on men or women."

"I do. Jim told me what to bring. I'll change when you are ready."

"Ah, good," Bearcloud said. "I'm just going to put more wood on the fire and bring out my sacred things for the altar. Did you bring your Chanupa, Jim?"

"I did. May I put it on the altar?"

"Of course. To the left of mine, near the buffalo skull. Okay?"

"I'll do that now," I responded, and went to get my pipe out of the car. I had asked Bearcloud if I could bring my pipe and lay it on the altar where it would absorb the energy of the lodge. I also had asked if we could bring rattles and he had welcomed this, so we each had a rattle for the lodge. These I also brought in from the car and carried to the altar.

Then I went inside as Bearcloud began to carry his Chanupa and tobacco and sage to the altar. I did this so he could prepare privately for the water pouring he was about to do. Sue was just coming out from the back of the house, having changed into her lodge clothes.

"I'm still nervous," she said very quietly.

"What?" I asked, not really hearing her.

"I'm still nervous. I like them both, but I'm nervous."

"That's okay. Just try to let it be and see how it works for you. Cool Beans?" I asked laughing.

One of the things Sue was working on—still is—is her voice. Sue is impressive. Six feet and thin and in very good shape for someone in their fifties. And she has long, blond gray hair. Her height, look and energy make her stand out; she draws attention. Just as I always have, even when I am trying to disappear into the background—which is often. She speaks however, very—VERY—softly. So quietly many people have to ask, "What did you say?" Worse, she refuses to recognize this and can get annoyed, especially with me, when I ask her to repeat something. Ah, we all have our areas to work on, people. I see some heads shaking. So, some of you need to work on your voice as well, eh? Good, then you know what I am speaking about. For Sue, this lack of voice lessens the impact she has on groups. Often others will talk over her, as her voice is so low. And often they do so because they see a chance to control. Sue, although a long-time walker with wolf people—having actually worked with them for years in the physical realm—walks her Walk more like a deer person. This is not good or bad, nor am I judging her Walk. You need to move away from those thoughts, circle; they always slow us down. It simply is what it is and I simply document it.

Those of you who walked with me in *White Man, Red Road, Five Colors* may remember I titled one chapter 'Into the Lodge of Two Bears'. That came to me as I wrote this part of the journey for us and I intentionally titled this chapter Into the Lodge of Bearcloud. It seemed to work—or as most often happens, I was guided to name it that. Into two lodges far apart in time—over twenty years—and in a different way, but for my spiritual grounding and growth while I prayed for all the people and creatures of the Earth Mother. In that earlier book; I shared a rather lengthy piece of writing I did shortly after my first lodge and a piece I wrote about my first lodge with Two Bears. I won't repeat all of this or cover Bearcloud's lodge in as much detail. The earlier writings are there for those who wish to read them, but I will speak to Bearcloud's lodge so you are there with me and understand a little more about this ceremony. And I also share so you can see the differences between this lodge and the earlier ones I was part of.

Over the past twenty minutes, several more people had arrived to go into lodge at Bearcloud's invite. Abbey was there from Bearcloud's gallery, in a colorful wrap, carrying two large towels. As was Jimmy, a friend of Bearcloud's whom I would come to know and like. Jimmy was in bathing suit, like me, with a heavy towel over his shoulder. Then two other women, Julie and Sandy, arrived. So we were eight to go into the lodge. A good number—the number of infinity.

Bearcloud came back inside and went to his room to change. In a few minutes he came out wearing his towel and sandals on his feet. He had tied his hair back in a braid, as was his way.

"Hmmm. I see the Grandfathers are ready. They are nice and hot. Let's go into the lodge," he told us all.

We followed him outside and stood around the fire. I went to the edge and saw the Grandfathers—the rocks for the lodge—were indeed glowing red.

"Women first," Bearcloud instructed. "Go in the lodge in the direction of the sun rising. Then move around the lodge and sit along the far side of the circle. Be careful of the fire pit in there. Then the men. I will go in last and sit to the right of the door, on the women's side. Then I will hand in the instruments and the herbs. Diana, will you put some of these herbs on the first seven rocks in? Thank you. When we are in, I will speak a little about the lodge and then I will come and bring in the first seven rocks and close the door. It is then we will begin."

Sue entered as the last woman and I entered as the first man, so we sat side-by-side. I thought this might make her more comfortable. Down the road I would become fire tender and rock carrier for Bearcloud and so would always enter last and sit in the lodge across the door from Bearcloud. And I would tend the fire, watching that the Grandfathers had enough wood to heat well and assisting Bearcloud in bringing them into the lodge. Of course, I had no idea of this now. I was a 'newbie' having been to a handful of Bearcloud's lodges. As we each entered we gifted Bearcloud sage or tobacco, as is the custom. He bowed and thanked each person, then bent and placed each bundle on the altar.

After Bearcloud brought in the first seven rocks, he pulled the flap down over the door and worked with it until there was no light showing. Then he began the ceremony. He opened with a song as he beat the drum for himself. The rest of us shook our rattles and those knowing the words sang along. As he finished the song he offered a short prayer and began pouring the water on the rocks. The rocks hissed and sang as he ladled on more and more water. The rocks sizzled and the steam billowed and I was more at peace than I had been all day—probably more at peace than I had been since the previous lodge. Lodges have this effect on me. Bearcloud welcomed the spirit guides and Ancestors he knew were with us and asked their help in this sacred place. Then he prayed in the seven directions as I have talked about earlier. From there he spoke of the animal guides with us, talking about raven, worm and bear specifically. As he poured he continued to ladle more water on the rocks. I sweated a lot and my towel began to gain weight from the moisture it was absorbing—so I knew it was hot, very hot. Yet I felt comfortably warm, as I had told Sue I would. When he had poured enough water he began another song, this one sending gratitude to Wankan Tanka. Again we shook our rattles and sang—or hummed. At the end, he asked for all of us to say Mitakuye Oyasin loudly and he would then open the door. We did and he did and the first round was over. The second round—or second door—would begin after he brought in seven more rocks.

"Is everyone okay?" Bearcloud asked.

"Great," I answered as others also affirmed they were okay.

"Ah, good. I will bring in seven more Grandfathers in a couple of minutes and we will begin the second door," Bearcloud continued. "It may get warm then."

In a few minutes our water pourer went out for the next seven rocks. I leaned over next to Sue and quietly asked, "Are you okay?"

"I think so. It's really hot and I had some fear at first, but I'm okay now."

"You staying in?"

"Absolutely. This is powerful medicine and I need some right now."

"Good. Remember, lay on the ground and breath from near the floor if you get too hot."

"I'll remember, thanks. But I don't think I will."

By then Bearcloud had brought in the rocks, thanking each for their service as he did so. Then he entered and again closed the door.

He began this round with a song about the bear—his totem and namesake. I knew this song from the past and was able to sing along. This I could do, I just could not drum, sing and pour water yet. Until my three years of mourning were over. As he finished he again began to pour and the steam got even thicker—the lodge even hotter. Bearcloud spoke for a few minutes about the changes coming at us soon and how we must stay connected to the Earth Mother in this time. Then he opened the circle and invited anyone to speak who wished to—moving again from east to west. If anyone wished to pass, they simply said Mitakuye Oyasin and the circle moved past them. Or, if they spoke, they also ended with Mitakuye Oyasin so the next person knew it was their turn. As we each spoke Bearcloud added more water to the rocks. Julie and Sandy each spoke at great length, out of ego I felt, causing the door to go long and the heat to really build. But, finally, the talking circle finished back at Bearcloud and he began another song. After the song the chorus of Mitakuye Oyasin was again asked for and the flap flew up.

"Ah, the polar bears are coming in with the door open," Bearcloud said, one of his favorite lines when he opened the door. "Everyone good? Anyone too cold?"

"All good," we responded in sync.

"I will get the next seven rocks and then we will begin the third door. This is a healing door so I will put sage and sacred herbs on the rocks as I pray. At the end of this door I will bring in my Chanupa and we will open the pipe. I will tell you then how we will do this."

And so, after he brought in seven more rocks, we began the third door. And again, we began with Bearcloud leading a song. This time as he sang, I spoke a prayer aloud into the rocks—a practice for prayer taught me a long time earlier in the lodge of Yellowhair. I prayed for all my brothers and sisters on the Earth Mother and for all other creatures in her realm. I prayed for the awakening of more humans, so we might change the way we were destroying our planet before the time was too late. I prayed for the Earth Mother's cooperation and help as we all tried to learn how to better live in harmony with each other and sustainably with her. And I asked that all those not ready or able to make the shift to the Fifth Earth of the prophecies be allowed to exit in an easy way. I finished by again committing myself to continuing to work with nature and to pass on the teachings of nature and the Ancestors to the generations to follow.

As I finished, the song was ending and Bearcloud began to pour once again. This was a really good lodge. A powerful lodge. I hoped Sue was okay and not in too much distress. I would ask again when the door was opened.

"I will now say a prayer for all the people's healing as I put the sage and herbs on the rocks. Then we will sing once more and I will bring in the Chanupa. If you do not wish to smoke the pipe, touch it to your head and heart and then pass it on. If you do smoke the pipe, take four puffs and blow them to the four directions as you pray."

The lodge filled with even more aromatic smoke as Bearcloud shaved the sage and herbs on the rocks. It was cleansing and pleasing to me. Then he prayed and sat a few minutes quietly, giving the healing smoke time to work. When quiet time was complete, he began another song and I sat quietly this time—not rattling—and just absorbing the music. After that, with Mitakuye Oyasin coming from us, the door was opened and Bearcloud went to get his Chanupa.

He came back in and asked me to light the pipe for him, which I did. Opening the Chanupa during a door was different than some of my teachers had passed on to me. Some open the pipe after the fourth door, but in the lodge. Some out at the fire after all exit the lodge. And some I have seen open the pipe just before the food after the ceremony. Further, some only open their pipe and others invite other pipe carriers present to open theirs as well. No rights or wrongs, simply different teachings of the way.

When we had sent the pipe around the circle and Bearcloud had smoked it to ash at the end of this circle, he took it outside and laid it on the altar again. It is important to smoke the pipe to ash, since it is thought that any unburned tobacco in the pipe were prayers not sent to Great Spirit. After laying the pipe on the altar, Bearcloud turned for the pitchfork so he could bring in the final seven rocks.

I again leaned over. "Are you okay? You look really hot," I asked Sue.

"I am. I have never been in such a hot ceremony. Even yours was not this hot. But I intend to stay. Just one more door. I did breathe near the ground a few times. That helped. Thanks."

"Okay, just take it slow leaving the lodge at the end. Some people fall when they try to rise because they don't realize how spent they are."

She smiled as Bearcloud reentered and closed the door. We began with another song and I again sat and quietly listened and absorbed. Then he poured more water—but less than in the previous doors. He may have been taking it easy on us or, more likely he felt it was enough. He then asked any who wished to speak again to do so now—again moving east to west. For my part I gave gratitude for this powerful lodge and was thankful to be included. I sent my thanks again to Great Spirit and again affirmed all I asked for in this lodge was not for me, but so that I could help to heal the sacred hoop wherever it was broken. Sue gave thanks to Bearcloud and Diana for inviting her and to Bearcloud for pouring the water and leading the ceremony. She also thanked me for giving her the space to be in the West and for bringing her to the lodge tonight. When we were all done speaking, Bearcloud began to beat his drum and sing the final song—"Don't You Know the Eagle Loves You?" I knew, and really liked this song, so I sang along loudly.

Then the door was opened and the polar bears were allowed to enter, as we prepared to exit. As we came out, Bearcloud stood by the door to thank us and send us into the house for the feast. Sue staggered a little as she rose, but got her balance, stood and accepted Bearcloud's thanks for attending in a good way. Then she went across the lawn and lay down next to Sandy, who had done the same. I went in and got a large glass of water, which I brought to Sue. She was very thankful and drank the entire glass. I asked Sandy if she would like some, but she declined—wanting to wait a while.

Bearcloud showers right after a lodge and when he was finished I went into the bathroom and wiped down a little and then changed into the clothes I had brought. Sue did the same in the ladies restroom at the other end of the house. After a little while we had all gathered in the kitchen, putting food on our plates as we drank glasses of water to replenish what we had lost. Sue was serving herself some chicken and fruit as I approached her.

"Are you okay?" I asked.

"I am. I made it through all four doors! I was unsure at the end of the third, but I hung in. It feels really good. But I am hungry and tired."

"After you eat, I'll show you some of the artwork Bearcloud has around. Some you've probably noticed as you've walked around, but some are almost hidden in the halls."

"Okay. Good," she answered.

After we all talked and ate in the living room I looked around and saw Bearcloud was missing. "Where is Bearcloud, Diana?" I asked.

"Oh, he usually vanishes shortly after the lodge. He is up by three AM every morning painting or writing, so he turns in early."

"Well thank him for us, again."

"I will."

It seemed odd that Bearcloud would disappear this way—without a word. But this too is his way and so I respect and honor it. I began showing Sue Bearcloud's art and explaining the Chameleon Project when we came to his work on that project. Then, as we went to look at a painting in the corner of a room, we saw bags and bags of sage, sweet grass and tobacco piled there. All the gifts from the lodges he had run. There was no doubt judging by the piles of these gifts, he had been doing lodges for many years. He could open a sage shop if he wished. This pile was a nice tribute to Bearcloud's spiritual teachings.

Bearcloud is a truly gifted artist. Great Spirit has given him creative abilities in painting, in computer-generated art and in writing.

I truly love his work—it speaks to me stronger than any art ever has. Happily he has not wasted these gifts of Creator, but is always bringing forth new offerings. His home holds a large collection of his works—spillover from his gallery. His gallery in Sedona is well-known and well-loved by locals and tourists alike. Over time I would see tourists who each time they came to Sedona, would stop in and visit Bearcloud and look at his work. I was glad to be working with him on his non-profit and hoped our connection would grow.

After another thirty minutes had passed I could see it was time to leave, so we gathered up our things, hugged and thanked Diana once again and went out to the car. Diana was gracious as always, thanking us for what we had brought to the lodge. I liked Diana the first time I met her and felt a connection even before we realized we were both born on 11/11. I was glad she had liked Sue and Sue had liked her. I would not want to bring people to the lodge who were not in alignment with the sacred nature of the evenings there. It was difficult enough the night I had brought Seth, and I did not want to repeat that event.

We went to the car, put our things in the back, got in, made the circle turn to get out of Bearcloud's parking area and began heading down Oak Creek Canyon towards my house.

"Boy, that was magical," Sue began.

"Yes, it was. Want to see something else magical? Wait a few minutes until we approach Sedona. So are you glad we went?"

"Oh, yeah. I know I have to live here now. I hope I will be invited again after I make that happen."

"That won't be a problem."

Then we maneuvered around a rock face and began the final descent into Sedona—whose lights sparkled and shone brightly below us. Like an airplane coming into a small town airport at night for a landing.

"Wow, that is impressive," Sue enthused.

"Always moves me," I agreed.

"We are still going to the Birthing Cave tomorrow, aren't we?" she asked.

"As long as you are up to it—you bet. Onyx will be pissed if we don't—he's ready for a long run."

"Good. I really want to go there."

"Okay. So you think you are ready for your move eh? Ready to go through the Golden Door? You've been trying a long time, but maybe the timing is now right."

"I know I have to. I can't wait forever. It will be hard, but there are things I need to do. I need to look at myself and give myself things I need, so I can be of help."

"Good. We'll talk more of these things later. Let's get some sleep so we don't sleep in too late. Okay?" I asked as we drove into my garage.

"Sounds good. Thanks again. For all of it."

"You're welcome. It's partly what I'm here for. More people will come—I know it."

13 | Womb of the Earth Mother

JESSE WAS IN THE BREAKFAST ROOM EATING HIS BREAKFAST FRUIT WHEN I got up in the morning. Sue was in the guest bathroom showering. Onyx, out back when I walked into the living area, saw me and dashed for his doggie door and through the house to greet me. And reminded me I had promised him a good hike today. I have said it before and I repeat it—anyone who uses the term 'dumb animals' are, themselves, dumber than bricks. Animals may not have the reasoning power of humans, but they are far from dumb. In fact they are much smarter than most humans give them credit for.

"Okay, buddy," I said as I rubbed his ears, "We'll be going in a little while. I need to eat and get a shower and then we're off."

"You going to the Birthing Cave, Jim?" Jesse asked.

"Yes, and maybe Shaman's tomorrow before Sue gets ready to leave. You're welcome to come, Jess."

"Thanks, no. I am picking my daughter up in an hour and we are spending the day together."

"Ah. Great. She's a beautiful little girl, Jess."

"I know," he answered. "You and Sue have some kind of relationship starting?"

"Why does this question keep coming from people? I have lots of men and women friends; and lots of both I help with their healing or learning. Are you going to ask this every time a woman comes and stays here with us? I told you—Onyx and me. That's it. I don't want to walk with anyone and certainly don't want any relationship. That's it," I spouted, a little angry.

"Sorry. It just seems you two are good together. I didn't mean anything. I would give anything to have a long-term relationship, as I've shared with you. Mine are always intense, but short. Never last."

"Sorry, Jess. But several people have now asked that and you just triggered me. I had my long-term relationship—thirty-two years. Don't need another. And I never want to risk going through this kind of pain if something ever happened to a partner again."

"So nothing between you and Sue but friends? Okay," he repeated.

Circle, two things here you may want to note, as they will probably affect things that happen down the road. Although I am never sure, as I write and share with you as it comes to me. Spirit is sending the thoughts and words and allowing me the gift of writing them down. Anyway, the first thing is what I just said to Jesse: The key to all of it is in the words—"And I never want to risk going through this kind of pain if something ever happened to a partner again." That's the heart of it. What if something happened to a relationship? What if a new partner sickened? I did not want to face the agony and the loneliness of that possibility again. It was pure fear talking here, which I justified as 'doing my work with no distractions if I only walked with Onyx'. I begin to see that now and I can accept it. When I write the walk I took through the dark time of my soul I believe you will understand as well. And possibly use my walk to aide your own or the walks of those nearest you. Well, that's for another time.

The second thing I would share is a little more about Jesse. I spoke of his duality—the Jesse when he was playing his magic flutes and the Jesse in everyday life, but I need to expand on that a little. The Jesse in everyday life was nervous, sometimes frantic. That's okay; we all get that way at times. But the trait he did have, which drove many people nuts, was his constantly repeating things or asking you the same question three times in a row. Sometimes more than three times. I don't think he ignored the answers he got, but there was some physical or emotional block he had, which did not allow him to register the answers. I say this out of my observations and my sense with the reading of his energy, but also because so many people would get angry with him over this. If he had conscious control over it I am certain he would shift it. But, much like Sue's denial of her very low voice volume, Jesse would not accept this fact about himself. Just as I would not accept my fear was what held me from any kind of relationship with anyone. This is the reason Jesse had few, if any, long-term relationships. It is maddening to be around this type of behavior. As much as I like Jesse, and I did and still do think of him as a good friend, sometimes I had to leave his space so I didn't blow up over this. Eventually it did play a role in him no longer rooming with me, but I'll probably say something about that later.

As always when we talk, circle, there is no judgment implied in my words—and I hope there is none in yours as well. Great Spirit is fully aware of all the nicks and dents in my mantle, as are those close to me I am sure. I share my own failings with you as readily as those of the people I know. I do so to advance the understandings we are exploring together, not to point the finger.

As Jesse and I finished this discussion I was putting out some food for Onyx and Sue came out, outfitted for a hike—jeans, t-shirt, hiking shoes, sweatshirt over her shoulder and a western hat she had bought in Flagstaff.

"Good morning, guys."

"Morning, Sue," Jesse spoke up.

"Morning. How are you?" I asked.

"Fine, but I sure slept after that lodge."

"You guys did a lodge?" Jesse asked, even though I had told him about the lodge at Bearcloud's twice yesterday and once again this morning.

"Yep. It was a good one, Jess. Hot," I answered, fighting back the desire to remark on how many times I had told him.

"I'd like to do a lodge with Bearcloud again. I did some years ago, but not for a long time. Maybe another time, huh?"

This he had also said earlier, but I answered without mentioning that as well. "Absolutely. I'll let you know when Bearcloud tells me of the next one and I'll ask if I could bring you along. Okay?"

"Good. Thanks, Jim."

We had some breakfast as Onyx polished off his meal in typical Onyx fashion—he would carry pieces into another room, put them down and then proceed to eat them. Then he would go back for more. I, on the other hand, laid my fruit, bacon, eggs and cheese out on my plate, separating them as I did so and then ate one after the other—not together. Like dog—like man. When animals and people share their walks, they also share their traits and quirks. This I guarantee.

After our meal I took a quick shower and then packed up water and some food for the hike. I made sure to include water for Onyx and a handful of his favorite chicken strip treats. Then we went to the car and got on the road to the parking place for the hike to the Birthing Cave. It was only a fifteen-minute drive from the house, but we did stop for some grapes along the way. Within thirty minutes of leaving the house we were stepping out on the trails that would take us to the side trail to the Cave. It was a perfect day—cool and sunny. Ideal for this hike, which was almost totally in the sun, with little shade. We talked about the flowers and shrubs along the way, trying to identify the desert growth around us. I was getting better with these identifications, but was not quite there yet. Then we worked on the birds we heard and saw. I was at maybe fifty percent on identifying the birds. I still had too many LBJ's—little brown jobs—in my repertoire of bird names.

After about forty-five minutes of walking and identifying plants and birds I saw the old, leaning, twisted piece of fence line that tells me where to turn cross-country. We followed the old fence for a few minutes and then turned north towards a notch visible between the red rock mountains. That is where we would find the Birthing Cave, the medicine wheel and the sacred circle above them both. And where Sue would find the next piece of her puzzle.

We hiked another half-hour or so and I was then able to point out the Birthing Cave to Sue—still in front of us and a that climb above us I had taken many times before.

"That's a powerful place—I can already feel it," Sue said, wonder in her voice.

"Yes. I told you, the combination of the three sites is strong medicine. You released some things you no longer need at the Wisdom Lodge and now here at the Birthing Cave, you can allow new things to grow in your spirit if you desire. Then Shaman's tomorrow, if you like. For me, that is the most powerful place around here. But they may be different for you."

"I think we are coming to the place that will be strongest for me. I can already feel her working on me. That Cave is special and sacred. Do we climb up soon?" she asked.

"Yes, we'll begin climbing up in about ten minutes. It's a slippery, rock strewn-trail bordered by a lot of cactus, so watch your step."

"Will do," she agreed.

As we continued along the trail I told her of one trip I had made here with Jesse and a group he was taking out for some spiritual work. It was a group of six, plus Jesse and me. He had asked me to bring sage and my Chanupa for ceremony down by the medicine wheel after the group had time at the Cave. He would climb the rocks and play his flute as I conducted the prayers and journeying. This was a model Jesse really liked and he was correct—it was very powerful. The group was made up of German tourists, here to experience the vortex energy and release some old emotional pains. A fun group, but a group with three members who spoke only German. They had a smattering of English words and I had some memory of German words from old college courses to get us through. The other three spoke English, so it was easier for them to interpret for those of us who were mono-language users. Two of the women were Valkyries—big, strong women. Not fat at all, but tall and big-boned: The historically stereotypical Germanic stock. They were 'attacking' the trail on the way up—moving fast and energetically, apparently trying to reach the Cave as quickly as they could. When we got to the ledge below the cave, they immediately began trying to climb up to the cave mouth, before Jess had time to share some safe, effective means of getting there. They laughed and chuckled as they kept sliding back down the rock face they were trying to scramble up.

Jesse reached the ledge and waved the women over, and then he began explaining the two ways you could reach the cave mouth and boost yourself up into this womb of the Earth Mother. As soon as the interpreters finished sharing his words, the two women got up and went at the rock face again. This time they followed Jesse's advice on approach methods, but not on being slow and careful. After an hour or so, everyone who wished to climb up to the Birthing Cave and get in it had done so. Some, as always, were unable to do so. Physically or emotionally unable—who knows? And it doesn't really matter; it was not yet time for them. I myself have not yet gone into the Birthing Cave womb. My fear of falling has stopped me and my spirit has held me back, saying it was unnecessary for me now. As at Shaman's Dome, where I do most of my spiritual work up above, I do a lot of my spiritual work here down at the medicine wheel or, with special groups, up at the sacred circle above. With this group, three of the six went into the womb, including one of our German warrioresses. All who went there, I noted, were women—none of the men went into the womb.

We gathered on the ledge below the cave mouth when the group had climbed back down and burned some sage and I opened the seven directions. Then we prepared to head back down. Jesse told everyone to be slow and careful heading back, as a misstep could put you on hard rock or painful cactus. Then we started down. About halfway down, as one of our warrioresses was taking long strides, I heard a commotion and looked back just in time to see her falling off the side of the trail and landing—butt first—in a huge cactus. This was a connection to nature she would not relish. We gathered around her and helped her to her feet and Jesse told her to turn around so we could see if there were any cactus needles in her back end. And, oh boy, were there ever! She had hundreds of needles poking through her hiking pants, which meant there would be as many or more tiny ones embedded in her legs and buttocks. She was laughing at her full volume, obviously enjoying her own clumsy fall, but wincing as one of her friends pulled out a few large needles. We hiked the rest of the way down to level ground and Jesse got out his tweezers, as did one of the German group. They said something to our pierced comrade and she dropped her pants, allowing the two with tweezers to begin removing the spikes from her posterior. This caused her to laugh even more, until she was red in the face, which, in turn, got us all laughing. Eight people in a circle, laughing like lunatics as two of us pulled small cactus needles out of the ample butt of a third. A good reminder not to take life too seriously.

As we go out in nature and connect with the Earth Mother it is important to enjoy our time and absorb all we can from the experience, but it is equally important to listen when the Mother speaks. We need to pay attention to the words of others or the signs from the creatures around us. Then, perhaps, we won't end up with our pants around our knees examining the spikes protruding from our butts—or worse. It is all too easy to get into a tight spot and not always so easy to back out. As I have had to do many times. Trusting, not foolhardy; cautious, not leery. I guess that captures the thought here.

Let me share a cactus story of my own to demonstrate how a lack of attention can 'bite you' in the great outdoors. Months after the incident with the German group I was again at the Grand Canyon. It was a hot day and I was tired and emotionally spent. I decided to sit and burn some sage, close my eyes and connect with Great Spirit. I needed help and wanted to go right to the Source. There were rocks and bare ground all around, so I had a choice of places to sit. Wanting to get off my feet, I simply sat on the bare ground I was standing on and began my ceremony. After a while I wanted to journey more deeply, so I laid back on the bare ground and let my spirit wander where it would. I rolled from my back to my side at one point, as I often do because of my sometimes-painful lower back. Sometime later, I mentally returned to the present, thanked the Earth Mother for her bounty—realizing I had not asked permission to do ceremony here before I began—got up and brushed myself off. Ouch! It was then I realized this was not bare ground—but ground covered by almost invisible tendrils of a variety of cactus. Tendrils covered by microscopic needles. Needles now all across my back and along my side. I tried my best to remove them, with little success. A friend back in Sedona, a medical woman, used duct tape to pull them out some days later. I had not paid attention before lying down and so had paid a price. At least I had no need to pull my pants down like my German acquaintance, but the pain in my back and side was bad enough. No matter how experienced we are in nature, it is nature in charge, not us. Good to remember. It sometimes allows us to avoid pain.

Okay, off this side trail here and back to the Birthing Cave with Sue, Onyx and I. We had reached the winding way up to the cave by the time I finished sharing my story of the German lady's behind, and Onyx went bounding up, knowing the way well.

"He sure knows his way and doesn't hit the cactus," Sue remarked.

"Oh yeah. Natural animal instinct and coordination. That and four feet instead of two, which really makes a difference."

It took about fifteen minutes to carefully wend our way to the shelf below the Birthing Cave and we were somewhat winded when we got there.

"God, this is beautiful," Sue exclaimed looking out over the red rock edifices, hills and desert we could see from our perch.

"It is. How are you feeling?" I asked.

"Good, but a little nervous. I want to climb up in the cave, but not just yet. Okay?"

"Sure. Let's burn some sage and smudge and you can play your new flute if you feel like it."

Sue had bought a flute at a shop in Sedona Jesse had recommended and was learning how to make it sing. So we sat—and Onyx 'plopped'—and I brought out my shell, sage and feather. I smudged us and said a few words; then Sue brought out her flute and began to play. It was another powerful time. Soon, she was ready to go into the womb. She carefully began picking her way upwards; using the hand and toeholds Jesse had taught me, until she stood just below the cave. She was flushed and her eyes were wet, so I knew her emotions were running full tilt. After standing there with her hands on the cave rock and head bowed, she began to slowly leverage herself up and into the womb created in the rocks so very long ago. Into the place countless women had gone before her. Woman about to give birth in a real, physical sense and others there to birth new dreams and new directions, like Sue. And men as well, those connected enough to their feminine side to sit in the energy here. And then—she stopped partway in. She lounged back into the outside embrace of the space and I turned, called Onyx and slowly began going back down the trail towards the medicine wheel below. Sue needed time and space alone with the Earth so I would do some prayers on her behalf from the wheel below. I don't think she even realized I had gone.

A couple of hours later, I heard Sue beginning to work her way down from the cave. I had sent my prayers and then just sat and connected with the nature all around me. It had been very pleasant, but I was ready to get up. I stood and, realizing my legs had gone numb, I leaned on my walking stick for a few minutes waiting for circulation to return. When it did, I moved towards the faint path that led from the trail to the medicine wheel. I waited until I heard Sue reach the trail and then called out to her.

"Sue, up this way. Go past the turnoff for the cave. I'm waiting here on the side."

As I called out Onyx shot by me and back down to where Sue was. No need for shouted directions when this four-legged was on the job. A minute later and he raced back to me, whipped around me and back Sue's way once again. This time he walked with her to the spot I waited.

"Powerful place, huh?" I asked.

"I've never felt anything like it," she agreed. "This must be the most powerful place anywhere in nature for me. I felt so much I don't now where to begin. When I came down from the cave mouth I saw you were not on the ledge. It threw me for a minute."

"Sorry, but Spirit let me know to come down here. You needed time in the Womb of the Earth Mother alone."

"That's what it is too. I felt her presence all around me. I didn't get all the way in. I guess I'm not ready for that yet, but I got far enough in that I felt cradled by the rocks. I'm moving here for sure. I'm going back home, telling my husband 'That's it' and coming here. Now I'm certain. I knew as I sat up in there. As the tears came, so did the certainty of this."

"That's the reaction I had on top of Shaman's Dome when I went with Jesse during the retreat in January. I knew I would go back to Pennsylvania and put things in order quickly, then return. It was not to be the mountains right now, but here, to Sedona."

"Will you open your pipe so we can pray now?" she asked.

"Of course. I waited for your return. Thought you might wish to do that."

We went back to the medicine wheel and opened the Chanupa and prayed to the seven directions. Then Sue spoke with Spirit quietly while I simply held space. After that we decided it was getting late and much cooler, so we would skip the sacred circle this time and head back to the car.

The next day we went to Shaman's Cave and Sue ventured along the high, narrow rock trail into the cave, while I went above and sat quietly listening to the breeze. She spent some time in the cave before I heard her playing her flute. I knew she had made another connection with her spirit and the land all around her. When she came up to where I was she shared how powerful she found this place to be as well, but not as powerful as the Birthing Cave had been for her. It made sense—the powerful feminine energy of the Birthing Cave was for her what the powerful masculine energy of Shaman's Cave was for me.

The following day I drove her to the airport and saw her off. I hated seeing her leave as we had done some powerful work together while she was here. But I expected she would get through the Golden Door before her this time and move this way before too long.

14 | Along the Creek and Into the Rocks

After Sue left, I immersed myself into finding new natural places to explore as well as working with Bearcloud and Kim on their respective projects. That, and looking forward to the calls when Bearcloud would say, "Ho. Lodge Friday night. Can you make it?" The answer was always yes. These lodges had become, once again after so many years, part of my spiritual life and my road to healing my mind, body and spirit.

Kim had submitted her papers for non-profit status months before, unfortunately as the Sedona School of Medicine. When you send 'school' and 'medicine' the IRS's way, you are going to get a thousand questions back at you. I never liked the name—finding it confusing. It was to be a gathering place for alternative teaching, learning and healing. This name she chose sounded to me like a teaching college for Western doctors. Kim could not see this and argued that this was the humor in the name. I tried to tell her the IRS had no sense of humor or any understanding of irony. I lost the argument and the name was submitted on the new documents she was sending. And, in a month or so, the pages and pages of questions and elaboration forms came back to her. I met with her many times to wade through these requests, especially with the issue she sometimes had in understanding the nuances of some English words. And so this project moved ahead with the speed of an inchworm. Kim was, however, inviting me to parties and gatherings with her friends, many of who were also German. I enjoyed these parties somewhat, but was never a party animal and found it hard to just 'mingle'. I did meet a few interesting people however, some of whom I took out to the sacred places I had discovered.

Kim had not been pleased when I asked Jesse to share my house. The relationship between the two of them was strained at best and confrontational most times. I told both of them I would not ever take sides or get in the middle, but I know Kim took it personally when Jesse moved in. Luckily I realized that was about her, and not me, so I could ignore any comments about this decision.

I was often still functioning in my old paradigm—move hard and fast and once I had made up my mind, I did all in my power to get others to agree. Very much in ego. This caused friction between Kim and I—Kim being even more dogmatic and sure of her decisions than I was—and Bearcloud and I. It would take another year before I started to pull back and let flow whatever was needed to flow. Support the circle, but do not always stand up to lead—or coerce others into following. This changes so many things so dramatically; I wished I had learned this years—decades—earlier.

The fact that Kim did not really understand indigenous ways did not help our relationship, either. Even though she claimed to have been taught some of her alternative healing ways by a Native American grandmother, she was not kind to Native ways. My sense of this from some things she did say, was that she had insulted the Native people she had connected with because of her very rigid, non-Indian demeanor. And spiritual healing was not in her vocabulary, even though she said she wanted this at the Sedona School of Medicine. She had heard of some of the healings that had occurred around me when I had practiced my spiritual healing techniques, but found it necessary to discredit them. An interesting person—Kim. An enigma at many levels. Yet, with both our rough edges, we remained friends for some time. Although the distance between us widened slowly, but steadily.

One day while having coffee with Kim, I answered my phone and it was Bearcloud inviting me to a lodge. I said yes, as usual, then hung up and saw Kim was looking at me, so I asked if she wanted to come to a lodge and see what this healing work was about. She said she would like that, so I called Bearcloud back and got his permission to bring her. Whew! Worse than when I brought Seth. She sat through the entire lodge, but I felt her energy totally disconnected from the circle. Okay, her choice, even if I don't like it when someone breaks the energy circle of a lodge. But, hey, it was what it was. But when we went in and ate afterwards it got worse. Kim proceeded to be negative about multiple aspects of the lodge and kept making references to the strength of her methods over these ways. I am certain she would maintain that she was having an intellectual debate with Bearcloud and the group, but what she was really doing was letting her ego shine through, highlighting her own insecurities. She asked me several times after this lodge to invite her and her friend Pat to a future lodge, which I never did. I did tell her she needed to call Bearcloud and ask his permission to come to a lodge and bring a friend. I assume she did not as I never saw her at any future lodges. After this evening I helped Kim with the non-profit, which I still believed in, but stopped bringing any of my healing ways into our interactions. Not judging, just easier this way.

One thing Kim did give me in this time period was a list of places where long hikes were possible and which had the creek and red rocks to navigate over and around. Just what I wanted! And these hikes started in or near Sedona so I did not need to drive all the way up the canyon to hit a trailhead. One morning, about a week after Sue had flown home, I decided to explore one of these trails. I drove down Route 89A as she had instructed and turned left just outside of town driving past the high school. Then downhill to a left at the bottom and on to the Chavez Ravine parking lot. Later in the summer, I would find this place jammed with teens and families picnicking by the creek and swimming in her waters, forcing me to find other spots along the creek. But now there was only one other car there. I parked and opened the back door so Onyx could bolt out. He shot out of the car, hit the ground running, barreled down the hill and launched himself straight out off a rock and into the creek. There he began swimming in circles looking back at me for the sticks he trusted would come. I followed him down the slope—at a much slower pace—and began tossing sticks his way. He retrieved them and brought them to the bank as quickly as he could so he would be ready for the next stick. After fifteen or twenty minutes I called him to me and he came, head slung low in his 'no, we can't leave now' body language. I went back to the car and got my pack and walking stick and started up the trail, which bordered the creek. Onyx saw we were heading away from the car and bounced happily after me.

Just a short walk up the trail and I came to a place I needed to ford a side stream if I wanted to get back on Oak Creek. Onyx danced across in high glee, then sat looking at me as if to say, "The holdup is what? Just run through it!" Instead I carefully navigated some five or six boulders and reached the other side. From here I took a branch of the trail, which seemed to angle towards the creek. Sure enough we reached the creek in just a few minutes. After another five-minute stop to gather and throw sticks I headed back upstream. This was a rocky trail, which obviously flooded on a fairly regular basis. I walked at a decent pace along this stretch, but did watch where I put my feet. These rocks were prime sprained ankle facilitators and I would prefer to avoid that. Onyx ran ahead and then circled, getting some quality exercise. As I stopped to listen to the sound of rapids in the creek next to me, I thought I heard a snuffling sound. I listened for more of the sound but only heard the creek coursing over the rocks this making the rapids. Onyx came slowly back down the trail towards me—a speed he seldom used. I thought nothing of it and picked up a stick so he would know another swim was in order. I arched it into the rapids and he dove after it. He swam to the creeks center, spotted the stick and then allowed the current to take him to it. He grabbed it and turned into the current again, allowing it to carry him back to shore twenty feet downstream. Once again he had surprised me with his ability to 'figure things out'. He came over and sat next to me. I thought he was tired from all the swimming and, since we wanted to take a long hike, I let him rest while I leaned back on a slanted tree trunk and just let my senses take over.

Have you ever just sat in nature, even for only twenty or thirty minutes, and cleared your mind and just paid attention to what your senses brought to you? It's amazingly powerful and a great way to begin to connect with the Earth Mother and all the Creator's work. Once you relax a little you close your eyes. We rely too much on sight and this dilutes what all the other senses bring us. Sit, friends of the circle, and try this while I tell you more of my hike that day. Find a comfortable place and lie down or lean back against something. Perfect, that's it. Now clear your minds, close your eyes and let you senses roam as you listen to my words. Good—a hands-on story, with you participating by concentrating. That's the kind of tale I like telling.

I leaned back into this tree stump, closed my eyes, cleared my mind and let my spirit roam as I had been doing for years. First I heard the rapids in the stream get even louder—at least to my ears now that my eyes did not steal the rapid's show. I let my consciousness flow into the water and among the rocks and soon I could hear the little sub-waves hitting individual rocks. And I could feel the moisture on my skin; tiny amounts kicked up as the water leaped over the rocks, but enough for my sense of touch to now feel. It was stronger on my left side—the side facing the water. And I could smell the water as it moved by. And the sage and ferns around me. And the stubby pines on the hill across the creek. I smelled the collage of these odors all together and I could also focus in and smell each one separately. And now the wings of two birds heading in for a landing came into my awareness and the sound of their bodies striking the creek. Ducks—I could tell by their landing style. A few seconds later some quacks confirmed my guess. I let my heart roam and my spirit fly as I quietly leaned against the Standing Person. Not seeking any more stimuli for a while, just letting all these things I just described sink into my being.

As I did this I was gathering energy from the Earth Mother, just letting all her sounds, smells and feels massage my weary spirit. And then I would store this energy safely in my heart for use later. I was suddenly aware of motion and knew it was my four-legged companion shifting position on the ground next to me. I felt his snoring before I heard it and allowed the strength of his sleek muscles to move under my hand as I stroked his side. Then I heard a soft snuffling sound once again and another just behind it. I reached out with my spirit to see if I could 'touch' whatever made the sound. And I sensed another four-legged animal not far off: Actually more than one. And they were not dogs, but I sensed no threat. So I simply waited for more sensory input as I continued to lightly stroke Onyx. This always soothed me as much as him—maybe more. As I again drifted in nature I heard a grunt from over by the rock face, maybe two hundred feet to my back. And I felt air begin to waft through my hair, moving it ever so slightly. A movement I would never feel except when I was connecting this way. The snuffling sounds seemed to be closer, the low grunts further over the next few minutes. So I relaxed and continued this journey of the senses.

I let my spirit and senses shift up into Father Sky's realm above and as I did I heard the screech of a hawk. A large hawk by his call, most probably a Red-Tail. And again, another screech. I could 'see' in my heart's eyes his talons extended and his eyes sharp on his prey below. I could feel his heartbeat as he worked his wings for position. And, as I felt a very slight temperature change on my skin I knew Father Sky had some of his Cloud People moving through. Just moving through as the temperature dropped minutely and then raised again—just as minutely. Could we ever feel this circle of energy when we were not this connected? Never, I assure you. All these messages we never receive if we do not slow down and connect. All these messages that it will be ever more important for us to 'hear and read' in order to reconnect to our environment in a healthy way. All these ways of 'hearing' we need to teach our kids and our kid's kids so they do not become so dependent on technology—especially since so much of our current technology is not sustainable in the long term. But we can use these senses of ours and listen to the voices of nature that ready are willing to talk to us and guide our actions in a sustainable way.

What are you feeling friends? Stop reading and try this if you like. I can wait and you can catch up. That is a nice thing about speaking my words in the symbols on these pages. You can come and go, as you like: Good options to have.

After a while I slowly opened my eyes and allowed my mind to awaken and come back into focus. And standing thirty feet away were two deer—does making the snuffling sound I had heard. Onyx started to wake as well, but he just watched the deer, failing to run after them as he usually would. The deer looked up, startled and confused, saw us and took off in the opposite direction. I found this fascinating. I had been leaning there for thirty-five minutes I saw by my watch, and the deer had been there most of that time judging by when I first heard them making noise as they looked for food. Yet they had not fled. They had not either seen or sensed us by their reaction just before they did flee. Why? What had changed after thirty-five minutes of being very close to us? Easy, circle. I was directly connected with the Earth Mother—the environment all around me—as are the animals all the time. So I was as connected as they were, therefore I was another part of the creation and nature—not a threat. When I began to return to my more thoughtful, focused human mode, they sensed me and fled. Likewise with Onyx who slept beside me. While asleep he poised no threat, so he was not 'seen'. We were invisible while in that state. With all due respect to my relative Bearcloud I ask you, "How's that for cool beans!"

As I pushed myself up and stretched my back I heard a grunt again and felt Onyx darting out before I saw the black streak move by me. A large Javelina was working the ground about a hundred feet from me—poking for food and moving my way. Onyx ran toward him at full speed, barking three times. The Javelina jerked up seeing Onyx and lifted his tusks. Oh hell, those were weapons against a dog. I yelled for Onyx to stop, but knew I would go unheeded. Luckily, just ten feet from the Javelina, he pulled up and just stared at him. He must have sensed the danger in those tusks. The Javelina snorted several times loudly and then turned and rumbled off towards the rocks, which I saw him begin to scale a couple of minutes later. Whew, close one.

Before starting off, I wanted to do another connection exercise a little different than this first one. Instead of using the senses on all around me I will focus all my senses on something very small. Possibly a fern seed. Or a small insect. Or a drop of water. Ah, I saw this blade of grass sticking through a fern by the water. And so I sat and focused my full attention on this one blade of grass. Eyes open this time so my sight would begin to look into and through this grass spear. Moving in deeper and deeper. Seeing the color of green, which really varied as you moved from bottom to top. Again, nothing anyone would see unless they 'tuned in' this way. And as I watched, a tiny little insect slowly began a lurching walk up the blade. It was a slow, stop and start, swaying kind of motion—much like Johnny Depp in one of the Pirates of the Caribbean movies. He appeared to be some sort of tiny aphid like critter. Then the blade bent forward ever so slightly as the aphid moved up, even his almost weightless body having enough mass to move my blade of grass. I could almost feel the energy of that motion and move with it. The more I shut down my brain the more I could become one with the blade of grass and the bug walking its surface. If you take the time you can also go this deep—maybe even deeper if your skills are sharp in this type of work.

When I came back from this looking into my small world of a blade of grass and aphid, I felt refreshed, as I always did. And I felt I had learned some valuable lessons as I also always did. These lessons did not always become clear at once, but came into my consciousness over time. So I would wait and see what came to me over the next few days. For now I looked down and saw Onyx looking up. I knew it was time to move on and explore this natural world and its lessons further.

We began working our way north—up stream. For a while it was just a nice, wooded walk; then I was facing a rock face with the trail just visible on the other side. If the creek were lower and slower I could have waded the sixty or so feet around this rock wall, but not today. So we backtracked a short distance and took a trail I had seen— a trail that climbed up the cliff. It was an easy climb; except for the places the trail narrowed and hugged the edge. In these spots my fear of falling came to say 'hello'. I slowly edged by these with cold hands and sweaty neck. Then I hiked higher up the hill we had reached, but soon realized it was taking us inland—away from the creek. So back we went. I worked my way to the edge of the trail I had been on and carefully looked over. Below me was a way to climb down—with rocks jutting out, which would serve as handholds. Not much of a climb down—for someone without the fear of falling issue. I dropped my walking stick over so it would be waiting down below, realizing that committed me unless I wanted to lose a walking stick I had used for years. Onyx gave me a look and then looked towards the creek below. With that he bounded over the edge and jumped his way down— jutting rock by jutting rock. Then he looked up with "okay, the hold up is what this time?" in his eyes. I gingerly worked my way over the edge and slowly inched down. In a few minutes, I stood below my rock torturer picking up my stick—still sweaty and shaky, but ready to continue.

For the next thirty minutes I walked along the bank of Oak Creek, listening to the gurgle of the water and whoosh as it crested rocks. I saw no one and welcomed the solitude. I don't think too many people hiked this way. It was out-of-the-way and didn't offer a lot of views of the red rocks, which most people came here for. But it was beautiful and the water and greenery were a welcomed contrast to the sparsely covered rock terrain all around the area. Onyx leaped and ran, jumping in and out of the water and generally having a high time. Sometimes he disappeared for a few minutes, but would come leaping my way soon enough. It was idyllic in my eyes and so I decided to continue.

I began crossing and re-crossing the creek several times as rocks and cliffs made this necessary. Easy crossings with just slightly wet feet to testify I had indeed crossed the wet trail. After another hour or so I saw several trails—seldom used by their look—branching away from the creek and into trees and brush.

"What do you say, Onyx old buddy? Time for something different?" I said to my four-legged companion as I rubbed his ears. He leapt up one of the trails, as if in answer, turned and ran back to me. "Okay, as good as any. I'm sure the trails will lead back to the creek at some point or we'll climb up and see where we are. Let's do it. Come on boy," I called as I headed in the new direction. He turned, looked at the creek with some sadness, and then romped after me.

About an hour later—mid-afternoon—I realized I was completely turned around and had no idea where we were or where the creek was. And no opportunity to climb up and survey my surroundings had materialized either. I still had a half bottle of water and dark was several hours off so I was not panicking, but I was getting uncomfortable. It seemed as if each time I turned one way it led to other choices, all of which seemed to lead equally nowhere I was familiar with. I sat for a few minutes to catch my breath and give this adventure of mine some thought. I was feeling quite stupid, even though I didn't see how, at some point, I wouldn't break through to a developed area. We were too near town not too. I hoped. I checked in with the sun and thought I had my directions straight. I began heading towards what I thought was west, which would eventually take me back to Oak Creek.

Thirty minutes later and no sign of creek or land that looked familiar started to test my nerves. Suddenly Onyx went tearing off up a side trail—like a streak of jet-black wind. I worried that he was on the trail of something he was not prepared to handle, so I began following and calling out to him.

"Onyx, come on buddy. Heya, Onyx. Here, boy. Come on," I called, to no avail. "Hoka hey," I yelled. This usually got him to return, but all I heard was a breeze rummaging through the trees and high grasses I was in. Hoka Hey, in Lakota, is said to be what Crazy Horse yelled to exhort his men forward. Its meaning was, "It's a good day to die." Others say it simply means "let's go" or "come on". My spirit teacher Black Elk has always told me it means "welcome to the soul", meaning it is time to go into your spirit and meditate on some lesson. With Onyx I generally meant—"Come on, buddy—I mean it". And for whatever reason he has always responded to this Lakota phrase quicker and more intensely than anything else I might call out to him. Coincidence my friends? Please don't force me to share my thoughts on coincidence again, people. I will bore you and myself. Let's just take it for what it is. Remember Onyx was and is one of my primary healing guides. When I was sure I would not take many more steps on the Red Road, he appeared to guide me and give me a reason to be alive. So why wouldn't he respond to a phrase my Lakota teachers both here and in the spirit world know and use often?

I waited a few minutes for my black canine pal to reappear and, as I prepared for another good yell, he came popping through the grasses—followed by a German shepherd.

"Oh, a friend, eh buddy? Where did you come from?" I asked Onyx's guest.

The shepherd came up to me and began rubbing himself against my legs, much as Onyx did. Then he and Onyx turned and bolted off together—once again into the grasses and shrubs. I shook my head and followed, tiring of yelling and now aware there was no danger.

"Oh, hi," I heard a voice say from the side of me. Onyx and his pal were jumping around a tall, thin, very attractive, Native-looking, dark-haired woman who was rubbing both of their heads. "I was writing in my journal over on the rocks there," she pointed as she spoke, "when your dog came running in to meet Dakota here."

"I'm sorry. He does go where he wants to and sometimes is a bit of a pest. And he loves women, so he had a double draw your way."

"No, no. Not a pest at all. He's such a sweet dog. Such a gentle, but connected spirit! And he and Dakota have hit it off as good friends. Something Dakota doesn't do often. What is your dog's name?"

"That black arrow is called Onyx. He is my friend and companion. We chose to walk with each other."

"That is beautiful. You understand dogs. My name is Rena. Yours?"

"Jim. Good to meet you, Rena."

"Yes, me too. Where are you headed, Jim?"

"Good question. I am still fairly new to this area and Onyx and I decided to head up Oak Creek out of the Chavez Ravine parking area—just to see where we might go. Then, after side trails and back tracking and pushing my way through shrubs and around deadfall, I admit I have no idea where we are. I was trying to find the creek again so I could follow it back to our car. It's getting late and I don't want to be here in the dark with no light and some tricky rocks to navigate. Anyway, where did you come from? And do you know the way to the creek?"

"I don't think we are anywhere near the creek, Jim. In fact we are much closer to the Village of Oak Creek then we are to Sedona. You have been heading east, not west, is my guess. Dakota and I hiked in a little over an hour from a parking area north of the town and were just about to hike out. It will be getting dark in about an hour— maybe less. Want to hike out with us? I could give you a lift back around to your car. And Onyx and Dakota could have some more play time as we head out."

"Oh, wow. I really am turned around. But I don't want to put you out. It's a good half-hour drive from where you are parked to where my car is."

"No trouble. I am going to a friend's in West Sedona anyway. Your car is not far from there. And it's too late for you to try and find the creek, especially since you don't know which way to go."

"I think I could move the right way now since I see which way you came. If I push it I can probably be out before it's too dark."

"Sounds like a poor plan to me, but your call," she said honestly.

"Okay, it is. I think my ego is hurt. And maybe my pride," I said with a smile.

"So. We'll walk my way then?"

I thought about it for a minute and spoke, "You know, you're right. It's a foolish plan. And no guarantee I will find the creek quickly enough. So I will walk with you—with my thanks."

"Better choice," she laughed as she gathered up her journal and backpack for the walk out.

The shadows were beginning to lengthen as we headed back the way Rena had come in. The play of light and dark on the rocks I stepped over was providing me a lot of beautiful moments. The shadows of the pointed grasses, lengthening with the approach of dusk, also caused me to think of other times and other places—some pleasant, some painful. Luckily Rena began to speak so I did not begin sinking into my too frequent state—a depressed zombie-like demeanor.

"Live here, Jim?"

"I do, Rena. Just a couple of months now and I am loving it."

"More than you loved Colorado?"

"Different. Both have wonderful natural areas and. . ." I stopped, as I had said nothing about Colorado. "Why do you ask about Colorado? I said nothing of that. Do I know you from there?"

"Yes, I'm sure you know me, just as we all really know each other in some way," she smilingly said.

"You know you sound like one of my Native teachers with that comment."

"Thank you, Jim. That is a beautiful compliment," she replied.

"Are you Native?" I asked.

"I have Navajo blood—mixed with other lines. So I am part Native. As are you."

"Nope. I am of the olive skinned tribe—my people came from Italy, where they were nomadic shepherds. I have worked with and learned from Native American teachers—and others."

"Then you know we are all one—or have you forgotten what you were taught? So, you are also part Native."

"Okay, in that sense—yes. And I have not forgotten the teachings. They are sacred to me and part of what keeps me going."

"I know. I meant no offense. You just seem in a lot of pain and I don't think you are ready to release it yet. I am sorry about that, but the time will come."

"You are very intuitive, Rena. You seem to see a lot. Many people tell me I am intuitive as well, but I am not reading you. Maybe you threw me with the Colorado comment."

"Sorry, I did not mean to. Just know there are those here to help you if you just ask. Well, enough heavy talk, eh? Let's enjoy the beauty all around us. Okay?"

"Sounds good," I answered.

Soon we were skipping over small rivulets of moving water, whether coming from springs or the creek I did not know. They trickled here and there for some time along the path we took. I liked watching them weave their way through the grasses and rocks strewn about by the Earth Mother's hand. They sparkled in the late afternoon light as they disappeared below ground and then hopped back up a few feet further on. It was like walking through a water garden—but a naturally occurring one. Quite special. After we left the water trickle spirits behind, we began carefully picking our way through some wet, muddy areas. When the soil in this environment does get wet it tends to cling to your shoes like cement, so I was rapidly hauling an extra ten pounds on my soles. I stopped to clean the mud several times, but noticed Rena stopping only once.

"You seem to do a much better job at missing the clinging mud than I do, Rena," I called over to her since she was eight or nine feet to my left.

"Well, maybe I have fewer things clinging to me that I need to be rid of. And so less new mud sticks to me as I go through it."

"Okay, I got that. Where are the dogs?"

As I said it the two dogs came running back towards us. Obviously tired of waiting for the slow two-leggeds to keep up, they were racing down the trails and then back our way, probably playing tag as they went.

"Thanks again, Rena. I would have been in trouble trying to hike back to the car. Careful, watch that web," I said loudly as she almost stepped into a huge web strung between two trees.

"Oh, I didn't see it, Jim. Thank you. I would hate to destroy something that beautiful."

As she spoke the light continued to fade away, but as it poked between some trees to our left it illuminated the web in a shimmering way.

"I can certainly see it now," Rena said. "The light going through it is so beautiful. How did you see it? It was hardly visible before."

"I think I get a burst of energy from natural things when they are near me. At least that's the best way I can describe it. I usually spot animals, or special trees or birds before others. It's as if they reach out to me, I sense their energy and then I begin to look for the source."

"It's nice that whatever else you are going through you have not lost that gift."

"Yes, I would miss it horribly I'm certain," I responded. "Where are you staying in West Sedona?"

"At a friend's, Lillian. Off of Navajo Road; nice place—good energy. We've been friends for a long time."

"Do you know Kim Moonson? She lives just around the corner from there."

"I think I have heard of her, but I don't know her. I don't know many people. Does she do some type of energy healing?"

"Yes, she does," I agreed. "Where is home?"

"You know, it seems to move and shift depending on where I am needed. I've lived in Washington State for the past two years. Near the coast. Beautiful, but very wet."

"I know what you mean. I have moved often over the years. Sometimes too slowly I feel, when I don't listen to what Great Spirit wants me to do. I'm trying to sharpen that skill and be ready when I am called to shift."

"That's probably a good idea. But I can't believe you've moved too slowly if you have moved many times. I'm sure you didn't," she said.

We had stopped for a short rest and to allow time to admire the web while we had this conversation. Now, as we spoke, the light coming through the web was even more beautiful—more spectral, more fine. And, for a minute, the shaft of light seemed to shine directly on the web and nowhere else. Almost as if Spirit was calling our attention to something. Or maybe just allowing us the gift of this beautiful dance of light and web before us.

"Wow," Rena said, watching the play of light on the web. "I am so completely thankful that you saw this work of eight-legged art and had us stop. Thank you, Jim, for this beautiful gift."

"You are welcome, but I simply stopped you from walking through the web. All the rest of the credit goes to the spider who created it and Spirit who created the spider," I said.

"True, but you know it is better to say 'thank you' than to argue about deserving thanks."

"I do. I'm just not very good at it. Let me try, Rena. Thank you, I am glad I was able to show you this work of natural art. I would have put a ribbon on it, but the spider-person already had."

"Beautiful. Thank you again," she replied smiling.

We continued on our way shortly after this exchange as the light was fading quickly and the beautiful glow was no longer on the spider's magic web. In fifteen minutes we reached Rena's car and got the two four-leggeds in back, where they continued to play. Oddly enough, Rena had the same car I did—a silver Toyota Highlander. It reminded me of the times I had rented cars here in the West and also gotten a rental match for mine.

In another twenty minutes we were pulling back into the Chavez Ravine parking area so I could get my car and head home. I had promised Jesse I would come and hear him play at the Hilton and time was getting short.

"I'm sorry if Onyx and I ruined your meditation and journaling time. But it was really good to meet you and share the wonder of the web together," I said as Rena pulled beside my car.

"No, I was done writing. In fact, you made my day better. Between the time at the web and giving Dakota a friend to play with, you added a great deal to this day. I'll be staying with Lillian, my friend in West Sedona, for a few more days I think. I can't think of her number, but it's the big sandstone red stucco house at the end of the Navajo Road. If you have time take a run up and I will introduce you. We can all have tea or coffee maybe," Rena said.

"I will. I am going to Cottonwood tomorrow about my license plate, but the next day, Wednesday, looks good."

"Bring Onyx."

"That's a given. I almost always do. Maybe we can drive around and I can introduce you and Lillian to Kim as well."

"I'm not sure about that. Let's see, okay?"

"Sure," I agreed, thinking it a strange response, but forgetting it just as quickly.

"You will heal more completely later. Try to have patience. And I hope you share those gifts you have out in nature with more people. They are special. I'll remember today's web for a long time and think about what it taught me."

"I guess we will all heal more as time goes on as long as we are aware of the need and willing to put in the work," I replied. "Thanks again. Enjoy your evening."

"You too, Jim. Onyx, you are a beautiful boy. I am so glad you walk with Jim and Jim walks with you. You are both fortunate. Just like Dakota and I. You be a good friend now. Okay?"

As she spoke Onyx nestled his head in the crux of her arm and allowed her to stroke his snout—something he allowed few people to do. I said goodbye to Dakota and we got out and headed to my car. Fifteen minutes later we were pulling into my garage—hungry and tired. But oh so amazed by the way the day had played out. It was only then that I became aware I had not gotten a cell phone number for Rena, nor given her mine. And although I had told her where I lived, I had not given her an address. That is also strange for me. An interesting meeting, for sure. And one I would explore in dreamtime.

Two days later, I was on my way to Kim's to go over more documents she had received from the IRS. The coffee was on and we were going to try to make sense of what they wanted. I remembered telling

Rena I would drop by and so I swung around the block further over to where her friend, Lillian, lived. I thought I knew where she meant and went to the dead end street with the house like the one she described. Her car wasn't there, but I thought nothing of that. She was probably out hiking again. I walked up and rang the door.

"Hi. Jim Petruzzi here. I am looking for Lillian and her friend, Rena, who is staying with her. I think I have the right house. Do I?" I asked the thirty-something man in a long gray robe who came to the door.

"No. Not here. Lillian you say? Can't say I know a Lillian along here, but then I'm new and don't know everyone. Do you know her address?" the man politely answered.

"No, I don't. Rena couldn't remember it, but she told me Navajo Street and described a house like this one. Of course now I see at least six houses like this one."

"And more further down the street. Sorry I can't help you."

"Thanks for your time," I answered and turned away as he closed the door.

This was odd because the location of this house was the location Rena had described—I think. And the house looked like the house she described as well. But, as I noted, there were many more similar houses. So I headed to the next likely suspect three houses down. And left with the same result. As I did with the next similar house—directly across the street. Now I was feeling stupid and frustrated. And confused. Rena had seemed sincere about wanting Onyx and I to drop by and was not putting me off since she suggested it. It was not something that would ever enter my mind. I don't make friends quickly and am often slow to connect with people. This is due to my introvert personality. Now this would shock a lot of people, since I am so often in front of groups—large to small—or leading ceremonies or meetings. And it is something I have often been told I am very good at. I guess it's another part of my gift from Great Spirit—communications: In writing and speaking. This gift was given to me so I can do what he wishes me to do. But with all gratitude to those who compliment me on my speaking, I am an introvert functioning as an extrovert at these times. And this takes a toll on my energy and nerves. So I don't look for quick connections with people or groups, but rather wait for them to come to me.

I walked around a corner and up another cul-de-sac to a house near the end, which also looked like the house Rena had described. I was sweating from approaching all these houses and the people they held whom I did not know, so I promised myself this would be my last try. A woman, probably in her sixties, came to the door.

"May I help you?" she asked. And I repeated my story and quest.

"Well, I don't know. I have lived here twelve years. There is no Lillian I know of on this street or Navajo. There was, I think, a while back, but she moved at least two years ago. She was around the corner there," she said pointing the way I had come, "in the big house at the end if I'm right. Always had a lot of people around, as several of the houses up there do. Wish I could help more."

"No, thank you. That's a big help. I'll stop looking now. Have a good day."

Friends, what are your thoughts here? I was baffled, I admit. Maybe I still am. Maybe not. But I certainly accept now that the truth of this meeting doesn't matter. The purpose does. So, come on, help me here. What? Ah, yes. Good. I agree with you. That was the young woman in back who offered that the learning 'I would heal someday' and being made aware my gifts in nature were still strong were what I needed to hear. Yes, so right. Thank you sister. Who else has thoughts? Come now, some of you are walking through a second journey with me here. You, the tall man back there. You seem to have something to share. I'm listening. Ahhh. . . Yes. Was she a teacher sent my way? And if so, was she a teacher in the flesh here on the Red Road or was she a spirit teacher? As is Black Elk and others I have told you about. Nice. And it doesn't matter. I have had spirit teachers come to me many times—some I have told you about before. Once I realized I was not nuts, I came to welcome their lessons as much as those of my corporeal teachers.

Okay circle, you are thinking the same way I was then. And I did quickly move to a place of—"I don't care what the truth of Rena's being is, she told me some things I needed to hear and we saw some things I needed to see. That is enough." The other piece of this story is that I was forty-five minutes late getting to Kim's and she was not amused. I apologized, as I do not like being late when I commit to a time and place. Then we drank coffee and did our work. I did not share my meeting with Rena with her. I don't know why—I simply didn't.

The next day I was preparing to take a hike with Onyx when Jesse walked into the house.

"Want to hike up to the Birthing Cave, Jim? I have a group next week and want to go and check the energy."

"Sure, I was just going to go up the canyon, but the Birthing Cave is always a powerful place for me."

So we drove to the parking area and started hiking in. It was another nice warm, but not hot, day with a gentle breeze blowing. The kind of day you can sit up on the rocks around Sedona and not fry. We walked and talked as Onyx ran and sniffed. A great morning to head out and connect with the Earth Mother.

"How is Sue doing? Have you heard from her? This was the most powerful place for her I think she told me. Yes? Anything going on with you two yet? Is she still coming out this way? Wasn't this the place she felt the most healing at?" Jesse rattled out his questions in typical Jesse fashion, allowing no time for response.

"Jesse, ho!" I broke in. "I'll forget everything you've asked man. Cool it. Yes, Sue is coming this way—in about a month. And there is nothing between us. How many times will you ask this? We are friends and I am a healing guide. And yes, this is the place she really resonated to. Okay?"

"Sure. So is she coming this way?" I shut off my ears at this point and, in a few minutes we reached the side trail to the cave.

We climbed up and Jesse climbed above the cave, where he perched on a tiny ledge and prepared to play his flute. I took out my drum and some sage and prepared for some music and prayer. In a couple of minutes the beautiful sounds of Jesse's flutes began flowing down around me. The sound of moose and eagle—of waves and surf—of running water and geese—and more came from above me. I began quietly beating a one-two rhythm on the drum—the heartbeat of the Earth Mother. It put my soul at rest for a while.

After a few minutes I heard another flute from up higher: Possibly from the cliffs above the Birthing Cave. The player was matching Jesse's flute and my drum and the sounds coming from three directions were extraordinary. We all played for a good half hour and then Jesse hiked down to my perch.

"Wonder who is up there? It was a beautiful connection," I shared.

"Yeah, a good flute player. Maybe he will come down while we are still here. Want to hike up to the sacred circle above?" Jesse asked.

"Yeah. That feels right today. Wonder who won't be able to see us there today?" I said with a chuckle.

And so we hiked the additional twenty minutes to get to the rock face, which we scaled, brushed ourselves off and walked on to the circle. I left tobacco and sage as I got out my Chanupa.

"Want to do flute and drum a little more first?" Jesse asked.

"Yep." I agreed.

And so Jesse again climbed another hundred feet up a rock face behind me and we began the dance of the flutes and drum once again. After a moment, from up a mountain in front of me the second flute chimed in. This time we played even longer, caught up in the sounds of nature coming from Jesse and our unknown friend. Finally our friend stopped as did Jesse and I waited for him to climb back down to the circle. I watched two big, beautiful red-tail hawks circle over me—listening to their calls and marveling at their flight patterns. They would soar up, circle as they screeched and then bullet down towards the ground. As they got to within fifty feet up the ground they pulled up and began soaring on the breezes until they began their next climb. I had not seen this behavior from hawks before. Almost as if they were hunting, but then breaking off into play. It was truly beautiful. Jesse made it down in about fifteen minutes; since he can scamper down the rock slopes—part goat, part man.

"Shall we open the pipe, Jess? I have it out."

"Yes. That's you and me—sucking in and blowing out," he said laughing. This was a little joke Jesse really liked. His blowing out into the flutes and my sucking in the smoke of the pipe was the joke he made often, especially with the groups he took out.

So I began preparing for opening the pipe to the seven directions followed by some journeying. A full ceremony agenda. Why not on such a beautiful day? As I prepped Onyx went running up one of the trails. In a few minutes he came racing back followed by a man and a woman. The man was about fifty, slender, dressed in jeans and flannel shirt and was easily identified as Native American. The woman was about the same age, a little heavier, with a bright, smiling face. She did not look Native, but I learned a long time ago none of us necessarily looks like what we are. What I really was pleased to see, was that the man carried two flutes; our friend from above.

And, as has happened often, they began walking right by us, not fifteen feet from where we sat. I got up and walked to the trail they were on.

"Ho, friend. Were you the one playing the flute?"

They stopped and paused and then he responded, "I am. And you are the flute from the other side?"

"No, I am the drum. My brother, Jesse, over by the circle, is the flute."

"He is a wonderful flute player," the man responded.

"We are sitting at a spirit circle over here. Would you two like to join us?" I asked.

"Yes, we would," the woman spoke up. They followed us to the circle and took seats in the two directions Jesse and I did not sit in. Onyx, being spirit dog when ceremony was about to begin, walked around checking each person and then went to the middle of the circle and laid down, with a humpfff of escaping air as he so often did.

"He is a beautiful dog," the woman noted.

"He is a dog with a lot of spirit," the man put in.

"Yes to both," I agreed.

"We did not see you two here from the trail. Don't know how we could miss you. You are in plain sight from there," the man proffered, sounding confused.

I told him of the difficulty many people had in finding this place or seeing it when they were near. I told him I was certain they would have seen us before going by as no one who could play the flute that way was without good, white energy and spirit.

"Thank you," he said to this. "Do you two live here?"

"Yes," I answered. "I just moved here and Jesse's been here a while. I am Jim Redwolf Petruzzi and this is Jesse Kalu."

"I've lived here twenty years. Making and playing my flutes for nineteen," Jesse put in. "What are your names and do you live here? I have not met you."

"I am Myra and this is my partner, Sam," the woman answered. "No, we are visiting, but I would love to move here. We are from Gettysburg. Sam is from a tribe in the East and he does teachings and flute making demonstrations at state parks there. We live on a small farm south of Gettysburg. That's about sixty miles west of Philadelphia."

"I know where it's at, Myra. I am from Kennett Square in Chester County—maybe thirty miles from your place. I left there a couple of months ago," I said.

"Boy, small world, Jim," she smiled at us.

"Are you about to open your pipe?" Sam asked. "We will leave. I do not wish to interrupt."

"We are," I answered. "But you are welcomed to join us if you wish. It would be good to have people in each of the four directions on the circle here when we do our prayers today."

"It will be an honor," Sam nodded. "May I put some sage in the shell?"

"Yes, thank you brother," I agreed. "I will open the pipe and we will pass it. Then I had thought to drum quietly so we might do some journeying. Will this be good for your spirits?"

"Wonderful," they answered together.

We spoke around the circle and each of us set our intentions for the Chanupa and then I opened the seven directions as I loaded the pipe. I offered it to Sam to start the fire in the bowl. He seemed very pleased and lit the pipe and then passed it back to me. When we had smoked the pipe and I had emptied the ashes into the sage fire, I picked up the drum and began a slow, steady heartbeat rhythm. The others lay back and closed their eyes, allowing their spirits to go where they wished. After ten minutes I put the drum to the side and joined them.

My wolf guide immediately showed up and sat beside me. I looked at him and he stared back at me. He was telling me now was not the time, but that it was coming soon. And he showed me more people in my circles and more work I needed to do. Then he rose, nodded his head and walked away. A moment later I was coming out of my meditative state and sitting up. Only thirty minutes had passed, a short journey. I felt as if Wolf of Many Colors, my animal guide for so many years, was just showing me previews and that I needed to wait for the feature film. That was fine. It was so powerful to have my wolf guide back in such a clear visual way that tears ran down my cheeks. We invited Sam and Myra to come to Jesse's concert that night and then have some dinner. They agreed and we all hugged and went our separate ways.

That night, over dinner, Myra talked of how much she was engrossed by the Sedona area and hoped to convince Sam to move here. Sam shook his head and spoke about the teaching and sharing work he needed to still do back East. I suggested they might live in both places—spending time in either as needed.

"Yes, that would be good, Jim," Sam spoke. "But Spirit has clearly showed me I have much more to do back there. I have leaned to listen to these things. In the past I have not listened well and paid high prices in the things that happened to me."

"But if we lived in both places, we could shift as needed," Myra tried to move her partner.

"No, not me, Myra. Sorry."

"Well, I guess we will stay in the East. It is beautiful where we are," she capitulated to Sam.

They had all of Sam's sacred bundles, flutes and Native American tools for his programs stuffed in their station wagon. They were heading to Phoenix the next day, where Sam would be giving some talks. Then they would slowly start the drive back home, stopping at sacred places along the way. We wished them well and told them to be in touch if they came back this way. They offered the same if we got back East. A good sharing of music, prayer and talk.

About two and a half years later I was sitting in Bearcloud's gallery watching it for him while he went to a meeting. It was a very slow day and I was actually writing *White Man, Red Road, Five Colors* when a woman walked in. She began looking at the art and I asked if I could help—getting up as I did so. She thanked me and said no, not right away. I went back to writing and she to browsing. After a while she commented from across the room how amazing Bearcloud's art was. I agreed; it is. She asked if he was hiring, telling me she had just moved to town. I told her he was and she could leave a number if she wished. Then she turned and began walking towards me.

"Jim, that is you, isn't it?"

"Yes. Myra. Oh my goodness. You live here now?"

"Yes, I had to come. I left Sam. It was very hard. But Spirit guided me and here I am."

So we talked a while and I promised to put in a good word with Bearcloud.

This is what is happening now. Shifting, moving, migrating, new relationships, no relationships. We will visit this much more friends.

15 | The Golden Door Before Me

A WEEK OR SO AFTER JESSE AND I MET SAM AND MYRA AT THE BIRTHING Cave, I went back with Onyx. I needed some time alone at the cave to do some meditating and journeying. I was surprised the Birthing Cave came to me and not Shaman's Dome—my strongest power place in Sedona to date. But I followed what I felt in my heart and headed out for the cave. It was a warmer day so I brought two large bottles of water—one for me and one for four-legged. I started out early so the sand would not be too hot on Onyx's paws. I may have already shared how some dogs get very ill or die each year because their human partners take them out on the hot sands, not realizing how quickly their body temperature goes up with heat on the feet.

We got to the cave about nine in the morning and I spread out the breakfast I had brought—hard-boiled eggs, cheese, apples, coffee, some lunchmeat and doggie biscuits. What did you ask? Why only biscuits for Onyx? Ah, don't assume friends. Half of the lunchmeat and cheese was also for my companion. The lunchmeat was turkey, so it was good for both our systems. We ate like wolves—our usual—quick, big bites and drinks. That out of the way I shimmied up the rock wall to a position just under the cave mouth—the womb of the Earth Mother. I felt no need to crawl up into the 'womb' as I had not on previous trips— nor have I to this day. I don't question these things—I simply follow my spirit. So I sat and burned sage and bear root as I played my drum and let my mind clear—giving control over to my heart. After a few minutes I stopped, feeling as if I needed to go back down to the ledge below. I did so and again settled in with sage, bear root and drum. Onyx flopped next to me, enjoying the music and the warm rock. As I drummed I realized I was to start this journey with a pipe of gratitude to Great Spirit, so I unwrapped my Chanupa, loaded it and opened it to the seven directions. I thanked the Ancestors of each direction for their assistance and then thanked Great Spirit for all he was about to give me. Before setting the Chanupa against the red rocks—my makeshift altar—I asked all my animal guides to join me this day and give to me whatever understanding I needed. Then I carefully placed the pipe on the altar and again picked up my drum.

One nice thing about the Birthing Cave is that there is almost always shade at the cave—even if the sun burns hot on the hike to it. So I spread my blanket—the healing blanket that had been gifted to me about a year before—and sat on it as I lit more sage. Onyx moved next to me on the blanket as well. And I began drumming in the one-two heartbeat of the Earth Mother. As my mind emptied and my heart matched the beat of the drum I began 'reaching out' with my spirit to all the natural things around me—the rocks, cactus, critters, wind, sky, earth and anything else my spirit could encompass. Soon I did not need the drum any longer and I laid it down and stretched out on my blanket. And let my spirit move wherever it wished. I became more and more aware of the things around me, especially the sounds that moved over me. As I lay there I sensed my animal guides gathering around me, ready to honor my request. The sage and bear root was pungent in my nostrils and I was breathing deeply of their healing smoke without even being aware of it. Then I felt my wolf guide— Wolf of Many Colors—approaching me. I could see nothing at first; just sense the energies of the various animal guides present. This was the opposite of what I usually encountered when journeying, but I re-laxed further and just went with it. Soon I could make out the spectral presence of Wolf and welcomed him with my mind and heart. He sat looking at me with wise eyes. I felt Onyx, lying next to me, shift several times and wondered if he was also sensing Wolf. I had learned over the years to never rush these encounters, so I just remained connected with the Earth and waited for anything else that might come.

After some time Wolf rose and approached even closer. As I looked into his eyes I felt Eagle flying above and knew he would also visit my perch here on the ledge. Something in the way Wolf stared at me let me know he had things to share, but that I would soar with Eagle first. As this thought passed though me I suddenly felt myself aloft in the presence of Eagle. This had not happened for many years in quite this way, but it was like riding a bike—you never forget how. I was totally comfortable and joyful as we flew together. We soared over the desert landscape above where my physical body lay and whooshed up and over the high hills around me. Eagle screeched as he banked to the south and began moving that way. I sensed nothing that I intentionally did, but I found myself moving beside Eagle towards the south. Soon we swooped down over a long, snakelike train that was wending its way through a mountain pass. Eagle dove and streaked along the length of the train. I followed with him. Four times he flew the length of the train, each time coming from a different direction. We came in from the east first, then the south, the west and the north—in the way of the medicine wheel. After the fourth fly over we rose once again and Eagle looked me in the eyes and again screeched—loudly!

His screech seemed to echo and vibrate all through my body and almost putting me into a fearful state. Yet there was no malice in the screech, just a reminder to heed what I was seeing and feeling. As I realized this he/we shot back down and flew the length of the train once again—from west to east. Eagle screeched as we did this and then shot out over the desert, swooped and turned and began flying away from the train in a east to west line. I was still with him for each wing beat. I am unsure if I was one with Eagle or he was carrying my energy and spirit, but it was a glorious ride either way.

Almost without any connecting space we were suddenly back above Wolf and then, just as quickly, I was back on the rock ledge, next to Onyx peering into Wolf's eyes. Eagle circled above us, screeching as he flew. I sent my gratitude and appreciation for his time and all he had showed me. And my thanks for honoring my 'ask' for help and guidance. I then asked that he continue to appear and guide me as was in the best interest of the service I was to provide on the Red Road. At this he again screeched, banked and headed towards Shaman's Dome, many miles away to the southeast.

The train was a key piece of what Eagle had shown me. That, coupled with the swoops in various directions, seemed to hold the message he had delivered. As I mulled this over I sensed Wolf lowering his head in confirmation. Then I saw that Eagle had given me directions from Great Spirit through our flight today. Again Wolf lowered his head in confirmation. I had not journeyed in this fashion for a long time and began wondering "Why now?" "Why here?" and then as quickly released these questions as they had come. This was brain trying to reassert his lead over heart and that is not where you want to be while journeying. I looked back to Wolf as Onyx got up and stared at the exact spot where my spirit animal guide stood. Wolf looked at Onyx and then back to me. I no longer wondered how much Onyx experienced when I was in the spirit plane or doing ceremony. My answer was here, with Wolf and Onyx staring each other in the eyes.

After a long time of this fairly static tableau of Wolf looking at me—Onyx had re-flopped down—and me looking at Wolf I asked Wolf if more was to come? He lowered his head, but just continued to stare in my eyes. I was confused, so I continued to sit there and look at Wolf as I stroked Onyx. I sensed the Golden Door behind Wolf and asked if I was to go through another such door so soon? Another lowering of the head, but nothing else. I sensed the door was gone and the acute connection of my senses to all around me was weakening.

"Am I to receive more guidance later?" I asked through my heart. Wolf stood straighter and was gone in an instant. My guess was that was a yes.

I suppose I could say a little more about journeying for those unfamiliar with the word and the concept. For those who travelled with me in *White Man, Red Road, Five Colors* I ask your understanding as I do so, since I know I shared quite a lot about this on that walk and took you through many journeying experiences I had. But, remember, repetition means importance—at least in the way I was taught. Journeying in the way I know it—where to begin. I guess with my understanding and use of the word and the process. I 'journey' in a spiritual way like I was taught by my indigenous teachers, which may differ from the common spiritual understanding of this great gift. I worked for years to master my mind and heart to the point my spirit could journey, so I don't subscribe to a lot of the fashionable throwing around of the word. Just as I hate what has been done to the word and practice of shamanism. But that's for another time. Not all ideas on journeying have been commercialized and there are some very good thoughts on the subject by those who follow various spiritual roads. I just know, for me, the Native use of journeying is my experience.

Spiritual journeying, as I was taught, is most often accomplished by allowing the spirit to disconnect from the physical body, at least in part, keeping some anchor back in the physical world. This is important or you may go into a state of panic, especially if you are a beginner at the practice. Panic, or even just simple fear, can 'cut the spirit line' and cause someone to be unable to reintegrate with their physical body, or to do so ineffectively, causing various disorders. I worked with teachers and guides for many years before trying to lead a journeying group and even longer before doing individual journeying, as I did this day below the Birthing Cave. When I journey I am liable to go anywhere in time or place. As I shared in the earlier book, when this first occurred for me I thought I had lost my mind. Especially since it happened suddenly, without the ceremony around my previous journeying experiences. The journey may also be within—a journey of your spirit and being. Meeting Ancestors, animal guides and spirit guides while journeying is also commonplace for me now, as I know it is for many who have learned in a fashion similar to mine. My visions, in fact, came to me while I was journeying as part of my first vision quest many years ago. Again, this is something others have shared with me they have also experienced. Many pooh-pooh journeying and the gifts it provides, saying drugs must be involved. That, or insanity coming to the surface. This, my friends, is their fears talking with, unfortunately, some help from the mis-users of this skill who do use drugs and other mind altering substances.

In the minds of other spiritual and even alternative healing practitioners journeying has some of the following traits, which I gather from various sources.

1. Spiritual journeying is an unfoldment—a journey to discover what is within.

2. Journeying involves exploring the self in relation to the Universe.

3. The soul becomes free to travel during journeying.

4. Journeying is done within, sometimes alone, sometimes with others.

5. Those who journey may go into the earth, or above it.

6. Those who journey often physically leave their body to explore the realms of the spirit world.

7. Those who journey often then help others heal.

I don't judge these comments and even agree with some of them, but I think they miss the totality of the journeying experience. The total is certainly greater than the sum of the parts. Many people seem to list the parts, as those above.

So why journey? For several reasons. One is for pure pleasure and joy—something often in short supply on our walks here. This is a valid reason as I was taught and so I share it first. More practical reasons include being receptive to visions, which allow you to walk your best road with your best healing gifts. I have often been given a healing approach to share with someone who has come to me for guidance from what I experienced while journeying. Connecting with the Ancestors is another valid journeying goal. Those now on the Blue Road of the spirit realm have a wealth of information they will share if approached in a good way and for positive reasons. Journeying provides one means of connecting with these Ancestors. Play with this for a while, circle, and see what other uses you may find for journeying.

Journeying in the way of Native people also often begins with a spiritual ceremony—as I open my Chanupa to the seven directions. And it involves intention, much as meditation does. As when I asked my animal guides to come and provide whatever it was that I needed next. It most definitely involves quieting the mind, emptying it of distraction and allowing the heart to take control of your being. I have never spoken with someone adept at journeying who does not attest to this part. And it most often involves drumming or chanting to get your being in sync with the Earth Mother and the spirit realms.

With all of this explanation you need to remember it is a spiritual practice and so really not controlled by any human devices. Sometimes I have found myself journeying with no conscious action on my own part. At times with other people as we do something physical. These are the exceptions I am certain, but they do occur. For now this is enough for you to consider. I will share other journeying experiences on this walk and other similar experiences I have been through. Now, at least you have some basis to assess whether this explanation makes sense to you or you, just think I may 'slip my gears' every so often.

After Wolf disappeared I slowly gathered my things together and Onyx and I began the hike back to my car. We had been at the cave over four hours, at least three times as long as I had imagined. This is another common trait of journeying—time distortion. You will also hear more of this later, but it is common for much less or much more time to pass then your human brain seems to register when you journey.

I got home and ate a big dinner, being hungry after journeying as I sometimes am. Jesse was playing a gig so I had the place to myself. I put on a movie and tried to get interested—with no luck. So I sat at my computer and began answering emails. I had several emails from people I was currently working with on their healing journeys. I was surprised they had not called as they most often did when they felt in a state of dis-ease. I took out my cell phone and saw it was turned off. I had turned it off when I began my ceremony at the Birthing Cave and forgotten to turn it back on. As I turned it on, six messages appeared. My mind had been working through the time with my animal guides today and I would not have been in a good place to assist these folks who had called anyway. So, I had 'forgotten' to turn on the phone again. Coincidence? Ah, I love playing with this word and the concept of it! Now I was more centered and ready so, as I brought up emails I was aware of who was trying to reach me. I began to play the messages and almost simultaneously someone rang through. So I pushed the save button on the messages and took the incoming call.

"Hi. Jim here."

"Hi, Jim. It's Sue. I tried to reach you a while ago but there was no answer."

"I was just checking my messages. I had the phone off. How are you?"

"Okay. I'm driving home. Let me pull off the road and call you back in a couple of minutes. Okay?"

"Sure. I'll stay off the phone. You know, call my landline. It's a much better signal."

A few minutes later my house phone rang and I answered.

"Hi."

"Hi. Sue again. I'm off the road. Can you talk a few minutes?"

"Sure. I just had dinner a little while ago and I was just going to catch up on emails. Then I saw a number of people had called. So, anyway, nothing pressing. What is on your mind? Better yet, in your heart?"

"The heart. How is it you know before I tell you things?"

"Sometimes I see, sometimes not," I answered, wincing, as I knew I sounded like one of my old teachers.

"I'm coming to Sedona to stay. The divorce is in the works and I'm looking for a car to buy. My old one has had it."

"Sounds like you will actually walk through the Golden Door this time," I responded. "Are you ready for that now?"

"Yes, I have to be. When I got home and my soon-to-be ex picked me up, I told him I was going West and soon. And that I was going to get a divorce."

"How did that go?"

"Okay. It's been coming a long time. Not like it's a surprise."

"And your son and grandkids?"

Sue had a son and four grandchildren who lived a short drive from her place.

"That's much harder. But I can't live my life for them. They can't be my life. I love them dearly, but I need to do what I am being called to do. And I sense from Spirit it needs to be done—or not—quickly. There is a short period of time I have to go through this door. And then it will be too late."

"Ah, a narrow window of opportunity," I spoke back. "I understand that. Had it happen several times. Okay, so when do you see this happening?"

"Quickly. Five or six weeks. Is there room at your place when I get there? Until I figure things out."

"Sure. Just Jesse and I right now. I'll make sure I don't invite anyone once I know when you might be here."

"I want to leave by the end of June. Can I mail some things there? Then I'll pack my car and head out."

"Yeah. I'll stick your things in the hall closets; lots of room there. You're going to drive it? How will you come?"

"I'm not sure yet. I'll look at some maps. What do you think?"

"Depends what you want to see. It's a long drive no matter which route you pick. Do you want help with the drive? I can come out and drive back with you."

I had absolutely no idea where this offer came from; I was amazed I had spoken the words. Eagle came to my mind for a moment and then Sue was speaking again.

"You'd come all the way here and then drive back with me? That wouldn't be too much? Do you really mean that?"

"Sure. I said it. It would give you a friend to split the driving with and we can do some work on your healing road along the way," I said, seeing no way to take back the offer and, surprisingly to me, not really wanting to.

"Well, okay. Yes. But just tell me if you change your mind later."

"Okay, but I won't. I have always make quick decisions and I stand behind them. At least until life proves to me I was wrong."

"How will you get here? Fly?"

"I'll figure that out later. What else is happening with you tonight?"

We talked for about another twenty minutes and then Sue hung up. I played my messages and decided to return two more calls that night.

I called another Susan, whom I had been working with for about three years. She was currently in Wyoming living with and learning from some Lakota Grandmothers I had asked to aide her. Susan was the one who had gifted me my healing blanket a couple of years earlier. And Susan is also a person who always came to mind when I thought I could not take any more pain and suffering. A Wiyot Grandfather in California had asked me to meet with her and see if I could help her heal her pain. This was at the same time my wife was taking her last walk and I now think Grandfather was asking this of me to help both of us with our healing. I met with Susan first over coffee in northern California in a small coffee shop near the coast. She carried one of the darkest, deepest black energy blankets wrapped around her I had ever seen. Her energy so sad and dark you could almost see it in fact, I could, as I am often able to do. Susan had lost her three children in a horrible car accident involving a van they were travelling in about a year and a half earlier. All at once—all with no warning. About a month after this happened her husband, unable to cope with the tragedy, left her and moved across country. She had walked in total depression and chronic pain ever since. Her one wish was to die but, being a strict Catholic to this point, she would not do anything to cause this; although, as she told me, she wanted to. So she was greatly conflicted. Each time we met she would thank me for my words and actions and then tell me I need not waste my time since she was only waiting to die. This went on for months. Then she told me her priest had informed her, in a chiding manner, that her children might have been killed because of some past wrong she had done; some sin she had committed. I could not believe my ears—although this should not have surprised me, given some of the things priests had told me in the past.

We spent a long time working through the words the priest had assaulted her with and finally, slowly, she began to tell me more of her suffering road. She asked me if I would perform some of the healing ceremonies I had learned from my Lakota and Mayan teachers.

The Wiyot Grandfather who had sent me to her had been asked to intervene by a social worker who knew him. He had met with Susan three times and realized he was not the one to help her. That was why and when he had asked me. Now, as I called her, I marveled at how much she had moved forward over the past few years. I had been the one who had suggested going to live, work and study with the Grandmothers and she had been there over a year by this time. It was working for everyone, as the Grandmothers told me on the rare occasions that we spoke.

"Susan, it's Jim. How are you? Sorry I missed your call, but I was out on the rocks and had my phone off."

"I'm fine. Nothing wrong. Just wanted to check in. You've been coming into my dreamtime a lot lately. How are you?"

"Okay. Good days and bad days. You know how it is. But very busy with new things and spending a lot of time with the Earth Mother on the rocks and by the water healing my spirit. Just as I guided you to do. I'd be a pretty poor healing guide if I didn't follow my own advice."

"Oh, you're not that at all! Without you I would be long dead; or still wishing I was. Is the healing blanket helping?"

"Yes, it is wonderful. I had it on the rocks with me today. A wonderful gift I will always use with myself and others I am sure."

"Oh good. Well, I am learning so much now that I feel over-full, but I keep finding room for more! I see why you so thoroughly entered this spiritual road. I can never give you enough thanks for showing me this way—no, pushing me this way. And finding the Grandmothers for me to be with. I just asked to stay another year and they all smiled and laughed—said they already knew this from Spirit. Ah, I have so much more to learn."

"No more thanks needed. You will learn and pass on any help I gave you to others. This is the way. Let's talk again soon. But I need to try and get some sleep now. Okay?"

"I'll call next week. Bye, Jim. Keep healing yourself first. Be a little selfish for now." And with that advice she hung up.

So you hear the main reason for sharing a little of Susan's story with you, friends, she lost everything and was beginning to rise like the Phoenix. She lost three children and then a husband, followed by her health. Even though she said she wished to die, something kept her going. This is very close to my story that I hope to be able to share with you another time. Remember Susan when times seem unbearable, if this will help you.

I did make two other calls and worked with two other people I was assisting with their healing. Then I took Onyx out, came back in and rubbed his belly for twenty minutes and went to bed. A moment later a heavy weight hit the mattress top as Onyx jumped up beside me. I had given up trying to 'train' him—read that as control—to curl up on the floor and decided he would do this on his own later. And he has—he now curls up on his bed pad across the room from me. Once again, a demonstration of the futility of trying to control things.

As I lay there with my head spinning, my fears and anger welling up, I still managed to feel a presence around me. My sinuses were so clogged I could only breath through my mouth, but I also felt a 'blanket of spiritual peace' on my chest. It's very difficult to share how these opposing feelings coursed through me, but I can assure you it was not pleasant. I got up and paced and then sat and did some puzzles. Once I had begun to find it impossible to read or write for more than a few minutes, I had taken up puzzles as a means to relax—or a means to mask what I did not want to address in myself. When that failed to calm my nerves, I burned some sage and played one of my eagle drums. Then, about midnight, I went back to bed and scratched behind Onyx's ears—as much for me as for him.

Finally, about 1 AM I drifted off into sleep. I saw Wolf padding towards me as dreamtime took me in. He seemed very large today and was one solid color—gray—not the usual mix of colors I generally saw him in. He came and I sensed I was to follow. So my spirit rose from the bed and stood next to him. Then, as had happened so many times in the past, I became Wolf and he became me. And yet we were both separate and distinct beings at the same time. Unless you have walked this particular road it is a very difficult thing to understand—being yourself and another creature or thing at once. It is, as I was taught, where the stories of shape shifting originated. Those stories that writers and Hollywood then changed to people actually turning into animals—most often wolves. Those mean, deadly, scary, awful, fearful wolves. Groan!!! So far from the truth. Ah well.

Wolf and I entered the garage in this spirit journey together and stopped for a moment by my car. A simple feeling of 'no' came to me and we journeyed forward. I felt us 'swooping', but saw nothing and was not sure if we were at ground level or aloft. Not that it mattered—just my brain trying to make sense of things that were meant for the heart. So as we moved along, I worked on having my heart take over the lead once again and quieting my antsy brain. Usually when I journeyed with my animal guides, the animal who existed in the realm I was to visit took me along. The eagle, hawk or some other Winged One in the air; wolf, bear or other four-legged on the ground; whale or shark in the water and so on. Not always, as Wolf was liable to take me anywhere in any time through any medium, but often the guide's realm was honored. Things began to clear as I felt us moving down, so I assume we were aloft. Below was, again, one of those long, long western trains that always fascinated me. This one had three engines in the lead and two behind, so its load was sizable. We entered the train from the top and I had the same fear well up as I had each time in the past when a guide brought me 'through' something solid. This even though I knew when I journeyed it was all spirit—no flesh.

My journeying almost always occurred out in nature—sometimes seeing manmade objects and people, sometimes just the artwork of the Earth Mother. But being 'in' a manmade thing was new to me. And as my spirit roamed through the train with the guidance of Wolf, I saw a man writing in a journal. He was bent over it in concentrating on his work. As we got closer he bent back to stretch his muscles and it was me. This seeing me in a different place or time had occurred at least once before—actually three times, which were part of one. That was in my vision I shared in *White Man, Red Road, Five Colors*. This was a fairly contemporary 'me' I looked at now—looking as I did in physical time at that moment.

As soon as I became aware of the fact that I was looking at myself, Wolf and I began to move again. And again things hazed and clouded so I could not say where or when we were. Then my vision cleared and it seemed as if we were running at an incredible pace across the North Country—South Dakota, I thought. As we neared Wounded Knee I knew I was correct. We stopped by the old sign reading "Wounded Knee Massacre", as Wolf stared at me and then we were in motion again. And then we were in wolf country, above Yellowstone National Park. We watched the Yellowstone wolves play for a while and then we were suddenly standing on the banks of the Yellowstone River. Wolf howled—long and loud. And then again three more times. With this we were again moving and, in almost no time, we were travelling through Colorado. I saw images from my past there and then un-familiar images. 'Future' flashed in my spirit as I looked at these pictures to be. And I got a sense that these images were further in the future, after I had done the things I needed to do after stepping through the Golden Door in front of me. As I understood this, we again shifted and I could see a Golden Door—a huge one—hovering in front of Wolf and I as we moved. I reached for the handle and was whisked back to my bed and out of the journey as Wolf vanished.

This was fairly abrupt for a journey ending, but then I heard Onyx barking out back and knew he had called me back. He had gone out his doggie door and was barking at the coyotes I now saw on the other side of the fence. They howled back and all the four-leggeds sang together for a few minutes. Then the coyotes ran off and Onyx came back in, jumped up on the bed, looked at me a minute and curled up—ready for some more sleep.

I sat with the images and thoughts of the journeying, which were totally present in my mind and heart. Several things came clearly—I was to take the train east to assist Sue in driving back; we were to go via Pine Ridge and Yellowstone, especially along the river as we drove and we would drive down through Colorado to Sedona. These were the messages for the present coming through the journey—the ones lodged further into the future were not clear to me. As I needed their clarity, it would come. That evening Sue and I spoke again and I told her I would be taking the train east. I sensed surprise—she had not gotten to know me enough yet to be surprised by anything I did. As I had learned long before not to be surprised by the things I was guided to do. I made a train reservation, which would get me to Concord, New Hampshire on the morning of June 25th, after a two and a half-day journey.

I talked to Jesse about caring for Onyx while I was gone and, while he was more than willing, I felt I needed a second person because of his busy schedule. So I put a call in to Abbey and she was more than willing to help. Between the two, I knew he would get enough walks and stimulation to keep him relatively happy until I got back. I thought I would be about ten days, maybe two weeks if we stopped anywhere along the way. I never suspected we would be about four weeks on the road. Serves me right for planning!

On the evening of June 22nd Abbey drove me to Flagstaff and I booked a room for the night across the street from the train station. The train departed at 5 AM, so I could trundle across the street at 4:30 and be ready. I had one bag and my Chanupa—that's it. I knew Sue would want to bring her things and had no idea how much room that would take, so I didn't want to fill her car with too many of my things. I had piled about twenty boxes she had shipped into the closets around my house, so I assumed it would just be her personal things in the car.

I got up at 3:30 AM, showered and walked over to the train station. At 4:45 the train rumbled into the station and I climbed on, hauling my bag behind me. At 5, right on time, it pulled out clanging along the tracks as it rocked from side-to-side. I was on my way to help a friend move West. Travelling back the way I had come less than four months earlier, but in a whole different way—on a train. I was looking forward to the train ride. I had always loved trains. Getting a Eurail pass and taking trains all over Europe was my preferred way of travel overseas; I always met some interesting people with whom to share stories when I did this. Stories I will share on some future walk. For now, I was set to enjoy the three days on the tracks, with nothing to do until I got to Concord. I assumed I was stepping through the Golden Door I had seen in my recent journeying with Wolf.

16 | Through the Looking Glass

I WHEELED MY BAG TO THE SLEEPING CAR I HAD RESERVED AND STOWED it below the narrow bed. At six foot one plus, I am always challenged by the room sizes on trains, but I've learned to adapt. Give a little to get a lot. I laid my ditty bag next to the small sink so I wouldn't need to rummage through the large bag for it later. I closed my room's door and headed up the narrow aisle towards the dining car. I hadn't eaten much the night before and, with getting up so early, I was starved. I rocked back and forth with the motion of the train as I navigated the path before me. Then I had excellent coffee and a veggie omelet along with a large bowl of berries in front of me in a few minutes. Once I had worked my way through this, I ordered some coffee to go and went back to my room. I had brought a copy of *Black Elk Speaks* with me, so I got it out and read until I fell asleep. After another hour of so of sleep, I felt more refreshed and ready to explore the train.

There were not too many people on the train, which had originated in Los Angeles two days earlier. Maybe thirty I guessed. I found a chair all to myself in one of the viewing cars with a glass sides and roof. I sat and enjoyed the desert scenery gliding by me for a couple of hours. Suddenly the train lurched, lurched again and slowly came to a stop. I thought we had pulled into a siding, waiting for another train to pass, so I sat and read the *USA Today* the conductor had brought me.

After about a half-hour, and no train passing us, I was getting curious. I began to get up when a conductor came into the car and announced we had a minor problem and might be there an hour or so while they worked on repairing it. Five hours and three announcements—and apologies—later, we still sat where we were. "They had to send parts to the train" was the latest. Ah, well. In the past I would have been angry and argumentative. Now I sat, read and relaxed. Shortly after another apology the train started up and we continued on our way.

A man had sat next to me and we had talked briefly. It turned out he was also going to New Hampshire—the only other passenger going that far, although I didn't know it at that time. After another couple of hours we again came to a stop—not at a station. After fifteen minutes the conductor came in and told us another train was broken down in front of us and we were going to be disembarked and bussed to a train sixty miles further on. Now things were getting funny. Unhappy, but resigned, we passengers gathered our belongings and trekked out to the waiting buses. We were near a large city—although which one escapes me at the moment—and it was late afternoon. We immediately got stuck in traffic. Then there was a huge accident on the highway and we were detoured off to side roads—also clogged by traffic. About four hours later we finally made it the sixty miles to get around the broken down trains. Except in the time it took on the bus in traffic and on side roads, the train tie up had been fixed and our original train awaited us. Now I did laugh, as did a few others, loudly. But the majority of the people were either very angry, and voicing their anger, or quietly shaking their heads in disgust.

After dinner I retired for the night and lay there, awake, listening to the clack, clank of the train going over the rails and feeling the sway and rock of my sleeping car. And loving every minute of it. Finally, after a bout of anxiety and pain that came out of nowhere, I slept.

The next day we were moving along our way, eating lunch, when we again stopped in the middle of nowhere. Yes, we had broken down again. Train staff began coming through the train and apologizing for all the mishaps. "The worse I've ever seen," one said. "Unbelievable," chimed in another. But there we were, stopped again. After a couple of hours they came through suggesting buses again. Many gathered up their belongings and departed, but a small group of us opted to stay on board and wait. An hour or a day, we had no idea, but I at least, had a gut feeling this was the way I was to go.

After about five hours the train was again repaired and we moved on, but now we needed to stop at the next city and wait to be rescheduled since we were so far behind our original schedule. After another few hours, we moved on again. They were comping us our meals by this time, so some of us sat in the dining car eating and drinking coffee while we moved further east. That night, just before my bedtime, the conductor came and told Lou, the other passenger going to New Hampshire, and one passenger going to Boston and myself that we would now be off-loaded in Washington, D.C., where we would spend two nights until the next train north came through. Lou and I simply said, no, that is not acceptable. The staff told us there were only three of us, so they were sending our train to New York City for maintenance. The man going to Boston disembarked, but Lou and I stayed on board. After an hour of going back and forth, they decided they would send the train on through to New Hampshire with us on board and then berth it in New York for work. I admit I was amazed. Just two of us and we had won our point.

The train was originally going to get into New Hampshire late morning of the third day, but we were many hours behind schedule. I called Sue and told her I would be in touch when I knew more, since she was meeting me at the train station. The good news was, with two passengers on the entire train I was allowed to move to one of the largest sleeping cars for this second night. After some time tossing in the bed I slept. What I didn't know was, since they were so far off schedule, they re-routed the train and bypassed towns and cities and rolled all night, skipping two long stops on the original schedule. Other trains had already dealt with passengers expecting this train. In the morning over breakfast with Lou, we were told we would make New Hampshire near the originally scheduled time, if nothing else went wrong. As we laughed, Lou shared he was a retired railroad employee and maybe that was why they were more willing to carry us through. I don't know if that was so, but we were getting where we needed to be—my only concern.

The train was originally scheduled to arrive in Concord on June 25th at 11:30 AM. I had travelled with it through a break down, a bus re-routing, a bus stuck in accident and work traffic, a second breakdown, rescheduling, twelve hours behind schedule at one point, rescheduling again and, oh well, you get it. With all of this we arrived at Concord on June 25th at 11:35 AM. With everything that had gone wrong we were five minutes late. See any lessons in this, circle? Hmmm? Well, yes. If you are meant to be somewhere you will arrive. Good, I like that. Anything else? No? Okay, sit with it a while and maybe other things will come to you. For me the biggest take away was that, with everything that went wrong, I still arrived for the next part of my journey on time. I would remember this often in the near future as things began to shift and change for me.

Sue was waiting as I disembarked, waving as I hauled my bag off the platform and over to her car. She had the car fairly well packed already, so I knew we would be hitting the road before too long.

"Wow, you made it on time," she said as we hugged. "That's amazing."

"More so than you know. There must have been ten things that went wrong and yet we pulled in on time. Interesting, huh? Well, I guess I was meant to be here now. It feels like part of the vision quest I knew I was on when I drove to Sedona."

I felt tired, but also somewhat uncomfortable, wondering why I had offered to do this. But we were going to head to Pam's and I was looking forward to seeing her. She was living with Frank, about my age, who walked a path similar to mine. He was white, but had walked the Red Road with the tribes in the East and Midwest for a number of years.

It was hot and I was sweating quickly. "Boy, I forgot what a difference the humidity makes back here," I said to Sue as I sweated my bag into the back of her car.

"Not like Sedona," she answered. "I can't believe I'm actually moving there. Or that we are taking this trip together. It's almost unreal."

"Oh, it's real. I'm not sure what we will encounter on the way, but I'm to be here helping you drive out. That was very clear to me—especially after the train mess to get here."

"Why did you take the train? You could have flown and been here in half a day," Sue asked.

"Spirit made it totally clear to me I was to take the train. My spirit animal, Wolf, showed me to take the train. And he showed me something of the route back. Through a lot of places I know and a few new ones."

"I hope we go through Yellowstone. That is my most sacred place; I love it there."

"We are definitely going there. It's a special place to me as well."

"Well, Pam's expecting to go to dinner with Frank and us. She'll be home from work about four."

"Good. We going straight there or somewhere on the way?"

"It's lunch time. I thought we would get something to eat. Okay?"

"Great. I'm hungry."

We went to a local café and had some lunch as we continued to chat and I tried to get more comfortable.

We took a ride around Concord and looked at some of the sites and then stopped at a park for a walk. It felt good to stretch my legs after the days on the train. We then drove the forty minutes to Pam's, which was out in the country. Frank was there and came out to greet us. I had suggested Pam and Frank meet when I was in New Hampshire for the retreat the year before. And they had hit it off. Pam's two boys were home doing chores and, as we carried our bags in, Pam drove up.

The four of us went to dinner in Concord and then went back to Pam's to do some ceremony together. Sue and Pam drummed the heartbeat of the Earth Mother one-two beat while Frank and I prepared our Chanupas. Frank was also a pipe carrier, so we would open our pipes together to the seven directions. We opened the directions, taking turns and then prepared to light them. I was suddenly guided to have Sue open mine—something I had never done before. We were both surprised, not for the last time. Bearcloud had had me open his pipe once in his lodge and Two Bears occasionally asked this of me before he gifted me a pipe, but I had always opened my own. I was still certain we were friends, about to walk a quest together as I helped her along her healing road. As I had told anyone who asked.

Sue and I got the sofas in Pam's living room. They were too small for us and it was stifling hot, so I did not sleep well. I don't think Sue did, either. She was about to step through a huge doorway—stepping off the cliff without a safety net, as I often put it for people. Her life as she knew it would never be the same again. That's a huge step to take, I know. Especially when all you have to go on is trust and faith.

In the morning we had coffee and Pam headed off to work. Frank also had some business to do and the boys had left for school. Sue and I discussed what was next and decided to spend the day seeing the natural areas around us. I had spent a great deal of time in New Hampshire when I was much younger. I came up and camped with two other friends well into our thirties. It was good to have some time to see some of the wonderful mountains, streams and meadows again. We decided to stay another night at Pam's and then head out. Going west—all the way.

We headed out to some of the more popular tourist areas and quickly decided this would not do. We stopped at a diner in Tilton for some breakfast and Sue got a call from her ex. It triggered a huge reaction in her—anxiety, fear and a nervous jerking. So we sat for a while as I asked her some questions for her to work on. Slowly her reaction subsided, she took some deep breaths and then we drove into the mountains. We took a side road and soon found a fast moving stream, decorated with beautiful grasses and ferns. We pulled over and got out, heading upstream for a walk. An attack of fear hit me as we walked. My nerves and brain trying to make sense of things, a very powerful assault. Slowly it passed and I began feeling giddy like a kid. I was making little jokes as we walked and laughing too loud at them myself. Sue must have thought me nuts. I'm surprised our trek did not end right there. Now I see it was deep, deep pools of emotions buried within me that were spouting as I walked the land; as if a valve had been opened.

We came to a place where two streams merged, so we stopped and got out my sage, shell and feathers. We burned sage and smudged ourselves thoroughly and then sat and talked awhile.

"Okay, we are both stepping through some major doors with this journey," I began. "And our emotional selves and nervous systems are trying to stay in balance as our brains are in distress, trying to 'figure out' what's going on in their previous safe worlds."

"I know. The way I freaked out when my ex called. And you are like a boiling kettle," Sue said.

"Understanding some of what is going on is easy, knowing we can't control the process and accepting that is hard. Let's drive further and see what we see. Okay?"

We drove up some other back roads and suddenly saw a mother bear and her four cubs coming down a slope towards us. Sue pulled over, turned off the engine and we quietly watched. The mother saw that we were there, but did not go into fear. Four is a lot of cubs; I have usually seen one or two in the past. The cubs rolled and played and then two of them climbed a tree in the field they were romping in. Momma stood below and watched—and checked on us periodically. We sat there about twenty minutes watching the 'bear show' until the cubs gathered around Mom and the family slowly lumbered up the mountain. As they crested a ridge we lost sight of them as I was giving thanks to their being with us.

As the bears left I felt an energetic shift inside again—emotions welling to the surface. Again I began laughing loudly—for no apparent reason—almost hysterically. I got out of the car and walked along a trail; and simply let the feelings come. I had no other choice; there was no control here. There never is. Right?

When we started back to Pam's I was still constantly breaking out in emotional outbursts, mostly in the form of loud laughing and making jokes. We had a good two-hour drive, maybe more and I watched the forests flow by as I waited for each new outburst. Sue's side hurt as she was laughing not only at my jokes, but also at the cartoon character I must have appeared like.

When we arrived back at Pam's, she and Frank were there, getting dinner ready. We ate, chatted and decided we would spend another evening drumming and doing ceremony—for Sue and I to help center our energy and clarify our intentions for the upcoming journey. We again got to bed late and I tried to get comfortable on the sofa—with little success. I heard Sue move her sheet and pillow to the floor, trying to find more room to stretch out, I assumed.

The next morning Sue went to visit with her grandchildren—four of them—before leaving. She returned very out-of-balance. I could sense her whole spirit was in conflict. Big changes—stepping through Golden Doors—are empowering, fascinating, powerful times; but they are not easy, especially the first few steps. Frank took her hands and did some energy balancing work, trying to get her into a better place where she could begin to work on the emotions of the moment for her. I then told her of the part of this quest I was to step forward in that I did understand—picking and following our route and acting as 'tour guide' for her. She began to slowly come into balance and I felt her 'ground' more firmly as we prepared to leave. I think she had tears in her eyes as we headed out.

Pam and Frank were happy to see us come and, I think, happy to see us go. I had said nothing of the sweat lodge—Inipi—we had built the year before for the retreat. The lodge I had led the circle in building at Pam's request and where I had done two nights of sweat ceremonies for the group gathered. Pam and Frank had taken the lodge part way down—leaving the 'ribs' of the lodge still connected and lying to the side of the lodge site. This is not anything you ever do. An Inipi is a sacred place. I shared with you all how we had built it with prayers and ceremony throughout. And then how we had used it and I had poured water in the ways taught me. Taking it down without the permission and participation of the ones who built it is not a good idea. And, even if it is agreed to remove it, it must be done with the same permission, respect and prayers as those used building it. Pam might not know this, but Frank certainly should have. To do otherwise is to invite some very dark medicine to come your way. I sensed some major ego involved here and maybe some fear. But I had said nothing, as I was not asked about it and it is never my place to offer in a case like this. As we stood saying our goodbyes, it finally came up.

"Jim, you saw we took the sweat lodge down. I hope that was okay?" Pam asked.

"You did what you needed to. I would not have done this—at least this way," I said.

"Well, Frank is doing ceremonies here so it seemed like what I needed to do," she continued.

"Do you want to hear more from me? If not, as I said, you did what you felt you needed to," I answered.

"No, just wanted you to know, that's all."

Frank said nothing and so we finished our goodbyes and went to the car. In a few minutes we were heading towards Vermont and the first leg of this joint vision quest.

"Why did Pam take the lodge down? I don't think it was a good idea," Sue said as we drove out.

"It wasn't," I agreed. "There is ego at play here. To do this, in this way, invites many hardships and negative energies to come in. But I was not to tell them this unless they asked. As it is with anyone in a situation like this."

"I guess with Frank now doing ceremony there it was bothering one of them; or both. But why would it? It's more energy," Sue added.

"Ego gets in the way and things happen. I'm not sure either. But there it is. Did you see the way it was not fully taken down? The bones— the willow branches creating the lodge—were still tied together with the four-color cloths and the whole structure was laid upended next to the place the lodge sat. They uprooted them and put them to the side. But they could not finish dismantling it. The energy or the guides we called to help us build it stopped them. There is some power-ful medicine working there now. I hope too many negative things don't fall on them. I will say prayers around it, but it's not my call, of course."

The lodge was not ever fully removed. The place we dug was still there the last time I visited, about six months ago. Pam had put the lodge willows back in their original holes over the land we first built the Inipi on. I had sent prayers to Spirit asking for understand-ing around the Inipi being dislodged and guidance for anything else I might do to remedy this action. I received no signs, so I dropped it, as clearly I was not to be involved. Not many months after Sue and I left, Frank and Pam began having serious issues and she finally went her own way. Still with issues she is trying to work out—as we all do. But Pam seems to stand in the same space she has long been in—inviting problems like this as she goes along. And, as I said, the skeleton of the lodge is again in place. If the 'ask' ever comes I will help her re-do the lodge in the way I was shown and end this circle of negative energy. Or, hopefully, she has worked through this event and the skeleton now being in place is a sign of that. As Sue's friend and mine, I hope this is so. But it seems it is not for me to know.

As we headed across Vermont my inner child again broke free and I began telling joke after joke. Both Sue and I were laughing soon. I felt fear and confusion—probably thinking I had lost my mind once again. I am glad these particular doubts no longer assail me. We took back roads most of the way across Vermont, as we had decided to do throughout the trip as often as we could. When we hit New York, however, we decided to make some time on Route 90. We stopped to stretch, use bathrooms and get gas—but that's about all. Almost as if we knew what we were heading for was past this area. Sue began sinking into dark moods and fear and I began doing some healing work as I drove. I opened the seven directions in my heart and then got her speaking about her feelings and physical sensations.

We looked for a place to stay as we headed through Pennsylva-nia and along Lake Erie with no success. Being summer season and approaching July 4th things were booked up. Finally, a little further on we found a place with a room. I was going to try and find two rooms somewhere, but Sue said it had double beds, so that was okay. My pain—mind and body—were coming at me in a big way by the time we brought our bags in. Sue had bought a stick shift car, which only made my lower back issues even worse. And all the emotional clearing I had been undergoing was also taking a toll. Sue began doing some reiki on me—as she is a Reiki Master. It was helping, but the pain and feeling of disconnection built even more to the point I was trying to force it down and so reacting in strange ways. Sue panicked a little not knowing what was happening, nor my intentions or mood. I had gone through this, as the healer, with many others I have aided in the past, so I understood what was happening even while in my pain. When I saw she was getting fearful, I talked the whole process through with her and told her of how others I had helped had gone through a similar process. It was very strange being the patient in this process—yet teaching and counseling at the same time. I was used to my role, as healer and healing guide, not pain-riddled dependent. Good for my ego. And I realized how much trust I did have in Sue, since I would normally seek out one of my elder healers for help on something this large.

I slept little that night and the next day Sue drove, since my back was spasming in pain. We talked again over breakfast about the processes we both were going through and how I had not expected my inner healing to surface on this journey. I had come to help her drive and work on the fears and doubts I knew she would have. I offered her the option of turning back as her fears were so deeply rooted. She said no, we would go forward. And so we headed out spending another long day driving, wanting to get into the West where I had seen the real power of this quest starting.

That night we got a room with separate beds so I could do some healing work on Sue. My pain had now gone all physical—mostly in the lower back and knees. The mental and emotional segments had disappeared once again. Sue, however, was a mental, physical and emotional basket case. I began doing some spiritual healing work on her. It was a combination of my Lakota and Mayan teachings, with a dose of Garifuna medicine thrown in. This is the medicine I had learned from the Gaifuna people of Belize, Central American; these people are of African descent. So I had a good mix of cultural medicine with me that night.

Much of my healing work is a mix of what I have learned from many cultures. Lakota, as with my ceremony, is usually the primary thread throughout, but not always. Great Spirit had shown me a long time ago that this was the reason I had learned healing arts from so many diverse people. I wrote more about this in my earlier book.

As I worked on Sue the energy began building on itself, doubling every few minutes. It built in a way I had rarely seen and I was glad I was in good mind and body shape that night. I could feel the fear and doubt coursing through her and knew her biggest issue was trust of anyone or anything. Her's was a deep-seated, very old mistrust. And now she had to decide if she trusted me. Working on her from a distance was very different than bringing all my energy to bear where she was. And the other issue of my own healing coming out to be clearly seen was also throwing her. I decided to give it all I had and then we would see what happened. It was her time to do this now, as she had told me. She had shared several times how she saw a narrow window of opportunity to act through—and I knew she was right.

So here we were, the wounded working on the wounded. Me with more breath and variety of healing approaches in my bag, but both with strong energy in this realm. I began some of the deep clearing work my Mayan teachers had taught me. These can be very difficult to take, since they go to the very core of one's being. But again, I knew this was the way. After an hour or so I saged and let her rest for a while. Then, as she roused I spoke to her about her trust issue. And about the huge energetic gap between her base chakra and the crown of her head. It was causing many disconnects in her spirit growth. After we talked I asked to work some more, focusing on this gap and around her crown chakra, so she might receive some spiritual focus that night.

As I worked I checked in with my own spirit at times, making certain I was still grounded and strong. Luckily I was, so I continued. I was functioning as a total 'hollow bone' that night, allowing all the healing and energy to come through me directly from Great Spirit. Not that I don't always function this way, but this night I was able to completely subjugate my self from the powers of the Universe. It was amazing and a bit scary, but just what was needed. And as I was bringing this energy through I thought, out of nowhere I believed, "Oh shit, I love her!" This did throw me. I wanted to stop the work and run away from her as quickly as I could. Then I stilled my panic and listened to my healer inside—my own inner voice. And I knew I was to continue my work and allow Spirit to direct us. It was not my decision to make—what would happen next.

Finally I had done all I thought was good for that night and I went to the other bed and stretched out. My fears came at me quickly— then subsided. The emotional turmoil then reared up for a while and that also receded. I could feel Sue's energy from across the room and began sending healing energy her way, as taught me by several different teachers. I knew as I lay there Sue loved me—had from the very beginning. I had blocked it so I did not have to deal with the reality of it. And I would have had trouble helping her with her healing if I had known love was in the equation. I would also have most probably disconnected from her quickly and completely, as I truly had no desire to ever walk with a partner again. But my heart had known better all along and, most importantly, Great Spirit had other plans for me—and for Sue. And, quite possibly I now had to admit, for us.

I had truly stepped through the Looking Glass now. What would be next I didn't know, but I knew it would be big.

17 | Wandering in Wonderland

THE NEXT DAY AS WE CONTINUED TO DRIVE OUT ROUTE 90, WE TALKED about the energy of the night before and the feelings we had for each other. Once I faced what I had been pushing away I had no problem talking and listening. I had faced the mirror once again and admitted what I saw, so now it was time to learn more about each other and our past lives in a whole different way. As a couple—a pair—a team. One that had not existed the day before, at least not in an acknowledged way. Still wanting to leave the East behind, we once again only stopped for gas and bathroom uses but, with all the talking we needed to do, we didn't mind the long drive at all. There was energy 'sparking' between us as we rode, a different energy than the healing energy generated in the past. And when we touched, jolts of heat and light shot through both of our beings. I expected this scenario about as much as I expected to be King of England and President of the United States at the same time. But my spirit seemed to be adjusting to this new reality quickly, so I again realized some part of me knew this connection was present.

In the late afternoon I called Wendy, a friend from healing work-shops, as I had promised and told her we were near her. She, her husband and three children lived in Wisconsin and we had expected to stop and say hello. She invited us to stay the night and gave me directions to her house. Wendy was an energy healer and she and her husband ran a healing clinic. After a few wrong turns we found their road and, a few minutes later, pulled up to their house.

We had a nice dinner and Wendy, John (her husband), Sue and I retired to their hot tub afterwards. We soaked and chatted for a couple of hours, enjoying our new friends and the warm water. That night we slept on an inflatable air mattress, which was very large. I only rolled off a few times.

The next morning we had breakfast together, then Wendy and John left to open their office as we packed to head out once again. It was a good night we spent with Wendy and her family and gave us a chance to relax our bodies and minds. As we packed our bags back into the car Jewell, the youngest daughter came out to say goodbye. She was very pleasant and kind, especially for one so young. After she left, we got in the car and drove off.

"Jewell is really a special child, isn't she?" Sue asked.

"Definitely. She is an Indigo Child or Crystal Child—or whatever name you would like to apply to her. Don't you think so?"

"Oh, yeah. No question," Sue replied.

I had been exposed to Indigo Children several years before and, I admit, was confused as to what exactly they were. In fact, I pooh-poohed the whole concept for quite some time. Now I have been around many of these children since and no longer deny their existence, even if I don't have full clarity yet as to their role in these times of change. I may introduce more on these children later, I am unsure. For now consider the description below.

There are many definitions and descriptions of star children—or crystal children—out there, some of which I accept, others I do not. I am sharing the following one, from the website www.starchildren. info.html because I think it does a fine job of describing these radiant ones. And it gives another voice, not just mine; describing something Sue and I were experiencing.

"The Crystal children began to appear on the planet from about 1990-2010, although a few scouts came earlier. Their main purpose is to take us to the next level in our evolution and reveal to us our inner and higher power. They function as a group consciousness rather than as individuals, and they live by the "Law of One" or global oneness. They are also advocates for love and peace on this planet.

The first thing you will recognize about Crystal children is their forgiving nature. They are very sensitive, warm, and caring. Don't mistake these characteristics as a sign of weakness as Crystal children are also very powerful.

The Crystal child is incredibly sensitive, which stems from the ability to feel universal consciousness. You won't be able to hide anything from these children. You won't be able to lie to them either, as they will know immediately what the truth is. It is important to mention that Crystal children know what is in your thoughts and even more importantly, what is in your heart. This is another reason why they are so sensitive.

Children with a crystal vibration have the ability to reflect things back to the universe that are of no importance to them. Not only will they reflect this energy back, they will reflect it in such a way that it is stronger than when it was taken in.

Doreen Virtue, noted author and expert on Star Children, has written about the characteristics of Crystal children. She says these characteristics may include:

Have large, communicative eyes and an intense stare.

Are highly affectionate.

Begin speaking later in life, but often uses telepathy or self-invented words or sign language to communicate.

Love music and may even sing before talking.

Are extremely connected to animals and nature. Are often very interested in rocks, crystals, and stones.

Are extremely artistic.

Are highly empathic and sensitive.

Are forgiving and generous to others.

Draw people and animals near them and love attention.

Often have good sense of balance and are fearless when exploring high places.

Often see or hear angels and spirit guides—both they're own and others'. Dislike high-stress environments with many distractions.

Dislike loud/sharp sounds.

Dislike bright, unnatural lights.

Often enjoy choosing their own meals and/or when they eat them.

Often speak about universal love and healing.

Sometimes show healing gifts at young ages.

Don't react well to sugar, caffeine, or unnatural foods/chemicals.

Dislike fighting or refuse to keep an argument going very long.

Often show strength in telekinesis (or Psychokinesis).

Often amplify emotional energies they gain from their environment (such as negative energies).

Can become uncomfortable when around electrical devices too long (watching TV, computer, etc.), sometimes resulting in a trance-like state.

Sometimes seem 'clingy' to their parents until 4 or 5.

Often stare at people for long periods of time (this allows them to read a person and find out more about them through their own personal memories and energy).

Can sometimes be manipulative and throw tantrums if they cannot create a reality that is good for them.

Are easily over-stimulated and need to meditate/be alone often to
replenish themselves.

Don't usually have trouble with fear or worry.

Enjoy discussing spiritual or philosophical topics.

May appear to be looking at nothing or talking to no one (sign of
clairvoyance and/or clairaudience).

Indigos and Crystals work together to tear down archaic systems and
build up new ones. Again, parents of these special children need to
realize that they agreed to bring these wise and powerful children
into the world whose mission reaches out to the globe as a whole
and not just individuals or individual families. They are also here to
work on the energy grids, raising vibrational frequencies to help fa-
cilitate global changes for a more peaceful earth."

As I always advise—as I was advised so often—take from this what
you need and leave the rest behind. We will be seeing soon enough,
exactly what role these special ones play. On our journey to Sedona,
Sue and I ran across a number of these children, more than I ever had
prior to this journey in such a short period of time. And in the time
since, we continue to cross paths with these children. So I am fairly
certain we will play a role with them or they with us as the future
unfolds for all of us.

As we followed Wendy's directions I soon realized I had missed
a turn and had gotten lost. As I was about to pull over and look at a
map, I saw a river to our right, so I turned that way, down a winding
lane. This was a wide, fast-flowing, steel grey river. With flashes of
blue as the sun caught the tumbling waters. The mighty Mississippi as
it is known in literature and song. I checked the map and saw I was
correct and also saw a winding road along the river that we could
roam if we wished that would eventually dump us out on a western
heading highway again. We decided to invest the time and connect
with Grandmother River this morning, so we continued south along

the river until we saw a little pull-off. A bench sat directly beside the river at this pull-off so we got out, grabbed some sage and went to the bench. We burned some sage, smudging the river and ourselves and thanked the Earth Mother for the beauty of the morning. As we sat there we talked about next steps and what we might do and how things had changed—and agreed to just 'go with the flow' and see where it took us. Then I looked up and at the river and laughed, realized with our flow analogies, why the river had called us over.

When we hit the road again we meandered down river for another hour or so and then picked up Route 90 West for another leg of the journey. We drove all the way to South Dakota, finally stopping in the Black Hills in Deadwood. We found a 1950's motel and checked in. Deadwood is a gambling town, but right in the heart of the Black Hills and a short ride from Pine Ridge, Wounded Knee and the Crazy Horse Monument—all of which I felt we had to go to. For me—revisits, for Sue—first time energy.

We drove downtown—a small, casino-packed downtown—parked and began a walk through town. We stopped at a steak house for dinner and listened to the phony, ersatz cowboy playing equally phony music. But we were enjoying the energy of the Black Hills, even if we were sitting in a restaurant. When we had ordered I felt my energy begin to rise. This happens to me on occasion—especially in places this special to me. My vision quest—the first one—had taken place out in these hills and the vision that had come with it. As did the first time I met the spirit of Black Elk in the flesh. I won't recount these things as I recorded them in detail in *White Man, Red Road, Five Colors*, but I did want to make you aware of the intense spiritual connections I had here. My energy continued to rise and I could feel vibrations going up and down my spine coupled with heavy feet and dancing fingers. In a moment the table between Sue and I began to rock and then vibrate. It lifted up and down in a tat-a-tat rhythm as Sue looked confused, then amused.

"I know you're doing that so you can stop," she laughingly said.

"I am making the table dance, you're right about that, but not in the way you think. This happens sometimes when my energy soars.

Look under the table and you'll see I'm not touching it except where my arms are resting on it."

I know she doubted what I was saying—most people would. But she looked under the table and saw I was speaking the truth. The table continued to 'dance' for another five minutes or so and, as I felt my energy peak, it hit the floor and stopped. I felt my 'charge' dissipate in a moment and then our dinner came.

"Boy, you are a strange one for sure," Sue said, shaking her head.

"I know. I told you, I have no idea what may come at us in the future, but I can promise you will never be bored."

"I guess so."

The next day we got up early to a cloudy, rainy day with some wind kicking things around. Our intention was to head to Wounded Knee, where I wanted to face this place once again and see what came to me. Some of you will remember the first time I was here when I was slammed by such energy and darkness I fell to my knees and just cried for a long time. While the other times I had visited here also affected me strongly, there had never been another like the first visit. I was curious what might come to me now, ten years since my last visit.

I am hearing your questions my friends. Yes, this area has always been sacred to me and a place of major spiritual awakenings and direction for my life. While I don't like repeating what I have shared before, there are enough new friends with us here that I may ask forgiveness of those of you who have walked with me before, and re-tell some of the story of my first trip here. I see by your nods that is okay and I thank you.

Here then, is a little of my first visit to Wounded Knee with Two Bears, my Lakota teacher and guide when we travelled from Rapid City to the rez. I'm taking this from *White Man, Red Road, Five Colors.*

"It was not a long ride to Wounded Knee and we sat, silently, except for Two Bears pointing directions out as we drove. I was enjoying

the rolling hills and cuts through rock faces we drove through, so I almost missed his finger pointing to the left. I braked and pulled onto a side road, going just a few feet to a sign—an old sign—next to the road.

"This is the sign about Wounded Knee," Two Bears finally spoke. "See where the word on top has been nailed over what was below?"

I looked and saw the sign said the Massacre of Wounded Knee. The word 'massacre' was the word he spoke of.

"The sign, when it was put up, read "The Battle of Wounded Knee". This was no battle. The army butchered men, women and children. So, with much anger from the people, it was changed to massacre—as it was. Soldiers from this battle were given medals and still these have not been taken back. These were hard times for white and red. For some they still are," he explained as we got out of the car.

"I will wait here," he said leaning against the Jeep, "Go and read the sign and listen to your spirit as you do so. See what comes to you," he instructed.

I approached the sign and suddenly felt something welling up in me. I looked at the sign a few moments, then stepped around it and began walking to the side—to some open grass as I remember. In a few seconds I was doubled over in pain, driven to my knees. The pain was centered in my gut and it felt like knives trying to get out. I went forward on all fours as the pain built even stronger. Then I was overcome by sadness and grief and began wailing out loud. Tears poured down my face and onto my hands. I lay down and continued to moan and wail as I also tried to understand the pain. Colors crossed my eyes—red, brown and black I remember as the primary hues I was seeing. Then that was gone and I felt sharp pains in my back, like pointed stakes being driven in. I thought I was dying and had no idea what to do, so I asked Great Spirit to help me, as I was powerless to even move. More gripping pains in my gut forced me to focus on just bearing the pain and tears continued to roll out of me, like a faucet left full open. I was scared—no, petrified. I had never felt pain like this and did not know what was happening. After a while I began to also feel pains around my heart, like a fist closing on it. The pain was strongest in the bottom area of my heart and I remember thinking, "Is this what a heart attack feels like? Is it my time— so suddenly?"

Two Bears was not far away and I thought he must see me, yet he did not approach. This onslaught of pain and tears lasted about twenty minutes Two Bears told me later. Then everything stopped at once, as quickly as it had come. I lay panting, afraid to trust my legs yet as they felt like rubber bands. Slowly I pushed myself into a seated position—legs under my torso in the inipi position. My brain was running like a racecar trying to make sense of what had happened. And I was soaked in sweat, my shirt hanging off of me dragged down by the perspiration it had absorbed. I wasn't even sure I was still alive for some seconds until the energy of the things around me made me accept I was. My mouth was so dry I could not even swallow. So I sat, moaned softly, wiped sweat and breathed in big gulps of air. Trying to stop the panic I felt inside of me.

After what seemed like an hour Two Bears approached me with a bottle of water and a very serious look on his face. A serious look mixed with concern and sympathy. "I gave you a few minutes before I came. Here, drink slow," he said as he handed me the bottle.

"What the hell is wrong with me! Do you think it's my heart! Did you see me on the ground? You must have heard me," I gasped out in a rush.

"Yes, I saw. I did not expect anything like this. I thought this place would touch you, but not in that way. I was very worried for you but knew I could not come to you. I hold sorrow for that but I know it is so. I do not think anything is physically wrong with you, but it is your heart you feel. This place came to you as it was then. You were there

*now as you were then. These things happen sometimes. Not often,
but they do. I begin to see why I was guided to bring you here. But
not just for this I see. We need to open the Chanunpa and ask for
guidance from above. This is big and I do not pretend to understand
much of it. Are you able to stand?"*

"I think so, if you help."

*I got up and Two Bears helped me to the car. I passed the keys to
him—not wanting to drive yet. "Will this happen again, Two Bears?"*

*"I do not think so. I do not know anyway. I have spoken about the
pain that would find you as you walked more on this road and into
your power. This is occurring with some now as the time of the
prophecies nears. I will speak of my Hanbleche one day soon. It
is the only time I had an experience like yours here. But not as in-
tense, I think. You howled and wailed as the tears came and the pain
grabbed you."*

Reading this you may understand why I was drawn and pleased
to be going back to Wounded Knee and, at the same time, fearful of
what I might experience. I also thought if I had another strong reac-
tion to this place Sue might go on 'overload' and ours would be one
of the fastest relationships ever. But, no matter, I knew I was to go
back on the rez and back to Wounded Knee. We headed out from the
motel with that intention, stopping for some breakfast and a pot full
of coffee, on the way. The rain was coming down in sheets as we left
the café, so we headed to the Badlands National Park Visitor Center,
which centered its displays on the grasslands of the region. The clouds
were even heavier and darker when we pulled up to the visitor cen-
ter, but the rain had slackened a little. We went in and spent about an
hour with some very educational displays and then met a ranger at
the desk.

"Hi folks, where are you from?" he asked with the question virtu-
ally all rangers opened with.

"That's a really good question," I responded. "I am currently from Sedona and, Sue?"

"I'm just moving to Sedona from New Hampshire," Sue chimed in.

"What brings you here?" he then asked. The second most asked question from park rangers.

"We are heading to Wounded Knee and then we will drive around Pine Ridge and the parks down that way," Sue answered.

"Oh boy. I don't think you want to go that way today. These heavy rains are going to keep coming in bursts and a lot of the roads down there are dirt. That means mud—the kind of mud you can get stuck in," the ranger shared, concern on his face.

"Thanks. Okay, we won't go that way. Maybe we can make it tomorrow," I said.

"No, we are going there today. We'll be fine with the weather," Sue countered me. This was unusual because Sue, at this time, was quiet and rarely spoke her mind this way. This was an interesting shift in her.

"Well, be really careful and if you see the big storm clouds coming I suggest you get off the dirt roads as fast as you can," the ranger added.

"Thanks, we will stay alert," Sue answered him and we headed out.

We went to the car and headed towards Wounded Knee, where darkening skies and mounded clouds loomed.

"Okay, I'm glad you spoke and we are going. I didn't need an easy way out of not going back to Wounded Knee," I said.

"I thought so. We'll just watch the weather and what roads we are on. It's cells of weather so it may not catch us," Sue replied.

We entered the Badlands National Park as we drove towards Wounded Knee. I wanted to give Sue a chance to see some of this beautiful landscape and, okay—I might have been postponing arriving at Wounded Knee. I felt the pull to stop and I turned to the right and pulled into an open area. When I feel these urges to stop or go a certain way I have learned to listen. Often I come upon something or someone I need to see.

It was not raining at the moment, so I thought we could get a walk in between cloudbursts. We headed out on a dirt path that ran between some gigantic rock boulders. As we got ten minutes along the trail the rain began once again—just a trickle at first. But we turned to start back and as we did, the deluge began. In seconds we were mired in thick, slippery, gooey, paste-like mud. We slogged towards the car, trying to kick the ten-pound masses off of our shoes as we went. As we got near the car the winds began to blow and, in another few seconds, hail began to fall. These western summer storms often include wind, rain and hail—and sometimes snow. But they usually only last a short time, often followed by sun breaking through the shroud. We made it to the car, pulling ourselves in out of the elements. Cleaning the mud out of the car would be a task for later. We were wet, muddy and our hands and faces were stinging from the hail, but we were also laughing—enjoying the display Father Sky had sent us.

We drove out of the storm in five minutes and continued on our way to Wounded Knee. I now truly feared seeing Black Elk again. And I think Sue feared not seeing him and getting affirmation for some of the things I had shared with her about my journey and myself. We continued the drive and again entered an area of heavy clouds, but no rain. The heavy, dark clouds above reflected for me what I felt in my heart—a huge sense of loss and guilt. Finally we pulled off the road next to the sign I had stopped at so often in the past. The sign where Massacre had been cemented over the word Battle—The Massacre of Wounded Knee.

I felt darkness and sorrow as I stood here reading, once again, about the massacre on that day so long ago. And felt part of it as I also had on my past trips here. But it was not the fall down, sobbing reaction of the past I experienced this time, but rather just a deep, painful sorrow. And I saw no spirit guides—including Black Elk—nor did I feel any. I found this confusing, since I had expected some spirit presence here. Sue saw the pain on my face as I turned back to her—away from the sign.

"Are you okay?" she asked.

"Just really sad and also confused. I sense no presence here. And it doesn't feel right to me—for us—to go deeper into Pine Ridge right now. What do you feel?"

"Whatever you think. You are the one with the intense history here," she answered quietly.

I nodded and we headed back to the car. We decided to drive through the rez to Custer, where we could spend a few days. Staying in Custer, SD, near Little Big Horn, always made me smile—the sheer sense of irony. We looked at the map and decided on an alternate route to Custer so we could see some different scenery and see what might come our way. I was still confused that no spiritual energy had appeared to me and no messages had become clear. But I was shrugging it off figuring, "Hey, this is a brand new day."

We followed the road on the map and after a half-hour, realized we had missed our turn off to our left—west, towards Custer. Just as we realized this we saw a narrow dirt road off to the left and decided to take it, assuming it would also lead the way we wanted. This was County Road 24, which we only knew from one small, battered, shot up sign bent back from the road. The road got increasingly narrower and rougher as we travelled up it, but at least there was no rain. In fact the nearest cloudbank was far off to our south. So we had no concerns about being on this dirt road—track, really. We came to a Y in the road and opted to go left, since there were no more signs and it just seemed to more closely point in the direction we thought Custer to be.

The track got even tighter and more deeply rutted as we drove and several times we had to stop and wait for horses or cattle to clear from our path. We were also climbing higher by the minute—gradually, but steadily. After what seemed like well over an hour, we crested a hill and popped out on a very high, open, rolling landscape. We could see for miles in every direction and there was no sign of civilization anywhere. It was like being in the middle of some unimproved, undisturbed land from long ago. Only the track we followed—which we could see disappearing into the far distance—and the livestock gave any clue that people did come onto this land, even if they did not live here.

Flowers decorated the hills to our right, so I stopped the car, pulling it to the far side of the track, and we got out. I couldn't pull off the road—track—completely, as it was rutted to three or four feet deep in this spot. But so what—traffic here? Maybe we would be in a cow's way? Or a horse might whinny at us? We climbed out of the rut we were in and began walking through the beautiful meadow. Friends, I just realized the implication of that last sentence as it flowed from me—"climbed out of the rut we were in." I love when Spirit sends me double meanings this way. Two Bears, my teacher, calls this Coyote medicine—as Coyote is the trickster in Lakota lore. We were, in fact, climbing not only out of the rut I stopped the car in, but also the emotional rut we had been in most of the day—especially me.

I was feeling torn—the pain and doubt I was going through and the happiness of suddenly, unexpectedly walking with another partner—an interesting place to be. As we walked we both connected stronger and stronger with the amazing nature all around us, and each other. We heard a few birds voicing their joy and a hawk high overhead. The aroma of the wildflowers we walked through massaged our noses, even if they did trigger a few good sneezes. And a soft breeze stroked our faces and heads. Off in the distance we saw the huge, ominous, black thunderclouds growling and barking at everything below them. Still far enough off we were not going to stop this side road on our journey because of them. While our senses were being bathed, I was also aware of the quietness of where we walked—the only sounds being the birds and an occasional noisy gust of wind. It was heavenly—as was looking down on so much landscape below and around our high loft. We just walked the fields and enjoyed the solitude—with no need for words between us. Hoka Hey—it's a good day to die!

Maybe twenty or thirty minutes later we heard some noise coming from below and behind us. It sounded like clanging metal and something very heavy bouncing its way along. We could not tell where it was coming from, but sensed it was getting closer—quickly. I began walking back to the car while Sue continued to sit among some flowers, where she had been for the past few minutes. As I approached the car a huge cattle-hauling truck broke the ridge on the track we had come up. It looked like a big, red, fire-breathing dragon as it wove its way among the herd of cows behind us, speeding toward us as it came. Sue had come a little closer to where I was as the truck lumbered closer—with me standing maybe ten feet from the car and she thirty feet up a slight rise. I hoped old 'fire breather' would clear the car because there was no way I could get back into the ditch, get into the car and move it before the behemoth was upon us. So we just watched and hoped.

Just seconds later, as I assume the driver saw our car, amidst the blast of air brakes, screech of metal scraping metal and a huge billow of dust, the truck came to a stop just behind our car. I couldn't really see the driver and could hear nothing with the truck engine rumbling in a deep, mechanical growl. In a second the door near me screeched open and the driver leaned out.

He yelled over the roar of the engine, "What are you looking for?"

I could barely hear him, but got the gist of his question. I pointed at the ground as I yelled, "Is this Route 24?"

He couldn't hear me—cupping his ear to let me know that, so I yelled my question again. And this time he shook his head, as if to say, "Still can't hear you." I did 2 and 4 with my fingers and pointed to the track we had both travelled and he shook his head 'no'. Then he waved me up on the running board of the truck. I jumped up on the running board—a good four feet off the ground, and hoped we could now hear each other. I didn't even think about why he didn't just turn the truck off, but he didn't. Sue watched us from her perch on the rise beside us—smiling as we talked.

Standing on the running board I could look into the truck cab and see the driver. He smiled and put two fingers to his forehead in a 'hello' gesture. I just stared and began sweating and yet feeling cold at the same time.

Wonder and confusion welled up in me as I heard, "How you doing? You alright?"

The driver was short, which I already knew, and thin; with a sun and wind weathered face. Unmistakably a Native American face. He wore a red bandana around his throat and had a beaded necklace hanging to mid-chest and an old, sweat-stained cowboy hat on his head. He was maybe sixty—old to be driving such a big rig I thought. And his smile. An honest, from the heart, welcoming smile. It was a smile I had seen before and a voice I had heard. Black Elk had come to visit once again.

As I looked at him I was registering he was the same size and shape that I remembered, the same wonderful smile and voice, the same intense energy surrounding him and, most especially, the same eyes—eyes that saw you and in you at the same time.

The truck engine had idled-down as we stood facing each other so we could now hear each other.

He continued to watch me and then he began laughing, as he said, "No, this is not 24, nephew, this is ranching land. The cows, the horses, the solitude and me and my boys."

"We were on a narrow dirt road that I thought said 24 back a ways, but when we came to a Y we came this way. Trying to get to Custer."

"No, it's important you take the right road now. You need to take the low road," he told me, eyes crinkled and shining.

"Down below?"

"You are doing much better now, but you need to continue to take the low road," he repeated, as he looked over to Sue. "Who is that one, nephew? Ah, I see. It's good your woman is with you," he continued as he smiled even bigger and nodded in approval.

"Yes, that's my mate, Sue," I surprised myself by saying.

"Good. Yes, good you speak that," he said back to me. "You are both doing much better now. Just stay with the low road and you will both get where you need to be."

I stood on the running board, not even hearing the growling of the truck engine any longer; wanting to say more, but fearing I was imagining this and would appear a fool. So I simply thanked him for the directions and prepared to jump down.

"Ho, nephew," he said laughing. "No problem at all. Can I help you with anything else?"

"No, we will follow your advice on the low road. It's not that far back."

"Good, good. You will both get there. It was really good to see you," he beamed, as he put the truck in gear and I jumped down so he could continue along his way.

He smiled big again as he looked at me with those truly unique eyes and I wondered how I had doubted for a second who it was. But that's the mind telling me it couldn't be so—even as my heart immediately knew the truth. He waved as the truck lurched into gear, swung around our car and rumbled downhill to the West—following the only road—track—anywhere in sight. There were no turns and no other way out of this land except the road behind us and in front of us where Black Elk had continued forward.

Sue was coming towards me as I climbed back out of the road rut. In seconds we were side-by-side. "Did you hear us?" I asked.

"No, too much noise and too far away. But it looked like you had a fun talk."

"Fun, oh yeah," I said, still amazed by what had just happened. "That was Black Elk," I fumbled out, half laughing and half crying. "Damn, Black Elk again. I thought 'forget it' after no one showed at Wounded Knee. And here, in the middle of no-damn where, he shows up. In a huge red truck to boot," I laughed out the words, tears running down my cheeks.

We hugged and laughed, walked a little and hugged some more, with me saying, "Damn, Black Elk," I don't know how many times.

I told Sue all that he had said and we decided to head back to the 'low road' he had suggested, as the road ahead went nowhere. We knew he was not just speaking of the road we were on when he showed, but was telling us to stay on the low road as we continued our journey together. And assuring us if we stayed on the low road we would get where we needed to be. Notice he did not tell us where that would be, only that we would get there. More affirmation about the journey, as Black Elk was again affirming it was all about the journey, not the destination. This would have more meaning soon, and in many different ways. Actually, we may rest for a while soon, friends, and I will share one of those ways with you, since I think it will assist us all as we continue our walk together.

I am having a hard time telling you of this encounter. In fact, you can see the tears coming as I do. After all these years, after all the pain and all the loss and all the time spent walking through the dark time of my soul, Black Elk appeared to me in the flesh once again. I knew I was stepping back up, even if I understood from his words it would not be easy or even pain-free for now. "You both will get where you need to be." Maybe not where we might want to be—but where we need to be. Good thing I have finally learned from strong men that tears and emotion are strength in warriors, not a weakness. I wish I had understood this truth decades ago, I could have saved myself a lot of inner work now. But of course, I needed to go through the pain to understand. Ah, we humans and our stubbornness!

As we walked ahead, Black Elk would begin showing up in human form—different human forms and at odd times. I have had no more long talks, as the one I am telling you about here, since Pine Ridge, but Sue and I have had short 'check ins'. It's almost always the same thing—someone shows up quickly, with "How you guys doing?" coming from him as he approaches. When we say fine, the person nods and keeps going. This has happened at least six times. It's nice to see he's watching over what we are doing. I wonder what would happen if we answered in the negative to one of these manifestations of Black Elk. Would he stop and follow up? Interesting question. I also think since he has not paid me any longer visits we must be walking the Good Red Road in the way Spirit wishes. I promise if he shows up in any person's form with a frown on his face and head shaking I will let this circle know first. But I don't expect that. Hope I'm right.

We finally turned, smiling and headed to the car. As we got near it we heard a commotion once again—something else rumbling towards us. A few seconds later an oversized white pick-up truck came shooting over the rise, up the track we and then Black Elk had come. It was a stretch cab pick-up truck with two Native American men in the front seat—Black Elk's men. They were looking ahead and pointing after the truck Black Elk drove, which was now throwing up a cloud of dust off in the distance. They looked to the side and saw us and as they did so, gave us huge grins and expressive waves of their hands. Then they picked up speed and shot after Black Elk.

Sue took a few more pictures and then we climbed in the car and began retracing our way down the dirt track looking for the 'lower road' we were told to take. We stopped often for cows and a few times for horses, watching for the Y we saw on the way up. We assumed the 'lower road' was literal and that Black Elk was not speaking only metaphorically. We finally found the Y about an hour later and hoped the lower fork was Route 24, as it was not marked and it was another narrow dirt road.

"Do we head out the way we came in or take this lower road our Ancestor told us of?" I asked.

"Take the road Black Elk told us to, I think," Sue said.

"I don't like the look of those huge cloudbanks coming our way," I commented as I pointed to masses of clouds coming from the south. "If they hit us out here on this type of road, we may stay the night. It turns quicksand-like quickly."

"I still think we go ahead," Sue held firm.

And so we turned and headed up the new dirt road, hoping it was 24 and hoping it would take us where we needed to be. After all, it was the low road, eh?

Once again we were dodging cows and the occasional horse as we wound our way down this road. After some time the road began getting even more narrow and rutted, with tall grass growing up in it—obviously not many took this road. The clouds began moving in all around us and I was getting nervous, but we kept moving forward. After what seemed a very long time, we came upon a lovely old church and schoolhouse—long abandoned. We thought this meant we were approaching civilization and this gave us the heart to continue. After another twenty minutes or so we bounced over a slight rise and saw a farmhouse across a field. Wow, we thought—people! But as we approached we could see it was a very, very old farmhouse and we saw no signs of people inhabiting it. Sue was certain we would be fine and should continue. I was more than ready to turn around and hope we could outrun the storms coming our way. We continued forward.

After another fairly long ride, bouncing over ruts and circling deep holes it began raining—lightly, but this was just the beginning judging by the clouds, which continued to mass around us. This time we both decided it was time to turn around—although Sue did so reluctantly. The sky continued to get darker and darker as we edged our way back the way we had come. The rain got a little heavier and we could smell ozone in the air. We no sooner noticed the ozone, then lightning bolts began cutting the sky. A few minutes later dust began kicking up, making it hard to see. For some reason I reset the odometer so I could see how far we had come once we made it out of here. In a few minutes we were re-approaching the old farmhouse.

"How can that be?" I asked. "Didn't we go much, much farther going the other way? I thought we went fifty miles or so beyond this place."

"Not fifty, but twenty at least," Sue agreed. "I don't understand how we got back here so fast."

"Well, let's be thankful we did, the way this weather is picking up," I responded.

As we got closer our mouths dropped open, our hearts started beating faster and our eyes went wide as Sue said, "That's his truck! Look, over there next to the barn."

Sure enough, the truck the rancher who was the embodiment of Black Elk was driving sat next to the barn, with the white pick-up behind it. And there was no one visible anywhere. Not quite sure what to think or do, we drove by in disbelief. There was no way for these trucks to get back down here from up above, especially given the direction they had been going. If there was a way back down they would have needed to pass us coming from the other direction—assuming there was another dirt track coming down past where we turned around. Damn, this was getting unbelievable and interesting, but not scary.

"Okay, I have no explanation at all," Sue said.

"There are no logical explanations when these things happen," I told her. "I will tell you more of past occurrences I have had like this as we drive. But not now, I need to really concentrate."

So I began carefully navigating our way back down the road. It was going to be a long ride and I didn't know how far we might make it before the deluge struck. Maybe we should have pulled into the farmhouse and seen if anyone was there. But I wasn't turning around again. Worse case, we would sleep in the car for the night.

In just a few short minutes I thought I was seeing the paved road we had taken from Wounded Knee. But that was impossible. In another minute I saw I was correct and we neared the road we had come on. I looked at the odometer and saw we had only come nine miles since I reset it when we turned around. That was crazy. Something was wrong.

"We only drove nine miles coming out," I told Sue. "How can that be?"

"It can't," she said. "That would mean maybe forty-five minutes for the total trip, yet checking our watches, we had been on these two roads for three and a half hours. Even adding thirty minutes for the meeting with Black Elk we had almost two and a half hours unaccounted for. Where were we? Where did we go?"

Sue had been sitting with the digital camera, fiddling with the settings, as we spoke. She stopped, looked at something twice and turned to me.

"You know the pictures I took up on top after your meeting with Black Elk?"

"Yep. I see you looking at them."

"I took twelve pictures, but only one came out. Yet the camera has worked fine all along. We have hundreds of pictures on the disks. Look at the one that came out," she said as she handed me the camera.

This photo was on top of the ridge, looking out over the flowers and the hills in the distance, with the dark clouds forming overhead. Beautiful picture, but for the play of white light in one corner, which seemed like an outline of some flying being.

"One more thing with no explanation," I said, handing the camera back to Sue.

"Where the heck were we? And who else was around? Or what else," Sue said; wonder, but not fear, in her voice.

Having no answers, but knowing we had lost an entire afternoon, we quit trying to 'figure it out' and turned north on the road and back towards the Badlands we had crossed earlier. Sue took several pictures out of the window of the huge storm about to hit us. All of the pictures came out; as did the hundreds of others we would take over the next four weeks.

We were on the road no more than two minutes when the now gigantic storm engulfed us. Rain came in sheets and the wind gusts rocked the car. Hail began beating on the roof and hood, while lightning again cut across the sky. This was a mighty storm, but I continued forward slowly. We thought we might be in this for a long time, but after about twenty minutes we rode out of it and into sunlight. Another of those fabulous desert summer storms. Interesting though how it held off until just after we left the dirt roads. Coincidence?

A short time later we saw a group of Native American teens on the side of the road thumbing a ride, holding a gas can. Since we were loaded like a gypsy wagon of old we wouldn't be of much help; there was nowhere someone could sit—let alone five people. They waved and we waved and we continued on. I still wish we had stopped. In our defense it had been an eventful, emotion-laden day and we were not thinking straight. I don't know how we could have helped, but we could have at least stopped and acknowledged their presence. Well, we can't always make choices we are happy with later. I take this moment, as I share this with all of you, to send my apologies to this group by the road.

Let's take that break now and I will share a little more about the low road as it relates to Hopi stories. About a year after we met Black Elk and heard his advice to "take the low road", we were in Hopi land—on the First Mesa—with a Hopi woman who was showing us around. We had been with her a couple of times before this day on cultural and service missions, but this time she was just playing tour guide for us. This woman, Tilia, was well-connected throughout Hopi land and involved in many community improvement efforts. So we were thankful to have her take us out.

"Would you like to see the Hopi Prophecy Rock?" she asked us.

"Sure, Tilia," Sue answered.

"Okay, let's go. You will be with me so it will be okay. The tribe doesn't want just anybody wandering in where it is. It is very, very old and sacred. They fear damage done to it or a lack of respect shown it," Tilia told us.

"We would love to see this, if you are certain it's okay," I followed up.

"You two will be seeing it for the right reasons. It will be fine."

We followed Tilia's directions and shortly got near the Prophecy Rock.

"Okay, turn right here and just drive across that open area of dirt. Then park on the far side," she instructed.

A few minutes later, we were out of the car walking around a hillside of boulders. It did not take long to reach the Rock but, without someone guiding you or giving good directions, you would never see it. I stood looking at the drawings on the rock face before us, absorbing the details of the images I was looking at. A few short minutes later a pick-up, driven by a young Native American man, came wheeling up to where we parked. The youth jumped out and headed our way. Tilia went to meet him and they spoke for a few minutes. The youth shook his head, looked at Sue and I a little suspiciously, walked back to his car and began to drive away. He gave one more frowning look at us and wheeled out of the parking area.

"He was seeing who was here," Tilia told us. "He will go back and tell his uncle it is okay."

"Wow, your people really do watch," I said.

"Oh, yes," she answered. "We take our sacred places very seriously. So, look at the picture there on the rock and tell me what you both see."

"I see people on two different lines—one straight and one jagged. And some animals and corn," Sue said.

"The two lines are joined here on the left, but separate as they go along," I added.

"Good," said Tilia, nodding solemnly. "These are the two roads of man. This one, the upper one—the jagged like, is modern man with all his technology and all the things being created which hurt our Earth Mother. This other one, the low road—the straight line, is man in a more natural way of living. Less stress, less need to control and destroy. Planting crops in a good way, without all the chemicals. Showing respect to the animal people—and to other humans. See what happens to the two lines?"

"The top one—modern man—seems to just stop here," Sue said, pointing. "The low road continues on around the rock face."

"That is it," Tilia agreed, smiling. The prophecy tells us if we humans continue on this high road of development and waste, we will no longer exist—suddenly and with no warning. If we again seek the low road and walk there we will prosper and our children's children down to the seven generations will prosper even better. We are to take the low road and we will get where we humans need to be."

Tilia showed us many other things that day and then took us to her home, where she, her son and daughter played drums and sang some of the old songs of the Hopi as we all sat in circle. Then we went for food at the Hopi Cultural Center. While I could spend more time on things we saw and learned that day, the Prophecy Rock and her last words about the low road are more than enough for now. She put walking the low road as the means we humans would again walk in harmony with the Earth Mother and each other—getting where we as a species needed to be. Just as Black Elk had told us in walking the low road, Sue and I would get where we needed to be. And this connected message came to us immediately as Tilia spoke that day. More coincidence, brothers and sisters?

Okay, back to South Dakota. We entered the Badlands from a different direction than we had earlier and headed back to 40 west and to Custer. Custer is an historic town, very popular with visitors in the region. It had good restaurants, shops and craft stores and was close to Wounded Knee and the Crazy Horse Monument. We went to the largest motel in town, ready to check in for a few days. And we were quickly told they had no rooms and they doubted we would find a room anywhere in town. The tourist traffic was heavy in the summer and there was a conference going on as well. At first we thought to drive on, but decided to try a few more motels, just in case. I really wanted more time in this area and had yet to visit the Crazy Horse Monument, which I knew Sue would find interesting.

I went into a smaller motel and asked about a room.

"Sorry, no rooms for the rest of the week," the clerk told me, as I noticed he was working on a hand-painted "No Rooms" sign as he answered me. "I just called all around town for some other visitors and there is not one room anywhere."

Oh, well. I really thought we were meant to stay in this town. And with taking the low road, I thought we had 'gotten where we needed to be'—in Custer. But we would just move on. I thanked him for his time and turned to go as his phone rang. Something made me stop and wait as he spoke on the line. He had turned away from me so I could not hear what he was saying. As he prepared to hang up, he turned to me with a finger up. Then he smiled and said someone had just cancelled—a three-day reservation. He wanted to know if I still wanted a room. This was a nice large room with a queen-sized bed and kitchenette. I signed for the room and went out to tell Sue this new story. I smiled as things just continued to manifest for us when we needed them. And gave thanks to the Creator for all that was being gifted us.

Sue had never seen the heads of the four presidents in the rocks—Mount Rushmore—so we decided to go there the next morning. It was hot—really hot, so we took a lot of water, some cheese and fruit and headed towards the monument. About seven miles from Mount Rushmore the traffic began getting very heavy; and about four miles in, it came to a stop. A three-mile wait to get close. We sat in line about twenty minutes, looking at the president's visages from afar as we moved about two-tenths of a mile. The car engine was getting hot and so were we, so we hung a U-turn and headed away from the chiseled leaders, which we could see in the distance.

"I have a better rock monument for us to visit," I told Sue, as I turned left and headed towards the Crazy Horse Monument. We pulled into the parking lot about thirty minutes later and walked up to it and then to the little museum and store. What? You want to know a little about this monument? Here is some information gathered from multiple sources.

The Crazy Horse Memorial is a monument complex in the mountains 17 miles from Mount Rushmore. It was begun in 1948 by Korczak Ziokowski after being commissioned by Henry Standing Bear, a Lakota elder. It is being built on private land held in the Black Hills, Custer County in South Dakota. The memorial is run by the Crazy Horse Memorial Foundation, a non-profit.

The memorial encompasses the carving of Crazy Horse in the mountain, the Native American Cultural Center and the Indian Museum. The monument is being carved out of Thunderhead Mountain, land sacred to the Oglala Sioux. The final dimensions are to be 641 feet wide, 563 feet high and Crazy Horse's head will be 87 feet high.

Crazy Horse was born c. 1842, near present-day Rapid City, S.D. He was an Oglala Sioux Indian chief and much-respected warrior who fought against removal to a reservation in the Black Hills. In 1876 he joined with Cheyenne forces in a surprise attack against Gen. George Crook; then united with Chief Sitting Bull for the Battle of the Little Bighorn. In 1877, Crazy Horse surrendered and was killed in a scuffle with soldiers. He ranks among the most notable and iconic of Native American tribal members.

Much of what is known about Crazy Horse comes from his own people. Even today, they still talk about him. To the Lakota, he was both a warrior and a holy man. In nineteen thirty-nine, the tribe asked an artist to make a statue of Crazy Horse. The Indians wanted a huge statue cut into the side of a mountain. It would show Crazy Horse riding a running horse, pointing his arm to where the Earth meets the sky—to the lands of the Lakota people. The tribe told the artist: "We would like the white man to know the red man had great heroes, too."

We spent hours roaming the museum and walking around the grounds—just absorbing the energy of the land and of Crazy Horse. The next day we decided it was time to move on, so we packed up and headed—where else?. . . West, always West. We took a back road, Route 16, as we slowly wended our way westward. As we approached the interstate, Sue saw a natural monument off in the distance—the Devil's Tower. It was forty miles off the highway we sought, but we felt the need to go there, so we headed north for the massive tower we could see before us. Devil's Tower was a name given this edifice by Europeans—much like Standing Eagle Mountain in Sedona was known as Coffee Pot. The Lakota name was Matho Thipila or 'Bear Lodge'. The Bear Lodge rises 1,270 feet above the land around it in a conical formation geologists have never fully explained. There are many stories the Lakota share about the structure and the long incisions down its sides. One of these stories tells of how a great bear chased two little boys up a hill and then proceeded to grab at them with its paws—building the tower and creating the incisions down it as it did so. However it was created, it is a sacred place for many tribes, including Kiowa, Sioux and Cheyenne.

We parked in the lot below the Tower and began walking the trail around it. There were a fair number of people around but as usual, after we walked five minutes most of them had disappeared. It's a sad fact, but a fact, that 90%+ of people whom visit National Parks, Monuments, State Parks—natural areas—walk no more than 150 feet from their cars. At least they visit, but it's a surface visit at best. I always want to take their kids in hand and have them walk a few miles with me. Oh well, we walked on as ravens wheeled overhead and stood sentry on the fence posts and tree stumps we passed. We didn't go too far ourselves at this stop, since we expected to go all the way to Yellowstone, but we did sit on a bench and absorb the energy for a long stretch of time. The views were stellar staring out over the low lands around the monument and up the scarred sides of the monument itself. We decided to turn back after we got the feeling we had connected with the energy here as we were meant to. As we walked back down the trail a couple asked if we would like our picture taken. We thanked them and posed with the natural setting in the background. Later, it evolved that this would be the photo we used for our mission as healing guides. And so we had gathered the other thing we were meant to here—this photo. This photo we didn't ask for, but rather two people approached us with the offer to take it.

We drove away from Devil's Tower down a dirt road and as we looked back, we watched a huge storm approaching it. We pulled over, got out and walked into a field beside the car. It was sunny, with birds flying and chirping and butterflies wafting along all around us. So we stood in the sun and nature as we watched the storm encircle the tower not that far away. After a while we restarted our day's ride, heading towards Route 90 some thirty miles south of our current position. We were both feeling some major emotional releasing, which was draining our energy and our spirits, so we stopped often for short walks and stretching. Soon we realized we were not to make Cody, Wyoming, outside of Yellowstone National Park this day, so we headed to Buffalo, Wyoming as dusk approached.

The West is full of trains—trains of all sorts—an element I have long loved. Most of them are very long and slow moving—and they generate sounds. Some would say noise, but I find that a negative word and I don't find the noise they generate to be negative at all. But it can be pervasive—filling all the nooks and crannies of the space around them as they come through. Buffalo was no exception to this, with a large number of tracks crossing the town. The room we took—and we in it—was serenaded by the sound of trains all night long. But, since we both felt miserable this was almost a blessing. We spent hours doing energy clearing and healing work on each other, trying to find places of more peace. I guess we had some success as we finally slept awhile.

18 | Yellowstone Magic

THE NEXT DAY WE FINISHED THE RIDE TO CODY, WHERE I HAD ALSO stayed many times in the past. Again we found most motels and hotels booked, but we found a room—the last they had—at a motel outside of town. Unfortunately this 'only room they had left' was a smoking room that had been converted to non-smoking room, which still smelled like a smoking room to us. We called an attendant who came and hooked up a machine to remove the smoke odors, which helped a little—although we now had to tolerate the noise of the machine.

I drove around Cody and the surrounding area to give Sue a sense of the people and place, then we parked near the small downtown and went out on foot. Cody is an interesting place—a place I have had numerous connections to over time. It is the western gateway to Yellowstone, from which a twenty-mile drive through ranch land and forest takes you to the gate of the park. And it is the largest town on the perimeter of the park, housing some historic buildings and the Buffalo Bill Museum. A place many tourists pass through but also a place locals live and work. An interesting mix of energies. It is here I first met Randy, the man who we would buy the horse packing business from and later connect with him when he led the trips for us. It was here I came with Two Bears twice before going to Wounded Knee. And from here I stationed myself while I did some projects while at Colorado State University. And, most powerful for me especially at this time when Sue and I were birthing as a couple, it was here that Bonnie, my deceased wife, and I came many times before our sojourns into the park. So, as with everything, it was no coincidence we were here before going into the park.

As we explored town on foot we began to get hungry and since it was early evening, we went to Buffalo Bill's Irma Hotel for dinner. I have spoken of this place in the previous book, so I will only share a little here. From that book. . .

". . .the Irma Hotel, built by Buffalo Bill in the early 1900's. It was here we would meet Randy for breakfast, but Shirley remembered the large steaks and plentiful fries they served and wanted to experience them again.

The Irma Hotel was out of the Old West, both in décor and in the look of some of the patrons. There was a large contingent of tourists—cameras swinging, bright-colored shirts blazing and brand new 'cowboy' hats cocked atop heads. But there were also a good number of locals there to order big steaks and, probably, to enjoy watching the tourists as much as the tourists watched them. Some of the locals were dressed in genuine 'just off the back forty' garb and others were not so genuinely dressed with spurs; leather leggings and deer hide vests. But we enjoyed watching the scene unfold as we ate, wondering what niche we might fall into for those looking at us."

This night was no exception as Sue and I walked in for dinner. A group of rancher types lounged at a table near the buffet, one with his chair tipped back and another working a wooden matchstick in his mouth. Several other tables housed ranchers and land workers, while two other tables seated groups of flamboyant 'cowboys'—decked out to meet the tourists. The remainder of the tables consisted of tourists speaking many different languages. We got a table just after we arrived, being seated near the front windows so we could look out at those walking the main street and back at those eating in the room with us.

As we were leaving the Hotel full of roast beef, pork, potatoes and veggies, we saw they were setting up for the 'shoot out' they re-enacted for tourists this time of year. They held this in the streets outside of the hotel. We had no desire to be in this area while that was happening, so we walked back to the car and took a drive up the highway towards the park. We drove up by the dam and through the tunnels near the Cody end of the road, and then on into the area where summer homes had grown—festered—during the economic booms of the past. Actually, some of the older places nestled in the hills with respect for the land, were not bad—even inviting. But other areas had the circumscribed four-acre ranchettes—most standing empty. We talked about what it would be like to live in this region, near the park and in among some of the most spiritual land I have walked, even if it has the footprints of humans on it.

About ten to twelve miles up the road we came to an old dirt road to our left and, as my spirit again pulled me that way, we pulled up it. This dirt road had not been used much of late, with grass growing in the ruts of the passage. This side road wended down to the branch of the Yellowstone River, which entered the park along this route as well. This river and the rivers on the north side of Yellowstone were to play a strong role in our quest. But especially this branch of the river that we now approached. We parked as the dirt road ended near the riverbank and got out for a walk. It had been clouding up as we drove and now a good-sized shower began. It felt good so we continued to walk, as we got wet—but not cold. As I looked to one side I saw a rainbow forming. I turned to face it full on, as I called Sue's attention to it at the same time—in a moment it was a full-arched rainbow, stretching from the land not far from where we walked to many miles away; where we saw it again meet the land on a hillside. We started running as if we could reach the base of it near us and, energetically, we did. As we stopped for a moment, Sue grabbed my arm and pointed in the other direction, where another huge, complete rainbow grew. A double rainbow—and both full, complete arches.

"Wow, is this amazing?" Sue said as we stared at the heavenly painting.

"Yep, two at once. What energy that is. I wonder what it might be affirming for us?" I asked.

"I'm thinking how, long ago, I left a large part of my spirit here when I passed through," Sue began. "I just knew this would be a homecoming for me and a chance to regain that part of my spirit that dropped out."

"Good. Yeah, and for me it's eleven years since I have been here. And I thought I would never be here again—or even back to the West. Yet I had a dream, so many times, of being here once again. Short, but very powerful dreams. Part of what got me through the dark times. And now here 'we' are. I never saw that!" I said.

"No, me either," Sue agreed. "I hoped maybe one more trip here with girlfriends, sometime in the future. Now it's you and I as a couple. Moving into the future, towards whatever is there."

"An interesting future I'm sure. And this is the start of the Yellowstone connection this time and for down the road. This rainbow extravaganza is one hell of a start to that."

After a while, and some tears of joy and pain and loss and renewal, we headed back to the car and returned to Cody, where we attempted to get some sleep. Not very effectively attempted, but at least we rested.

The next morning we checked out and returned to the Irma Hotel and feasted at the breakfast buffet while we watched the early morning cowboys eat and prepare for their day. After breakfast we headed towards the park. We again took Route 14 and in about forty-five minutes we reached the park entry station. We had our annual National Parks pass, so we moved to the right and glided through after showing the pass to the ranger stationed there. We were here now; in the magical embrace of Yellowstone—the country's first national park and the home of the wolf packs. Finally reintroduced into the environment that was theirs before humans encroached on their lands. Long before even the Native American two-leggeds walked these sacred mountains and valleys. The spirit brothers and sisters of both Sue and I—the Wolf People. The people my primary animal guide, Wolf of Many Colors, was a member of. Ah. . . . . Hoka hey—it is a good day to die. At least a good day for some of the dark energy in us to die—energy we no longer needed.

We drove around the park like all the other visitors for a while and then stopped at the Rainbow Bridge Visitor Center. This seemed a very fitting place to stop after the panoramic display along the river the night before. We ended up in the gift shop, picking our way through the offerings. Sue found a large sun-catcher with a wolf theme she was examining, while I found a wolf-themed healing blanket whose energy I explored. I bought the blanket for Sue, knowing it was time for her to have a healing blanket for her own healing and for those she would now work with. We also purchased the sun-catcher—which is currently in a box awaiting our next stop on our current journey—and several other things before heading back to the car. As we carefully stowed these purchases, most of which were wolf-related—in our increasingly overstuffed vagabond car—we talked and decided to head for the north end of the park, the home of the wolves. Sue and I wanted to spend some days in the midst of this wolf energy.

We crossed over some of the high roads with no guardrails lining their sides, so I was rigidly focused, eyes straight ahead, white knuckles grasping the steering wheel. Heights, if I have not shared this before, are one of my great fears. In fact, I learned some time after this quest, I am not afraid of heights, but rather of falling. This it seems, is past life trauma coming back at me. Whatever the reasons for the fear, I am always physically, emotionally and mentally wasted after a high altitude outing. Sue, on the other hand, was looking out over the steep drop-offs, oohing and aahing all she saw. She was enjoying telling me just how steep and deep the drop-offs were, until I asked her to go quiet until we navigated through this area.

Once we cleared this mountainous region, we approached the North End Lodge, where we thought we might get a room. We booked no lodging this entire journey, knowing a quest required shift and change, not control. Being the height of tourist season, we knew we might have to leave some areas where there were no rooms. Yellowstone was one of those places we wondered what we might find. But we also knew that Great Spirit would again provide, as had happened in Custer, if we were meant to stay here awhile.

We went into the inn and got in line at the check-in counter. I began losing my patience as the woman at the counter was asking all types of questions, rather than checking into her room and allowing the long line of people to move forward. Total arrogance on her part and insensitivity to those in the line, both by her and the park clerk. Finally, the woman left and the line moved slowly onward. When our turn came, the woman behind the counter told us there were no rooms available and probably none anywhere in the park. I asked why they did not post this, rather than having people wait in line for twenty minutes? Especially since she was answering questions that the rangers could answer, which would not tie up the line as long. She did not welcome my advice and we left with me angry. I sat in the car trying to release this anger, which I knew did me no good and changed nothing. It was old 'Jim' surfacing—Jim who planned and controlled the moment. After a few minutes, I let it go and Sue and I looked at our options.

Sue wanted to be near the Lamar Valley where the wolves roamed, which was one reason we had tried the North End Lodge, located on the western side of the Lamar. We now headed to the Northeast Entrance to the park, near Cooke City, Montana, to see what we might find in accommodations. We had both spent time in the Lamar Valley in the past; Sue when she attended a wolf and bear workshop some years back, and me when I did some work around wolf education while at Colorado State. The Lamar Valley was also on the highway that went through Red Lodge on the east side of the park, the place where we ran our horse-packing business.

What a small, interconnected circle this planet and its creatures inhabit when we are awake to seeing the constant connections. Now is a time it is especially important to stay aware of these connections and ask Spirit how they are to help shape your Walk. I offer this to you for your consideration and use, brothers and sisters. Look for the spider webs of life. It will change many things for you in ways you might not anticipate, but change is good. Sometimes difficult, but not bad as much of our modern culture seems to preach.

We found no place to stay as we drove through this end of the park, nor did we expect any since only campsites were along this road and they were also full. As we approached the Northeast Entrance we hit road construction, which slowed us down and made us question this route. We saw a sign telling us the highway was closed four miles ahead due to the construction. We knew we needed to find something in Cooke City, just outside the Yellowstone Gate, or go back through the park and out the north end—something we had no intention of doing. We pulled into a small place with a handful of cabins and went in to see what was available. What we found was a very unhappy lady renting some very unhappy cabins. The energy was not good and the woman's 'heaviness' did not resonate with Sue. So even though she had one cabin left, we got in the car and drove off.

"We are probably nuts," I shared as we drove off. "We may find nothing now, but that place did not feel good."

"No, we couldn't stay there," Sue agreed. "It was so dark and heavy, and we don't need that. We have enough emotional turmoil in ourselves, we don't need to be in anyone else's negative energy, as well."

"How about this place across the way?" I asked as I saw a little store with a sign saying 'Rooms' almost hidden by the construction trucks.

"Sure, let's try," Sue agreed.

The little store—a few groceries and newspapers—was also the check-in place for the rooms they offered. A very nice man told us he had two rooms available—one in the old building that housed the store and the other was a cabin behind the building we stood in.

And he said, yes, we could have either for three nights. We looked at the re-modeled cabin and knew that was what we wanted, so we rented it for the three nights. That now put us just minutes from the park entrance and the Lamar Valley in a cabin with woods and a river behind us. Why had there been no rooms at the crowded, noisy North End Lodge? You answer.

This whole quest was about surrender and trust and honoring our spirits. That's why we made no plans and knew we would get what we needed each day, even if it was not always all that we wanted. In the case of this cabin, it was more than we had hoped for, so trust in Great Spirit had rewarded our efforts to stay in this region. Even choosing the cabin involved an additional level of trust. We could have rented the room in the main building for less money, at a time when our funds were very low, but we listened to our hearts and rented the cabin. Surrender and trust are not always easy, but they are always re-warding; I guarantee you this—and I guarantee very little in this life's journey.

We unpacked—prying what we needed out of the stuffed car—and rested for a while, then walked back to the store and asked about a place to eat. We didn't expect much in this tiny village, but it was worth asking. We had seen some lunchmeats and cheese in the store, if all else failed. Our host told us the little restaurant across the street was the best place to eat, so we thanked him and drove up the road to the center of the village first, to buy some food at the local store. Since we had a small kitchen in the cabin, we decided to cut expenses by doing our own cooking. We went back to our cabin and settled into its cozy, warm embrace for an hour or so and then walked across the street to the little restaurant we were told about. And had a great meal, served by a young girl with very happy, positive energy. All the vegetables were fresh out of their garden and the food was lovingly and expertly prepared. We gave thanks before and after this feast, then left the restaurant ready to explore Yellowstone at dusk.

Sue wanted to see the wolves this first night and wouldn't budge from that desire—so we began driving back through the Lamar Valley to the places I remembered where people waited with telescopes hoping for a look at the wolves. Volunteers would spend the summer there documenting and reporting the wolf activity they to the park for their databases. My excitement also began to grow as we drove through the beautiful valley to the 'wolf zone'. As we approached the area with the wolf watchers, we found a place to park; not an easy task, since dawn and dusk was when most of the wolves were sighted. We grabbed our binoculars and crossed to where people waited with their eyes trained on the stream and hill below them.

Several people became animated as we approached and we asked if they had seen anything. Sure enough, they directed us to the streambed off to our right. Training our binoculars, we picked up a pair of wolves walking the streambed in an area where there had been a recent kill. As I looked down at my first wolves in the wild in many years, my eyes teared up and I felt my throat tighten. I was finally once again where my heart and soul wanted to be—had to be to survive—in the wild watching nature and her creatures in action. I looked over at Sue and saw similar tears and knew she was experiencing feelings much like mine. This was the connection that had dictated we become a pair—ready and willing to do our work together whenever and wherever that was required. And for the first time these thoughts were not followed by my mind saying, "What about just Onyx and me up on a mountain at peace"? I knew when I had asked Spirit to allow me to continue my walk I was committing to whatever work was meant for me to do, not to sitting in safety and peace up on a mountaintop—no matter how alluring it may be.

Ironic that now Sue and I sit atop a mountaintop doing our work out of the fray—at least for this winter. The difference is, as I just said—"doing our work". Do not worry about where you are, friends, if you are serving the way you were meant to and feel you are in balance and harmony with the Universe. It's when you feel out-of-balance you need to begin questioning your place.

A few minutes later a third wolf, a large black one, joined the first two and the three trekked along the streambed. After another ten minutes or so, they disappeared over a ridge and down a gully. We finally breathed easier, without constantly holding our breath in awe of these magnificent animals. These animals that have played such a huge role in my spiritual growth from its very beginning; and who had played an equally big role in Sue's spiritual and emotional growth.

It was getting dark and we knew we had three more days here, so we headed back to the cabin for some hoped-for sleep. Our plan was to rise early and head back into the park.

As we drove and talked about the wolves and talked about the future, a huge black wolf sprinted from our left side and crossed right in front of the car and disappeared into the blackness of the woods beyond.

"God! Do you believe that!" I exclaimed.

"So beautiful; so powerful. And so real and grounded," Sue said.

We were again in awe—knowing this was a real, physical wolf and not one of the spirit wolves who visit us regularly. A wild wolf and it was just feet away from us; close enough we could have touched him if we were not in the car. A wolf whose pack's spirits had kept both of us connected to the Earth Mother in special ways for many years. And would continue to connect us with all things wild for the remainder of our walks—of this I was certain. Another gift and blessing from our Creator and our spirit guides; and another reason to be thankful.

We had had a full day—and then some—so we drove straight back to the cabin and got ready for bed. But first I asked to do a prayer of gratitude to Great Spirit. Sue was in total agreement, so we sat, burned sage and both spoke our words. Then we lay down and Sue covered us with her wolf-healing blanket and we closed our eyes, hoping to sleep. Sue actually was asleep quickly, as her breathing told me. I lay there with my mind spinning, trying to give control to my heart. I was so conflicted, my nervous system again began going crazy and pain visited me in ever-growing waves. I was grieving my wife and working through the guilt of my failure to 'heal' her, while joyous that Sue and I now walked together. Even if part of me still wanted no partner—ever. And so my mind whirled and my emotions leaped and my brain hurt.

Slowly I worked on the rocketing brain and felt my body back off the intensity of the pain, allowing me to examine all the pieces of this current puzzle of emotions I walked. I had no doubt Sue and I were to be a pair, even though I also had had little doubt I would take my spirit walk shortly after Bonnie took hers. That was different however, as I was given that chance and had passed on it.

My body was twisting and turning as my mind worked through these things, so I moved to a bed in another room and just let things come. I moved into wolf as Wolf of Many Colors came into my awareness and roamed the nighttime landscape. Then bear showed up and I entered his realm in his form. We walked the forest around the cabin and clawed a tree as we passed it to keep our claws sharp and ready. Some night fishing was next in the river on the Yellowstone River just behind the cabin. We waited patiently for grandfather fish to come by, passing on his smaller brethren as we did so. Then, with a quick but mighty sweep of our front paw, we scooped up our meal for the evening. Even as a bear, we gave thanks to the fish for providing this food so we might flourish.

My spirit and body shifted back to the bed I lay on, the pain going up and down my spine, which caused me to twist and turn. Then I was with bear again, suddenly, just sitting on the banks of the river—playing with the moonbeams hitting the surface. I seemed to be waiting for something—as bear—and my human mind told me it was big. Also that I would know it when I saw it. With that I was back in the cabin in Jim form. This night, I was in no way trying to induce this shape-shifting, but rather it was occurring on its own. Possibly the mental and physical pain I was in while in my human form, was seeking relief by having my consciousness and spirit shift to an animal guide. I don't know, but the sudden changes were a bit disconcerting, although they did not cause me any fear. When my mind, body and spirit pain gets as intense as it sometimes can, there is little I can fear. What, after all, can be worse than the wrenching, twisting, pulling pain I experience in these times? When I experienced this type of pain for days—even weeks—on end when I was journeying through my dark time of the soul, I wanted relief any way I could get it—just beseeching Spirit to let me end this life's walk. That never came, but the meaninglessness of fear from those times has stayed with me. Not that I don't still have fears—only a fool would claim that—but the fear of death was gone. Death, which had been my biggest, deepest fear, no longer could control me. Fear of falling—absolutely. Fearing I might not be able to help someone who asked—you bet. Fear of walking with Sue lest something happen to her, repeating history—I had that fear in a big way. Fear that the continuous, mind-snapping pain of my dark time was returning—oh yeah—I feared this to the point of dread. But fear of my own death: No—not any more.

My twitching and jerking muscles and limbs made me appear like a puppet on a stick I am certain, but when the pain gets this intense I never try to suppress it. I try to take the pain and move it to understand what it seeks to tell me, because every pain, every ache, every wound tells us something. We are free to listen and look at what it is telling us and usually, in so doing, release it or suppress it and ignore the messages, in which case it usually comes even harder and faster. Our choice—our human free will. Having gone both routes I assure you, circle, looking at what the pain is there to tell you and working through the messages is the much-preferred way to go in the long run. Although you might curse your own stupidity for going this route in the short haul, as you deal with the dis-ease the messages bring.

And suddenly I was one with Tatanka—buffalo. The buffalo that roam freely throughout the park in their slow, stately, unperturbed way. We—the buffalo and I as one—moved with measured grace through a field, munching high grasses as we went. I sensed we were very near our cabin, but could not see it as the buffalo was focused on the grass and not the human constructs near him. I seemed to be in this form for a long time—moving slowly, meticulously about my business; knowing no hunger or fear. Not rushing to anything or fleeing anything else. Just content with 'being'—a skill I had been trying master for a long time. With my ability to be in the past, present and future simultaneously it was difficult for me to just be present. This had frustrated my healers for many years now, but it was not something I could change quickly or easily.

Finally I found my awareness back in the cabin lying on my bed, my agonized gyrations greatly lessened. I got up and went to a window, pulling aside the curtain in one corner and looked out at the beginning of sun-up. That made it about six in the morning. I quietly approached the bed Sue was on—covered nicely by the wolf blanket—and heard her light snoring as she slept deeply. So I went back to my bed and stretched out, clearing my now fairly pain-free mind and relaxing. We had intended to get up at sun-up and head to the park, but I needed some rest and Sue was obviously getting the sleep she needed. I must have drifted off, because the next thing I knew we were both awakening at eight-thirty.

"You had an awful night," Sue said, approaching my bed.

"A painful one at least," I agreed. "The pain was really intense and I was shape-shifting half of the time, so I got little rest."

I had taught Sue the true meaning of shape shifting—as I had experienced it that night—not actually turning into an animal as some early settlers thought the Native's meant. So she asked, "Really. I'm not surprised the way you were twisting and groaning. What animals were you in or with?"

"My wolf guide first, as usual, then some others."

"Wow. I hope I learn to do that some day," she responded.

"You will if you really wish it and if it is for your best and highest good of the things you will serve," I answered, sounding like one of my old teachers again. Teachers I always wanted to rap in the head after they made statements like this. Ah, what goes around, comes around.

I didn't tell Sue much more than that, just because my spirit didn't seem to find it necessary. And when she asked for no more details I saw this was correct. So I went to the front door to see what the day was like, as Sue went to wash in the bathroom. I opened the door and stepped out on the front porch, stretching some of the pain out of my joints as I did so. And there not six feet from me directly in front of the cabin, stood a large, brown, imposing Tatanka. The buffalo I entered as I shifted—still munching grass and content to be what he was and where he was. I turned back into the cabin as he watched me with only slight interest.

"Sue. You got to come here. We have a visitor."

"In a minute. I'm washing my face."

"Okay, but you don't want to miss this guy."

And so she came out, wiping her face as she approached the door where I stood.

"Okay, what is it?"

"Look," I said, pointing.

She saw Tatanka and her eyes lit up. After the wolves, the buffalo of Yellowstone captivate Sue the most.

"He's handsome; and beautiful," was all she said as she stood there staring at him.

"Hmmm. You told me I was handsome. Now you call our shaggy-faced, pointy-nosed brother here handsome. I'm not sure if it was a compliment to me before," I said smiling.

He stayed in the front of the cabin until we left for the park—just enjoying his breakfast feed. And that evening and the next morning; he would be back—welcoming us to his home. I began some breakfast and Sue began filling water bottles for the days jaunt. I still didn't say anything about bear or buffalo from my shape shifting. Not for any reason—it simply didn't come up again as we prepared for our day. We were planning on heading into the park to explore as many areas as we were able. We had intended to begin with by looking for the wolves at dawn, but now that would obviously have to wait for dusk. But we still had a myriad of places to go and things to see; we expected a really eventful day. How eventful—neither of us foresaw as we sat over our morning coffee.

As we entered the park we saw a picnic area and pulled off to explore it. It was next to the river and deserted, so we stopped. We walked off in opposite directions along the river enjoying the beautiful morning and the energy of the place. I saw an eagle circling across the river from me as I walked. Sue, when I reached her again, told me she watched a deer moving along a small island in the river. Air and land relatives—fierce and gentle; predator and prey. Some nice differences there. Sue told me she had walked along the river feeling the energy of the park and the excitement of watching the wolves the night before. And I had watched the eagle thinking about my 'handsome' Tanaka brother of the night before and this morning. We were enjoying a nice break at this spot but as someone drove in, we headed to the car and pointed back into the park.

We had no destination in mind—we were just enjoying the journey. As we drove, a black bear ambled across the road in front of us and we began talking about the number of bears—in different places— we had already seen while on this quest. In a few more minutes we saw an area off to the side of the road where Sue wanted to take some pictures. A beautiful meadow running down to the Yellowstone River—all back-dropped by an imposing mountainside, which had whetted her appetite for photos. So we pulled over, she grabbed the camera, and we began to walk into the field. Sue began lining-up a shot, while I saw a path and began walking up it. Something was talking to my spirit about stopping longer here and following the path I had found further. But to explore further with more than I was carrying—which was simply water—and with Sue walking with me.

So I went to where she had just finished shooting some pictures and asked, "Hey, I'm getting a hit to follow that trail I was on for a ways. Are you game? And I also got we were to bring some 'things' with us."

"Sure, but what do we bring? The camera?"

"Yes, but more. Let's go back to the car and see what we feel," I answered.

When we got to the car we gathered up my Chanupa, sage and bowl, feather, and Sue's drum and tobacco, and began hiking the trail. Not too far along we could see the Yellowstone River down below where we stood. We hitched our regalia up on our shoulders and began hiking down to the river.

When we got to the river we found a large log to sit on directly beside the rushing, foamy water. Sue sat and took out her drum, which she began playing as she sang lodge songs in accompaniment. I decided to walk a little bit further to an area where deer and elk obviously came often, judging by their prints and droppings. While I was looking this area over I saw some dried bark near a log. I picked it up and realized the Earth Mother was gifting it to me to put in my Chanupa. I gave thanks, pulverized it between my fingers and added it to my tobacco pouch. This is often the way with sacred tobacco—being gifted tobacco, herbs or, like here, some bark, by a friend or the Earth Mother and then adding it to your pouch. The energy of the pipe expands and grows in this way.

I walked back to the log Sue sat on and sat, cross-legged, on the ground next to her only two feet from the river. Sitting cross-legged is something I have always been able to do—from when I was a little child. Long before I began walking the Good Red Road with my Native American friends. I can sit for hours with no pain or edginess. People ask me how I do this and I have no answer; it simply always has been so. And in a case like this, the ability served me well.

I began gazing around me—at Sue now drumming and singing, at the Yellowstone River, at the mountainside nearby, at the plants around me and up into the sky where Winged People swooped and soared. I was feeling very content, with less pain and emotional angst than I had felt in a long time. I unwrapped my Chanupa and slowly began loading it, praying to the seven directions for guidance as I did so. Sue continued her drumming and singing and, after the pipe was ready, I lit a large pile of sage in the shell—smudging the pipe, then the drum and finally Sue and I. I said a prayer of gratitude for this day and for Sue and I having come together.

I let my spirit enter the river, letting go of the bank and moving to the center so I might flow where the river took me. I cleared my mind as best I could and just let the sensations of the day wash over me. After about ten minutes, Sue put the drum aside and moved to sit next to me. I asked her to open the pipe and as she did, I said a prayer to the four directions and to Wankan Tanka asking them to be with us. Asking the Ancestors to come and honor the couple we had become added their energy to the circle. Thanking Father Sky for this wonderful day and for his connection to the Earth Mother was next. Finally as I began to speak to Mother Earth things shifted dramatically. My words changed and my prayer to the Earth Mother became the words of the Lakota wedding ceremony I had learned years before. Sue had begun drumming softly again and, as I told her what this ceremony was, I asked her to speak her heart. She tried, but could not voice any words—probably even more surprised than I was. If that was possible. But she nodded as she played her drum—letting the drum speak for her.

Sue's major issues with her throat chakra didn't stop us here. I understood her nods, her wet eyes and her drum speaking, so I again picked up the pipe and finished the words of the wedding ceremony. I puffed the pipe back into life, as it had sat between us for several minutes after Sue opened it, and let the good white smoke lift skyward. Then we passed it back and forth until it was complete. I said more prayers of gratitude as I emptied the ashes into the smudge shell and, lifting the pipe to Father Sky, asked for Sue and I to be as complete a couple as he was with the Earth Mother. Then, touching the bowl to the Earth Mother's mantle, I asked her to continue to walk with us and guide the two of us as she had guided me to this point. Now with the ceremony over, Sue and I moved close and hugged each other, crying as we sat on the banks of the Yellowstone River, now married in the Lakota way. We both realized, as we shared later, that we would remain a couple for the remainder of our walks here on the Earth Mother. This being less than two weeks after we had just been friends.

"Did you know you were going to do this for us?" Sue asked through her tears.

"Not until I began speaking to the Earth Mother. No idea at all; I am still stunned."

"I am thinking about the failed relationships I've had in the past," she continued. "But this is different. Our souls are joined; and our spirits can walk as one."

"Yes, it will be an amazing journey from here on I think," I told her. "Shall we go as Jim and Sue Graywolf?"

"Yes, of course," she answered.

We sat about an hour longer, just allowing ourselves to meld into the natural land around us—saying little more, as there was no more to be said. Then, we got up and slowly headed towards the car. I was still in shock, wondering what had prompted me to do this. And knowing of course, that Spirit had this in our paths and was just waiting for the proper moment. And, when it came, allowing the Earth Mother to facilitate it—the Earth Mother whom I had served my entire life.

Sue took some panoramic shots of the area as we left so we might have them for later. As if we would ever forget the land or the moment—but it is always good to have some tangible reminders of major events. And there could be no more major event for me than being married again. In the way of my Lakota family. I am a minister from an earlier part of my walk; a minister of the Universal Church. But the ceremony that came forward was the Lakota one—never any doubt or questioning of that in my mind. We knew we might decide to do the legal paperwork at a later date, but the wedding I just conducted for us was all we would ever need for our spirits. All of this and the day was still young!

We decided to take an auto tour of the park for a while, so we began by driving to the museum on the north side of the park, in Mammoth Hot Springs. It was a beautiful ride along the east end of the Lamar Valley and then up the road towards Mammoth where we saw deer and elk in groupings scattered everywhere. As we parked in Mammoth, a herd of elk surrounded the car, so we waited and just enjoyed their presence and their energy. Another visitor who had parked three cars down from us decided to get out and walk to the middle of the herd for a good picture. This in spite of the fact there were signs everywhere warning against this. So many tourists, especially those who are novices in the natural world, seem to think they are in Disneyworld and nothing can hurt them. I may have shared this before, circle, but it's worth repeating. Nature is not Disneyworld, which this tourist found out a minute later. A huge bull elk turned and faced him, with lowered head—a sure sign you are in the elk's 'space'. But Mr. Tourist, Mr. Totally Oblivious Tourist, did not have a clue. In fact, he seemed to think that this was the opportunity for a great elk photo—probably thinking the bull was posing just for him, as Mickey Mouse in Florida might do. In a few more seconds, the elk charged and the camera-toting two-legged fell over backwards in his shock. Luckily for him the elk was just making a warning run and not attacking. He stumbled to his feet, grabbed his camera from off the ground and shot to his car, where he sat for a few minutes and then took off.

Park Rangers at our National—and State—Parks have a name for tourists of this type: "lunchmeat". And a descriptive term for this type of behavior: "natural selection". Sometimes the names become brutally real, with some tourist posing his kids on animal's backs or approaching a bear eating his dinner with a camera. Each year 'natural selection' accounts for a number of tourists becoming 'lunchmeat'. Nature is beautiful, majestic, healing, vibrant, alive and revitalizing, but it is also dangerous at times and demands the respect of all creatures. Especially we humans, who are one of the weakest species of the animal kingdom. What? I'm, sorry—do some of you still think humans are somehow different? That we are not animals—intelligent animals—but still animals? Really? Oh, I see—you know people who still think this. Well if you do, just have them take a long hike in the wild lands of our Earth Mother. They'll lose that arrogance quickly—or become lunchmeat. I know, brothers and sisters, I preach to the choir here, but it is good to remember so you can give others guidance in how to view nature and the world in a more peaceful, sustainable way.

We had some lunch in Mammoth and then headed down the southeast side of the park—towards Old Faithful—and into the traffic. Everyone who comes to Yellowstone visits Old Faithful. Understandably so, as it is magnificent. But this causes heavy traffic in that section of the park during the tourist season. We were lucky this day that the traffic never came to a halt, but it still took an hour and a half to get there, stopping for views and short walks along the way. I had seen Old

Faithful many times, but Sue never had, so we waited it out. When we got there she decided we didn't need to fight the crowd and so we viewed the geyser from a little further back than was allowed—to the west of it. We watched her spout twice—allowing Sue time for some great pics—and then turned back to the car and a ride back through the center of the park.

We drove further down the west side to Grants Village and then turned up the center road and into a region of the park unlike the rest. The huge Yellowstone Lake is on your left as you travel this way, but so are many other lakes and waterways, making this the 'water element' of the park. We stopped at Fishing Bridge, got gas and some drinks, then decided to head up the middle road back to the Lamar Valley. As we drove we passed yet another black bear, playing some personal game on the side of the road. He held his foot and rocked—then got up and paraded up the hill behind him. Shortly after watching the bear we saw a side road we were again 'pulled' to take it. We parked at a railhead at the end of the road and decided, what the heck, let's take a hike. We began hiking uphill on the trail and were soon walking through meadows and very high grasses. It was beautiful and smelled like a dream, but it was fairly steep and we were high up and tired. As we thought about turning back a woman came our way from above, and told us of the beautiful lake at the top. That ended our talk of turning around.

When we reached the lake we sat on the ground and let the grasses caress our arms and legs—but not for long as the mosquito militia came out from their watery refuge and attacked us from the flank. It was truly a beautiful place and we sprayed some of the natural, plant-based insect repellent on ourselves and stayed a while longer. We drank our water as we slowly hiked around the lake and then began the downward trek to the car below. We hiked about three and a half miles and I had the requisite—for me—two hundred mosquito bites to prove it. But it was a fantastic way to spend the afternoon.

When we regained the car, we drove back to the Lamar Valley region where we had seen the wolves along the streamed the evening before. We lucked out again and found a parking space, got out and approached the swarm of humans with telescopes, binoculars and cameras who again lined the roadside. They looked like a milling, invasive mass of paparazzi hoping to get a shot of Johnny Depp or Winona Ryder. What they did get to see—and us with them— were two black wolves down below, possibly the same two from the night before. We watched them run and play across the fields next to the river, down a slope from the human horde. My eyes teared as I watched their joyful interactions. Two of the wolves our kind had almost hunted and harassed to extinction—still hunted with a hatred and vengeance without reason—lucky to see them here in the park, where only cameras now were aimed at their heads. I gave thanks to Creator for allowing me this visual gift.

I wondered what the wolves thought of the massed two-leggeds looking down at them? Maybe. . . . .

"Ah, crazy humans. They hunt us, but it is they who face extinction if they do not change their ways soon. And we will still be here. We will always be here. Here to welcome those humans who do change and live in harmony with nature. Here to hunt, eat and raise our young—helping maintain the balance of nature for the Earth Mother we had before the tall, slow ones came. The human 'unbalancers'. For now—let them gawk, let them take their pictures—we will simply ignore their energy and their presence."

We stayed and listened to one of the wolf enthusiasts speak about the movement of the packs this summer. It was interesting, but when he finished it was 8 PM and we were tired, so we headed for the cabin. We made and ate some dinner and did some healing work on each other, as we both had emotions running wild. The healing blanket I had purchased for Sue was already coming in very handy.

The next day we slept in, got up and spent some time with our relative Tatanka, who still worked the land around the cabin. Then we ate and gathered our supplies for another day in the park. We drove and hiked all day and again went to the area where we had seen the wolves in the evenings. This time although we waited a couple of hours, we saw no wolves. We had used our allotment of 'watching wolves in the wild' for this trip, I assumed, and so we went back to the cabin for our last night in Yellowstone—at least for now. The next morning we got up early, finding our wooly buffalo friend right outside our door. We made coffee and threw some bacon and eggs in a pan—letting them fry as we began packing. It was time to move on to the next adventure— the next part of this quest—and we were ready.

After breakfast we drove the short two miles to the picnic area we had visited the first day and went for one more walk along the Yellowstone River before we left. In my mind, I went back through the wedding ceremony I had conducted and connected with that moment when I said the final words with my heart. I was walking this stretch of the river as I did this, but my spirit walked that other—where Sue still sat drumming and singing, unaware I was about to give us both one of the biggest surprises of our lives. And I again thanked Creator for allowing this to happen, as I asked the Ancestors on the spirit road to look after us as we walked forward—especially Bonnie, my wife and resident of that realm for a little over a year and a half, and my dad, Jim, a resident there much longer. I felt the energy of those two, and others circling around honoring my request, even as I thought it.

Back to the cabin and a farewell blessing for our hairy friend, bags crammed back into our ersatz gypsy wagon, a stop at the front building to buy water and drop off the keys and we headed West over the pass to Red Lodge, which was now open. Out of the magic of Yellowstone and into the magic of. . .whatever was next.

19 | Horse Whisperer Speaks

As we drove up and over the pass to Red Lodge, my cell phone signal reappeared after being absent for three days. I decided to call home to Sedona and see how Onyx the Soap Opera, was working out. When I had first gotten to New Hampshire I had called Jesse and Abbey to see how they were making out with Onyx. I didn't worry about the four-legged behaving, but the two-leggeds gave me some concerns—and I was right. They had gotten into a battle the day I left. Abbey had asked her daughter and grandson to stay with her for that night and Jesse had come home and was furious. Abbey and her family left in a huff, and she and Jesse had not talked since. I asked questions of both and asked for some help since it would be a long time from that point until I got home. Before I left Sedona I had told Abbey she was welcomed to sleep over if she wished while helping with Onyx—but never envisioned her 'bringing the family' along, if only for a night. And Jesse had flown off the handle, making things worse. I'm sure Onyx made some popcorn and watched the Jesse and Abbey Show with a smile across his face.

I finally got them to agree to take turns walking Onyx until I returned and was told they had worked out a schedule when I called this day. Jesse had decided I had sided with Abbey and was angry with me now as well. What I had attempted to tell him was—"hey, why such a furious explosion from you"? Telling her calmly that you also rented there and a whole family moving in invaded your space might have been a better approach. Then again, Abbey is bullheaded and often righteous in her opinions—maybe that would have failed. But at least it would have been a better starting point. As we spoke I heard they had a truce—if an uneasy one. But at least, Onyx was being cared for and I would deal with the humans when I got back. After hearing everything was okay, I hung up shaking my head.

"What's wrong?" Sue asked.

"Just Jesse and Abbey at each other again. I swear Onyx is the only one in that house right now with any sense. Jesse is really out of control with his anger, but I can't do much from here."

"Is he alright?"

"Yeah. They have written a schedule so Onyx is cared for and so they don't have to see each other. So childish. Oh well, Onyx is okay."

"It will be a mess when we get there, I'm sure," Sue said.

"I know, but I hope to just let it go. We'll see. Anyway, I had this vision of Onyx making popcorn and sitting eating it as he watched the Jesse and Abbey show. Smile on his face—in wonder of human behavior—or misbehavior."

Sue laughed and we continued on our way. Soon we passed through Red Lodge and on up the Chief Joseph Highway—the highest highway in the country, reaching altitudes of 8,900 feet over its forty-five to fifty mile length. Although the highway is fairly short it takes a couple of hours due to the switchbacks along the way. And I don't see how you can drive through the beauty of this region without stopping for the views or some pictures. So we slowly inched our way along, stopping as Spirit moved us. Finally we approached the southern end, very close to Cody where we had stayed just four nights—and several lifetimes—ago. We turned and headed to Thermopolis, cruising through the badlands along the way. The jagged, rugged, harsh badlands; beautiful in their own way—much like the stark beauty of the desert.

We stopped for lunch in Thermopolis at a little café, where we had an unexpectedly good meal. Thermopolis is another town I had been through many times—and had stayed in a few times as well. Thermopolis was at the head of the Wind River Basin and a good place to explore. It was a town of hot spas and water. Sue and I walked around, looking at the spas and the land around them. After a while we decided not to stay in Thermopolis for the night, which was fine with me since past memories were already giving me emotional pain. We headed down the Wind River highway, through another area of rivers and peaks whose grandeur is breathtaking. As we began heading down the road, we looked to the river and saw an eagle landing on a treetop. Sue immediately fell in love with the views, so we stopped several times as we traversed the road. As we came out the bottom of the ravine—about fifty miles later—we decided to try and get to a town near where Stanford Addison, the horse whisperer, lived. Looking at a map we saw Lander, Wyoming was our best choice.

We had first learned of Stanford about nine months earlier when a friend gave me Lisa Jones' book *Broken: A Love Story*. Stanford was a Northern Arapahoe tribal member but, more importantly, an extraordinary healer and medicine person. He was in his early fifties when we met him and a quadriplegic since a terrible auto accident had left him that way as a teen. Stanford had amazing healing gifts, which Spirit gave him when he lost the use of his limbs. He was a horse whisperer— he could speak to and hear the horses—and a horse gentler as well as a traditional healer. People came from all over Turtle Island—and beyond—seeking his aide with their horse's problems as well as their own cancer, bipolar disorder, back pains and all other ailments of the human mind and body. He was, we would soon find out, a gentle but strong man, sure in his abilities and powers. And here we were attempting to connect with this man—unannounced and without even a clear idea of what we sought from him. But that was now how we walked—in the moment with little planning, but a great deal of trust in the Creator.

We arrived in Lander later that afternoon and realized it was the only place to stay in the region, surrounded by desert and Indian lands. So we went looking for a motel, with a limited number of options to explore. The first motel we entered had a line of people waiting at the check-in counter. A young woman asking the clerk about a room did not speak very good English and the clerk was being totally disrespectful and rude. This clerk radiated depression and anger, which she was obviously taking out on someone she felt 'beneath' her. And her energy and face spoke to someone who was also disrespected often.

Has anyone ever seen this behavior before, circle? What do you think of it? Yes, yes, you are all correct—we see it all too often. Those who seek to control and those with low self-image denigrate anyone they see as different or weak. Ah, the things we humans must change!

The clerk finally told this woman she could have a room, but would have to pay cash in advance. Why? Because she did not speak English well? An excuse to allow this poor, pitiful creature behind the counter to exert some semblance of control over another. As people waited, many with disgust showing on their faces, I watched the entire group thinking about these things I am sharing. Two people in the line turned and left, their displeasure obvious. We left and decided to walk around town to release some of the dark energy of that place. As we walked, we found everyone we met seemed angry and dark. Not the kind of place we would ever want to live—or even stay except for our desire to meet Stanford.

We found a motel room near dark and carried our bags in, not knowing if we were staying a night or longer. Not even knowing if we could find Stanford's ranch, as directions were not available to us, except a general county road number. After unpacking, we went to the laundry on the first floor. We washed the clothes and when we tried to dry them we saw the dryers were old and not drying things quickly. We would need another forty minutes or so to have our clothes come out dry. A man came to lock the door as we stood there, since the room closed at eight. Sue explained the problem with the dryer and he behaved as if we spoke another language. Finally he agreed to allow us to feed more quarters in the machine, but we would have to retrieve our things in the morning as he was locking the door right then. Another very angry person taking the chance to control someone else in a small, petty way and so demonstrate to himself that he 'was someone'. What a truly negative place we had landed in. But still we felt we needed to try and meet with Stanford, so we fed our quarters in and went back to our room as the warden locked the cell door where the dryer was housed.

In the morning we stopped at a café for some breakfast, where we again felt unwelcomed and barely tolerated, and then headed in the direction of the Northern Arapahoe reservation and Stanford's ranch— very happy to be driving away from Lander. We began breathing more easily as the car moved out of the town and headed across the prairie to the north. When we reached the rez we took out the address we had, but quickly realized none of the roads had any name signs. I had a GPS function on my phone, but was unsure how to enter the address. Sue wanted to stop somewhere and ask people if they knew Stanford and where his land was, but I did not wish to do that—an odd quirk I had always had. I always hid this quirk with, "Men don't ask directions, we find things", but I knew it was my oddity at work here. We agreed to try to find Stanford on our own before stopping and asking our way—if we could even find someone able and willing to direct these two white faces in the red land. We decided to do a 'drive about' first, getting a lay of the land and an idea of where things were located.

We hit a paved road and turned to our right towards a hill in the distance. As we crested the hill we saw over 100 tee-pees spread out in a valley to our left. Our mouths dropped open and we looked at each other in awe. "Where" were we? "When" were we? This looked like a village out of the past, especially here on the prairie.

"Oh wow. We are going to get a chance to attend this gathering," Sue immediately said. "and we get to meet Stanford."

"No, I doubt that luck. Stan will be down there at the gathering I suspect. It's big. Must be a hundred tee-pees or more. I doubt it's an event open to the public, but let's go check it out," I said.

We drove down off the hill and lost sight of the gathering as we did so, but in a minute we saw it again as we got closer. We turned up a side road, hoping to drive around it looking for a gate. We came across the gate with a sign above it proclaiming 'Northern Arapahoe Nation Sundance'. Sue was excited to go, but she knew someone would have to invite us as guests. The people entering the gate were almost all native and in groups—probably the families of those dancing. For those of you unfamiliar with the Sundance, let me add some information here. Some of these facts I found in books, while the rest is from the teachings of my elders.

The Sundance is a tribal ceremony primarily used by Great Plains Indians, although it's practiced by many other tribes today as a prayer for life, world renewal and thanksgiving. On a personal level, someone may dance to pray for a sick relative or friend, or to determine their place in the universe, while on a larger scale, the Sundance serves the tribe and the earth. Indigenous people believe that unless the Sundance is performed each year, the earth will lose touch with the creative power of the Universe, thereby losing its ability to regenerate.

The Sundance was outlawed in 1895, partly because certain tribes inflicted self-mutilation in the form of piercing as part of the ceremony, which settlers found gruesome, and partially as part of a grand attempt to westernize Indians by forbidding them to engage in their ceremonies and speak their language. Sometimes the dance was performed secretly. But as a rule, younger generations were not being introduced to the Sundance and other sacred rituals, and a rich cultural heritage was becoming extinct.

The Sundance consists of various elements. There is the ritual of the sacred pipe—the Chanupa, the purification ceremony, monthly prayer ceremonies, and a yearly ritual. Different tribes honor and practice all or some of these ceremonies based on their tribal practices. The Sundance chief offers the prayers from the sacred pipe to the four directions, as well as the earth and sky, on a daily basis. The purification ceremony is performed before the Sundance and again afterwards. Monthly Sundance prayer ceremonies take place twelve times a year, at the time of the full moon. During this ceremony, two medicine bundles are brought in and opened, and ritual objects are taken out and placed on an elk or moose skin in the middle of the floor. Heated coals are brought into the lodge, incense is placed on the fire, and special songs are sung to help carry the prayers of the smoke to the spirit world.

In addition to the twelve monthly ceremonies, there is a three to four day Sundance that takes place each summer, usually in July. The preparation is too detailed to describe here, but involves building a lodge from a large Cottonwood tree, with a forked branch in the middle. Twelve upright poles are placed about thirteen paces from the center pole in a circular fashion, with rafter poles connecting the outside of the circle to the inner pole. From an aerial view, this appears as a wagon wheel with a hub in its center. This symbolizes the tribe (on the outside of the circle) trying to find their way straight to the center.

It was the four-day ceremony and dance of the Northern Arapahoe we had come upon, a dance a full year in the making and a dance some Native Americans want no non-natives at. Knowing this is why I thought we had no chance of attending the Sundance and only slightly less than no chance of meeting Stanford Addison, a Sundance attendee I was certain.

"What do we do now?" Sue asked.

"I don't know. My cell phone wouldn't work when I tried it, so GPS is out," I answered. "Maybe I'll try it again—that was an hour ago when we were on the other side of the rez."

So I turned my phone back on with little hope of any signal. Cell phones almost never work on any reservation. Seems the phone companies often deal with these lands like separate entities, which means the primary carriers often don't cover them—but I tried anyway.

"Hey, look at this," I said, holding the phone towards Sue. "The darn things picking up a signal. A weak one, but a signal. The address we have is so vague, but the phone is a surprise, so let's try the GPS."

Surprise number two came when the GPS started spewing out directions. "I'll be damned, we're getting something. Let's follow, eh?" I said.

"Nothing to lose," Sue responded. We pulled out of the Sundance property and turned up the narrow road the GPS indicated. We followed the directions for about fifteen minutes, getting in increasingly less populated areas. Finally, as we pulled down a lane with several horse properties off of it, I thought we might be getting close. Sue spotted a trailer with a wheelchair next to it, thinking it was probably Stanford's.

We pulled in and a native woman who was outside the trailer said, "No, this is not Stan's place. His is at the end of the road. Down that a way," she continued as she pointed at a small house at the end of the lane.

"Thank you," Sue told the woman and then we continued forward.

As we approached the house she had pointed out, we saw a horse ring behind it with five or six horses in sight. We thought we had the place now. It was a ramshackle building, as many on the rez are, with a small trailer off to the side where someone else obviously slept, since there was bedding hanging over its railing. Five or six dogs ran out from under cover as we pulled in—barking and growling in a fairly unfriendly fashion. They looked like pit bull mixes, so we needed to be aware of them if we got out of the car. A ramp was built on the side of the small house, leading up to the door. Stanford's way in and out I felt certain. The dogs disappeared around the side of the house and we got out—with Sue thinking we would get a Sundance invite and me doubting we would even meet Stanford.

We stepped out into hot, dry, dusty heat, feeling like we were stepping into another time and place—having no idea what an adventure we would have while at the Addison Ranch. We headed towards the house and began walking up the ramp towards the door. A pit bull appeared half way up the ramp, with a bloody muzzle, making Sue feel suddenly very uncomfortable and apprehensive about this whole visit idea. Sue is amazingly connected to animals, as am I. It is another reason we mesh so nicely. But her connection is at a level I have seldom experienced. That, coupled with having never seen this sort of occurrence before, put her in an emotional swamp. Unfortunately animals are not always as well-treated on the rez as would be desirable and I had seen dogs injured and killed in the past. I didn't like the savagery of it, but had learned I had to accept it if I were to spend time on Indian lands. Another dead pit bull lay dead further up the ramp.

As we went further up the ramp I looked down on puppies running all about our legs. This would be another harsh lesson in reservation life. One of the puppies over by the side was dead. It turned out it had been killed in a fight with the other dog and the family was unaware of it when we arrived. They took the dog off for burial shortly after, once they saw him lying there. The mother of the puppies, to make matters worse, had been killed by a car. The puppies—four of them left alive—were only four or five weeks old and too young to be without a mother. A sad introduction to the ranch.

A woman came to the door when we knocked who introduced herself as Stan's niece. "No, sorry. Uncle Stan is at Sundance—Daniel, his son, dances. But let me call him, I think he will want to meet you."

She picked up her cell phone and hit the memory button, waiting for Stanford to come on. She spoke to him as we respectfully moved further away, giving her some privacy.

"Uncle Stan will be heading this way now. His chair was losing power and he needs to charge it up for the dances later. He wants to see you and says you should wait."

"Thank you. We would be happy to wait," Sue told her.

"You can come in if you want," she offered.

"No, we'll walk and see the horses if that is okay?" I said.

And so we walked the land for about forty-five minutes while Stanford was heading our way. The heat was getting to us and we were thinking of going back to the car, not wanting to infringe on Stanford's niece in the house, when a pick-up truck, spitting dust and stones from its rear tires, came roaring into the parking area. Two young Native youth jumped out, whipped around behind the truck, pulled out a ramp and pushed out a wheelchair. The wheelchair was a heavy, bulky motorized model and these two young men—part of Stanford's posse—had to wrestle it to the ground. Then they were ready to get Stanford out of the car and into the chair and we were finally about to meet the horse whisperer himself.

One of the young men—Stanford's nephew we learned later—reached into the truck and lifted Stanford out and placed him, very gently, into the wheelchair. Stanford was very thin—skinny—with frail with arms and legs over which he had little or no control, but he had a stockpile of spiritual energy. Energy we could feel from the fifteen feet we stood away from him. His nephew walked to the front of his chair and took an unfiltered cigarette from a pack in his shirt, which he inserted into a makeshift holder attached to Stanford's chair. Then he lit it as Stanford gave it a puff to get it going. The nephew looked up at us and nodded and we approached Stanford to introduce ourselves.

"Hi, Mr. Addison, we are Jim and Sue and have come to meet you. Thank you for coming to see us. We understand your son is dancing at the Sundance down the road," I said.

"That's okay. Wheelchair battery went dead, so I had to come home a while anyway. Come on in the house and get comfortable or walk around the ranch, while my niece gets me comfortable in my bed."

At that point he saw the dogs and gave orders to remove them and bury the dead ones. The other young man from the truck jumped right to this task and we realized this was the norm at the Addison ranch—his family and friends jumped to the task as soon as the words left Stan's mouth; and they did it with obvious love for the man.

We hung around outside for a while so as not to get in the way in the little house and then Stan called us in. We went through the small living room and into Stan's bedroom. It was a small, cluttered dark little space, with a straight back chair to his right and fans pointed at him, blowing air over his body. We squeezed into the room and Sue took the chair as I stood behind her. Stan seemed to still be radiating energy, which seemed to almost light the room up a little—a phenomenon I had come across a few times before with elders.

"How do you know me?"

"Through the book *Broken: A Love Story*," Sue answered him.

"Did you like it?"

"Loved it," Sue responded.

"I've read it twice," I added.

"You like horses?"

"Yes," I said, "my sister has seven horses and I did some Eagala training with her—using horses as healing partners. I'm just a novice, but I experienced how powerful this type of work is."

"I love the clear energy of horses," Sue said.

"Good," Stan answered. "I would like you to stay. I have to get some rest now. I tire easily sometimes. Then you will go to Sundance with the family and me later. My son is dancing. You will sit in the Addison tent."

"Thank you, Stan," Sue said. "We would be honored. What can we bring?"

"Yes, thank you uncle," I followed up. "Will there be any lodge this week? It has been many weeks and we could use a cleansing."

"Yes, probably Monday. If you can stay, you will come in."

"We'll stay," Sue answered for us—no need for discussion between us on this.

"You could bring some fruit and some things to drink, maybe," Stan continued. "Something for the table in the family tent; something to share with others. Okay?"

"Sure," I said. "We would be happy to do this. Where can we get some food here on the rez?"

"My niece will tell you," he answered, obviously getting more tired. "So you will go to Sundance tonight and tomorrow, and Monday we will do lodge. And then we will see what more. Good. Let me rest now."

We edged out of the room and Stan called out for his niece. She went in and turned on the tiny portable television on top of his bureau. Then he called out for his nephew, who came running, went into his room and helped him light another cigarette. Over the next three hours Stan rested. During the times we were at the house, Stan would call out a name and the person would get whatever Stan asked for. A man in a wheelchair for thirty years—still a lucky man, blessed with those who loved him and never tired serving him as he served so many others. Do you see the teaching here my friends? The way the circle is meant to work? Just think on it and see all the lessons coming from this story of Stan and his family circle.

Stan was totally welcoming us—to the point of inviting us to spend the remainder of the Sundance in his family's tent. This is an honor, especially to people he did not even know. And yet we both sensed he knew us as soon as we sat together—the same way we felt about him. Our spirits had meshed in a good way. I was still feeling a little uncomfortable by this open welcome and fearing we were putting him out, but this was gone in a few minutes as we sat on the sofa in the living room getting to know the others in the house. As we sat there a lot more people began arriving, along with many children. We could hear Stan watching television in the other room and I tried to strain to hear what he had on. I thought Pow-Wow Highway or Smoke Signals or some other Native American movie. What I heard was an old John Wayne movie. The irony of my expectations and Stan's choice made me laugh inside, where my laughter would not be questioned.

As we sat there a little girl, about five years old with beautiful dark, wavy hair and deep brown eyes came in and immediately came over to us. Her name was Basile and she was one of Stan's grandchildren. And she was another Crystal Child. Looking us right in the eyes and crawling up on Sue's lap, she did not want to leave us. She radiated a glow of wonderment and freedom—a free spirit meant to roam where she felt the need to be. After a few minutes she got up and took our hands to take us out to see the puppies. The three of us played with the puppies for a while then she again took our hands to guide us down the dirt lane leading to Stan's ranch. It was a tour of the swimming hole she now took us on, pointing to the rope swing hanging over the hole. Next she took us to the horse corral so we could see the horses closer up. As we all walked she picked up small stones and flowers along the way and gifted them to us, one at a time. She stuck to us like glue the entire time Stan napped, beginning to talk a lot as we walked further and asking us questions, waiting patiently for us to answer. The other seven or eight children now at the ranch came and went, ran and played, laughed and cried—but not Basile, she was with us.

"You doing okay?" I asked Sue, while Basile went inside to use the bathroom.

"I guess so. It's a lot. I'm wondering what I'm doing here," she answered, a little nervously.

"You ain't in Kansas anymore, Dorothy," I said with a grin.

"I know and it's taking some getting used to it all. So much is happening here and my emotions are on a roller-coaster ride."

I had been with many Native American communities and families in the past, spending a lot of time on different reservations. So I was used to the culture clash you need to accept. This was a first time for Sue and so many things were coming at her, she was unsure how to react.

"I'll be fine, though. Just think—we are invited to the Sundance. Guess I was right on that one."

"You sure were," I said. "I'm still amazed."

"But for now I see the kids all running around doing things I would have been punished for—and my son would punish his kids for—and it's hard not to say or do something. But I am realizing that is not my place. They are allowed to be free. And that is good."

"I agree," I said. "I think if they got in real mischief, you would see the adults appear quickly. At least that's been my experience in the past, in other indigenous communities."

After a while we went back inside since it was getting very hot and dusty and we needed a drink. We sat back on the sofa, chatting and listening to Basile, who was still with us. Some time later, over the sound of another Western, we heard Stan call for his nieces. One helped him change his position and the other helped him light another cigarette. Most of the time Stan was awake he seemed to have a cigarette in his mouth, probably one of only a few pleasures his tortured body could enjoy. In a few minutes the television was turned off and one of Stan's nieces—the obvious 'drill sergeant' of the family came out and said Stan wanted to see us again.

We went in and squeezed next to his bed, the chair now full of blankets. It wasn't quite as dark now, with the curtain pulled aside, and we could see his face as we spoke. We gifted him sage and sweet grass we had brought along and he thanked us as he called out for his niece, who he had take the gifts and bring them to another room.

"What do you know about Native customs? Who were your teachers, Jim?" he asked, watching me as I answered.

"My first teacher was Little Thunder, a brother now, who brought Yellowhair, from Denver, in to run lodges for us. And I worked most with Two Bears. Out of Boulder. They are all Lakota. I've had Blackfoot and Wiyot and other teachers. And many others in other countries, especially Mayan."

"I know Yellowhair. He is a good healer. And I have heard of Two Bears, but I do not know him. These are good teachers."

"And you, Sue?" he asked.

He shifted his inspection to Sue as she began telling him of being a Reiki Master and the native people in the East she had worked with as Basile came in. Stan immediately broke the conversation and turned to her. She climbed up in Sue's lap and Sue made a comment about how Basile was a little angel.

Stan nodded solemnly and said, "Yes. She is."

Stan called Basile to come sit with him and the conversation now included the four of us. After we all talked for a while Basile slid down off Stan's bed and headed to the door. She stopped on the way to give Sue and then me a flower. Then she smiled and headed into the living room. At the moment she gave us flowers and smiled at us I knew we had "passed the test". She was Stan's barometer to see where our hearts truly were.

"Time to get ready," Stan, said. "Time to get back to the Sundance."

As the people in the house began gathering what they would need more cars began pulling in, including one driven by Stan's sister—Frenchie. We were saying hello to everyone and sharing names around as everyone was getting organized. It took another hour before everyone felt ready to go and Stan was comfortable we had all that we needed.

"I need to see if the puppies have food and water before we go," Sue said, in a tone I knew there was no point arguing with.

She was obviously struggling to understand and accept a new culture to her, so if checking on the puppies made her feel better, so be it. We went outside to look for the little guys and found them near the trailer. They had plenty of both food and water so Sue felt better about leaving—as did I.

Finally everyone, including Stan after his nephews got him into the truck, started leaving, heading for the Sundance. We pulled out and followed Stan's truck. We were really hungry, having only munched on a few corn chips all afternoon. When we got to the Sundance entrance gate—the same one Sue and I had pulled up to hours earlier—Stan spoke to the attendants and pointed back at us. We followed his truck through, waving to the staff as we entered. I was glad to see them wave back, a good indication we would be welcomed. We continued to follow Stan's truck, right into the middle of three hundred plus tee-pees. We bounced over a rutted road and pulled up next to Stan behind the Addison family tent. The food tent next to the family tent was surrounded by cut saplings, to keep some of the heat off of the food waiting inside. We entered and were welcomed by Stan's family members already there. We met Stan's brother, Tony, and a good-looking young Native man and a young man of mixed Native and black blood. We all stood chatting as Stan's uncle approached and said hello. He was a really pleasant man who wanted to talk. So we stood and shared our thumbnail stories for a few minutes. After some time we had met all those who were present when we arrived and those who continued to arrive after us. As we were getting ready to sit, three teenage girls said they were going to the food tent to get some food. The food tent sold food for the families who had not yet prepared their food in their family tents.

"Ladies, can I come along? We are really hungry," I said as the girls prepared to leave.

"Yes," one girl said simply and I followed them to the food tent nearest us.

To my delight this tent had Indian Tacos—one of my favorite foods. For those unfamiliar with Indian Tacos I offer my sympathy— and I will give a little description. First you take a hot fry bread and put it on a plate. What? You don't know what fry bread is? You must be new members to the circle, friends. I'm kidding. Fry bread is flour, buttermilk and a little water whipped into a dough and left to settle for a few hours. Then a flattened ball of it is dropped into boiling fat and allowed to fry that way—deep-fried. Then it is set to dry and is ready to eat in a few minutes. It can be eaten as a desert with cinnamon on top and honey dripping over the sides and down your fingers. Or as the base for Indian Tacos. For these you layer beef crumbled and fried with sauces and onions on the fry bread, followed by shredded lettuce, tomato, onion, beans and grated cheese. Then you take three large napkins—one for in your shirt collar, one on your lap and the third as a back-up and you prepare to taste something too good to describe. Ah, how my mouth waters now.

I told the girls to order and I would treat them, which made them much happier that I had come along. Then I ordered an Indian Taco for both Sue and I and a couple of bottles of water and headed back to the Addison tent.

Others were also bringing food back to the tent, so we ate and talked for a while. Then Stan said we should go over to the dance— it was time. We wandered our way through the teepees, following the sound of drums to the Sundance lodge—a big circular area surrounded by tall saplings with green, leaf-covered branches. The entrance gate was pointed to the East—the place Grandfather Sun rises in the morning. The gate was festooned by strips of cloth in the four colors—red, black, yellow and white—with other strips tied periodically around the enclosure. An arbor was built about fifty feet from the Sundance circle with two young women holding smudge pots next to it—one on each side. We got in line at the arbor and waited our turn to be smudged so we would be cleansed to enter the area around the Sundance lodge. There were people everywhere watching the dancers, talking and sitting on rugs on the ground—lost in meditation or prayer. Almost all were Native-looking people, with almost no obviously non-red faces in the crowd. Of course assuming someone's ethnic background is a fool's game—and I have been wrong more often than right. What I can say and just did, is that here, on this day, there were few non-red people.

This was a huge Sundance, with over 150 dancers and over a dozen drummers at any given time. A handful of dancers were returning to the circle, their helpers—or runners—with them. Each dancer has a runner who is their support should they require aid. And, when they leave to use the restroom, the runners also go with them for support. Sundancers prepare for this ceremony over the course of the preceding year and usually commit to dancing three years in a row. The Sundance is not a spectator pageant—it is the most sacred of the ceremonies with many tribes. It is for this reason that we felt so honored to be invited—and wanted to be so careful to respect all that needed respecting. The dancers had started dancing at sunrise on Thursday and would dance, non-stop, until sundown Sunday. Stop and think about that for a moment, friends of the circle. You dance without food or water, suffering for the people. Before the dance begins a sweat lodge ceremony is held to help the dancers purify and prepare. And often another lodge when the dance is over. This is the lodge Stanford had invited us to this coming Monday.

This dance is no small feat and no small commitment to make. You dance for all the people—their healing and well-being, never for yourself. This is much like sweating in the lodge or the prayers offered when we open the Chanupa. It was now Saturday, so these dancers were being sorely tested by this point-in-time. In the traditional way, the chest is pierced on the left and right and sticks passed through the holes—one on each side. Then leather thongs are tied to these and, some six feet behind, a buffalo skull attached. The dancers are to drag the skull as they dance until the sticks break through the flesh—which indicates rebirth and renewal. Most of the Sundances I have attended no longer had the dancers piercing in this way, although there were usually a few who did. Two dances I had attended in the past—smaller dances—did include the dragging of the skull. Dancers, helpers and drummers were all in full regalia, with the dancers painted in many colors. I have found it quite a stirring ceremony and one that quickly speaks to your heart.

"This is amazing!" Sue exclaimed, in awe of the beauty and energy of the dance.

"Sure is," I leaned over and responded. We had spread a blanket and were sitting on the ground, amongst many other people on blankets, to the left of the entry gate.

"Listen to the whistles. How they blend with the drums," she quietly spoke, gazing through the gate at the dancers within.

In addition to the drums and the singing and chanting that sometimes broke out, eagle bone whistles were played by various people around the site. The high-pitched sound issuing from these complemented the deep beats of the drums. The entire scene and all its components created a mesmerizing effect. So we sat and just absorbed everything around us.

"I feel completely comfortable and welcomed here," Sue whispered. "I'm surprised because I look so completely different than the others here."

At six foot tall, thin and blond Sue was right—she would probably never serve as a model for Native American pictures. I, on the other hand, could blend in to many cultures with my darker olive skin and black hair. The giveaway was my beard, which was not normal on Native American people and my height, at six foot one, which was not the norm when I worked with Central American cultures. But here, as Sue noted, we felt welcomed and that is always a good thing.

After we watched the dancers and listened to the drums for a couple of hours we decided to go back and socialize at the Addison clan camp. It was after dark by this time and not easy seeing where we walked, nor finding our way through the maze we had taken to get to the dance circle. I was really having trouble seeing, so Sue led the way and somehow we managed to miss the ankle wrenching prairie dog holes and tent lines all over the land. In about ten minutes we came up upon the Addison tent from the back. Sue went in as I went to the Indian Taco stand and bought us each another taco. We were hungry again and the tacos helped fill that void. It was only much later that night that we realized how much these rich delights would affect our stomachs. A lesson we remembered in the future.

We talked and shared with the people in the tent until about eleven in the evening and then returned with some of our new friends to watch the dancers again. Finally, about one thirty in the morning, as we struggled to keep our eyes open, we decided to head back to the motel. Stan invited us to stay at his house, but we knew with the limited space and the number of family members visiting we would take up needed room, so we thanked him and said we'd be back the next day with his permission. With that we carefully pulled out of the Sundance grounds and took a road towards Riverton, hoping to find a more welcoming motel.

As we headed down the road to take us off the reservation we became aware just how dark the night sky was. This was something not visible while we were around the fires of the Sundance. It was an amazing sight to see the twinkling stars everywhere and the Grandmother Moon smiling down on us. It was again easy to feel ourselves back two hundred years ago, leaving our extended family for the night to find our bedrolls and some rest. We watched the sky as we drove and just enjoyed the deep, dark, enveloping night. In about forty-five minutes—or four years energetically—we found Riverton and pulled into a nice looking little motel. A clerk appeared when we rang the bell, rubbing his eyes and we booked a room for three nights, telling him we might add more nights later. We wanted to stay for the sweat lodge and to spend more time with Stanford, so we threw our mental schedule out the window. We lugged only what we needed to the room, washed and turned in. We hugged and spoke of this amazing day until we dropped off—probably around three in the morning.

In the morning we had a big breakfast and several cups of good, dark, strong coffee at a little café down the street from the motel. Then we walked around the small town a while getting a little exercise as we knew this would be another glorious, but long and physically inactive day. Around noon we drove to the market and bought several bags of food—fruit, cheese, chips and lunchmeats. And a couple of cases of soda. With this packed in the car we headed back to Addison's place, where we arrived about one thirty.

As we brought the food into the house Stan called over from his wheelchair, which was positioned near the kitchen door. "Ho, Sue and Jim. Come see me here. I am glad you are back. We will go to the dance grounds soon. Thanks for the food there. Nieces! Come get this here food brought to us!"

We helped put the food out and grabbed some bowls and dishes to put beside it. Stan's family had made a huge pot of soup and heaped a tall stack of fry bread next to it. The aroma of the soup as the lid was taken off called people from around the property to come and eat. More people were arriving by the minute, so we took some fry bread and headed outside to check on the puppies. Sue gave them more fresh water and we filled their food bowls from the bags we had seen the day before. Then we played with them for a while as people appeared with plates and bowls, looking for good places to sit. As even more people arrived we decided to drive to a convenience store on the rez we had spotted that morning to get more food for the Addison tent later that day. And to get us more to eat before going to the Sundance grounds, as the food at Addison's home had disappeared without a trace. We bought more food for Stan's table, but decided to wait on our own food and get Indian Taco's at the Sundance. As we were checking out I saw travel mugs on the counter. My travel mug had broken a few days earlier and I like to have coffee or tea I can keep hot in the car. I picked one up and saw it was stamped with Northern Arapaho Tribe and a picture of a medicine wheel, skull and eagle feathers. I took this one and a second mug and put them with the food. As I share this story with you my friends, you may see it is one of these travel mugs I sip my tea and bear root from. A nice connection between the 'then' and the 'now'.

We again loaded food in the car and headed back to the Sundance grounds, excited to see what today might bring. I silently prayed— "Wopila Great Spirit for all you have gifted us on this quest. Grant us the wisdom to understand what we have seen, heard and learned on this journey when the time is right."

The gatekeepers again waved us through the entry gate to the grounds and we drove to Stan's tent, where we unloaded the food onto one of the many tables now set up. Then we walked over to the dance circle grounds and found many of the dancers having their bodies repainted for this last day of dancing. We stayed watching the dancers and absorbing the drums for several hours, then wandered slowly back to Stan's tent, where we again mingled and spoke with those there. We got our Indian Tacos to hold us until the feast after the dance ended and then went back to the dance grounds when Stan's uncle told us they would be preparing for the final dance soon.

The boughs on the west side of the Sundance circle lodge had been taken down so the dancers could see the sunset, which marked the end of the ceremonies. It also allowed more people to watch the final dance rituals. The crowd had swelled dramatically for these last rituals and there were a handful of other white faces now present. The dancers were all painted and dancing feverishly, as the drummers were beating a loud rhythm and the singers were belting out their supporting songs. As this extended final dance was occurring, a Giveaway was also being conducted. Blankets were being gifted to dancers and their runners and those who hosted the dance. And other gifts were being passed out among the attendees. This is a part of many Native American gatherings and other events in Native people's lives as well. You give away what you no longer need or what you know someone else may need more than you. Or you 'gift' to honor and recognize someone—as the dancers and runners were being recognized. You may remember, brothers and sisters, the giveaway I did with my possessions before leaving Pennsylvania to head West. It is a powerful thing to do—trust me, I found this out when doing my giveaways several times in this life.

As the final dance ended, the runners, one-by-one, took their bedrolls and all the ceremonial pieces of the dancers and removed them from the circle. Then, when the dance circle was bare of everything, the dancers prepared to come out to meet their families and all who had gathered. The exit from the circle was thronged by family members of all the dancers, so we respectfully left and returned to Stan's tent to await the family there.

All of Stan's family and friends soon began gathering at his tent and then Daniel, his son and Sundancer, returned. Everyone gathered around him and took turns embracing him and thanking him for dancing for the people. After the family had thanked him we also took turns embracing him, thanking him for the people and thanking him as guests of his father. He nodded and welcomed us quietly, as he was quite tired; as were all the Sundancers I was quite certain.

Stan came up to us as Daniel finished speaking and asked if we would like to go to the large food tent and get the food for the family. This was quite an unexpected honor.

"Thank you, Stan," I said. "It is an honor to be asked. But, respectfully, I think Daniel should decide this. He is the one who danced for all."

Stan nodded his approval as Daniel spoke, "Thank you. Yes, please, you two go with my uncle here and me to get the food and the blessing."

And so now we were to be two of the four to go to the big tent and gather the food for the Addison family feast. As I write this I am again amazed we were asked to do this thing. Even if I knew and experienced daily how this vision quest we travelled included such things along the way. Again, many thanks, Wankan Tanka.

Food for all the families of the dancers is prepared in a huge communal tent, with the women from the families doing the cooking after the men bring in the supplies. The women for this Sundance had been cooking since before sunup because there were so many families present. Each family chose a few members to go to the tent and gather the food for their Sundancer and his kin. Daniel, his uncle, Sue and I were the four to go for the Addison family. Elders would go to a few families at a time and invite them to come to the food tent. When they arrived there they were shown into a separate area in the rear of the tent. There they sat and the women served them some of each of the foods they had prepared. Before the family members ate, the Dance Master—the Grandfather who led the spiritual side of the Sundance—came and spoke some words to them and blessed them and the families they represented. The food is then eaten, the women thanked and as much food as is required is bundled and taken to the family tent, where it is put out for everyone. This is the honor bestowed upon us by Stan and Daniel.

We took the truck so we could bring back enough food for the fifty or so people now at Stan's tent and parked behind the food tent. Then we went in, pausing to smudge ourselves at the door first. Food was piled everywhere—enough to feed a small city by the looks of it. We were shown to the table in the back, where I sat cross-legged as the women served us. Then the Grandfather arrived with the Sundance Chief, the person responsible for the Sundance and all it encompassed. We did not expect this, but sat and listened quietly as the chief spoke a blessing and prayer in Lakota. Then he turned it over to the Grandfather who spoke of the loss of his wife of fifty years this past winter and how he missed her every day in all he did. She had been a large part of this Sundance—the Grandmother—especially in the workings of the women. When he finished, he did a blessing of the water and a ladle of water was passed around our circle—east to west. We felt honored and humble to be in this ceremony with these elders and thanked them profusely. I also thanked my teachers of the past for the knowledge about these things so I could participate in a good way. They liked this show of respect and nodded their approval. Then the Chief and the Grandfather left to go meet with the representatives of other families. We tasted food for a few minutes and then thanked the women as we rose to leave. We had been one of the first families called to meet the elders and gather food—an honor I believe was bestowed on the Addison family out of respect for Stanford and all the good works he did.

We gathered a large pile of food and carefully packed it in the truck for the short ride back to the Addison tent. Daniel thanked us for being there for the family and for being part of the blessing. We thanked him for the great honor and told him we were glad we had done this as he wished. Then we were back at the tent, where a group of young girls awaited us to help unload and serve the food. There was corn prepared in over a dozen ways—as corn has been a staple of many Native American tribes for generations. Pots of stew—bison and elk—steamed when the lids were removed. Elk and venison steaks were heaped on platters. Fry bread sizzled everywhere. And fruits and vegetables were stacked on each table. Hot vegetable dishes that were new to me also gave off amazing aromas. I found the tasting at the food tent had not lessened my appetite at all. We all ate, talked and celebrated Daniel's success long into the night. It was a glorious gathering of a circle—a circle of friends who, although different in culture and customs, were connecting as family with good intentions.

We finally helped with clean up and loaded our car, as did many others, to bring the remainder of the food to Stan's for some more talking and eating. We left Stan's after two in the morning with a re-peat invite to the sweat lodge the next day.

"Be at my place by three in the afternoon," Stan directed us. "We will light the fire to heat the rocks and begin to get ready for the lodge."

"Thanks, Stan," I said. "We'll be there."

We crashed when we got to the motel room and woke up mid-morning, having missed breakfast. We drove around town, found a café serving lunch and then went back to the market for more food and sodas. We finally made it back to Stan's at three, right when he had asked for us to be there.

Stan was napping and we saw there was no wood to get the fire going, so we carried the food into the house, where we found un-refrigerated food from the night before. Not a good idea in this heat. We put out the things we had brought and, as we were headed to the sofa, Stan came out in his wheelchair. Stan was giving orders as he rolled out of his room, pointing and gesticulating as he did. People jumped and began cleaning the place—putting food away or throwing it away if it had turned bad. Others began washing dishes and still others swept the floors. Stan ran a tight ship and his crew was used to it. We began help-ing with the dishes and later with the floors. In an hour the house was clean and neat. Stan looked it over and then rolled over to his bedroom door.

"Niece," he said to the niece nearest him, "get the old rocks out of the lodge and put them around the fire pit. Wood will come soon and we can start a fire. I'm going to take a short nap then I'll be outside." With this, he rolled into his room and pushed the door shut.

The niece he asked to remove the old lodge rocks headed for the door. I asked if she needed help and she smiled and said yes, that would make it easier. So we went out and began removing the pile of rocks from inside the lodge. When they were out we then stacked them around the fire pit as Stan had asked.

Shortly after we finished moving the rocks, Stan came rolling down the ramp. He rolled towards us and saw no wood had been delivered yet.

"Well, we got a little wood around the land here," Stan said as he reached us. "There's some pieces over by the stables and some old fence posts over by the far property fence. Everybody go get some."

So we all went and gathered wood. Sue, coming out after the inside work was done, headed out with me and we began salvaging all we could. The fence posts were big and long and really needed to be cut. There was a chainsaw in the shed, but Stan's nephew wasn't sure how to use it. I stayed quiet, figuring someone would ask if they wanted me to run it.

"Jim, you know how to run one of these?" Stan asked.

"I used a lot of them, Stan. Shall we cut the posts with them?"

"Good. Nephew, you help him. You three there, you start laying a fire. Sue and you two, start bringing rocks from over next to the trailer. Put them right here next to the fire," he continued, pointing.

In a few minutes I got the saw started and Stan's nephew and I got the posts cut into pieces that would fit into the fire pit in a few short minutes.

"Good," Stan said eyeing the new pile of firewood we had created. "Now, Jim, will you start to lay a fire and place the Grandfathers please. I like my fire with a layer of wood, a layer of rocks, more wood and so on. Okay?"

"Of course, Stan," I said. "I would be happy to set it."

"You've been a firekeeper, right?" he asked me.

"Many, many times Stan, especially when I was learning the ways. And many fires laid in the way you asked."

"Good. This way, as the wood burns, the rocks drop and the Grandfathers get good and hot," Stan shared.

Once the fire was laid out with all the rocks in place Stan rolled around it, checking it out.

"Put another log there," he pointed, and a nephew rushed to grab one. "And one here, where I can still see the Grandfather's side. And some more wood on top. Then we are good. Set the fire."

After we placed the final pieces of wood, I lit the pile from one side and his nephew from the other. In a few minutes we had a nice roaring fire. Now we could stand back, or sit, for a while. There was no need to tend the fire until the burning started shifting the pyre.

I am using 'Stan's nephew' or 'Stan's niece' or 'grandchild' because that's how we were introduced and how Stan addressed them. Names seemed irrelevant—family connection more so. So I say nephew, which could mean one of three nephews present. Basile was an exception. As was Frenchie, his sister.

As the fire roared I walked around the lodge to get a feel for the lodge. It was a large lodge, which could probably hold thirty-five people if it had to. And it was very low ceiling for a lodge, coming to my waist. This told me it would be a hot lodge, if Stanford poured much water at all. The most interesting thing about it was that it had two doors—one facing the east and the other facing the west. I had never seen a lodge with a 'back door' before, so this was new to me. Stan's nephew and I tended the fire, adding wood any place the rocks were exposed and keeping the fire within the pit. The rocks were glowing red-hot before long and I could see we were in for a hot lodge today. As the rocks were heating I asked Stan for permission to place my Chanupa on the altar so that it might absorb the energy of this ceremony. He told me I was welcomed to do that and instructed me to place it at the north with the stem facing the north. I went to the car, got my pipe and placed as he had directed.

Then Stan's nephew and I grabbed four large sheets of metal and placed them around and over the fire to help keep sparks from flying and to keep the rocks hot. With the dry, dry conditions of the land here, one spark could trigger an inferno—something Stan didn't want. Nor did any of the rest of us for that matter. Sue and several others stayed at the fire with us, as did Stan for some time, until he went inside for a while to prepare himself. Around dusk people started pouring in. Cars and pick-up trucks wheeled into the driveway and people started to gather. Stan came back outside and asked us how the fire was and were the Grandfather rocks ready? We told him the fire burned hot and the Grandfathers glowed red. He nodded and said it was time for lodge. I looked and saw it was about eight in the evening.

People began lining up to be smudged and then entered the lodge through the west door, women first in the traditional way. All ages were here to sweat tonight—from a one year old to a grandfather in his eighties. There were about twenty-five people, a very large lodge by my standards. Once everyone was in and settled into their place Stan was lifted in to the lodge through the door in the east. Now I saw why there was a second door—it was to make it possible for Stan to enter and lead the ceremonies. Stan's nephews were ready to now bring in the rocks for the first door—the first round—of the ceremony. They began bringing the rocks in and placing them in the pit in the middle of the lodge, while Stan said some words over each. After seven had been brought in—the number I was used to for each of the four doors—I noticed one nephew was bringing another rock towards the lodge.

"Will you bring in more than seven, Uncle?" I asked Stan in the break between the rocks coming in and his words over them.

"Yes, several more at least," Stan answered me. "I think we will have a hot lodge tonight. You all did a good job with the fire."

When we had eleven rocks in the pit Stan called out that we had enough and told the nephews to come and join the lodge. They entered and one of them closed the door. We all shared water from a ladle Stan passed around so we could purify ourselves in Stan's tradition. Then the remainder of this water was poured over the rocks. Some of the little ones were crying because of the dark and I had a young boy of six next to me that Daniel and his uncle were trying to control. Stan's lodge was much less structured than any I had ever been in, with people coming and going before the lodge began and between doors. Finally people seemed to settle down and the children who were too afraid had left, so Stan began welcoming everyone and thanking them for coming in a good way. He spoke of the large number of rocks he had had brought in and that this was to be a healing lodge, so many rocks were needed. Then he thanked Daniel for dancing for all the people and honoring the family. Then he began singing, with everyone joining in, as he poured water on the rocks. It got hot quickly as the steam filled the lodge. When he was done singing his song he spoke about how good it was to have the little ones in lodge with us. After another song and more water on the rocks, the door was opened so the nephews could go out to get more rocks.

Once again, between doors now, people came and went as the nephews brought in another eleven rocks. Then, when he was confident the rocks were ready, Stan began calling everyone back in. Once the door was closed for this second round Stan added sage, bear root and other herbs to the rocks, filling the lodge with an aromatic cloud. Then he again began pouring water and the lodge filled with steam. Sweat ran down my back and legs but, as usual, I did not really feel the heat. I knew how hot it was, however, by the fire in my chest. After a song, Stan gave everyone the chance to speak to Great Spirit in his or her own way. With twenty-five people speaking I knew this would be a long round, and it was.

The six year old between Daniel and me kept saying he wanted to leave, but Daniel would not let him do so. So he settled down a little as the people talked around the circle. Stan drummed as the people spoke and when the circle had gone around he began another song. Everyone's voice joined in and the sound was deafening. I loved it. Stan poured as he sang and the lodge was now totally engulfed by hot, humid steam. It was hot—even I could feel it. I breathed through my towel so I would not burn my throat with the hot air. Then, as the song ended the door was opened and some people again went out for a break.

There was a commotion coming from near the house and, in a minute, some yelling could be heard. Frenchie went to check and came back to tell Stan there were some guys in a pick-up causing trouble with the people in the house. Stan was pulled out of the lodge to deal with it. As Stan tried to talk to the young men in the truck I heard Frenchie yelling that she had called the cops and they had better get out of here. Then I heard the screech of tires and a vehicle—I assumed the truck—go wheeling off the property. Stan arrived back at the lodge and was lifted in once again. Then he called everyone in and, once they were seated, called for eleven more rocks. The third door—round—was about to begin.

Before the flap was closed for the third door Stan said we would begin this door with the Chanupa—the sacred pipe. Then he caught me by surprise.

"I will fill my pipe as I pray to the directions for all the people," Stan began. "First, Jim, will you bring your Chanupa in and open it here with mine?"

"I would be honored, Stan. Thank you."

"Get it then. And, Mark, I believe you brought your pipe as well. Will you also bring yours in? We will open three tonight. Very powerful," Stan finished.

The other pipe carrier, Mark, rose and got his pipe as Stan had asked. They all sang and Stan shared more teachings as Stan and I loaded our pipes. Mark had decided he was not ready to open his pipe and asked permission to hold it to his heart during the ceremony. Stan had agreed. So we did the prayers to the seven directions and then did the pipe ceremony with both of our pipes going around the circle. I almost wept I was so moved. Another great honor I had not expected and I did not understand why I deserved it. Some of the youngest ones who had left earlier had returned for the second door and this pipe ceremony in the third. Now they left again, not wanting to be in the dark. The six-year old sat next to me again, still being a pest and distraction to the circle, but Stan did not seem to notice or care. Stan's uncle sat on the other side of the boy and watched me as I talked to him. He and Daniel had been trying to get the boy to settle down the entire lodge and so far, with little success. I asked Spirit for the right words and energy for the boy to understand what I asked and then spoke to the boy. After a couple of minutes the boy settled down and moved even closer to me, sitting quietly for the first time. Stan's uncle looked at me, nodded and smiled and Stan asked for the flap to be closed. He looked at me as the door was closed and also nodded approval. He had seen. I don't think Stan ever missed much.

The third door was even hotter, with thirty-three rocks in the pit and a lot of water being poured. I was used to the traditional seven rocks in each of the four doors of a lodge—or a total of twenty-eight rocks. We had already exceeded that. It was a powerful door even if it was hot, with four healing songs and some people offering their prayers to the rock people to take up to Great Spirit. People were also releasing whatever ailed them into the heat. Then, after a good long door, the flap was again opened. Stan was again lifted out as the police had arrived during the third door. I had never experienced anything like the surroundings and occurrences of this lodge. People again got out and walked about as Stan talked to the police. I took my Chanupa, as Stan had instructed before going over to the police, out of the lodge and walked around the lodge before placing it in the north on Stan's altar. Then I returned to my place in the lodge. After a while Stan was wheeled back to the lodge and lifted in for the fourth door. He called everyone back and watched as my six-year old partner moved next to me again.

Stan called for rocks and a pile were brought in—I lost count of how many. Stan spoke of how he really wanted this door hot so we all might have some healing and then, as soon as the flap was closed, he began to pour—and pour and pour. Songs and prayers and a lot of heat kept coming as Stan continued to pour and lead the singing. And the steam seemed almost solid. The hottest, most intense door I had ever been a part of. I worried how Sue was taking it, but I also knew she would do fine. We had talked briefly between the third and fourth door and she said she was really hot but also really feeling the cleansing and the energy. Finally the flaps were both thrown up and Stan announced the ceremony was over—three hours after we had begun. I looked to my six-year old ward and saw he was sound asleep. Daniel picked him up, nodded to me, and carried him out.

"Come to the house. We have good food. And we will all talk," Stan invited the circle.

After we had eaten, Stan approached Sue and I.

"Sorry it was so busy with the Sundance," he said to us. "We didn't have as much time as I would like."

"No, it was wonderful. An honor. Every minute a special time," Sue replied.

"There is another lodge tomorrow night," Stan shared. "Some people coming from Colorado for healing. You are welcomed."

"We really need to move on, Stan," I responded. "We need to be in Fort Collins and then head to Sedona."

"Okay. But you come again," he said. "I need to rest up after tomorrow. I begin a speaking trip next week. But come back and we will talk and do more lodges. You will always be welcomed. You are family now."

"Thank you," we said together.

"We are proud to be of your circle," I continued.

"And to know you now," Sue added. "We will be back. Thank you for the invite and thank everyone for us. We will make the rounds with our thanks now, before we leave."

And so we did—shaking hands and hugging. Stan smiled as we thanked him again and reminded us again this was our place now, too. And then we left, heading back to Riverton, once again about two in the morning.

"What an unbelievable four days," Sue began as we drove away.

"Yes. If we had written a script we could not have made it as complete as this time was. We need to think on this, connect with Spirit in dreamtime tonight and talk more tomorrow. Okay?"

"Yes. I am so tired and overwhelmed I can't really talk now anyway," Sue agreed.

We fell into a deep, deep sleep of exhaustion and slept in the next morning. Then packed and hit the road for Colorado.

20 | Natural Balance

I WOULD LIKE TO SIT WITH YOU, BROTHERS AND SISTERS, AND THE EARTH Mother and explore some natural connections that have crossed my awareness lately. We will rejoin the journey Sue and I am on again soon, but for now I think we need to look at some natural world realities. They may also help us all on our walks later.

We have been speaking about balance in the universe—within our selves, between species, in the natural world, throughout the universe... everywhere. One of the reasons many humans have such disregard and disrespect for our home—the Earth Mother—is that the natural world has gone so dramatically out-of-balance, mostly due to human actions. We two-leggeds are holding our collective breath to see how the planet addresses it. It is no wonder this has occurred, with the value systems we have created in the world today. Money is king and the more you have, the better you are: The bigger winner you are at the crap tables of life. Greed rules the day and causes such a perverted view of reality that even people who might know better begin to believe the stories they are fed. Especially what they are told—mis-told—about the natural world.

As an indicator of this dis-ease we have created in the Earth, I start with my spirit family—my pack—the wolves as an example. One of the most misunderstood and under-valued species on the planet. Wolves are another species many humans are trying to make extinct, as we have with so many other species before them. Why? Because the wolves give some people's fears another great target to vent their hatred at—this hatred their fear creates. Stories and myths are created and even people who value wildlife begin to wonder if maybe—just maybe—there are too many wolves. After all, these politicians and 'scientists' are telling us that's so. I did some studies around Yellowstone while I was at Colorado State and found just this type of response in many populations. The haters—the truth-twisters—were doing their work well.

And lately, in some of the groups I am a member of on Facebook and in the real world, I have seen people ranting against wolves. And bears and any other predator they decided were fouling nature's nest or upsetting her balance. Telling people the wolves were decimating the elk herds, costing jobs and business to hunters and hunting group leaders. Ah—money. . . what role does that play in these remarks? Citing wolf attacks on people because there are too many wolves and not enough prey. And on and on. And, when you show proof to the contrary on all these false claims, they simply go into anger and lash out with name-calling and threats. Not how we need to be walking in these times, my friends. But let's look further at this phenomenon.

What is the reality of predator—prey balance? Look at the past; look at times before the Europeans came to the Americas. Let's go back and look. Travel with wolf guides if we like. Okay, good. Relax and go with the journey back to those days. Lie down and close your eyes, stare at a natural setting or whatever you like to clear your mind and let your spirit come with me. Great. That's it. Just go with it, at whatever level you are able. There is no right or wrong here. Look down below now. Look at the natural world on Turtle Island—the Americas—as it was then. If you are from another part of the world, know that similar processes occurred. Huge herds of buffalo running the plains below us. See them? If not, just listen to my descriptions. Grasslands as far as we can see, even from the 'altitude' of looking back. And on these grasslands Tatanka by the thousands. Over there, deer and elk in herds that fill our vision and also in smaller groups travelling across the landscape. There—there, by the towering trees, some wolves taking down an elk. Still others—a little further—taking down another. And some wolf pups over by that blue, free-flowing river eating their meal of deer meat Mom brought home earlier. Now focus in on that river. Deep, deeper into the flowing, coursing blue-white water. What do you see? See, there, in the current. Now jumping. Salmon. By the hundreds. Thousands. Moving upstream to breed. And see those large black animals? Look closely. Black bears. Six of them strung along the bank, dipping paws in and pulling out piles of fresh salmon. Over by the downed trees to our left—a mile or so—a mother and four bear cubs waiting for the feast to come. And people coming into our view now. Indigenous people making their way to their next village site. Their hunters are moving through the grasses and taking deer and elk for the tribe to feed on for the next week. The older hunters meeting in circle to plan a buffalo hunt for the following days, so that meat can be dried for later and the hides turned into clothes before the winter snows comes. So many trees of the Standing People Nations mingled throughout our land here, bringing in a rainbow of birds and insects. Let's hold these images while we look at things as they stand now.

The buffalo now all but gone. Almost wiped out by the white man for 'sport' and so that he might kill off many of the native people who preceded him on the land. The grasslands? Where? Except in a few parks they also no longer exist. Huge gatherings of trees? Not there either. Cut down for fuel or building materials or to clear fields. What about the salmon? At risk now in so many rivers. Wolves? We know that story. Protected so they can survive, with politicians and ranchers and others trying their best to re-open the season on the wolves. And bears? Fewer all the time. Less to eat and less land to roam. And we could continue, but enough. You see the contrast, I am certain. And, if you are like me, you weep over it. And you weep over what we are leaving our kids and their kids. A landscape, yes. Oil and gas rigs everywhere, damaging more habitats. Fuel and oil spills in our oceans. More trees cut. More cement. More homes. More greed.

And yet some people still wonder why nature is out-of-balance. Last week someone debated me on the wolves—that the wolves were killing off all the elk, as I said earlier. I asked if in the past, before European settlers arrived here, the wolves killed off all the elk? If his statement was correct, and there was no one to hunt these killer wolves, they must have eliminated all the elk. And then, I guess, the deer would be hunted by the wolves to extinction. Buffalo? Yes, the buffalo are all but gone, but humans, not wolves, killed them off. He would not answer me, but said it was a proven fact that the wolves were killing off the elk and reminded me no species had died out since humans began to 'manage predators'. I wondered if he had shared that with the species no longer with us. But, he didn't answer that. Two others joined the 'attack on the wolves' of this exchange. They also swore these wolf stories were all facts, proven by science. And this was not leaving any elk for the hunters, putting a hardship on the hunting provider industry. Okay, got it. I then asked why it was that hunters took all the 'trophy animals'—the biggest, strongest animals of the herd, decreasing the quality of the gene pool for future generations? Well, they were against that. They were talking about people hunting for food. My next question was since when did out-of-town hunters visit an area to hunt for food? They responded with "no one had control of that". Talking to people with this mind-set may seem an exercise in futility and many people involved in this discussion were beginning to believe the nonsense these hunters were espousing. I, at least, helped provide balance. As did several others with their comments. There it is again brothers and sisters—balance. Balance in the dialogue around the balance in nature. Nice circle.

This debate made me curious about what was happening of late with the wolves in the North Country, where their numbers had increased while they were protected. As I sat thinking about this I picked up a newspaper and saw—what? An article on wolf impacts on the Yellowstone landscape. It was just a few lines talking about a study in Montana. I Googled and found the article reported in multiple newspapers. Newspapers I can't quote here because they are in terror of having their copyright protections abused if we were to read what they reported about the wolves. I searched some more and found an Associated Press article, which allows for sharing on social media sites. And several other sources with similar articles. So let me share some of this material with full credit to the Associated Press and the *Observer-Reporter* (1/8/2012), which allows sharing as I said.

Wolves helping alter Yellowstone landscape

Associated Press

BILLINGS, Mont.—The return of gray wolves has dramatically altered the landscape in portions of Yellowstone National Park, as new trees take root in areas where the predators have curbed the size of foraging elk herds, according to scientists in a new study.

Stands of aspen, willow and cottonwood are expanding in areas where for decades dense elk populations prevented new growth, said study author William Ripple from Oregon State University.

While other factors may play a role, from a changing climate to wildfires, more than a decade of research has confirmed earlier assertions that the return of Yellowstone's elk-hungry wolves has spurred new plant growth, he said.

The findings from Ripple and co-author Robert Beschta will be published in the scientific journal Biological Conservation. The study already has been released online.

Wolves are "apex predators, on top of the food web," Ripple said. "They're more than just charismatic animals that are nice to have around. We're finding that their function in nature is very important."

Wolves have spin-off benefits, too, the researchers said: As trees grow taller, the stands provide more habitat for yellow warblers and other songbirds and more food for beavers, which in turn construct ponds that attract fish, reptiles and amphibians.

Some scientists dispute the claim that wolves have sparked a restoration among Yellowstone's aspen.

That's because elk alter their behavior only slightly to avoid wolves, concluded Kauffman (U.S. Geological Survey scientist Matthew Kauffman), who also heads the Wyoming Cooperative Fish and Wildlife Research Unit. Although elk numbers are down by about two-thirds in some areas of the park, herd numbers would have to drop even more for aspen to recover, Kauffman said.

"The weight of the evidence is certainly coming down in favor of wolves having a particularly profound impact on aspects of Yellowstone's ecosystem," he said.

Studies on other predators have found similar top-down effects on their surroundings. With fewer lions, researchers said increasing numbers of baboons in sub-Saharan Africa are pushing into settled areas where they raid farmers' crops more frequently and can spread intestinal parasites to humans. And fewer sharks along the East Coast has led to more rays, which in turn eat more scallops, wiping out some local fisheries.

One difference in those studies and the work in Yellowstone is that in most other cases, scientists have been left to study what was lost when a predator was gone. In the park, scientists have been able to track what happens after the predator came back.

Ripple said the results of his work suggest wolves also could have positive effects outside Yellowstone. More than 1,600 gray wolves now live in the Northern Rockies, and elk numbers have dropped as a result.

So let's see, our "let's manage the predators" people, whose belief that wolves kill many elk, are correct in saying the elk herds are diminished by predators, as they need to be. As is needed for balance. There are too many elk, which destroys trees and diminishes bird populations and on throughout the circle of balance in nature. We have the bounty on the head of the elk as hunters prey to kill for sport and the bounty on the wolves because they dare re-establish balance in their ecosystems. And that, according to some, is wildlife management. Sorry, it's not. It's seeking the highest financial return on our animal resources possible. It's greed and ego and a supposed entitlement by we humans.

I know I am mostly preaching to the choir here again, friends, but it is important to have this picture in our minds as I move us into a little discussion of the prophecies of many cultures. Cultures including Native American and prophecies that are coming of age now, in our lifetimes.

Earlier I shared a trip Sue and I took to Prophecy Rock in Hopi land. What we are talking about with this balance of nature trail is the low road. I do not mean we need to live as the Native people did generations ago—hunting and foraging—but I do mean we need to walk away from the greed and begin to work with the Earth Mother to provide some level of balance in our natural world. If we do not, our kids will inherit a global slum. It's that simple.

Nor are the Hopi the only people with a 'low road' prophecy. Sue and I would also attend an International Wilderness Conference later on our walk and see drawings and hear explanations very similar to the Hopi Rock prophecy. At that conference, in Mexico, during an indigenous people's session a man dressed for working in the fields, asked to speak. He was indeed a farmer—an indigenous farmer who lived in Mexico. He had travelled several days to get to the conference from his home and fields high in the mountains. And he had done this because a Native elder he did not know, entrusted him with some drawings the elder had uncovered at one of the ancient sites in Mexico. And asked him to share these drawings at the right place with the right people. He heard of this conference and knew he was to bring these drawings to this group. He carefully redrew what he carried on large sheets of paper and showed them to us. The elder had told him this was a prophecy about to unfold. I asked permission to photograph his drawings—which he gave. I still have these pictures and look at them on occasion to remind myself we are truly all one. The drawings mimic those on Prophecy Rock. Some of the images are different and the connection between these images serve in the way of the 'low road' images of the Hopi, but the message is the same: Humans will learn to again walk in balance with the Earth Mother and all her creatures and thereby inherit a better place to live or they will continue in their wasteful, damaging ways and face great pain as the Earth Mother exerts her will and achieves natural balance on her own.

Two prophecies so similar must be coincidence again, right people? I'm sorry; I can't resist playing with the coincidence button. But it's not just two cultures—it's many. I know of very similar prophecies in the Mayan teachings—as many of you have probably heard about. The Mayan prophecy that many people fear means the end of the world instead of the harmonious reshaping of it. And I have heard stories and prophecies of the same sort from my Australian aboriginal friends and my Garifuna friends of African descent in Central America. And that's just the prophecies I've been told directly—I have heard of many more in the same vein from cultures around the globe. Too many to pooh-pooh. Too many to discount. And all pointing to our current times. To now, when we all walk our walks. Does this sound like doom and gloom? I hope not, it's not meant to. I don't allow doom and gloom, or those wringing their hands over it, into my space.

The prophecies are not about the end of the world. They are about a world that will change, with or without our help as humans. And it will change in an easy, less destructive way or a harsh, very destructive way in large part depending on how we humans realign with the Earth Mother. This is the message and the power of the prophecies from around the globe. And with that time of change rapidly approaching, our time to decide how we wish to see it unfold is almost over. Every day, in every action we, as a species, are making that decision.

When I was first exposed to all the prophecies and many of my teachings, I went into fear—I actually ran away from what I was being told my roles would be. But I slowly came to understand that we all have our roles—our gifts to use—in this time of change. So, at first, I agonized over, "What I am supposed to bring to people and teach them about indigenous people and the balance needed of our planet and its creatures?" Now I do my job the best I am able, spreading the words and allowing all to make their own decisions. I stand with the Earth Mother and my relatives wishing to effect change in the least destructive way. I hope you all walk with me. It is important. For us and for those who follow. Enough now. Thanks for listening.

21 | Rocky Mountain High

We decided to take some back roads on the way to Colorado, to Fort Collins, my home for over eight years. Prairie and badlands were the views most of the time, but we relaxed and just went slowly—still recovering from our powerful time with Stanford and the Addison family and friends. A couple of hours after leaving Riverton we needed a bathroom stop and found an old, dilapidated, sheet metal covered gas station to stop at. In the middle of nowhere—many miles from anything, down the road from nothing. I filled the gas tank as Sue went to get drinks and use the rest room. She came out as I finished filling the tank with a bag of drinks and a big smile.

"Got drinks, but the toilet doesn't work," she said chuckling.

"That figures," I answered. "Well, we'll stop down the road and at least pee and hope we see something else soon."

We headed down the road and, just as I was going to pull off the road on a side lane, we saw a small sign with "food and gas—8 miles" handwritten on it. So we continued on and found a service station at the intersection with Route 285—the road we could take the rest of the way to Fort Collins. We stopped and went inside, leaving ten minutes later feeling much more comfortable.

"Let's take 285 now," I suggested. "It will get us to Fort Collins in the afternoon and we can take a walk before we find a room. Okay?"

"Sure, it's all new to me," Sue answered.

"So, what about our time with Stan?" I asked. "What do we make of that? So many things in such a short period of time. I almost wish we had stayed another couple of days."

"But we agreed it felt like time to move on," Sue reminded me.

"Oh, I know. No problem. It was just such a power-packed time; I wonder what else might have come at us. But, since we moved on, we must have experienced all we needed to."

"Spending those days at the Sundance, being asked to get the food for the family with Daniel and a sweat lodge different from any other—wow," Sue said.

"Yes. And I'm thinking about the number of indigo kids we've come across. Or who have found us. I wonder what that's all about."

"Basile was a special little girl, for sure," Sue agreed.

"And the way she stuck with us and then hearing she was Stan's favorite. She was the reason we were asked to do the other things. I'm certain of that. Stan saw the way she bonded with us and that was enough for him," I spoke as I worked it through my mind.

"Yes, I think so too," Sue, said. "The amazing spirit of Stan and Basile and the dance, lodge and horses—and yet the brutality of the dead dog and the young people who came to make trouble at the lodge. They seem like opposites."

"They are. The balance that is everywhere and in everything. Maybe reminding us of the balance in even the most sacred things being balanced by harsher things was part of what we learned? Balance is the Law of the Universe. I think we need to pay attention to this as we continue our journey."

"It was troubling. I had a hard time getting through the whole dog issue," Sue said, troubled.

"I know. I don't like it either. I have never really understood the relationship between some Native people and their dogs or cats. Especially those spiritually awake. Yet it exists. Most of my Indian friends care for and respect their pets, so I've never gotten a good explanation from them about this either. Yet even some of my friends who care for their pets tend to ignore them at times. Don't know why. I figured my way of animals as friends and companions just makes me a oddball."

"Then I'm also an oddball. And I don't think we are," Sue animatedly began. "I think it's a part of a spiritual road some have just not yet arrived at."

"Yeah. So we did get some teachings that we understand," I smiled and said.

"What was wonderful was you and I as a couple for only a week receiving spiritual gifts like Stan gave us," Sue so correctly said.

"This is a vision quest we are taking together. Not traditional in the way my past vision quests have gone, but just as powerful. So I think maybe it is because we are a new couple—a couple with a road to walk in service to the Earth Mother—that these gifts are coming."

"Well, let's be grateful and enjoy."

"Yes, and see what comes next," I agreed. "I'm looking forward to the next time we get to Stan's and back in his lodge. Maybe we can have him come to Sedona and give a talk?"

"Hmmm, good idea about Sedona. I hope we see him again soon, too."

We began the descent into Fort Collins from Laramie and I began pointing out landmarks and special places of mine to Sue as we drove along. I think we both felt complete in our talk about Stan and the happenings at his ranch and on the rez. I knew other teachings would come to me later—as they always do. And, of course, they have. Some of these may be shared by me later as we continue our walk, my circle. One thing we had strong intention about was re-connecting with Stan at a later time—actually as soon as we were able. And it was this past summer, when we went on a migration journey, that we had put time and energy to doing just that. This migration journey will be something I will need to relate to you on a future walk we take—whenever my spirit tells me to begin writing about that road. For now, know our intention was to spend extended time with Stan and to reconnect with some of my past brothers and teachers. So we again visited Fort Collins during this recent trip, the summer of 2011, and I was able to reach Lawrence Little Thunder, my brother and friend from my days in the Fort, Fort Collins, with Colorado State. Those from the earlier journey we took through my previous book will remember Lawrence well. Sue and I stayed with Lawrence for five days and we did much and talked together in circle.

Somewhere during the days we stayed with Lawrence—actually in his driveway in our RV—the conversation came around to Stan, and even though Lawrence and I had no connection to him together, it turned out Lawrence knew him. Had, in fact, spent time with him in the hospital in Wyoming that spring. Good, quality time before Stan passed away of diabetes—at fifty-two years of age. Sue and I were floored. Stunned, Stopped. Stan was gone. A man who lived thirty-plus years in a wheelchair needing others for aid—yet giving constantly to people, especially young people, on their road of healing and growth. Gone one year before the shifts of 2012—whatever they might be. And gone before we could again connect as he had invited and we had wanted. Why? No need to ask because there is no answer. Great Spirit decided his work was done and welcomed Stan on the Blue Road—the road of the Ancestors. Still 'present' to meet with us and teach and guide us from the spirit realm, just as he was when he walked the Earth Mother. I learned this as I acquired guides and teachers from the spirit realm during my spiritual learning. It is only recently that I truly accepted that this is just as true for our friends and relatives from this life walk as it is for those Ancestors who walked long ago. And so while we could not sit and talk with Stan nor go into his lodge and sing nor sit beside him and watch his son dance—we could connect any time we wished. Thank you Stan— Mitakuye Oyasin. Friends, circle, pause a minute with me and send a prayer of gratitude to Stanford Addison for all the people he helped, if you will. Many thanks.

As we reached the northern outskirts of Fort Collins I turned west up into the hills and pulled into the parking area for the fish hatchery and lake I knew well from my past. This was a place white eagles liked to visit and I wanted to connect with their energies, even though I didn't expect them there in the summer. We walked the trail along the creek and across from the pond enjoying the songs of different birds that were attracted to the trees and water the place had to offer.

"It's good to walk here again," I said as we strolled. "I would come here often since few other people were ever here. I could walk and listen to the water and the birds and watch the eagles in winter. Sometimes with Bonnie, sometimes alone."

"The water and the rocks across the way make for a mix of feminine and masculine energy," Sue mused.

I wondered, as we walked, how my system—mind, body and spirit—would react to being in Fort Collins this trip. I had had major pain issues and emotional distress on other trips here, after I had moved away. Fort Collins was and is a focal point for my spiritual road, my growth and learning, my serving as well as attacks and issues. A good place for me to do some personal healing—if I could stand 'walking through the flames'.

"What say we go walk around Old Town a little and pick a place for some dinner?" I asked.

"Sounds good, I'm hungry."

We parked near Old Town and wandered the shops and businesses, listening to the group playing guitar in the center square. Then we found the Mongolian Grill and prepared a good meal of veggies and meat grilled over their open flames. A motel room at the Holiday Inn near the Colorado State campus completed our work for the day. This hotel was one I had also stayed at before living in Fort Collins and after I had moved away. More connections—more triggers.

We listened to music and read that evening, as I also tried to get in touch with my emotions. I was feeling physically good—not experiencing the grinding pain that sometimes stopped my ability to do healing work on myself. Emotionally I was in a paradoxical state—happiness with Sue and myself mixed with deep sorrow for the lost past and Bonnie. All things that would take a long time to cycle through to a point where my psyche could accept the reality of the now and finality of the past. Something we all are 'working on' at different levels and in different specifics in these days, my friends. Something we must work through to be able to move ahead and evolve. And I tell you, from intense personal experience, that no matter how painful this inner work is it can be done and healing can be accomplished.

The next morning we went downstairs and had a hearty breakfast before starting out on a day of local trips and walks. We drove up the Poudre River Canyon and some of the other canyons in the area. We parked about ten miles northward in the Poudre Canyon and took a walk up a trail along the river for a while, then drove to Horsetooth Reservoir and took the twenty-mile road along its top. From there we headed across town to the east side and the Environmental Learning Center—the center you journeyers from the first book will remember well. We parked at the Center and walked over to see the birds of prey of the Rocky Mountain Raptor Center, which were housed there. These were birds that were injured and were being rehabbed. I looked around the Center as we connected with the birds. One of the volunteers arrived and took one of the hawks out on a tether, perched on her arm. Sue went to hear what she had to say and I walked around the cages—the cages I had helped raise the resources to build. Many things came flooding back to me and I knew I would need to do ceremony here today, with my half-side, Sue. I went back to the car and got my Chanupa, tobacco and sage and then rejoined Sue who was leaving the raptor area.

"Ready to walk around the Center?" she asked.

"Sure. We'll take the trail system for a while and then stop where Lawrence and I helped build the sweat lodge. Okay?"

She nodded and we started out, first crossing the suspension bridge over the Poudre River, which led to the trail system that meandered through the natural areas of the Center. It was very strange seeing the interpretive signs I had designed and had funded, crossing the bridge my staff had rebuilt and walking the trails I had worked on with the AmeriCorps youth to keep open and clear. Very, very strange—but not bad. We walked for about an hour as I told Sue about the projects and programs my circle had undertaken there and then we came to the area where the lodge had stood. Right on the banks of the Poudre. In an area not easily accessible to the general public. And I felt tingling along my spine and in the back of my neck. Well, time to face it.

"Across the river from us, right over there," I said, pointing, "is where the sweat lodges were."

"Are we going over?"

"Yes. I think we'll do our ceremony there. Too much water in the river to cross, so we'll have to go back through the visitor area. Back behind the raptor cages is a trail leading up that side of the river to the site. It's part of the reason we offered that spot—hard for people to get to. It helped keep the area respected."

"Makes sense. Two lodges you said. Right?"

"Yes, the women asked for one of their own, so a second was added. There are a lot of stories to tell around this place. One time I'll never forget is when Fort Collins flooded in '94 or '95. The whole city flooded. The trails we just walked were several feet under water and the old, historic farmstead, which was down that way, south of the lodges, was also flooded. Water ripped down the river here and flooded the parking area near the raptors. And the land to the west of the lodges, over there, was three or four feet under water. And yet the lodges and the land around them, in a hundred-foot circle or so, were totally dry. It looked like an island poking out of the ocean around it. During the days of the flood the lodges never got wet. I had photos, but don't know where they are now."

"Protected by Spirit I guess," Sue said.

"Yes. It was powerful. I called Lawrence and Yellowhair and they came to see it as well. Good energy in that time."

And I told Sue the rest of the stories about the lodge and the ceremonies and how it all evolved and grew. And then I told her of the attacks and negative energy that came much later. And how we fought it, but finally I decided I could no longer stay in Fort Collins. And so Bonnie and I moved to Chattanooga, Tennessee.

"I don't think it was a good thing that I left. It was more to run away from what my teachers were telling me about my powers and gifts than the lodge and the problems with it. But it happened. And I still think one day I will end up back here. That circle must be closed."

"We'll end up here," Sue corrected me.

"You're right. I'm still trying to get used to that. Remember it was Onyx and I up in the mountains where no one could bother us. That's what I 'knew' would happen. So, sorry, yes, you, Onyx and I will end up here—or in this general area of Colorado—at some point and I will close that circle. We will have work to do here."

"That's better."

Then we sat next to where the lodge fire pit had been and laid out the Chanupa and tobacco and burned sage and cedar in the bowl. We opened the seven directions with prayers as Sue played her flute and then I opened the Chanupa and sent our gratitude and requests to Great Spirit. I spoke an honoring of all of those who had been a part of this sacred place and those ceremonies we of the four colors shared, which came out from my heart, as tears coursed down my cheeks. We burned some more sage as I respectfully put the tobacco ash from the Chanupa in the center of where the lodge had stood. I then tied cloth in the four colors to a tree next to the site—cloth of the colors I had brought for this reason. And then we walked to the car as I let the emotions come. Sue commented about now understanding how much this lodge and this Center meant to me as we began the drive to the far side of the Center's land.

Although my emotions were in turmoil and my head was pounding I was feeling less apprehension and anger over what had happened here. It was as it needed to be, not how I would have wanted it to be. I needed to move on and learn and experience more before I could truly step up into my gifts and be a grandfather of the change coming towards us all. This, in spite of the pain, was gloriously beautiful in my heart.

We visited and hiked some of the lakes on the far eastern side of the Center and then sat and watched the fish. We watched from a dock I had helped build with the help of Volunteers for Outdoor Colorado and Division of Fish and Wildlife. Once again, very strange as I was here, with Sue, experiencing this and telling her the story, but also back then leading the effort. Past, present and future are all one, brothers and sisters. Never forget that. It will be an important element for each of us very soon.

The next morning we decided to go up into the Rockies so we packed our things and headed up the Big Thompson River towards Estes Park—the gateway town to Rocky Mountain National Park—and the Park itself. We found a cabin to rent about half way up the canyon and then drove into Rocky Mountain for a while. We drove half-way up to the visitor center at the top of Trail Ridge Drive and sat, just looking at the views for a long time. Then we explored the beaver ponds and the elk meadows before taking a hike in a backcountry area I knew. I was reconnecting with another area where I had a lot of background and, therefore, a lot of triggers for my emotions. Part of the healing, my friends, is walking through the fire in your bare feet. It hurts less and less each time you do it, but it never feels good.

At the end of the day we had dinner in Estes Park and then went back to our cabin to rest. That night was a restless one for me, with many visits from spirit guides and animal guides, but I have no real remembrance of the specifics of these visits. I suppose, as usual, I did not need to access whatever they had shared at that point. This was probably good, since I was on emotional overload as it was. The next day we stopped at The Egg and I in Estes Park for breakfast and then drove all the way to the visitor center on Trail Ridge Road. My fear of falling caused me to hug the side of the road furthest from the drop off as I gripped the steering wheel with all my might. After we spent time at the center we began the drive back down, sighting wildlife all along the way. We stopped each time animals appeared and watched them, sharing our energy with theirs. Later that day we stopped back at Estes Park and walked the town, checking out the shops and the little pocket parks. Then, after dinner, it was back to the cabin, as we had a long ride the next day.

I had another long night with little sleep and a lot of body pain and mental churning. I tried to 'shut my brain off', but had no success. So I lay there twisting and turning most of the night. Around three in the morning I showered and sat in a chair and watched the moon through a window, wondering how much longer I would need to suffer these stresses and pains. Yet, at the same time, realizing I could at least function during these mind, body and spirit assaults, which was a vast improvement over past bouts. I thanked Great Spirit for this and for the healing I knew would eventually come and finally slept a while, there in the chair.

At some point I must have gone back to bed because I awoke there at eight in the morning. Sue was already awake and looking out a window at the new day.

"I really love the Rocky Mountains," she said wistfully.

"Me, too. Always have—always will. The pain each time I came here over the past five or six years has made it too difficult for me to stay too long. But this time, although it was bad, we had some good times as well. Affirmation we will end up here some time down the road. Like I said, we will never get bored."

"You've been right so far. This has been an amazing trip and we still have a long way to go to get to Sedona."

"Yes. I think I want to go up the Poudre and over the pass at the top to Steamboat Springs. Okay?"

"You're the tour guide. I'm the tourist."

"Good. There is a place near the top where I made a little memorial to my Dad after he died and I'd like to find the spot. That's where I want to open the pipe today and see what comes to me about the remainder of the trip to Sedona."

"Great. But let's get breakfast at The Egg and I first and then I want to revisit a few of those shops. I saw some things for my grandkids I want to get," Sue said, finishing our itinerary for the morning.

Since I performed the Lakota wedding ceremony at Yellowstone we had been looking for rings—specifically rings with bear emblems; fetish style—on them. Rings to cement our bond as a couple. We had looked everywhere and found nothing so far, but we remained confident we would find them before we got to Sedona. We would keep looking. Sue had seen some shops she thought might carry rings in Estes Park, so she also wanted to stop at them. A couple of hours later we were ready to head out. We had found no rings, but Sue got things for her grandkids and I got a dress for my granddaughter.

"I guess we give up on the rings," Sue began. "They just don't seem to have anything like what we want."

"Yeah. I'm surprised, but I'm tired of looking too. Maybe we can have one of the Native artists in Sedona make us two."

"Great, but I was hoping we could find them while we were on this vision quest. I was sure if we looked hard enough, they would appear," Sue said.

"Me, too. But it's just not happening. So let's let it go. Worry about it in Sedona. Jesse will probably know someone. Or Bearcloud will." And so we agreed to wait for Sedona.

Since it had reached late morning, I suggested we shift our route and go through Rocky Mountain Park and then to Steamboat Springs. We could do ceremony in my father's memory at the far side of the park, at a special place I knew. And so we headed back into the park and took Trail Ridge Road through the park and out the western side.

We stopped at a lake—the spot I had in mind—and I got out the pipe and tobacco. It was hot—really hot, but we did not let this stop us. We spent an hour doing prayers and just connecting to nature and then continued towards Steamboat, crossing amazing mountains, driving along rivers and exploring canyons along the way. In the afternoon we reached Steamboat Springs and decided to stop for lunch. We went into a local café I knew and had salads and ice tea—lots of ice tea as the day had remained extremely hot. Then we ambled across the street to F.M. Light and Sons, an outfitter that has been in business over a hundred years and the place I bought my western hat twenty years earlier. It's a comfortable, brown, hat in the traditional western style—a hat I still wear daily. Probably be buried in it. We bought some t-shirts and Sue bought herself a western hat and we picked up a few more things for the grandkids and then we headed to the car.

But we really needed a restroom before we left and so we walked down the street to a little collection of shops, where we were certain they would have a bathroom. We looked on the first floor and found none, so we climbed the steps to the second floor, again not seeing any. A shop carrying Native American art was next to where we stood so we ducked in to ask about the restrooms.

"Hi," Sue spoke to the man behind the counter. "Are there restrooms in this complex?"

"Yes, there is one downstairs and around back," the man replied in a friendly way.

I was looking at some gaucho belts as Sue was speaking to the man, since Sue had wanted one for some time, but had not found one at a price she wanted to pay.

"Nice belts," I pointed out to her as she turned away from the man she had just finished talking to. She came over and looked.

"They are nice," she agreed. "But look at the prices. Too much for now, especially when neither of us has an income."

"You're right," I agreed. "Well, we better get moving, I still want to go further today. I'm sensing it's time to reach Sedona before too many more days are done."

"Sure, let's go to the bathrooms and then be on our way," she said and we headed for the door.

"Thank you," Sue turned back to the counter and said to the man.

"You're welcome. Have a good day," he nodded and replied.

As I continued towards the door, Sue stopped and took another step towards the counter the man stood behind.

"Wait a minute, Jim," she stopped me. "Look at this. This is really funny. Can we see these two rings in here please," she asked the man.

"Of course," he smiled as he took out the two rings—a man's and a woman's—in bear motif, fetish style and put them on the counter.

"I'll be damned," I said as I reached Sue and saw the rings. "Try it on," I continued as I picked up the man's ring.

"These are really good quality," the man began. "This is my shop so I can attest to their quality and who made them. They were made by a Zuni artist from the town of Zuni, in New Mexico. He brings a few each time he comes—once or twice a year. These are the only two I have now."

Trying the rings on we found, of course, that they both fit perfectly. Ten minutes later we had the rings we wanted—the rings bonding us together in yet another way. The ring I am looking at as I share this story here today with you, brothers and sisters. And I'm again reminded of a lesson I share often—when there is something you really feel you need, don't search too hard for it. Put it out there for Great Spirit and, if it is needed, it will appear. Whatever it might be. We had searched long and hard since our wedding in Yellowstone for these rings and had not seen anything even close to what we had envisioned. Then, after releasing the search and leaving it to Spirit to allow us to find a craftsperson later, we found the exact rings we sought in the sizes we both needed. And only found that because we needed to pee. Or did Spirit add the 'need to pee' to our agenda that day? The other interesting insight here is that I was looking at the belts Sue wanted, but we passed on, because it was not something she truly needed. It was something she wanted at a time when money was scarce. That had changed our course and given Sue a reason to turn back and thank the man again. And it was then the rings caught her eye. If we had bought what we wanted—the belt—would Spirit have even made what we needed—the rings—visible to us? I don't know, my relatives, but it's a great question.

We left the shop with our rings on our fingers and, after stopping at the rest rooms; we went back to the car to continue our journey. I turned right out of our parking space and we began moving in a southwestern direction.

"I really like this town and this area," Sue said as we started driving off.

"Me, too. It's a place I always enjoyed. We drove over here quite often when we lived in Fort Collins. It's only about three and a half hours between the two places. Maybe this is a place we may finally live," I responded.

"It could be," Sue began again. "The area is beautiful and the town not too big. And I really like the energy."

"But, it gets really heavy winter weather. Lots of snow, so we would need to be ready for that."

"Well, we'll see. We will know where when the time comes," Sue finished.

We took back roads as often as I was able—heading towards Rifle, Colorado on Route 70 as we did so. Somewhere north of Rifle we came across a natural area where we decided to stop and do some more ceremony. With this entire journey being a type of vision quest, it was important that we add ceremony into as many of our days as possible.

In the afternoon we hit Route 70 and headed west to Grand Junction and beyond. When we got near Grand Junction we realized the day was getting late and we couldn't get too much further, so we got off the interstate and headed for the Colorado National Monument just south of town. This beautiful land has a road through it, which climbs steadily uphill. The land is famous for beautiful and amazing rock formations and views of the surrounding desert. We drove up the road and stopped to enjoy many of the vistas spread out below us. When we drove back down we were rejuvenated, so we decided to go further than we were on our run to Sedona. We jumped back on 70 and headed west into Utah.

Not long after we crossed the border I turned south and headed down a back road to Moab, Utah that I knew well from many past trips. Moab is another of those places that speaks to me. A place I went often in the past to rejuvenate and connect with the Earth Mother. As we crossed the Colorado River on an old metal bridge I again turned, this time up a dirt road I knew, which followed the Colorado River into natural lands where I almost never saw any people. We bounced and lurched down the road about five miles when I pulled off under some impressive mountainsides and boulders—an area I had hiked often. I took my Chanupa, tobacco and sage and we hiked into the rocks a short distance and then lit sage and smudged the Chanupa, the rocks and ourselves thoroughly. When we were well smudged, I prepared the pipe and we did a ceremony of gratitude—our third ceremony of the day. Afterwards we drove further up the road and then angled down a track to the river. We walked, hand-in-hand, to the banks of the river and just stood listening to the song of the cascading waters for some time. When we felt refreshed, we turned and headed back to the car.

"Beautiful spot," Sue said.

"Yes, this whole area is pretty special," I agreed. "Look at the sunlight bouncing off the water," I continued, as I turned back to the water and pointed at a rocky stretch of the river. "And the way the light plays with the hillside on the far side. See those sticks and dark areas; nests, maybe eagles. And the trees down river there a ways— look at how they hug the river bank," I continued.

"It is a beautiful place. Are we far from Moab?"

"No, just a nice ride down another beautiful canyon," I answered.

"Dusk is coming soon. Maybe we should head that way?"

"Yep. I needed to stop here and walk with you. It's definitely a bittersweet experience, but the two of us here, together, now is a good thing," I shared.

As we headed to the car I saw some prints near a row of hills to our left. I pulled on Sue's hand and we walked over to them.

"Neat. A big cat," I said, as we looked at the tracks, which came down to the water and then back up into the hills behind us. "You're liable to see anything here. The water of the river draws all the critters out of the desert on these hot days. I saw really big bear prints one time, but this is the first big cat."

"What do you think it is?"

"Not sure, I'm not that good with my tracks. But I would guess a mountain lion from the size. And I know they are in these hills. The rangers around Moab used to tell me great mountain lion stories."

While living in Fort Collins and running Colorado State's Environmental Learning Center we talked about earlier, I learned that if you wanted to see a lot of wildlife, you would go and sit on the riverbanks—especially at dawn and dusk. Just remember all the creatures of the area will come for drinks—the cute and cuddly as well as the more dangerous. Try to find some trees or bushes to screen you when you do this and sit as still as you can. I've had coyotes and deer pass within feet of me when they were really thirsty and not even give me a look. At the Environmental Center, I went many evenings and sat on the bank near the beaver lodges. The beaver there were big, maybe four feet when they stood up on their feet, propped by their broad, flat tail. After a time they no longer paid attention to me—thinking me safe, I assume—and I could sit for hours watching them build their lodges and create their dams. No matter what I had had to deal with on those days, I left the beavers and their ponds feeling alive and cleansed. Nature heals and cleanses if we only take it in large enough doses. And we don't have to worry about any dangerous side effects, unless someone is holding dinner for you. But, I am digressing, or maybe not. I'm talking about Mother Earth the healer and that is one major piece of what I share with you.

We finally got in the car and drove back to the road—Route 128 I think, which would take us to Moab. Twilight was upon us and it painted amazing canvases of light and shadow on the cliff walls that soon lined our drive on both sides.

"Another amazing place," Sue exclaimed. "It's still hard to believe I'm here and you and I will be living in a place just this wonderful."

"Beautiful and amazing places all over the Earth Mother," I added. "And as long as we two-leggeds don't continue to destroy them, they'll be with us a long time."

When I first began coming to Moab in the early 1990's, there was almost no building along this road we were taking along the river and into Moab. Now we saw dude ranches and guest ranches in a lot of places—all too close to the river for my taste.

About thirty minutes later we passed Arches National Park—another special place we would explore the next day—and pulled into Moab. I stopped at a motel I knew and we booked a room for two nights. Then, still not tired, we drove along the Green River to an area that had some intricate petroglyphs, painted by the Ancestors who once lived here. I was feeling a little down, as I was not ready for the number of motels now in Moab. Again, on my past trips, there were only a few motels in the entire region. The only people who visited here were bike riders and people visiting Arches—and, of course, crazy people like me who walked out into the desert areas to renew and refresh. But, so be it. I could not change it or stop it—only, hopefully continue to exert any pressure I can to moderate the effects of these expansions near natural areas everywhere.

We went back to town and decided to eat at the Sunset Grille, which sat up a mountainside north of town. We put the car in second gear so it could chug and climb up the pitted dirt road that led to the restaurant and laughed as we were thrown about the car. We got a table next to one of the windows that looked out over the countryside in a grand vista way.

"My heart and spirit are so much a part of the West," Sue said when we were seated. "And we've seen some of all of it as we take this journey to Sedona—desert, mountains, rivers, plains—what a way to be certain I'm where I need to be."

"Just showing you the places that are a part of my spirit has given you a great over-view of everything."

"Your job as tour guide on this part of our quest, I guess," Sue said, smiling. "I know I have spent many previous lifetimes here, in this country. Maybe we spent some of those together."

"We probably have. I know I've walked these lands in different colored skins in the past," I agreed. "Moab is another place I could live and call home. Where we are meant to be will emerge, even if we are to remain mobile as I have my whole life."

"Oh, I know. I loved Sedona and can't wait to be there, but I don't feel like that's permanent for us," Sue replied back.

"Yes, nor do I. Odd, because I love it too, but I see us moving on in a few years. Whatever is to be, I guess."

"And that will be just fine," Sue finished.

The next day we drove into Arches National Park, parked and took a long walk along a little-used trail I knew from the past. It was hot out on the desert, but we kept drinking water and pulling our big-brimmed hats lower on our foreheads to stay slightly cooler. When we were done with that hike we drove to a short hike along some huge, flat exposed rock surfaces—a favorite place for visitors to go. There were a handful of people walking to the rocks this day, but not too many with the sun beating down the way it was. I brought my Chanupa and we clamored over the rocks to a niche on the far side, where we opened the pipe and did some prayers asking for clarity around our next moves. When we finished the prayers, we realized we were medium-well done on the frying pan of these rocks so we started back to our car. A couple stopped us on the way and asked what we had been doing on the rocks. I explained that I was a pipe carrier in the Lakota tradition—and what that meant—and that Sue and I had been sending prayers to Great Spirit, asking for guidance. They liked this idea and said they would sit and pray to God while they were out there. Sometimes the lessons we teach are simply through our walk, by just being.

The remainder of the day we spent in visiting natural areas around Moab. That evening we realized it was time to get to Sedona—the destination of this quest—but just the beginning of our journey together. Jesse and Abbey had been having a 'quiet' war since the day I left Sedona and Onyx was, I'm certain, tired of being a referee. So we agreed to hit the road early the next day and see if we made it all the way to Sedona.

22 | Completing the Circle

THE NEXT MORNING WE PACKED THE CAR AND HEADED ON OUR WAY TO Sedona and the completion of the circle for me that started the day before I boarded the train for New Hampshire. The day I had been driven from my home to Flagstaff—several lifetimes ago, so it seemed. Coming back not just with a friend who I helped move and some great experiences to interpret, but also with a life-partner willing to walk the Red Road at my side. Not only willing but excited to do so, knowing my road is anything but stable and planned. My walk is as Spirit directs it, sometimes with dramatic changes day-by-day.

We drove with several stops for walks, to Monument Valley National Park on the border of Utah and Arizona. This is another high-energy place with natural sandstone rock edifices rising from the land everywhere—in an assortment of shapes and sizes. A place where countless Westerns had been shot by the Hollywood crews of the past and a place the Native American people of the region hold sacred. In fact, some of the land preserved here is Navajo Tribal Park. We drove into the Tribal Park for a short distance, stopping at a hotel that served as a base for many of the old movies made here. We had some Indian Tacos and checked out the hotel and gift shop before moving on. We agreed that we needed to return here in the future and explore further. There were things we needed to see and feel here—that much I was sure of. What they were would become clear when the time was right. For now, I felt even more strongly we were to be back in Sedona.

We spent the remainder of the day and evening, driving the route to Sedona. Finally, about nine in the evening, we pulled into my driveway just below Standing Eagle Mountain. Or, as the new reality had unfolded for Sue and I, our driveway. As we got out of the car Jesse opened the front door and seventy pounds of unbelievably ecstatic spirit dog came bounding out, rocketing towards us. He leaped up on me, his manners forgotten for a while in his joy at seeing his primary human partner back in place. Then, twisting himself in a circle, he changed direction and began jumping on Sue as well. Having much more common sense than most humans and an uncanny sense of perception, Onyx already seemed to know that we were a couple. Since that would now provide him with two humans to take on walks and chase sticks for, he was all in favor of this.

"Hiya, buddy!" I exclaimed. "Ah, you look great. Jesse take you on good walks?"

"He knew you were coming fifteen minutes ago," Jesse shared. "He's been going from window-to-window just waiting for you to pull in."

"Dog sense," Sue said. "They always seem to know things before they happen. And these two," she said, pointing at Onyx and me, "are like a human/dog clone."

"How was everything coming back?" Jesse asked.

"Great. Surprising," I said. "We'll talk more, Jess. Let me just bring in what we need for now; we're exhausted."

"You know Abbey was walking Onyx today and I didn't like the way she brought him back," Jesse started.

"Oh hell, Jess! Can't we let that all alone until later? I don't want to start on that right away," I angrily affirmed.

"Sure, but you seem to be taking just her side. You don't want to hear me. I live here, too. And she just came in with her family and...," he started to rant.

"Jesse, enough! I'm not taking anyone's side. I don't know why you got so furious with her. And I don't know what she said, either. But not now."

I got madder as Jesse continued to beat on the issue, even after I asked for a reprieve. Finally, he said we would talk the next day. Here, my friends, is a good lesson for me—which you may remember if it serves you as well. I think I was taking Abbey's side because Jesse had that habit of repeating things many times without listening to the other side. When we finally spoke it got so bad I said I did not want to talk about it again. I thanked him several times for helping with Onyx, but the issue between he and Abbey was over for me. That arrangement would never again occur, so I asked what was to be gained by continued venting? Jesse decided that meant I was not listening to him and was siding with Abbey totally. Our friendship was damaged after this and took a long time to heal. Maybe because of his manner, I was siding with Abbey. A decision that was later proven incorrect when some of Abbey's intrusive and painful actions affected Sue and I. Maybe I could have listened to Jesse until he said what he needed to twenty or even fifty times. Maybe I needed to have practiced a little more patience.

When we had gotten things inside, Jesse asked if I wanted help moving anything to the guest room.

"No, no need," I answered. "But thanks. It seems we are a couple now."

"Oh, wow. Many blessings!" Jesse said with a big smile.

"Thanks," Sue said, with an answering smile.

We were both uncomfortable that night. Now we were at the place we would live together and the wedding ceremony I conducted and the trip—quest—were behind us. So it felt strange to both of us. I know for me, it was like a final admittance I would now share my life with a partner again. And as happy as I was with that, I was also nervous and uncomfortable as well. Over time these feelings of discomfort would dissipate and then disappear for both of us but for now they were firmly "in our faces".

The next day we began putting together our possessions, and listing our needs and wants in Sedona. We stopped by a few friends' houses, and then made plans for the immediate future. One of the first things I did was call Bearcloud and ask about a Lodge. Happily he was thinking of doing one three nights from then and I asked for an invite, which he immediately offered. That would assist us in starting our spiritual life here in Sedona, as a couple. Something important to both of us.

I had been in Sedona about nine months when Sue and I arrived that night. We would stay another two years, working on our own healing and receiving continued powerful teachings from Great Spirit through our spirit and animal guides. Even now, as I sit on the mountaintop above Santa Fe in Jack's house writing this, we still go back to Sedona to do work and be in circles when we are able. And, most importantly, to go into lodge with Bearcloud. But it no longer feels like home. Where is home? Probably, as least for now, it is where I have shared before—anywhere on Turtle Island I happen to be at the moment. At this time this house we sit in is our current home—even if it is not ours, but Jack's. The circle we three have formed has allowed us to create and manifest things together which make us a group—a 'wolf pack' if you will. No matter where any of us may be, that circle will stay intact, as it does with our other brothers and sisters. This is one of the powerful things about these times—those of us awake and working with the Earth Mother in a good way are connected as one, regardless of where we might physically be at any moment.

In the future I will share much more about our time in Sedona and the things we learned. Maybe if she is willing, Sue and I will do this together. If not, I am comfortable speaking for us with her editing. We shall see. And I most definitely will share, soon I think, the journey—the migration—we took in 2011. A trip all around Turtle Island we thought we took to connect with circles and do the work of Sanctuaries of the Earth Mother. But a trip that really was for us to connect with the Earth Mother and the natural world and with the two-leggeds walking on it so we might experience and better understand some of the immense changes already underway—before 2012. We recorded and documented these things in our hearts and spirits so I might write them down later to share with all who wished, on another walk together. Sue and I are still processing what we saw— the fear, anger, doubt and hatred in many places. And the joy, love, trust and warmth in others—without clear reasons of why we saw these opposite extremes when we were out there. Reasons that are now surfacing for me, that I know need to be shared soon.

We saw the "for sale" signs on half of the businesses, land and homes across Turtle Island combined with the virtual ghost towns so many communities have become. The things you do not see on television. The things not documented in the media. Yet, even with these signs of collapse, the other places—the 'balance' of this reality—with thriving shops, well kept houses and few vacant businesses or homes.

It's all here, friends, in our hearts, waiting to be shared. And it will be, as soon as Great Spirit wishes it to be so. But for this current walk we have taken together, I offer my great gratitude and appreciation for all you have taught me as we journeyed. If I have said things that may aid your walk, remember to take what you need and leave the rest behind. Mitakuye Oyasin—we are all one.

Afterword and Special Thanks

I'M NOT CERTAIN WHAT MORE THERE IS TO SAY HERE, BUT I'M CERTAIN Great Spirit will guide my fingers over the keys as I sit here with you for this wrap-up of our work; at least for now. This time as I wrote and we all walked together, Sue and Jack have been reading and editing as the circle moved forward. They've shared some thoughts and kept others to themselves for now is my sense of it. Redhawk joined the group today with some thoughts on the short piece of the book he has read to-date and Gerri Ann, our wonderful friend and proof-reader from the first book, has a copy winging her way. As does my mother, who has embraced the teachings and musings of our walks in the two books and brought them out to other Grandmothers and Grandfathers. This is an occurrence I never envisioned, but one I welcome with great joy. So, why this book so quickly after the first? Because Spirit has shown me it must be so. Sorry if this seems a cop-out; but it is reality.

As all these great hearts have read and made suggestions, I have just written—some each day, all depending on whether Great Spirit sends the words through me or not. I have not read any of the book, nor will I until I finish this piece with you here. From the pieces I have some memory of writing—as it was in *White Man, Red Road, Five Colors*—I marvel at some of what I have shared and wonder about other things not shared. With my gift of being anywhere past, present or future at any given moment I have relived this quest I have shared as it happened. But I can't tell you why I relived some incidents and not others. This will be seen as we all move ahead, I suspect. Or maybe not—as long as these walks accomplish what Spirit wishes.

I do know I feel as exposed in this book as I did in the first—but with less care about that. I am what I am—no more and no less. I ask others to accept this, so how can I accept less? And like all of us, I face my fears in the mirror each day, decide not to have them stop me, and move on. What peace there is in that, friends. Practice it—you will see. I worry that these walks I share will be misread or scoffed at. Why? Some vestiges of ego I assume. I worry about how Sue and I will live going forward, with little money and rapidly amassing bills. Why? Do I not believe my own teachings around surrender and trust? Of course I do, brothers and sisters, but I am a work in progress as we all are, so my abilities wax and wan from time to time. I could continue on with this, but you see my warts—my fears—and accept I am as imperfect as any. As we all must be. As I accept each of your imperfections.

What is next for Sue and I—and what is next for this circle we walk in with you all? With this circle that seems to grow daily. Well, for one thing, Sue and I will be going around the Earth Mother in 2012, inviting together circles and physically joining them so we might share what Great Spirit has directed and these circles might share back with us. We will bring our healing Grandmother Drum—Hoop of Many Colors—with us so we all can drum and heal together. How will we do this? Pay for it? Wow, more surrender and trust. Jack, as always, is part of the answer—having donated the air miles for us to fly. And working with us to fund this book. Having each in the circles that form as we travel contribute money will be another piece of this and . . . it will work out. This I do trust.

More walks together? More that I write as we see and experience things and share what I am told to share? Yes. These are important, even if I do not yet see exactly why. The book about Sedona and our migration trek last year I have already brought to your attention. This I will continue to write even as this walk here ends. And another book, about my dark time of the soul is needed, as soon as I am able to write it. In this time of shift and change—and perceived loss—my story of having lost everything, standing in the ashes of my life and screaming at Spirit to take me, to the point I again began to live is something I know will have value for others. But I am not quite ready for that yet. It will be unbelievably painful to write. I will write it—soon I sense. But, please, relatives, give me just a little longer reprieve on this. Many thanks.

I may need to write about Arizona and our time there. Arizona, which has become the Land of Hatred and Fear. A land that has evolved into a place that demonstrates all the wrong and hurtful ways for people to interact and for people to disrespect the Earth Mother. A place I believe, that will lead the way in systems collapsing as the changes of the prophecies come. One state controlled by people who despise and attack any not like themselves. And yet a place of astounding beauty, with pockets of people who are awake and connected in a good way. No judgment, the change needs to begin somewhere. Those in power who hate, must be doing so for a reason. Watch Arizona, friends, for you may well see the beginnings of the changes there.

For now, please continue to sit with all we have said and shared on this walk. Put the teachings in your heart and let your spirit work on them if you are willing and able. And report back anything that comes to you we might all learn from. Go to my email or the Sanctuaries of the Earth Mother website or Facebook Group and put it out there. Being exposed is not as bad as you might think. Trust me.

This book was harder for me to write than the first, so I wonder how the next books will compare in that way. Reliving some of these times brings up triggers and emotions that still need to be flushed. This is so important to do, circle. I hope it will help you in this way as well. I did not expect to share the story of Sue and I on a quest, becoming a couple. Yet I did. And my brother Jack, I know had a more difficult time reading this book because it triggered emotions and reactions in him as well. Jack's losses are much like mine, so my walk 'talks' to him. As did my sharing of John's story and his leaving this realm. This is not meant to be a bad thing for any of us, but rather some additional healing work we need to do as we approach the new times before us—no matter how they evolve.

Please, please—for the sake of the Seven Generations and beyond—consider walking with the Earth Mother in a good way. In a harmonious, sustainable way. You do not need to shift and move the way I have—maybe I even do that for the circle, who knows—but in your own lives and in your own places consider what we have done to the Earth Mother and what we now need to do with her to heal the wounds we have created. I know some will resonant to the love story aspect of this walk we are completing. They will ask things about Sue and I and how our love happened and has grown. We will welcome this and respond as honestly as we can. But be aware that if this is a love story, it is a love story at many levels. Sue and I—yes, that is obvious. But also my love story with the Earth Mother—a story that has spanned this lifetime, and I am certain other lifetimes as well. And the love story of the circles forming now between us all, asking us to effect change together. And the love of Great Spirit for all he has gifted me, even the pain and suffering whose purpose is not always clear. If we accept these love stories then we will be started on the road to a better legacy for our kids and our kid's kids—as well as more comfort for ourselves for the remainder of our walks. Let it be so. Be well, brothers and sisters.

SPECIAL THANKS

In my previous book I thanked my friend, Bearcloud, for the amazing cover he created and gifted me with. This time he once again used one of his paintings to create a cover that is a work-of-art: A work-of-art that adds so much energy and spirit to what I have written. I thank him with all my being for this gift to the book, my readers and myself. I am blessed to walk with such a good friend. And I again offer to you, my friends, the opportunity to hear his story and visit his art on his website www.bearcloudgallery.com. When you are there, please visit the Chameleon Project as well. This is a nonprofit Bearcloud's visions inspired and manifested. It is a project near to my heart, as it has a large role to play in this time of change.

I extend another round of thanks here as well. As I finished this book, I was shown to ask a circle of 7 to read it and contribute their thoughts and/or energy to it. I was to bring the "circle" to the creation phase of *Walking With the Earth Mother*. I pondered whom to ask for a few days—and nothing concrete came to me, so I released the idea. And—yes, I know you see it coming—as soon as I did, the 7 began to appear in my heart. Each of these 7 will do as they see fit with the copy I have sent them. Some will read it quickly and comment. Some will read a portion of it. Others will simply hold it and wait for the right time for them. It does not matter—each does as he or she is meant to. And each is putting his or her energy into it. These 7 from around the globe—these friends—I give thanks for your willingness to explore this "new way" with me. I am honored to have you as friends: Those of you whom I have known many years and those who I have met recently equally. Pilamaya—thank you.

Continuing Journey

As this book was being prepared for printing, Jack suggested I share a little on the path Sue and I now take.

First, the pictures. The picture on the back cover is the picture taken of me as I hiked the trail to the Wisdom Lodge. I thought it only existed on our website, but Sue was able to retrieve it from there. Voodoo to me, but she conquered the technology. The other picture I now share on this page is the picture we were asked if we wanted taken while at Devil's Tower. I hope they bring something to the energy of this book.

For Sue and I the personal journey takes new paths each day. In addition to the Native wedding ceremony I performed, we opted to ask a friend, Bishop Richard, to perform a wedding ceremony for us as well. Then we registered the license with the state. This summer we envision a Native American friend performing a ceremony—the third time. Why, I am unsure, but it must have energetic and spiritual meaning.

We now begin more travels sharing our energies, the Hoop of Many Colors drum and the teachings and ceremonies gifted me over the years. Part of our journey as a couple and part of our work of 'connecting the dots' of circles of people around the globe with the Earth Mother and all her creatures. I hope you are with us on these walks—and you bring friends.